The Metaphor of the Monster

The Metaphor of the Monster

Interdisciplinary Approaches to Understanding the Monstrous Other in Literature

Edited by
Keith Moser and Karina Zelaya

BLOOMSBURY ACADEMIC
NEW YORK • LONDON • OXFORD • NEW DELHI • SYDNEY

BLOOMSBURY ACADEMIC
Bloomsbury Publishing Inc
1385 Broadway, New York, NY 10018, USA
50 Bedford Square, London, WC1B 3DP, UK

BLOOMSBURY, BLOOMSBURY ACADEMIC and the Diana logo are trademarks of
Bloomsbury Publishing Plc

First published in the United States of America 2020
This paperback edition published 2022

Volume Editors' Part of the Work © Keith Moser and Karina Zelaya, 2020
Each chapter © of Contributors, 2020

Cover image © Bodleian Libraries

All rights reserved. No part of this publication may be reproduced or transmitted in any form or by any means, electronic or mechanical, including photocopying, recording, or any information storage or retrieval system, without prior permission in writing from the publishers.

Bloomsbury Publishing Inc does not have any control over, or responsibility for, any third-party websites referred to or in this book. All internet addresses given in this book were correct at the time of going to press. The author and publisher regret any inconvenience caused if addresses have changed or sites have ceased to exist, but can accept no responsibility for any such changes.

Library of Congress Cataloging-in-Publication Data
Names: Moser, Keith A., editor. | Zelaya, Karina, editor.
Title: The Metaphor of the Monster: Interdisciplinary Approaches to Understanding the Monstrous Other in Literature / edited by Keith Moser and Karina Zelaya.
Description: New York: Bloomsbury Academic, 2020. | Includes bibliographical references and index. | Summary: "A collection of fresh interventions into the field of monster studies that brings into conversation a wide variety of scholarly disciplines"—Provided by publisher.
Identifiers: LCCN 2020013049 | ISBN 9781501364334 (hardback) | ISBN 9781501364358 (pdf) | ISBN 9781501364341 (ebook)
Subjects: LCSH: Monsters in literature. | Monsters–Symbolic aspects.
Classification: LCC PN56.M55 M48 2020 | DDC 809/.9337–dc23
LC record available at https://lccn.loc.gov/2020013049

ISBN: HB: 978-1-5013-6433-4
PB: 978-1-5013-6929-2
ePDF: 978-1-5013-6435-8
eBook: 978-1-5013-6434-1

Typeset by Deanta Global Publishing Services, Chennai, India

To find out more about our authors and books visit www.bloomsbury.com and sign up for our newsletters.

To Addison and Andy Hélène,

May you one day inherit a better world less riddled with the visible scars of monstrosity.

Contents

Acknowledgments — ix

Introduction *Keith Moser* — 1

Part I Ecological Perspectives

1. A Portrait of Fictional Characters as Darwinian Monsters
   Dominique Lestel, translated by Keith Moser — 17
2. *Tokyo Ghoul* and the Trouble with Cannibalism *Tony Milligan* — 34
3. Monster and Victim: Melusine from the Fourteenth Century to the Age of *Homo Detritus* *Jonathan Krell* — 49
4. J. M. G. Le Clézio's Defense of the Human and Other-than-human Victims of the Derridean "Monstrosity of the Unrecognizable" in the Mauritian Saga *Alma* *Keith Moser* — 63
5. Strange Fish: Caliban's Sea-changes and the Problems of Classification *James Seth* — 85
6. Monster of Vacancy, Ghost of Culture, Instrument of Clarity: Cultural and Textual Analysis of the Function of the Sonoran Desert as Monster in Luis Alberto Urrea's *The Devil's Highway* *Mindy Adams* — 98

Part II Transgressive, Monstrous Gender and Corporality

7. Transgressive and Sovereign Authority in the Valois Court *Touba Ghadessi* — 109
8. "Maybe Something I Never Wanted Will Be Born": Etgar Keret's Monstrous Dream of Motherhood *Elisa Carandina* — 130

Part III Teaching Monstrosity in the (Post-)Modern World

9. Reading Monsters: How Mary Shelley Teaches Incels to Read *Paradise Lost* *Neil Barrett* — 147
10. "We Live in a Time of Monsters": Teaching Composition through the Representations of Monsters and Monstrosity in Literature *Devon Pizzino* — 163

Part IV Monstrosity in World Literature

11 Vamping It Up: Identity Performance and Intoxicated Bloodlust in the
    Poetry of Eduardo Haro Ibars *Alyssa Holan*   187
12 The Edges of the World in Classical Greece and Epic India:
    A Comparison of the Monstrous Races of Ctesias's *Indica* and the
    Rākṣasas of Vālmīki's *Rāmāyaṇa* *Albert Watanabe*   204
13 Satire and Monstrosity in African Diasporic Drama *Subbah Mir*   213
14 How a Monster Became a Hero: An Understanding of Camusian
    Morality through the Absurdist Hero, Don Juan *Scott Truesdale*   227

Index   239

Acknowledgments

First of all, we are truly indebted to Peter Corrigan (department head of Classical and Modern Languages and Literatures) and Rick Travis (dean of the College of Arts and Sciences) at Mississippi State University for their unwavering support of *The Metaphor of the Monster* conference that ultimately inspired this transdisciplinary volume. We would also like to take advantage of this opportunity to thank all the other members of the organizing committee for this symposium: Silvia Arroyo, Salvador Bartera, Robert Harland, Julia Kraker, Arleana Moya, and Rosa Vozzo. We must also express our gratitude to the external contributors who believed in this project. Moreover, we must acknowledge the pivotal role of the anonymous reviewers for each manuscript representing many different fields of study who took time out of their busy schedules to offer invaluable feedback that greatly enhanced the quality of the final product. On a final note, we would like to thank Katherine de Chant at Bloomsbury for her enthusiastic support of this project from the onset.

Introduction

Keith Moser

Departing from the notion that knowledge has no center from which it emanates, this edited volume seeks to expose the porosity of disciplinary boundaries. The eclectic group of researchers who comprise this volume represents many different fields of study including world literature, philosophy, environmental ethics, gender studies, and religion. Although Monster Studies is now a relatively established interdiscipline in many academic circles, this project contributes to the wealth of existing criticism in the field by breaking new ground and offering fresh perspectives related to various representations of monstrosity. In this regard, the innovative and bold theoretical frameworks proposed in *The Metaphor of the Monster* are a testament to how Monster Studies continues to bifurcate in many divergent directions near the beginning of a new millennium. In a concerted effort to transcend the ubiquitous "rhetoric of interdisciplinarity," we have united scholars from varied academic backgrounds who weave together meaningful connections between different kinds of epistemological discourses (Brown 1). Indeed, it is this radical transdisciplinarity that separates this (re-)investigation of monstrosity from previous studies such as Cohen's *Monster Theory* (1996), Scott's *Monsters and the Monstrous: Myths and Metaphors of Enduring Evil* (2007), and Levina and Bui's *Monster Culture in the 21ˢᵗ Century* (2013).[1]

In stark contrast to narrowly focused areas of study that have resulted in overspecialization and insularity, which reflect the inherent limitations of traditional critical theory, the contributors to this volume adhere to the basic tenets of the methodical approach that Edgar Morin refers to as "complex thought." As opposed to remaining within the confines of a tiny epistemological box, this volume strives to "reorganize knowledge and rethink the fragmented disciplines" (Morin 132). Adopting the Morinian view of knowledge and inquiry, this team of scholars deliberately engages in the sort of transdisciplinary "bordercrossing" for which Jacques Derrida advocates in his posthumous environmental works *The Animal That Therefore I Am* and *The Beast and the Sovereign* series (Derrida, *The Animal* 12). In this vein, the etymology of the word "complex" is quite revealing. As Morin often explains throughout his vast *oeuvre*, which is informed by the discoveries of modern science, the Latin declension

---

[1] This is evidently a non-exhaustive list of recent seminal works in the field of Monster Studies. A few others include Picart, Caroline, and John Browning. *Speaking of Monsters: A Teratological Anthology*. Palgrave Macmillan, 2012; Ken Gelder. *The Horror Reader*. Routledge, 2000; Mark Jancovich. *Horror, The Film Reader*. Routledge, 2001; Alain Silver, and James Ursini. *Horror Film Reader*. Limelight, 2001.

"complexus" signifies "that which is woven together" (Montuori 14). This vision of erudition embodies the spirit of *The Metaphor of the Monster* that (re-)connects disparate strands of knowledge that have been severed by "fractured thinking" in Western civilization in an attempt to understand the social construct of a monster more fully (Morin 130).

Before briefly contextualizing the renowned philosopher and ethologist Dominique Lestel's pioneering chapter that opens the volume, I would like to propose the following operational definition: "Monsters are exceptions to the doctrine of moral considerability that fall through the conceptual cracks epitomized by dichotomous, reductionistic thinking. They are reflections of both *limitrophy* and liminality inextricably linked to the concept of the 'human' and the history of normality in Western civilization." In *The Animal That Therefore I Am*, Derrida elucidates what his theory of limitrophy entails. In this influential series of lectures published shortly after his death, Derrida declares,

> Limitrophy is therefore my subject. Not just because it will concern what sprouts or grows at the limit, around the limit, by maintaining the limit, but also what feeds the limit generates it, raises it, and complicates it. Everything I'll say will consist, certainty not in effacing the limit, but in multiplying its figures, in complicating, thickening, delinearizing, folding, and dividing the line precisely by making it increase and multiply. (29)

From a Derridean standpoint, numerous Monster Studies theorists such as Mia Spiro, Tony Caesar, and Iris Idelsen-Shein posit that human and other-than-human monsters contest and problematize the oppositional thinking through which our sense of Self and the Other is constructed.

Given that monstrous entities are "not quite one thing, and yet not quite another" that do not fit so neatly into our preconceived representations of the world predicated upon reductionistic, binary logic, they undermine the mental structures upon which our collective sense of identity is forged (Caesar 287). In simple terms, monsters "threaten binary thinking by introducing a new category that refutes easy classification" (Spiro 27). In his Derridean interpretation of monstrosity, Colin Milburn theorizes that monsters are "denizens of the borderland [who] have always represented the extremities of transgression and the limits of the order of things [. . .] the boundaries of conventional thought" (603). Likewise, Iris Idelsen-Shein asserts that monstrosity is really a question of how we perceive ourselves and our relationship to both the human and cosmic Other. As Idelsen-Shein notes, "The monstrous is that which cannot be understood according to conventional notions of identity. It is an aberration, which in its very existence destabilizes epistemological boundaries and challenges the possibility of identity" (30). Monsters erode our stable sense of Self, thereby compromising the shaky edifice upon which our understanding of the biosphere and our place in it originates. From an ecolinguistic angle, the monster lays bare the artifice of the "cognitive structures in the minds of individuals which influence how they perceive the world" (Stibbe 6). It is our inability to think beyond the parameters of deeply flawed conceptual frameworks revolving around binary codes that breathes life into the monster who becomes a disenfranchised, ostracized, and marginalized Other that must be effaced from society at all costs.

After mental categories like *human and animal* and *man and woman* have been severely weakened, "it is in this liminal space where the subject experiences a crisis of meaning" (Phillips 20). The implosion of the dualities that serve as the cornerstone of our collective identity momentarily paralyzes the subject. When these identiary binary structures begin to collapse, we are confronted with an ethical choice. It is a matter of embracing alterity by redefining and multiplying conceptual borders, or "ridding society of difference" (Arrigo and Williams 178). Due to the prevalence of many different types of monsters from antiquity to the present who have been relegated to the status of social pariahs, Michel Foucault implies that it is easier to cling to bad dichotomous thinking than it is to reconstruct the veritable essence of our identity. As Emily Troshynski and Jesse Weiner underscore, "Foucault suggests that monsters are living transgressions, deviations from a preconceived idea of normal" (741). In order to bring the monster out of the shadows into the light of moral considerability, the question is how to implore more people to engage in the philosophical and ethical exercise of limitrophy. Instead of seeking refuge in categories that have been destabilized and discredited, Derrida urges us to go "back to the drawing board" to reexamine these fuzzy borders and to expand their dimensions (*The Animal* 76). When our reductionistic understanding of what it means to be human is replaced with richer cognitive structures that reject all forms of oppositional thinking, perhaps the monsters who have haunted human civilization for millennia will perish as well. For Derrida, the key is to uproot the monstrous thinking that divides "normal" people from the savage beasts and freaks.

Deriving a considerable amount of inspiration from Derrida, as evidenced in his recent article entitled "The Infinite Debt of the Human towards the Animal," much of Lestel's philosophical project explores the "long history of violence and discipline directed against non-human bodies," or those that are not granted the status of full-fledged humans (Chrulew 187). In comparison to Lestel's bi-constructivist paradigm that is infused with principles from philosophy, literature, ecology, ethology, ethnography, and biosemiotics, Derrida does not "go out of the text [. . .] even [. . .] with his strong interest in animals, he could not go out of that French theory, which is really a literary theory, literary ways to think about not the world but the text. Texts are very central" (Chrulew 192). As a maverick thinker who acts as if academic divisions do not exist at all in seminal works such as *L'Animal singulier* (2004), *L'animalité: Essai sur le statut de l'humain* (2007), *Les origines animales de la culture* (2009), *A quoi sert l'homme?* (2015), Lestel is the ideal choice to open this present volume. In Chapter 1, "A Portrait of Fictional Characters as Darwinian Monsters," Lestel adds even more new wrinkles to the transdisciplinary philosophical mode of inquiry that he has been honing for decades. Not only does Lestel's thought experiment offer an intriguing, interdisciplinary lens from which to examine the myriad of issues highlighted by other scholars, but it also reflects a unique way of thinking about literature and evolution. Specifically, Lestel compellingly outlines "*a general theory of evolution* [emphasis in original]" that considers fictional characters to be agents evolving in different kinds of ecologies within human mental spaces. Lestel's highly original study seamlessly blends all of the aforementioned ways of knowing into a cohesive whole. His theories related to the "operational existence" of the creatures that human civilizations have been conjuring up for countless eons concretize what is at stake in discussions revolving around monstrosity.

The renowned Scottish animal ethicist and philosopher Tony Milligan's chapter "*Tokyo Ghoul* and the Trouble with Cannibalism" follows Lestel's latest thought experiment. Similar to how Lestel is at the forefront of debates centered around environmental ethics in the Francophone world, Milligan has earned the reputation of being a key thinker in many Anglophone circles. Building upon the transdisciplinary, biocentric paradigms that he develops in *Beyond Animal Rights: Food, Pets and Ethics* (2010), *Love: The Art of Living* (2011), and *Animal Ethics: The Basics* (2015), Milligan further expands conversations related to veganism as a moral imperative by mingling philosophy, religion, theology, film studies, and popular culture in his analysis of Sui Ishida's manga series *Tokyo Ghoul*. In contrast to the voracious, monstrous appetite for daily meat consumption rendered possible by the horrors of industrial farming that is indicative of modern life, Milligan describes some ghouls as "vegan monsters" who even have *Homo sapiens* as pets. Drawing upon Foucault's ideas about cannibalism and sovereignty, Milligan also portrays the ghoul community in *Tokyo Ghoul* and *Tokyo Ghoul: Re* as a complex society characterized by rival narratives.

The selection of Lestel's groundbreaking reappraisal of the monster and Milligan's inventive reworking of ghoulish monstrosity as the lead chapters is strategic on another level as well. The ecological perspectives that they incorporate into their reflections enrich our understanding of the biocentric explanations of the monster conceived by Jonathan Krell, Keith Moser, Mindy Adams, and James Seth. These researchers start to fill a significant research gap by revisiting the metaphor of the monster from an ecological angle that is grounded in ecocriticism, environmental philosophy, ecolinguistics, and biosemiotics. Despite the fact that Monster Studies is a diverse interdiscipline that seemingly knows no bounds, research that takes advantage of environmental theory to shed new light on manifestations of monstrosity is rather scant. For this reason, this portion of the volume is one of the most essential contributions of the project as a whole. In this regard, this transdisciplinary initiative also invites other scholars from the environmental humanities and related fields to join this crucial conversation in the Anthropocene.

Krell, Moser, Adams, and Seth's defense of the cosmic "wholly other" recalls Derrida's "contemplation of monstrosity" in addition to the ecological thought of Edgar Morin, Michel Serres, Jean-Marie Pelt, Dominique Lestel, Tony Milligan, Peter Singer, Arne Næss, Pierre Rabhi, Philippe Descola, and Eric Baratay (Derrida, *The Animal* 11; Milburn 607). On the basis of the human-animal divide undergirded by chimerical fantasies like Descartes's "notorious *bêtemachine* theory," mainstream Western philosophy has long supported the untenable position that all other organisms are "biological automatons" that operate purely according to an internal machinery (Batra 116; Lestel qtd. in Chrulew 22). From such an extreme anthropocentric frame of reference, which has been utterly debunked by the scientific community, it is easy to paint the nonhuman Other as a vile beast that must be subjugated, tamed, and annihilated. The metaphor of the monster reminds us that "the worst, the cruelest, the most human violence has been unleashed against living things [...] who precisely were not accorded the dignity of being fellows" (Derrida, *The Animal* 108). In his deconstruction of the human-animal binary in *Musique*, Serres also argues that other creatures are subjects as opposed to being monstrous, non-sentient objects for many of the same reasons as Derrida. Compelling us to end what he calls the "world war" against the remainder of the cosmos before it is too late, Serres muses,

> Listen yet again to a *Requiem for Massacres*. As we are destroying many species every day, we are definitively extinguishing their voice. [...] Here is the true scale of human deafness. Responsible for this Babylonian destruction, deaf to this Pentecost, how can we pretend to listen to our language brothers if we are forever silencing the voice of our cousins? (*Musique* 62)

Beginning with the publication of his landmark essay *Le Contrat naturel* in 1990, Serres develops an ethics of compassion that unveils other-than-human subjects as sentient fellows with whom we share this interconnected and interdependent planet. Similar to Derrida, Serres realizes that the myopic "guerre mondiale" (world war) that we have launched against the rest of the biotic community of life is inseparable from the monstrous ideology that continues to justify the egregious, ecocidal violence that we incessantly inflict upon the earth.

After probing the ecological implications of monster literature that are overdue for more recognition, Touba Ghadessi delves into the connection between historiography and monstrosity. As the popular culture phenomenon of the freak show in Western society illustrates, monstrosity has always been a "metaphor for the exploration of difference" intimately tied to "historically established, coercive" norms that are not meant to be analyzed critically (Richards 378; Gyllenhammer 52). Consequently, the philosopher-historian "Foucault's *Discipline and Punish* has a broad interest in the way *power* operates on the body through *regimes* of behavior" (Gyllenhammer 59). In the larger context of public perception related to transgressive corporality that deviates from socially accepted norms, Ghadessi's study of representations of aberrant bodies in the late fifteenth and sixteenth century in France offers an excellent historical and theoretical vantage point for broaching contemporary debates linked to transgenderism and gender fluidity.

As Iris Idelsen-Shein highlights, monsters are "beings that challenge boundaries and hierarchies, and complicate binary pairs" (52). In her article "Transgender Theory and Embodiment: The Risk of Racial Marginalization" based upon field research conducted with gender liminal people living in the South Pacific, Katrina Roen discusses "the maintenance of the gender binary" (252). Roen's "deconstruction of the man/woman binary" explains why the decision to have a sex reassignment surgery is an agonizing choice for many transgender people (252). Celebrating her third gender, Roen chronicles how an individual, whom she refers as Tania, rejects the possibility of an operation because "she disagrees with the suggestion that she must have sex reassignment surgery to attain the legal rights of a woman" (259). On the reality show *I am Jazz*, the transgender star of the program legitimizes both sides of the debate before ultimately opting to have a gender confirmation surgery. Although Jazz indicates that it is the correct decision for her, she understands why some transgender women are vehemently opposed to the operation. In a political atmosphere in the United States in which the current president has made numerous attempts to ban transgender people from serving in the military, the struggles of this often-misunderstood community are far from over. As the transgender theorist Anthony Wagner underscores, transgender people still "live in a binary world that is divided into human and animal, and in which humanity is divided into male and female" (51). Furthermore, Wagner expresses the common transgender sentiment that "I am monstrous by simply being 'Other'" (51).

Building upon Ghadessi's historical backdrop focusing on alterity, Elisa Carandina and Neil Barrett (re-)investigate how the advent of the age of information and the dawn of modern science have generated new forms of monstrosity. In her exploration of the social and geographical context that inspired Mary Shelley to write *Frankenstein*, Elisa Carandina decries the pervasive misuse of science associated with technological monstrosities. Delving into gender theory, Carandina theorizes that the story of Frankenstein is a misogynistic tale depicting a kind of monstrous desire for male maternity that attempts to bypass the feminine body altogether. In his essay in which he contends that the novel *Frankenstein* could foster deep feelings of sympathy and understanding for the feminine Other upon which incels place all of the blame for their suffering linked to "involuntary celibacy," Neil Barrett notes how anonymous virtual environments like *4chan* provide a dangerous safe haven for toxic masculinity.

Carandina and Barrett's troubling reflections are reminiscent of the anxiety articulated by Michel Serres and Jean Baudrillard about the ubiquity of technological advances that they rather prophetically predicted at the end of the 1960s would one day concretize nearly every facet of the human condition. As a philosopher of science and epistemologist, Serres often lauds sophisticated forms of human innovation that have radically improved the quality of life for millions of people around the planet in optimistic works like *Petite Poucette* (2012), *Le Gaucher boiteux* (2015), and *C'était mieux avant!* (2017). Nevertheless, Serres avoids falling into the common ideological trap of describing human inventions as inherently good or evil. Adopting a pragmatic approach to dealing with the new philosophical problems posed by the technologies through which many of our quotidian experiences are now filtered in the digital age, Serres opines,

> Nothing is better, nothing is worse than the online environment. [. . .] Nothing is worse, certainly, but nothing is better than the virtual. As Aesop says about language, all media is assuredly the best and worst of all things. [. . .] Remedies for all poison, poison against all remedies, all of the channels start on an equal playing field. (*Atlas* 185)

In response to his many detractors who appear to be somewhat baffled regarding the "surprising turn" in the aforementioned recent texts in which he passionately highlights the positive aspects of the age of information, Serres unequivocally condemns those who take advantage of the internet to exploit, debase, and denigrate other people (Paulson 35). In his essay *Hominescence* (2001), Serres directly addresses the issue of online predation connected to a wide range of illicit activities including human trafficking, prostitution, drug smuggling, and terrorism. Explaining that the term "web" is the perfect word for discussing both the promise and peril of the internet depending on how it is used, or who controls access to this information superhighway, Serres (2001) declares, "The English term web designates a spider's web [...] upon which a formidable predator watches over every living being that passes by. Admission?" (*Hominescence* 256). It is perhaps in this sense in which the monstrous, heinous crimes committed by certain members of the incel movement outlined by Barrett should be understood. Anonymous online spaces are an ideal breeding ground for contemporary monsters who are cunning enough to lure unsuspecting victims into their web. Additionally, Carandina's chapter demonstrates that men with misogynistic tendencies have long been conceiving ways in which to misuse inventions in an effort to subdue women and to assert their alleged supremacy.

As I systematically explore in *The Encyclopedic Philosophy of Michel Serres: Writing the Modern World and Anticipating the Future* in a section entitled "The Distinction between Active and Passive Mediums: The Recent Break with Baudrillardian Philosophy," Baudrillard does not share Serres's cautious optimism regarding the digital revolution. For Baudrillard, virtual technology has ushered in what he refers to as "the final stage of simulation" in which the modern subject is now a passive consumer of commercial simulacra that find their origins outside of concrete reality (Barron 394). Summarizing Baudrillard's position, Douglas Kellner affirms, "the production and proliferation of signs, has created a society of simulations governed by hyperreality. [...] As simulations proliferate, they come to refer only to themselves: a carnival of mirrors reflecting images projected from other mirrors onto the omnipresent television screen. [...] No exit. Caught up in the universe of simulations" (128). According to Baudrillard, there is no escape from "the nectar of simulation" that bombards us nearly every waking moment in our edifices of wood, brick, concrete, and steel (Cline).

In the aptly named *The Intelligence of Evil* (2004), the postmodern theorist of hyperreality and "integral reality" boldly proclaims that the "reality principle" itself has been withered away by an enticing sea of empty signs in which we are constantly immersed (17). For all intents and purposes, "alternative facts" representing a parallel universe of simulation revolving around a fantasy-based structure have eclipsed the real, thus replacing it entirely. Baudrillard maintains that the "perfect crime"[2] has been committed in the shape of the erosion of reality and the imposition of an omnipresent realm of simulacra comprised of floating signifiers that have no real referents. Baudrillard's harrowing vision of a world that has been stripped of any semblance of meaning is an extension of "René Descartes's suspicions of the evil demon manipulating appearances" that is a recurring theme in the so-called social

---

[2] Jean Baudrillard. *The Perfect Crime*. Verso, 2008.

imaginary[3] in the philosophy of imagination (Stadler 9). In this vein, the simulators of hyperreality are the digital "beasts" that have "murdered" anything that exists "outside of their operational logics" in Baudrillardian terms (Abbinnett 69). Although other theorists would argue that Baudrillard's main premise is valid but overstated, a litany of recent events, including Kellyanne Conway's astonishing admission to which I alluded to earlier, lends credence to his theories overall. It is difficult to deny that many people have lost the ability to discern between reality and its representation on a screen. Given that the age of information is monstrous in the philosophical sense, these questions must be taken seriously.[4]

Baudrillard's concept of hyperreality, which has been revisited by numerous theorists such as Brett Nicholls, Pauline Sameshima, and Rupert Read[5] in the wake of the "post-truth" era reflecting an unheralded political landscape defined by the dissemination of an avalanche of simulacra, is applicable to the most salient example of contemporary monstrosity: the immigrant. In their (re-)examinations of timeless literary and philosophical issues that have been at the heart of the social construct of monstrosity since the beginning of human civilization, Mindy Adams, Subbah Mir, Devon Pizzino, Albert Watanabe, and Alyssa Holan lament the plight of many different kinds of individuals who are vilified as monsters because they do not correspond to our preexisting mental categories. Even if immigrants are not the only disenfranchised group of people whose very humanity has been called into question through the metaphor of the monster, Mindy Adams illustrates in her ecocritical reading of Luis Alberto Urrea's *The Devil's Highway* that they are currently the most vulnerable sector of the population. Devon Pizzino briefly mentions the precarious situation of immigrants in a political climate dominated by the politics of fear and hyperreal spectacle as well.

The fact that Trump's emergency declaration occurred during a period in which US-Mexico border crossings are at near historic lows supports Baudrillard's radical reworking of symbolic exchange in consumer republics[6] (Qiu). From a Foucaultian perspective, "difference must be suppressed as unsafe" in a disciplinary society whose hegemonic function is to remove the perceived "danger" that the Other represents

---

[3] In his recent book *The Cultural Imaginary of the Internet: Virtual Utopias and Dystopia* (2014), Majid Yar offers an excellent overview related to how theorists like Jean Baudrillard frame discussions revolving around the social-cultural imaginary.

[4] For a more detailed analysis of how the Trump administration has taken the phenomenon of hyperreality to an unprecedented level, see my recent essay "'Alternative Facts' Trump Reality in American Presidential Politics?: A Baudrillardian Analysis of the Present Crisis of Simulation." *International Journal of Baudrillard Studies*, vol. 15, no. 1, 2018, https://baudrillardstudies.ubishops.ca/alternative-facts-trump-reality-in-american-presidential-politics-a-baudrillardian-analysis-of-the-present-crisis-of-simulation/. Accessed February 25, 2019.

[5] See Brett Nicholls. "Baudrillard in a 'Post-Truth' World: Groundwork for a Critique of the Rise of Trump." *Medianz*, vol. 16, no. 2, 2016, pp. 1–25; Pauline Sameshima. "Post-Truth Simulacra: Inviting Mutable Meaning-Making." *Journal of the Canadian Association for Curriculum Studies*, vol. 15, no. 2, 2017, pp. 1–7; Rupert Read. "Richard Rorty and How Postmodernism Helped Elect Trump." *Philosopher's Magazine*, November 22, 2016, https://www.philosophersmag.com/opinion/147-richard-rorty-and-how-postmodernism-helped-elect-trump. Accessed February 25, 2019.

[6] The historian Lizabeth Cohen coined the term "consumer republic" in *A Consumers' Republic: The Politics of Mass Consumption in Postwar America* (2003).

(Segal 160; Comaroff 36). In what could only be described as "security theater,"[7] an American president has manufactured a media pseudocrisis through an incessant barrage of tweets and polemical diatribes about thousands of foreign invaders arriving in caravans. Labeling political asylum seekers as murders, rapists, and criminals, Trump has conceived a monstrous, parallel universe in which all "migrants or ethnic minorities are constructed as security threats" (Manokha 221). The Trump administration's obfuscation of the reality that both migrants and immigrants commit crimes at a much lower rate than the average American citizen reinforces Didier Bigo's notion of "Ban-Optican" inspired by Foucault's metaphor of the Panopticon (Ingraham).

As the derogatory word "alien" proves, the hegemonic tools used in the service of disciplinary power intentionally fuel the perception that immigrants-migrants are not fully human. In his article "Invasive Aliens: The Late-Modern Politics of Species Being," Jean Comaroff probes the etymological origins of the word "alien" being applied to human beings in legal and political arenas. Comaroff reveals that the expression alien was "enshrined in laws aimed most directly at barring Jewish entry in the 1930s" (35). In other words, the idea of a fellow human being an alien is a useful legal and political concept that permits people to absolve themselves of any ethical responsibility whatsoever for the trauma experienced by those who are fleeing discrimination, persecution, and ethnic cleansing. The doctrine of moral considerability does not apply to an "alien," or any other nonhuman entity that is denied personhood. As Kevin Johnson summarizes in his study "'Aliens' and the US Immigration Laws: The Social and Legal Construction of Nonpersons," "Immigrants are aliens, immigration is a flood, and immigration is invasion" (265). In this sense, the legal fiction of a human alien as an ideological device for scapegoating immigrants and imposing an alternate worldview grounded on the hyperreal construction of imaginary monsters.[8]

Given that all of the previous studies highlighted earlier posit that monstrosity is a social construct that dehumanizes the Other, Chapter 14 presents a different take on the metaphor of the monster. In his reflection "How a Monster Became a Hero: An Understanding of Camusian Morality through the Absurdist Hero, Don Juan," Scott Truesdale implores us to ponder what is a "real" monster. Although we have undoubtedly been conceiving fake monsters to avoid granting the status of full personhood to all of the members of the human and other-than-human community for millennia, Truesdale suggests a new path for Monster Studies connected to Camusian ethics. Since "Camus has long been neglected as a moral philosopher," Truesdale's exploration of Camusian morality through the writer's (re)-appropriation of the symbolism of

---

[7] For a more comprehensive explanation of security theater as it relates to immigration and migration, see James Welsh. "Border Theatre and Security Spectacles: Surveillance, Mobility and Reality-Based Television." *Crime, Media, Culture*, vol. 11, no. 2, 2015, pp. 201–21.

[8] In a recent interview, Trump's characterization of the migrant population as "animals" demonstrates that it truly is a question of personhood from a Derridean point of view. As Trump professes, "We have people coming into the country, or trying to come in—and we're stopping a lot of them—but we're taking people out of the country. You wouldn't believe how bad these people are. These aren't people. These are animals. And we're taking them out of the country at a level and at a rate that's never happened before" (Lind).

Don Juan in *The Myth of Sisyphus* is a welcome addition to the ongoing conversation (Starkey 144). Truesdale persuasively maintains that we are all saints and monsters, for it is impossible to live in a completely authentic manner without sometimes falling into the trap of what Sartre refers to as "bad faith." The "absurd hero who passionately" embraces his "earthly, sensual, existence" in Camus's writings is often confronted with an ethical quandary that cannot be solved in its totality (Starkey 148). In *The Myth of Sisyphus* and throughout the *pied-noir* writer's oeuvre, the Camusian hero cannot be entirely true to himself without turning his back on society or hurting those around him. Don Juan's actions are deemed to be monstrous and unacceptable according to social conventions, but this archetype reflects Camus's deep-seated conviction that we should appreciate every privileged moment[9] that life has to afford before we succumb to death as mortal beings.

In conclusion, Monster Studies is an interdiscipline that appears to have a bright future in the coming years based on the strength and diversity of the contributions to this volume. For better or worse, our predilection to create monsters has always been a part of us. Whether or not these fantastical apparitions that haunt humanity can be vanquished once and for all, thereby leaving no one to fall into the conceptual cracks, is thus debatable. Regardless, Monster Theory could play a major role in undermining the simplistic mental categories predicated upon dichotomous thinking that are at the core of the social construct of the monster. Perhaps, it is possible to live in a more humane and compassionate world that is less scarred by the visible effects of human and other-than-human monstrosity. As evidenced throughout much of recorded human history, social justice does not follow a linear trajectory. Even if certain monsters of the past are now considered to be full-fledged persons, the beast always has a tendency to rear its ugly head one last time. Monster Studies is emblematic of an unending battle against those who give birth to chimerical fictions in an attempt to ostracize, subjugate, debase, and exploit the Other. It is essentially a question of who we are and what sort of society that we want to bequeath to future generations in an age of information and at the dawn of the Anthropocene.

References

Abbinnett, Ross. "The Spectre and the Simulacrum." *Theory, Culture & Society*, vol. 25, no. 6, 2008, pp. 69–87.

Arrigo, Bruce and Christopher Williams. "Chaos Theory and the Social Control Thesis: A Post-foucauldian Analysis of Mental Illness and Involuntary Civil Confinement." *Social Justice*, vol. 26, no. 1, 1999, pp. 177–207.

---

[9] In my book *"Privileged Moments" in the Novels and Short Stories of J.M.G. Le Clézio: His Contemporary Development of a Traditional French Literary Device* (2008), I provide an operational definition of a privileged moment in the introduction. Moreover, I discuss this concept in the context of Camus's fiction as well in Chapter 1.

Barron, Lee. "Living with the Virtual: Baudrillard, Integral Reality, and Second Life." *Cultural Politics*, vol. 7, no. 3, 2011, pp. 391–408.
Batra, Nandita. "Dominion, Empathy, and Symbiosis: Gender and Anthropocentrism in Romanticism." *Interdisciplinary Studies in Literature and Environment*, vol. 3, no. 2, 1996, pp. 101–20.
Baudrillard, Jean. *The Intelligence of Evil*. Translated by Chris Turner, Berg, 2004.
Baudrillard, Jean. *The Perfect Crime*. Verso, 2008.
Brown, Steve. "Michel Serres: Science, Translation and the Logic of the Parasite." *Theory, Culture, and Society*, vol. 19, no. 3, 2002, pp. 1–27.
Caesar, Terry. "'Beasts Vaulting among the Earthworks:' Monstrosity in *Gravity's Rainbow*." *Novel: A Forum on Fiction*, vol. 17, no. 3, 1984, pp. 286–8.
Chrulew, Matthew. "The Animal Outside the Text: An Interview with Dominique Lestel." *Angelaki*, vol. 19, no. 3, 2014, pp. 187–96.
Cline, Alex. "Statues of Commodus-Death and Simulation in the Work of Jean Baudrillard." *International Journal of Baudrillard Studies*, vol. 8, no. 2, 2011, https://baudrillardstudies.com/international-journal-of-baudrillard-studies/, Accessed Feb. 23, 2019.
Cohen, Lizabeth. *A Consumers' Republic: The Politics of Mass Consumption in Postwar America*. Vintage Books, 2003.
Comaroff, Jean. "Invasive Aliens: The Late-Modern Politics of Species Being." *Social Research*, vol. 84, no. 1, 2017, pp. 29–52.
Derrida, Jacques. *The Animal That Therefore I Am*. Translated by David Wills, Fordham University Press, 2008.
Gelder, Ken. *The Horror Reader*. Routledge, 2000.
Gyllenhammer, Paul. "Normality in Husserl and Foucault." *Research in Phenomenology*, vol. 39, 2009, pp. 52–68.
Idelsen-Shein, Iris. "Meditations on a Monkey-Face: Monsters, Transgressed Boundaries, and Contested Hierarchies in a Yiddish *Eulenspiegel*." *Jewish Quarterly Review*, vol. 108, no. 1, 2018, pp. 28–59.
Ingraham, Christopher. "Two Charts Demolish the Notion that Immigrants here Illegally Commit More Crime." *Washington Post*, June 19, 2018, https://www.washingtonpost.com/news/wonk/wp/2018/06/19/two-charts-demolish-the-notion-that-immigrants-here-illegally-commit-more-crime/?noredirect=on&utm_term=.5e967655d542. Accessed Feb. 25, 2019.
Jancovich, Mark. *Horror, The Film Reader*. Routledge, 2001.
Johnson, Kevin. "'Aliens' and the U.S. Immigration Laws: The Social and Legal Construction of Nonpersons." *The University of Miami Inter-American Law Review*, vol. 28, no. 2, 1996–7, pp. 263–92.
Kellner, Douglas. "Baudrillard, Semiurgy and Death." *Theory, Culture & Society*, vol. 4, no. 1, 1987, pp. 125–46.
Lind, Dara. "Trump on Deported Immigrants: 'They're Not People, They're Animals.'" *Vox*, May 17, 2018, https://www.vox.com/2018/5/16/17362870/trump-immigrants-animals-ms-13-illegal. Accessed Feb. 25, 2019.
Manokha, Ivan. "Surveillance, Panopticism, and Self-Discipline in the Digital Age." *Surveillance & Society*, vol. 16, no. 2, 2018, pp. 219–37.
Milburn, Colin. "Monsters in Eden: Darwin and Derrida." *Modern Language Notes*, vol. 118, no. 3, 2003, pp. 603–21.

Montuori, Alfonso. "Complex Thought: An Overview of Edgar Morin's Intellectual Journey." *Metaintegral Foundation*, Resource Paper, June 2013, https://www.researchgate.net/profile/Alfonso_Montuori/publication/260603130_Edgar_Morin_and_Complex_Thought/links/00463531d465f68973000000/Edgar-Morin-and-Complex-Thought.pdf?origin=publication_detail. Accessed Mar. 10, 2018.

Morin, Edgar. *Homeland Earth: A Manifesto for the New Millennium*. Translated by Sean M. Kelly and Roger LaPointe, Hampton Press, 1999.

Moser, Keith. "'Alternative Facts' Trump Reality in American Presidential Politics? A Baudrillardian Analysis of the Present Crisis of Simulation." *International Journal of Baudrillard Studies*, vol. 15, no. 1, 2018, https://baudrillardstudies.ubishops.ca/alternative-facts-trump-reality-in-american-presidential-politics-a-baudrillardian-analysis-of-the-present-crisis-of-simulation/. Accessed Feb. 25, 2019.

Moser, Keith. *Privileged Moments' in the Novels and Short Stories of J.M.G. Le Clézio: His Contemporary Development of a Traditional French Literary Device*. The Edwin Mellen Press, 2008.

Nicholls, Brett. "Baudrillard in a 'Post-Truth' World: Groundwork for a Critique of the Rise of Trump." *Medianz*, vol. 16, no. 2, 2016, pp. 1–25.

Paulson, William. "Writing that Matters." *SubStance*, vol. 83, 1997, pp. 22–36.

Phillips, Robert. "Abjection." *Transgender Studies Quarterly*, vol. 1, nos. 1–2, 2014, pp. 19–22.

Picart, Caroline, and John Browning. *Speaking of Monsters: A Teratological Anthology*. Palgrave Macmillan, 2012.

Qiu, Linda. "Trump's Rationale for a National Emergency Is Based on False or Misleading Claims." *New York Times*, Feb. 15, 2019, https://www.nytimes.com/2019/02/15/us/politics/fact-checking-trump-emergency-border.html.

Read, Rupert. "Richard Rorty and How Postmodernism Helped Elect Trump." *Philosopher's Magazine*, Nov. 22, 2016, https://www.philosophersmag.com/opinion/147-richard-rorty-and-how-postmodernism-helped-elect-trump. Accessed Feb. 25, 2019.

Richards, Evelleen. "A Political Anatomy of Monsters, Hopeful and Otherwise." *Isis*, vol. 85, 1994, pp. 377–411.

Roen, Katrina. "Transgender Theory and Embodiment: The Risk of Racial Marginalization." *Journal of Gender Studies*, vol. 10, no. 3, 2001, pp. 253–63.

Sameshima, Pauline. "Post-Truth Simulacra: Inviting Mutable Meaning-Making." *Journal of the Canadian Association for Curriculum Studies*, vol. 15, no. 2, 2017, pp. 1–7.

Segal, Jacob. "Michel Foucault and Michael Oakeshott: The Virtuosity of Individuality." *Foucault Studies*, vol. 18, 2014, pp. 154–72.

Serres, Michel. *Atlas*. Julliard, 1994.

Serres, Michel. *Hominescence*. Le Pommier, 2001.

Serres, Michel. *Musique*. Le Pommier, 2011.

Silver, Alain, and James Ursini. *Horror Film Reader*. Limelight, 2001.

Spiro, Mia. "Uncanny Survivors and the Nazi Beast: Monstrous Imagination in *See Under: Love*." *Prooftexts*, vol. 35, 2015, pp. 25–36.

Stadler, Jane. "Cinesonic Imagination: The Somatic, the Sonorous, and the Synaesthetic." *Cinephile*, vol. 12, no. 1, 2018, pp. 8–15.

Starkey, Lana. "Albert Camus and The Ethics of Moderation." *Parrhesia*, vol. 21, 2014, pp. 144–60.

Stibbe, Arran. *Ecolinguistics: Language, Ecology and the Stories We Live By*. Routledge, 2015.
Troshynski, Emily, and Jesse Weiner. "Freak Show: Modern Constructions of Ciceronian Monstra and Foucauldian Monstrosity." *Law, Culture & The Humanities*, vol. 12, no. 3, 2016, pp. 741–65.
Wagner, Anthony. "On Elves and Beasts: An Intervention into Normative Imaginaries." *Graduate Journal of Social Science*, vol. 7, no. 2, 2010, pp. 44–56.
Welsh, James. "Border Theatre and Security Spectacles: Surveillance, Mobility and Reality-Based Television." *Crime, Media, Culture*, vol. 11, no. 2, 2015, pp. 201–21.
Yar, Majid. *The Cultural Imaginary of the Internet: Virtual Utopias and Dystopia*. Palgrave, 2014.

Part I

Ecological Perspectives

1

A Portrait of Fictional Characters as Darwinian Monsters

Dominique Lestel,
translated by Keith Moser

The Darwinian theory of evolution appeared in the nineteenth century. It could be succinctly characterized as a theory of the victorious monster. The monster thus appeared as the archetype of the predator, but this particular predator was less of a predator that consumed an individual than a predator that consumed the species itself. In other words, it was a predator that replaced the current version of the species with the one to which he belongs. Darwinian theory focuses on populations challenged by permanent, random mutations that continually appear among those who are a part of it. Most of these transformations do not present any adaptive advantage, and they disappear as quickly as they appeared. On the other hand, some of them turn out to be very profitable and are quickly adopted by the species. Darwinism (and contemporary Neo-Darwinism) could therefore be characterized as a theory of monsters that win. Nearly all of these mutations disappear because they are unsuitable. The only ones that remain are those that reveal themselves to be advantageous because they allow organisms that carry them to hijack some of these environmental characteristics of the developing environments they face. From this point of view, Darwinism is a theory of lucky and stubborn monsters that end up occupying space at the expense of the less fortunate. Neo-Darwinism (Darwinism plus genetics) does not modify this conception of evolution. The most recent trends maintain this general framework, even if they modify it by introducing elements derived from complexity theory.[1] The theory of evolution, or more precisely *a* theory of evolution, does it apply to other monsters in addition to biological monsters? Specifically, can it enable us to understand the phenomenon of fictional characters more fully by considering them to be semiotic, Darwinian monsters that strive to duplicate themselves in specific ecologies?

---

[1] This kind of approach, pioneered by biologists like Stuart Kauffman, stipulates that a mutation can only persist if it is inscribed in a viable biological system. This constraint simultaneously limits the space of possible mutations and maximizes the possibility of existence for those who enter into this space. The first appearance of this paradigm is found in Stuart Kauffman's *The Origins of Order: Self Organization and Selection in Evolution* (1993). He has more fully developed his original intuitions in several other publications.

The Theory of Evolution as a Theory of Triumphant Monsters

An evolutionary approach to fictional characters can only be understood in the larger context of what evolution has become today. Cultural practices related to species management (whether it is in the form of domestication or what is designated in a somewhat strange manner as an expression of preserving wild spaces) have evolutionary repercussions that are difficult to deny. From the Neolithic era, humans have played an essential role in the process of species selection. They favor the development of certain monsters while ignoring others. Humans have thus assumed a rather odd place in the evolution of species:[2] we are not only a monster that tries to sustain itself but also a monster that creates monsters that we allow to survive. A certain number of triumphant monsters presently owe their success to a feature, which has become increasingly important, that appeared rather late in natural history. "Attracting the attention of humans" is now a vital factor. This attraction manifests itself in a variety of different ways. For instance, it could take the shape of beauty, a certain type of touching vulnerability or interests that are more materially motivated including the production of meat or milk, the ability to run quickly in a race, or helping blind people find their way. Cultural organization has introduced corrective measures that are more or less efficient for managing emerging monsters without changing the mechanisms in the phenomenon of natural selection.[3] Beginning with the Neolithic revolution, the situation started to transform radically. It is possible to largely reconstitute the noteworthy stages that increased the role of humans in the evolutionary process.

Stage 1: Domestication as the Practice of the Subjugated Monster

The Neolithic era substantially changed the rules of the game by introducing several innovations such as domestication. This stage could be described as an industry of hereditary monstrosity to the exclusive benefit of one given species. Domestication is less concerned with dominion over an animal than it is with reproduction. The hunter-gatherer from the Paleolithic appropriates available resources: the peasant transforms the heritability of his prey in order to adapt them to his desires or needs. From an evolutionary angle, he also ends up with rather peculiar living beings that are unable to survive without the assistance of their predator to whom they are made available. They are subjugated monsters. Their reproduction and management should be understood as a gigantic "jeu infini" (infinite game), to borrow an expression from the American historian James P. Carse, between one given species (*Homo sapiens*),

---

[2] This is not to say that we are alone. The role of bacteria upon the evolution of living things is huge in this regard, even larger than that of humans.

[3] For that matter, the phenomenon of culture is not proper to humans. A great number of other animal species have their own unique cultures. For a more comprehensive explanation of the idea that we should think of culture as a plural phenomenon that has been independently verified in diverse forms in numerous species, see Dominique Lestel's *Les Origines animales de la culture* (2001).

several other selected species, and evolution.[4] The "finite game" is a game that is about winning. The "infinite game" is a game that one must make last as long as possible. From an evolutionary vantage point, domestication is a phenomenon that has been an extraordinary success. Nonetheless, the phenomenon of domestication has turned out to be only the first stage of a general transformation of the living by humans.

Stage 2: Comparative Ecology of Monstrosity

These domestic monsters are so well adapted today that they are quantitatively much more triumphant than the majority of wild species of a comparable size. The success of the phenomenon of domestication is evident in several statistics. In 2018, there were approximately one billion cows (*Statista* 2018). There were more than a billion sheep (*answers.com* 2018), 19 billion chickens in 2017 (*Quora* 2018), and more than 769 billion pigs in 2017 (*Statista* 2018). A comparison with large wild mammals even further underscores this impressive number from available data. In 2014, there were between 450,000 to 700,000 African elephants, and around 40,000 Asian elephants (*reference.com* 2018). There are between 50,000 and 100,000 whales. We could go on forever like this, but the following conclusion is obvious: the artificial monsters produced by livestock farming are much more abundant than most natural monsters of evolution. In the transformation of the planet brought about by humans, subjugated monsters have supplanted wild monsters. Some non-subservient species know how to play the same game admirably well, but they are rare. For example, it is impossible to quantify the number of rats that exist in the world, but there are already several billion of them, and they continue to proliferate blithely (*Worldatlas.com* 2018). It comes as no surprise that the biological monsters that take advantage of the presence of humans get by the best. Humans are also doing quite well. In 2011, there were around seven billion of them. The collapse of biodiversity should be understood in this context as the inevitable sign that monsters exclusively descended from natural evolution are no longer welcome in the present world.

Stage 3: From Hybridization to Biotechnologies

It is very true that subjugated, biological monsters are more and more artificial. The technologies of monstrosity have generally been placed in the hands of farmers, but a certain number of mavericks have acquired exceptional expertise in this field that has led to remarkable success. Chinese goldfish, Japanese carp, or all of the animals that are regularly exhibited in these competitions come to mind. For several years, researchers have explained the challenges that underpin this practice that has been pushed to unheralded extremes. They have explored the unprecedented possibilities of mobilizing biotechnologies that have induced a logical split in relation to the hybridization

---

[4] Cf. James P. Carse. *Finite and Infinite Games. A Vision of Life as Play and Possibility.* Ballantine Books, 1986.

techniques of traditional farming. With these techniques for manipulating the animal genome, it is not about influencing a reproductive program of monsters. Instead, it is a matter of directly fabricating monsters. In other words, it is a question of going from controlled hybridization manipulation to the mastery of the genome.

Stage 4: Butlerian Evolution

However, the role of humans in the evolutionary process does not stop at biological selection. According to the vast majority of experts, evolution is above all a biological theory, but there is no reason why it has to be restricted to such a space. The English writer Samuel Butler was the first person to apply the Darwinian theory of evolution to things. In 1863, he sent a letter to a New Zealand journal in which he explained that we are engaged in an evolutionary struggle with machines and they have already won the game.[5] This idea is not merely comical. It destabilizes our vision of evolution itself. The biological theory of evolution no longer appeared to be a special case (even if it is still the most remarkable). What should be considered a *general* theory of evolution applies to *all* evolutionary agents, whether they are biological or not.[6] The technologies for subverting living beings no longer even need to have biological connections.

Fictional Agents, Are They the Same?

The biologist Richard Dawkins gives credence to this idea of a Darwinism that focuses on artifacts suggesting that evolution is as much about "memes" (intellectual) as it is about "genes" (biological).[7] Furthermore, the Darwinian theory of evolution is not a unique case, but rather Darwinism is a much more encompassing theory. Whereas genes spread out through the reproduction of organisms that incorporate them, memes branch out by being copied or imitated by active agents. Dawkins's theory poses many problems, and what constitutes a "meme" is far from being the most trivial. Nevertheless, this theory has the advantage of envisioning the possibility that artificial, semiotic agents can be full actors in their own right in the evolutionary game by parasitizing biological organisms like the human brain.[8] Dan Dennett and Douglas Hofstadter popularized the theory of memes while noticeably transforming it at the same time, since they made memes selfish predators who take over our brains like

---

[5] This letter was taken up again in Samuel Butler's *Erewhon, or Over the Range* in 1872.
[6] In this vein, astrophysicists have recently proposed thinking about the dynamics of galaxies from an evolutionary perspective.
[7] Cf. Richard Dawkins's *The Selfish Gene* (1976).
[8] Expressing a similar idea, Jesper Hoffmeyer writes, "It seems more appropriate and more satisfactory to speak of living creatures as messages rather than as vehicles for survival" (46). He concludes, "The other dog is, in fact, a message" (Hoffmeyer 46). The original text appeared in Danish in 1993. I discussed this intriguing sentence in "Data" (2012).

prey.⁹ Susan Blackmore revisits this interpretation in *The Meme Machine* (1996) while simultaneously rejecting the intentional point of view. The meme theory poses a lot of problems; thus, its popularity has declined in recent years. Privileging the copy and reproducibility compared to variability and duplication has uncontestably neutralized its impact.

Evolution of Artifacts

Yet, the question of an evolution of artifacts insistently remains. Beyond memes, there is the possibility of an evolution of artifacts in the broad sense of the term, an evolution that includes ideas, beliefs, and so on which merits discussion. A certain number of theorists have explored this direction. Without going into all of the details of their studies, here are a few examples: F. T. Cloak, Jr. who evokes the possibility of a "cultural ethology" starting from 1975, D. T. Campbell who thinks about scientific theories in an evolutionary perspective, and David Hull who affirms that scientific theories have an evolutionary dynamic based on selection organized around a *conceptual inclusive fitness* that refers to the recognition of the originality of the researcher. Additionally, Hull theorizes about a "demic" structure referring to the need for each researcher to cooperate with others while also trying to assert their own originality.[10]

Thinking about Fictional Monsters from an Evolutionary Perspective

It is in this context of an evolutionary approach to nonbiological entities that thinking about fictional characters by considering them to be "literary monsters" becomes interesting. Literature, art, and cinema unite through sophisticated practices involving fictional monstrosity. They put into place ecologies in which fictional monsters proliferate that differ distinctly from biological ecologies, even if these two ecologies belong to a common evolutionary process.[11] Darwinism contends that an organism that is better adapted than another is one that reproduces itself more. Reproduction

---

[9] Cf. Hofstadter, Douglas, and Daniel Dennett. *The Mind's I: Fantasies and Reflections on Self and Soul*. Bantam Books, 1982. For additional reading about the transformations brought about in the organization of the text, without ever being indicated anywhere, which changes its meaning, see Jeremy Trevelyan Burman (2012).

[10] Cf. David Hull's "A Mechanism and Its Metaphysics: An Evolutionary Account of the Social and Conceptual Development of Science" (1988).

[11] Franco Moretti (*Distant Reading*, 2013) is a literary theorist who saw the potential richness of an evolutionary approach to fiction. However, what I am proposing is different. Moretti mainly derived inspiration from the evolutionary biogeography of Ernest Mayr, one of the principal theorists of Neo-Darwinism. This choice is problematic for two reasons. First, given that Mayr places the dynamics of genes at the heart of the evolutionary process rather than organisms themselves, what are the equivalents of genes in literature?

is the *only* criterion for success.[12] A similar analysis is equally applicable to fictional monsters who fill stories and more generally to imaginary monsters—and consequently to literary monsters. Yet, is the agency of fictional characters not illusory? This is the question that Marjorie Taylor and her colleagues respond to negatively evoking what they call "the illusion of independent agency" (Taylor, Hodges, and Kohányi 361–80). Two aspects of their work deserve to be expounded upon further. They first highlight that a massive majority of adult writers (published or unpublished) are convinced that their fictional characters have an autonomous life compared to them.[13] This empirical analysis is not only confirmed by a questionnaire but the data also reflects an overwhelming majority. Ninety-two percent of the authors who were questioned recalled this experience. In other words, nearly all of them! Hence, it is not a matter of a marginal phenomenon that only appears in the discourse of renowned writers. They additionally link this feeling to that of "imaginary friends" in young children. This comparison is interesting, but it is also a trap. It is interesting because it does not restrict the question of the autonomy of fictional characters to the sole domain of literary creation. Instead, it suggests that these characters are part of a much larger whole. It is a trap because the authors could have extended the question of imaginary friends to literary, fictional characters. They actually do the reverse by reducing fictional characters to childhood imaginary friends. In other words, they only discuss the psychology of the relationship to fictional characters instead of further developing their ontology. The reason for this choice is easily explained by the perspective they adopt. The authors place the autonomy of fictional characters into the category of "pretend play" (*jeu-à-faire-comme-si*). In the remaining pages, I will make the exact opposite hypothesis from that of Taylor and her colleagues. I will start from the position that all writers (or almost) think that their fictional characters have their own autonomy. The only difference is that the best authors are more precise. We should also attribute a real existence to such characters—as long as such a conception is not clearly refuted empirically. The question is not about knowing if these fictional characters truly exist but knowing how they interact with us. I will adopt *one* evolutionary model (not necessarily *the* classical Darwinian model) in order to do this.

"Imaginary Monsters," "Fictional Monsters," and "Literary Monsters"

Our chosen lexicon must be precise. "Imaginary monsters," "Fictional monsters," and "literary monsters" should not be understood to be synonymous expressions. An imaginary monster (*monstre imaginaire*) is a monster that inhabits the human

---

[12] It is the question of sexual selection that preoccupied Darwin and Wallace. Why are there still so many flamboyant male grouses when they attract the attention of predators? They are eaten more quickly than the others, but they attract more attention from females so they reproduce more.

[13] Joshua Landy (2015) offers several classical examples including Luigi Pirandello's play *Six Characters* in which the characters of the play complain to *their* author.

imagination, regardless of the nature of the monster in question. We have a hard time understanding what is at stake here. We underestimate the importance of this discussion, because we remain in a largely representational, Platonic paradigm in which the world is divided into the idea and the entity including its concretization in specific instances—between monsters on one hand and the representation of monsters on the other hand. Likewise, just as the concept of a dog does not bite,[14] the imaginary monster is not supposed to be a "real" monster. This sort of attitude, evidently that of reason, is not so straightforward. Many imaginary monsters have an operational existence. For instance, monsters from urban legends have real effects on people.[15] On another level, a certain number of monsters have an ambiguous existential status. What are we to make of the example of an animal like the Yeti or the sea serpent that no one has ever found, but that many people are still seriously trying hard to find?[16] As for the existence of ghosts, anyone who has lived in Asia knows that this is a subject that should be broached with a great deal of caution.[17]

A fictional monster (*monstre fictionnel*) is a specific type of imaginary monster that dwells within literary and cinematic fictions in addition to role playing games and video games. A fictional monster "who succeeds" duplicates itself into many other fictions, interviews, newspaper journals, periodicals, discussions among people, and so on. I am using the term "success" (as in all throughout the text) in a strictly Darwinian sense. *Harry Potter* is a shining example. Above all, J. K. Rowling's fictional agents reflect this remarkably adaptable success—her novels have sold millions of copies around the world. Whether or not this is good literature is not important at this stage. Rowling is an excellent duplicator,[18] and the fictional monsters to whom she has given birth have been multiplied by billions across the world. Following multiple translations, cinematic or theatrical adaptations, and comic books that have drawn inspiration from these monsters, the characters from the novel have transformed themselves in order to adapt to multiple cultural ecosystems. A "fictional monster" is not a monster in the sense in which this term is generally understood in monster literature, but rather it is a monster in the sense in which the theory of evolution should be understood. There is *one considerable difference*: unlike Darwinian monsters, the fictional monster is not a product of random mutations. It borrows a lot from the Lamarckian monster that transforms itself based on specific environmental characteristics that I will come back to a little later.[19]

---

[14] Gérard Genette writes, "le mot chien ne mord pas" (the word dog does not bite) in the prelude to *Mimologique: Voyage en Cratylie* (1999).
[15] Cf. Campio-Vincent, Véronique, and Jean-Bruno Renard. *Les légendes urbaines. Rumeurs d'aujourd'hui*. Payot, 2002.
[16] Bernard Heuvelmans created a new branch of zoology in his time called "la cryptozoologie" (cryptozoology) that was interested in such creatures.
[17] The recent exposition at the *Musée du Quai Branly* in Paris about Asian ghosts was very interesting from this point of view.
[18] I am deliberately using the term "duplicator" instead of "replicator" (that one finds in meme theory) or the word "reproducer" that one finds in Darwinism. I will revisit this point later.
[19] David Hull does not think that we can talk about Lamarckian evolution. We need to develop this point further regardless.

Literary monsters (*monstres littéraires* [or movies?]) comprise a third category of monsters, that of monsters who are identified as such in literature-like Dracula or Frankenstein's creature. All literary monsters are fictional monsters, but all fictional monsters are not literary monsters (e.g., Tarzan). Even if all fictional monsters are imaginary monsters, the opposite is false.

Imaginary monsters	Exist in the human imagination
Fictional monsters	Exist in works of fiction
Literary monsters	Comprise a subsection of fictional monsters that represent monsters

In this chapter, I am especially interested in fictional monsters, and I am proposing a slightly odd evolutionary approach *that adopts the point of view of fictional monsters*. However, this operation is to be taken from an evolutionary point of view and not from a psychological point of view that could lead us to suffer (or to celebrate), for instance, *with* fictional characters. For a long time, Noël Carroll has opposed the idea that the reader could feel something like empathy for fictional monsters.[20] Nevertheless, he himself remains locked in a psychological trap, when he posits that even when we care about characters, we do not want what they want because the truth is that *they want nothing at all*. Here we are dealing with an absent referent.[21] A fictional character has no mental state. It has no emotion, nor proto-emotion; it only exhibits these symptoms.[22] We can relate to these fictional characters through pseudo-empathy:[23] we can suffer with them, be worried about them, celebrate with them, and so on, although these characters feel nothing.

The Central Issue Warranting Attention

In the evolutionary perspective that I just discussed,[24] fictional monsters are "characters" that duplicate themselves by occupying media ecologies and parasitizing humans. What emerges from this is a very strange form of heterogeneous hybridization.[25] It

---

[20] Cf. Noël Carroll. *Beyond Aesthetics: Philosophical Essay*. Cambridge University Press, 2001.
[21] We should make reference here to Alexandre Kojève's reading of Hegel in which he supports the idea that it is the desire of desire that drives history.
[22] But what is a symptom that refers to *no* phenomenon at all? It is Baudrillard's simulacrum, for instance: "A copy without an original." The logic of simulation appears through a paradoxical circuit in which "that which is real" is lost at the very moment in which it can be perfectly simulated (Baudrillard, *Simulations*, 1983).
[23] This notion of "pseudo-empathy" that I am taking up here refers to a way of relating to the *nonexistent* emotions of an agent. It is very different than what we talk about in psychology when we evoke the ability to understand the difficulties of others without being able to relate to them and without doing anything to improve the situation, or when we manipulate the Other for our own gain.
[24] Even if it is humans that have created them. See J. P. Dupuy's revealing group that talks about these phenomena that we have not fabricated, those who have no longer been born, but of which we are the cause.
[25] The virus that infects the brain of a cat that starts liking mice perhaps belongs to a closely related category.

concretizes itself through a particular human ability that plays a preponderant role in the systems that are put into place. These fictional monsters do not take up residence in the human brain in order to exist,[26] but they parasitize their *attention*. The relationship to fictional monsters is thus understood through an ecology of attention. Paradoxically, attention has been rarely studied in an evolutionary perspective, even in a cognitive approach that focuses more on how an agent sees a fellow as opposed to what it is attentive to in an environment.[27] Economists have been a little more interested in this subject.[28] They understand that it is attention more than consumer products that properly determines all rare objects. Nonetheless, attention has always been present in literary practices. The Polish writer Stanislaw Lem quotes Witold Gombrowicz for whom writing a book is nothing; it is forcing others to read it that is art (Swirski 31). A work of art is thus incorporated into an economy of attention, to whose transformation it contributes in return. As Yves Citton writes, "The analysis of the economy of attention offers a unique perspective for understanding in a new light the multiple interactions that have been established during the last three centuries between the material production of our existence(s) and the cultural production of discourses, images, stories, and spectacles that have captivated and oriented our attention" (78). Citton thus brings to mind the definition of literature provided by Philip Watts:[29] a specific practice of attention to details. After Barthes, Citton focuses on this practice, but he could have just as easily examined the attention projected upon the characters. Moreover, he brilliantly reminds us that in French *être attentif à* (to be attentive to) also means *porter son attention sur* (focus one's attention on) and *prendre soin de* (to take care of). However, it is less about "care" (caring) than it is a type of virtuosity that we mobilize to take care of a delicate, fledgling fire so that it does not go out. A fire does not suffer. It feels nothing just like a fictional character, even if the latter can pretend the opposite, which a fire could never do. An ecology of attention and an economy of attention share at least one common principle: attention to the Other in relation to oneself is a rare resource that must be carefully cultivated. From this perspective, a fictional monster is someone who catches the attention of a large number of humans, who arouses their curiosity and leads them to take care of him like one would take care of a fire (taking care of a fire is not to be preoccupied with feelings but to pay attention so that the ongoing process continues). Knowing *why* fictional monsters spark our attention is yet another question, as is the question of knowing why *these monsters* and not others. I will come back to this later, but two questions need to be presently addressed: Can we think about fictional monsters based upon their own point of view, and do they have their own interests?

---

[26] It would be absurd to think this way. These fictional monsters are not viruses.
[27] Therefore, there is no consensus in evolutionary psychology about attention, even if we can find case studies in ethology dedicated to this theme. One of the most famous is that of Cheney and Seyfarth.
[28] Michael Goldhaber's article "The Attention Economy and the Net" (1997) ignited a polemical controversy.
[29] Cf. Yves Citton. "Literary Attention: The Hairy Politics of Details." (2013).

(Their) Own Point of View and Interest in Duplicating Themselves

One characteristic of evolutionary thought is its non-anthropocentric nature adopting the point of view of other organisms. For instance, the evolution of canines starts with the perspective adopted by canines. This is why we attribute so much importance to the choice of a sexual partner, which is described by the choices made by canines that are not dependent upon those of the biologists that observe them, and to the ways in which preys are spotted or predators avoided. Conversely, we would find it absurd to judge the attractiveness of female dogs for male dogs by adopting human criteria. This kind of censorship can be largely explained, but it does not cause us to avoid doing it from the point of view of imaginary monsters or fictional monsters. The idea that these monsters have no point of view falls under a largely imaginary psychology. We can certainly imagine that animals like mammals have preferences that we can more easily access, but this is not the question. From an evolutionary standpoint, this point is secondary. What is taken into account is the assessment that every living being "tries" to multiply itself. This is also true for elephants, moss, as well as fictional characters. The fact that elephants mobilize cognitive abilities that neither moss nor fictional characters possess is too trivial to be mentioned other than in passing. The evident objection that fictional monsters have no interest in duplicating themselves fades away when faced with the difficulty of characterizing what this "interest" could be in a clear and convincing manner outside of a fundamental evolutionary mechanism that could be explained as follows: when a fictional monster can duplicate itself, it duplicates itself. This is incidentally the attitude that biologists adopt when confronting the question of knowing what is the "interest" of an earthworm, a bacterium, a flower, or a meme in reproducing itself. We would not be able to find an earthworm that says to himself: "I have to reproduce" any more than we would be able to find a fictional monster that would think (to himself) "I have to duplicate." In this instance, interest alone is the only theoretical principle that has no reason to receive psychological support. The notion that fictional monsters lack cognitive abilities is therefore not a relevant objection.[30] A theorist of the evolution of fictional monsters has no reason to want to complicate his life more than a theorist of biological monsters. Biological evolution and the semiotic evolution of fiction ultimately participate in the same phenomenon. Biological evolution is organized around the reproduction of organisms, whereas the semiotic evolution of fiction is organized around the duplication of fictional characters—and the stories in which they find themselves caught up.

---

[30] A fictional character has at its disposal simulated cognitive abilities. "Simuler" (to simulate) has two meanings in French that are strangely complementary in this case: "reproduire" (to reproduce) and "faire croire que" (to make someone believe that). A fictional character "who thinks" does not think like a professor (*Homo universitae*) thinks: he only exhibits a few of the symptoms of thinking. Yet, he can make one think, and we can thus truly engage in "dialogue" with him and find answers that we did not have initially.

Biological Evolution	Reproduce	Search for energy sources
The evolution of memes	Replicate	Multiply identically and automatically
The evolution of fiction	Duplicate	Seek to capture the attention of humans and duplicate by transforming contingent upon opportunities

The ecology of this fictional duplication is far from simple. It takes shape at the interface of three distinct spaces that have nothing to do with the abstract: the space of human mental worlds, the realm of the materiality of literary production, and that of networks of transmission and evaluation.

Ethology of Fictional Monsters

This ecology differs from the ecologies in which biological monsters evolve, which is not very surprising at all. For this reason, it is not that easy to characterize it adequately. As a first approximation, these fictional monsters evolve in very odd environments in which material spaces (like the pages of a book), social regulations, and cognitive parameters that are proper to humans mingle. These fictional monsters are not biological, but the material characteristics of the ecosystems in which they live must be taken into account anyway. These fictional monsters are transitional agents that exist on many levels at the same time. (1) They exist on sheets of paper or parchment, in handwritten notebooks, in digital spaces, in libraries, or in bedrooms. (2) However, they also exist in other human mental spaces. One of the major distinctive features of fictional monsters, which biological monsters do not have, is that they are parasitic agents who take up residence in the mental spaces of humans capturing our attention. Many other biological species parasitize other species in order to survive without us attributing to them a lower intensity of life. (3) Finally, these fictional monsters take advantage of social networks—whether it be the printing press, periodicals, reading clubs, literary prizes, or the internet today. The main difference with biological organisms is that fictional monsters are entities that only secondarily, not exclusively, occupy metabolic spaces. They are also rather passive (like mushrooms[31]) as opposed to being active (like animals). These monsters are fictional like others are hairy. This characteristic is part of their specific ontology. The mental spaces that accommodate these fictional monsters are just as real as the geographical spaces that accommodate biological monsters, but they are situated at other levels of reality. They play a major role in monstrosity *as a general rule*, and it makes sense to develop their role further in the *global* evolutionary process. The combination of human mental spaces, cultural specificities, and types of media technology generates ecosystems in which fictional monsters evolve. These ecosystems can vary from one time period to another and from

---

[31] Mushrooms could represent a good model to think about some of the fundamental characteristics of literature.

one culture to another. We are thus dealing with a mechanism that is comprised yet again of three levels: (1) There is an *ethology of fictional monsters* that allows us to understand that certain fictional monsters duplicate themselves and others do not, which shows how those who duplicate parasitize human interests and take advantage of available natural resources at the same time (books, films, conferences, etc.) in order to do this. (2) There is also a *cultural anthropology of fictional monsters* that recognizes the fact that the category of fictional monsters and their nature vary from one culture to another and from one time period to another. (3) Finally, there is a *biological anthropology* of the human that makes up the main medium of fictional monsters, owing to specific cognitive abilities including that of being able to *tell stories* (to be more specific, fictions in which the narrator is not the hero Lestel, 1997). There is also the power to conceive material mediums into which fictional characters can place themselves.

Ethology of fictional monsters	Why do certain monsters proliferate and others do not?
Cultural anthropology of life shared with fictional monsters	How do humans develop different relationships with fictional monsters depending on their cultures?
Biological anthropology of the human	What are the biological abilities mobilized by humans to be parasitized by fictional monsters?

We like these imaginary fictional monsters for the same reasons that we like video games today. It is very exciting to interact with them and to feel "interesting" and "interested" through them.[32] The important point is that the reasons why we prefer such and such a fictional monster has no reason to be evolutionary. It is the fact of being parasitized by fictional monsters that is, providing that we adopt their point of view as we have seen.

Why Do Certain Fictional Monsters Parasitize Humans More than Others?

How do fictional monsters that take the shape of customized, fictional characters like Dracula or Frankenstein's creature capture the attention of humans? Critics usually reformulate the question in a more functional and apparent fashion, whether it be by making it into a sociopolitical problem or making it into a psychological problem. Sociopolitical explanations of literature appeared with Marx in the nineteenth century, but literary Marxism emerged with diverse theorists like Walter Benjamin, George Lukacs, Lucien Goldman, or even Fredric Jameson later. It blossomed at the end of the twentieth century in the work of Pierre Bourdieu. It positioned itself from the point of view of class struggles maintaining that the attraction for certain kinds of fiction

---

[32] Cf. Lisa Zunshine in *Why We Read Fiction* (2006) demonstrates in particular how actors can advantageously mobilize the techniques of the "Theory of Mind" to intensify the pressure on readers.

(literary or cinematic) is explained by the desire of the dominant class to distinguish itself from others, or to legitimize its relationships with the power in place. Conversely, this attraction could also be explained by the desire of the subaltern classes to emancipate themselves.[33] At the end of the twentieth century and at the beginning of the twenty-first, it became more diverse by adopting feminist, *queer*, or postcolonial points of view—but the principle remained the same. Fiction has always been instrumentalized by a particular social group through these approaches. Psychological explanations evolve in another space. They themselves are divided into two very different categories. Psychoanalysts assume a point of view reflecting the intimate, personal psychology of individuals. Bruno Bettelheim, the psychoanalyst of fairy tales, is a standard example.[34] He explains that fairy tales respond to children's anguish and prepare them to become adults. Evolutionary psychology, which has surfaced more recently, distances itself from psychoanalysis by assuming the point of view of the species. A sign of the times is that the influence of psychoanalysis is fading away, whereas Darwinian approaches to literature are gaining traction, knowing that it is ultimately a question of the same method, apart from a few parameters.

Darwinian Literary Studies

These Darwinian literary studies argue that fictions are comprised of tools that enable humans to exercise their adaptability in the real world.[35] These fictions thus constitute ways in which certain humans acquire adaptive advantages in *the evolution of the human*. A representative example of this is Matthias Clasen's treatment of Bram Stoker's *Dracula*.[36] For the Danish theorist, horror stories are dependent upon evolutionary properties of our central nervous system, and our understanding of them requires us to take the evolutionary history of humanity seriously (Clasen, *Why Horror Seduces* 4). From this angle, Stoker's novel provides a "strong emotional shape to conflicts and fears that are deeply ingrained in human nature" (Clasen, "Attention, Predation, Counterintuition" 381). When we adopt such a position, we run into numerous issues. I will limit myself by highlighting four of these problems. First of all, it should be understood that we have entered into a kind of Molieresque, dormitive virtue. Humans like this novel because it is in our nature to appreciate this kind of literature. But what are the evolutionary characteristics of humans that a novel latches on to (with the constant ambiguity of knowing that the reader latches on to the novel,

---

[33] The fact that two types of opposing explanations are just as easy to defend demonstrates that they explain nothing at all.
[34] Cf. Bruno Bettelheim. *The Uses of Enchantment: The Meaning and Importance of Fairy Tales* (1976).
[35] The literary critic Ugo Angelo Canello (1848–83) is considered to be a pioneer of this approach that blossomed at the end of the twentieth century and at the beginning of the twenty-first with theorists like Stephen Pinker (1999), Geoffrey Miller (2000), Brian Boyd (2009), Ellen Dissanayake (2000), Joseph Carroll (2004), or Denis Dutton (2004) to cite only a few of the most known.
[36] Cf. Mathias Clasen's article "Attention, Predation, Counterintuition: Why Dracula Won't Die" (2012).

because he "recognizes" an evolutionary theme, or he latches on because the novel teaches humans to understand a useful evolutionary theme)? Moreover, if the novel is successful because it latches on to a major evolutionary preoccupation of humans, why don't all novels that deal with this theme enjoy the same success? Afterward, when Clasen explains that humans have mirror neurons that allow us to feel what the Other feels including when it is a fictional character, he embarks on an adventure whose outcome is uncertain. A fictional character does not have a brain. Likewise, when Clasen asserts that our disgust in regard to pathogenic substances is coded in our genes, making Dracula a carrier of infectious germs is a judicious choice. He is playing with our attraction/repugnance of the character, and thus of his interests. We could remain skeptical and think that resorting to a genetic form of causality is hardly a satisfactory explanation in this instance. Finally, the question of monsters interests Clasen who makes it an evolutionary theme par excellence. But it is not because we are concerned with the great predators that the history of the predator and predation fascinates us—otherwise, we would be more interested in archery than soccer matches. Additionally, the interesting question is the one that we have a hard time answering: Does the evolutionary approach to literature teach us anything *interesting* about literature that we did not already know?

An Evolutionary Approach to Fictional Monsters Versus an Evolutionary Approach of Their Reception

Psychological, sociological, or classical Darwinian approaches transform fictions as a pretext for something else. They instrumentalize them as a way of achieving goals that are external to literature. Conversely, the evolutionary approach that I am proposing here takes them very seriously. Monster literature participates not only in the phenomenon of monstrosity but also in the phenomenon of evolution. Ultimately, we need to reverse this process here as well. It is not about applying the theories of evolution to fictional monsters, but rather understanding how they force us to transform our theories of evolution. What happens when fictional monsters contribute to the evolution of evolution itself. The fact that the human is an animal haunted by the company of diverse, imaginary monsters is part of who we are, and it plays a role in our adaptivity. Our "fuzzy interest" for novels or films about monsters should be perceived as a reproductive medium for cultural agents that parasitize our imagination just like agents dwell in any other ecosystem. There are not necessarily any complex reasons why we are so attracted to monsters. Perhaps, it is a reflection of our curiosity for *different* kinds of living beings, which could find its origins in our status as a predator, without this explanation being sufficient in and of itself. In this vein, we do not need anything more than gravity to explain why fruits fall on the ground. The error in psycho-evolutionary approaches to literary monsters is to believe that it is possible to find causal reasons that lead us to like specific monsters (e.g., Dracula), whereas other monsters force themselves into the ecology of our attention for *random* reasons that largely take place by chance.³⁷ Triumphant monsters are not victorious because they possess something specific; they are victorious because they got lucky (like rich entrepreneurs vs those who went bankrupt). We are in a state of retrospective illusion when we look for inexistent causalities.

Conclusion

Biology should not be a pure source of metaphors or a model to follow in literary studies, but rather a very rich intellectual resource from which new ways of thinking about fiction emerge. What I have tried to propose here is an evolutionary ethology of fictional monsters to be taken at face value. Monstrosity in literature resides as much in the signification of fictional characters as it does in their existence itself—the existence of "fictional monsters." The term "monster" should be understood in the Darwinian sense of an agent who receives random mutations, some of which enable him to impose himself into specific ecological spaces. I have conceived these "fictional monsters" as forms of symbiotic or parasitic agency to take at face value, endowed with a life of their own, thrown into material mediums like the book, capturing the attention of humans who traffic in these artifacts who mobilize themselves in human social networks to move about—like fleas or viruses. It is not only about determining to what extent a theory of evolution could apply to fictional characters but also about understanding to what extent wanting to grasp them therefore modifies the significance of what is or could be a theory of evolution. Biologists assimilate the theory of evolution into a biological theory, which very different authors like Butler or Dawkins have contested. By applying it to fictional characters, this approach forces us to think of evolution itself in another way. Literary Darwinism should be credited with the intuition that literature and evolution have convergent features. Nonetheless, its approach is comparable to that of saying that flowers exist because men can pick them in order to offer them to women and seduce them. Let's move away from marshaling evolution to understand literature and really do it and not by clinging to an approach that was referred to in its time as "human sociobiology," and which has since been discredited.³⁸ The human attention that I have evoked in this chapter is not proper to fictional monsters; it is already found in traditional forms of domestication. The difference resides in the fact that in the domesticated space, this attention is essentially utilitarian. In the case of fictional monsters, it falls under another phenomenon that is more complex. In domestication, the point of view of the human parasitizes that of the animal in question to the point of rendering the latter insignificant. In the evolution of fictions, it is quite the opposite.

---

[37] For a discussion of the importance of being lucky to be successful and the manner in which successful entrepreneurs transform this luck into personal qualities, see Nassim Nicholas Taleb's *The Black Swan* (2007).

[38] Its origins are found in E. O. Wilson's *Sociobiology: The New Synthesis* (1975). In this regard, it should be noted that the notion he refers to as "consilience," which is popular among many literary theorists, is a form of scientism that establishes the *biology* of evolution as the most important discipline.

It is fictional agents who manipulate the point of view of humans—perhaps even in an unprecedented form of *semiotic domestication*. Pretending that it is not fictions that manipulate other humans but other humans would be as trivial as pointing out that it is not parasites that manipulate the infected bodies of their hosts, but evolution. How far can we push this evolutionary perspective about fictions? It is too early to answer this question. Any answer would be premature, given that we are not necessarily taking into account the right agents. An alternative version of the story would be to consider that it is ultimately *words* that are the true agents of evolution and that fictional characters are only useful human vehicles to make these words desirable. Fictional characters would thus be a part of mediums through which they could develop and spread out. Theories representing an ambivalent position like philosophical theories could have a closely related status. In this context, we could also consider Greek philosophers, such as Plato and Aristotle, as a very efficient method for allowing a certain number of Greek words (like *phronesis*) to survive. Otherwise, they would have been forgotten after the collapse of Greek civilization. Conversely, we could ponder whether these problems of translatability would not be the equivalents of species that are incapable of adapting to changing ecosystems—the word is disappearing because it does not manage to impose its meaning and utility upon very different semantic ecologies than that to which it is accustomed.[39] One last question, albeit essential, has not been discussed in this text: Why fiction, which fictions? This could be the subject of another text, since the subject is so complex. A non-anthropocentric response would be interesting: it would suggest that it is the same question as that of knowing why there are animals and not only plants. Evolution is itself scalable. It takes on the task of creating previously unseen forms of living beings when it has the possibility of doing so. By allowing fictional characters to exist in a more or less autonomous fashion, humans would thus assume a closely related position to that of the *Tiktaalik rosae*: the fish that lived 350 billion years ago which was the first being to emerge from the water and the ancestor of all terrestrial animals.

References

Answers.com. "How Many Sheep are in the World?" 2018.
Baudrillard, Jean. *Simulations*. Translated by Phil Beitchman, Paul Foss, and Paul Patton, Semiotext(e), 1983.
Bettelheim, Bruno. *The Uses of Enchantment: The Meaning and Importance of Fairy Tales*. Knopf, 1976.
Blackmore, Susan. *The Meme Machine*. Oxford University Press, 1996.
Burman, Jeremy Trevelyan. "The Misunderstanding of Memes: Biography of an Unscientific Object, 1976-1999." *Perspectives in Science*, vol. 20, no. 1, 2012, pp. 75-104.

---

[39] For a more optimistic vision of the problems associated with translatability in philosophy, see Barbara Cassin's *Vocabulaire européen des philosophies - Dictionnaire des Intraduisibles* (2004).

Butler, Samuel. *Erewhon, or Over the Range*. Trübner and Ballantyne, 1872.
Campio-Vincent, Véronique, and Jean-Bruno Renard. *Les légendes urbaines. Rumeurs d'aujourd'hui*. Payot, 2002.
Carroll, Noël. *Beyond Aesthetics: Philosophical Essay*. Cambridge University Press, 2001.
Carse, James P. *Finite and Infinite Games. A Vision of Life as Play and Possibility*. Ballantine Books, 1986.
Citton, Yves. "Le point sur l'économie de l'attention." *La Revue des Livres*, no. 11, mai–juin 2013, pp. 72–9.
Citton, Yves. "Literary Attention: The Hairy Politics of Details." *Romanic Review*, vol. 105, nos. 1–2, 2013, pp. 111–21.
Clasen, Mathias. "Attention, Predation, Counterintuition: Why Dracula Won't Die." *Style*, vol. 46, nos. 3–4, Fall/Winter 2012, pp. 378–98.
Clasen, Mathias. *Why Horror Seduces*. Oxford University Press, 2017.
Dawkins, Richard. *The Selfish Gene*. Oxford University Press, 1976.
Genette, Gérard. *Mimologique: Voyage en Cratylie*. Seuil, 1999.
Goldhaber, Michael. "The Attention Economy and the Net." *First Monday*, vol. 2, no. 4, April 7, 1997, https://firstmonday.org/article/view/519/440.
Hoffmeyer, Jesper. *Signs of Meaning*. Indiana University Press, 1996.
Hofstadter, Douglas, and Daniel Dennett. *The Mind's I: Fantasies and Reflections on Self and Soul*. Bantam Books, 1982.
Hull, David. "A Mechanism and Its Metaphysics: An Evolutionary Account of the Social and Conceptual Development of Science." *Biology and Philosophy*, vol. 3, no. 2, 1988, pp. 123–55.
Kauffman, Stuart. *The Origins of Order: Self Organization and Selection in Evolution*. Oxford University Press, 1993.
Landy, Joshua. "Mental Calisthenics and Self-reflexive Fiction." *The Oxford Handbook of Cognitive Literary Studies*, edited by Lisa Zunshine, Oxford University Press, 2015, pp. 559–80.
Lestel, Dominique. "Data." *A More Developed Sign: Interpreting the Work of Jesper Hoffmeyer*, edited by Donald Favareau, Paul Cobley, and Kalevi Kull, University of Tartu Press, 2012, pp. 93–5.
Lestel, Dominique. *Les Origines animales de la culture*. Flammarion, 2001.
Moretti, Franco. *Distant Reading*. Verso, 2013.
Quora. "How Many Chickens Are There in the World?" 2018.
Reference.com. "How Many Elephants Are There in the World?" 2018.
Swirski, Peter. *A Stanislaw Lem Reader*. Northwestern University Press, 1997.
Taleb, Nassim Nicholas. *The Black Swan: The Impact of the Highly Improbable*. Random House, 2007.
Taylor, Marjorie, Sara Hodges, and Adèle Kohányi. "The Illusion of Independent Agency: Do Adult Fiction Writers Experience Their Characters as Having Minds of Their Own?" *Imagination, Cognition and Personality*, vol. 22, no. 4, 2003, pp. 361–80.
UNWO. "Number of Cattle Worldwide From 2012 to 2018 (in Million Head)." 2018, Statistica.
UNWO. "Number of Pigs Worldwide from 2012 to 2018 (in Million Head)." 2018, Statistica.
Wilson, Edward O. *Sociobiology: The New Synthesis*. Harvard University Press, 1975.
Worldatlas.com. "How Many Rats Are There in the World?" 2018.

2

Tokyo Ghoul and the Trouble with Cannibalism

Tony Milligan

Ken Kanecki wanders the streets of Tokyo, hungry and disconsolate. Food has turned to dust in his mouth. Burgers cannot be eaten. Suddenly, he wonders, what is that glorious smell? When he turns the corner and sees that it is a corpse, it is a moment of visceral realization. He has become a ghoul (*Tokyo Ghoul 1* 21).

This scene is from Sui Ishida's *Tokyo Ghoul* (2011–14), one of the most successful manga to have transitioned from Japan to the West. Continued in the sequel series, *Tokyo Ghoul: re* (2014–18), available in some slightly less-convincing novellas for teenagers (not written by Ishida), in a three series anime, and more recently as a live action film, the plotline has held together through several formats and sharp transitions. Not easy in a genre notorious for discontinuation and mid-story publisher cut-offs. Superficially, it is an inversion tale, a world turned upside down, where we humans are on the menu. In what follows, I do not want to focus upon this aspect of the tale, but rather to use it as the backdrop for some comments about cannibalism as a dietary practice and, more particularly, for observations about the concept of "cannibalism." These observations will tend to reinforce a sense of the strength of the practice as prohibited even where practitioners are sympathetically understood. There will be a "not just inversion" argument, but this is primarily a structuring device, a way of proceeding, and not the main thing that is going on.

Ishida's Ghouls

The crux of the story is simple: ghouls walk among, and sometimes eat, the inhabitants of modern Tokyo. Cannibalism is just around the corner. For most of the time, these beings look like everyone else. But they are not us. Indeed, the series opens with a fairly sharp contrast of ghoul and human, with the latter preyed upon for food, for revenge, and occasionally for psychopathic pleasure. The latter theme strengthens as the series progresses and key characters discover the even darker side of the ghoul community.

Some ghouls, like Kanecki and the slightly more experienced Touka, are young, naive, and vulnerable. Their portrayal is sympathetic. They care for one another and they avoid or limit their harm to humans. Under the guidance of a wiser older ghoul, they prepare suicide meat, rather than reluctant victims, for distribution to the desperate and tormented. And they cluster around Anteiku café, where the only normal thing that a ghoul can consume is served. That is, coffee. These are the good ghouls who fight an intermittent, hidden or open, battle with their ghoul side. In the case of Kanecki and Touka, the inner struggles are superimposed upon the regular problems of growing up, with its ambiguities and associated loss of moral certainties. They are not exactly good, but better than the other ghouls. Just who these better ghouls are becomes less clear over time, as loyalty to friends and dependents tends to displace any absolute sense of right and wrong. What helps to sustain the broader narrative during these developments is a reluctance to engage in moralism or superficial nihilism. There may well be a right and wrong to these matters, a right or wrong about what to do in this awful predicament, but Kanecki and Touka are poorly placed to know what it is. Instead, they respond to immediate events and turns of fortune.

Kanecki, even more than the others at Anteiku, bridges the worlds of ghoul and human, having transitioned from ordinary human to ghoul following an accident while defending himself from a ghoul (Rize). The subsequent transplanting of ghoul organs into his body contaminates, then takes over and helps to reconstitute his being. Kanecki's ghoul predicament is not, then, his fault, although it may be someone's fault. The status of his accident is later brought into doubt (*Tokyo Ghoul 10* 172–83). Yet, although this transformation sets him apart from those born into ghouldom, his status as a being caught between two worlds is also typical. The story may begin with a sharp ghoul/human contrast, but this erodes over time. These nonhuman ghouls are, in multiple respects, still very much human in the broader sense. Biological differences are limited, and they share many of our vulnerabilities and longings. They can be emotionally wounded and crave love and companionship. Without this, any sense of ghoul community would be impossible. They may not be, strictly, *Homo sapiens*, but might easily fall within a nonbiological conception of "a shared humanity," albeit with exaggerated capability for recovery and special fighting strength. This proximity to us is required in order for their consumption of biological humans to be truly cannibalistic. Their status as cannibals is then reinforced by predation within the ghoul community, and by occasional self-consumption in order to gain strength.

Touca attends high school, officially to fit in, because she is angry at the humans and is not looking for friends. Unofficially, because of her yearning for a life more ordinary. The relationship with Kanecki is complex. At a feeding site that opens the story, he says, "I'm not like you monsters," which causes her eyes (already manga sized) to widen in shock. "I can't eat human flesh!! Don't confuse me with [. . .] monsters like you guys" (*Tokyo Ghoul 1* 142–3). She, in turn, lambasts him for a reluctance to truly accept what he is, for his cowardice in refusing to eat meat: "There's no place for someone who can't decide [. . .] between being one or the other" (*Tokyo Ghoul 1* 146). But still, she eats alone in the shadows or in her room, hidden away from colleagues at Anteiku. Touka wants her unavoidable flesh-eating to be strictly offstage. Others, such as the ghoul members of the more rapaciously cannibal Aogiri Tree, live more in the way that she only speaks of, and it is terrible. They are less torn. Loyal among themselves, up to a point, but contemptuous of humans as food, pets, and inferiors. Their presence makes the picture of Kanecki and Touka's otherwise monstrous cannibalism more sympathetic, more palatable.

The limited inversion aspect to this story is simple and familiar. The reader is invited to imagine what would it be like if we were on the plate, the hunted, the consumed. However, pressed too far, we can see how this might easily slip into moralistic critique, a play upon all manner of human insecurities and guilt, condensed down into a concern about eating practice. From an ethical point of view, the limits of such inversion stories are also clear. They have a tendency to represent harms which differ significantly as if they were equal. In particular, the harms of death which may be dreadful for animals, but which (in the case of humans) are often to do with the frustration of complex desires which only humans have, rather than levels of pain that any given creature might experience. It may still be wrong to kill animals for food. Generally, I think it is. But the wrongness in question is bound up with harms which are not obviously the same as the varying harms involved in killing humans.

An appreciation of the difference is built into our practices. Even vegans, like myself, routinely break bread with the killers and consumers of animals but would be reluctant to break bread knowingly with either cannibals or murderers. Whatever kind of species egalitarianism we might then commit to, it is not one where an absolute equivalence of responses and equality in all things might be embraced. Cannibalism and meat-eating are not down on all fours with each other from an ethical point of view, and there is no agenda in Ishida to draw more than a rough parallel between forms of preying upon the other. Tokyo's ghouls are not, then, thin devices for moralizing critique. Instead, they are something more ambiguous, caught in between being one thing and another. Touka critiques her own predicament. She and her companions are something monstrous and threatening, yet also attractive. Not an unusual combination. Seductive vampires spring to mind.

Tokyo's ghouls are, then, like us enough for cannibalism to be a possibility, but also strikingly unlike us. They are unsettling, a hybrid at the margins of conceivable dietary practice, caught between cannibal and herbivore or even vegan. Although, apparently rotting cheese is still initially palatable. More tolerable than fresh food, but far from ideal (Ishida, *Tokyo Ghoul 1* 71). Their diet is like all diets. It has exclusions as well as inclusions. They cannot eat animal flesh or animal products more generally. Or, at least, they do not do so, out of a sense of disgust at the appalling taste. When Ken Kanecki becomes a ghoul, his familiar diet and beloved burgers make him ill. This drives him to consume human flesh, just as it drives vampires to drink human blood for their sustenance. Yet Touca, in the final installments of the story in *Tokyo Ghoul: re*, does manage to eat human food in order to prevent her body from consuming the child that she is carrying. In extremity, her body finds a way for her and Kanecki to reproduce. He, by contrast, does not have the option. Animals are simply off the menu. Even the coffee that ghouls routinely drink (and often in excessive quantities) is black, no milk. The identification with the animal is reinforced in other ways. Masks worn by ghouls, for attack or defense against the ghoul hunters of the Commission of Counter

Ghoul (the CCG), often have animal faces and are used by the CCG to name their unknown enemy. Touka is the Rabbit. Kanecki is distinctively caught between two things and wears a mask with a monstrously exaggerated human mouth.

The cannibal theme is present throughout, and clearly more pronounced than the brief hand waving at animal-free diet. Yet the association with the latter is nonetheless difficult to miss, the sense of threat in the face of something new. And this marks a further dimension to their sympathetically portrayed monstrosity. Although the key characters are simultaneously attractive and repellant, these ghouls are in other respects very different from the familiar vampires who disrupt a modern world as a demonic force from the past. Rather, they are coffee drinkers at home in the most modern of cities. Yet gathered in a cafe whose name suggests the search for a compromise with the past and, by implication, with the human both inside and outside.

Manga and Depth

My focus upon manga to write about these matters, and especially cannibalism, may benefit from some preliminary comment. Especially so, given that the monstrous nature of the cannibal makes sense only if we regard the prohibition or taboo on eating human flesh as a deep one rather than a superficial dietary preference. Some people like frogs, some like snails, some prefer animal-free, and others consume human bodies. But the latter cannot fit, with any ease, within the range of available choice. For monstrosity, the taboo must place it beyond such availability. Yet, how can such depth be explored effectively through a shallow medium? And there is certainly something shallow about a good deal of manga and about graphic novels generally. Commentary on series such as *Bleach* and *Naruto* should not displace analysis of Tolstoy any time soon.

Here, I offer two considerations in defense of the approach. First, a negative consideration: there is simply no reason in principle why graphic novels and manga cannot tackle deep themes. Art Spiegelman's *Maus* (1980–91), for example, explores the Holocaust effectively, from a personally engaged standpoint and is not a simple moralizing tale for children. But if the medium is capable of depth, then it is worthy of commentary. In the case of *Maus*, it would also be difficult for commentary to match the depth of the text. However, as a qualification in the case of *Tokyo Ghoul*, this might be more of an issue with the novellas, written by another author and crafted for more of a teen audience. My suggestion here is not, however, that they are bad instances of what they try to be, but simply that they are trying to be something else, without the same level of reflection upon the human condition.

Second, a more positive consideration: there may be something about manga as a cultural product that happens to be particularly apt for the present discussion. Manga is demotic. It is geared to mass production and to the ephemeral. It is not just there to be read but to be *consumed*. In its pages, the idea of consumption is multiply present. Images of humans who are physically swallowed by monsters and oneida are common. An obvious and comparable example is *Attack on Titan* (2009 onwards), where humans are besieged by creatures which would physically swallow them, take over and eat their bodies (which are, of course, *our* bodies). And then there is lolicon, where sexually immature girls are reimagined with exaggerated adult characteristics. The image of the adult lolicon reader as someone who wants to physically consume such bodies is a familiar one. Masahiro Morioka is a rare example of a philosopher who writes about this, and rarer still for doing so biographically, and as a warning about lolicon culture, breaking down his own sexual urges to devour, consume, and become: "Lolicon men consume the images of cheerfully cavorting young girls they see on television as public displays of underage pornography" (Morioka, *Confessions of a Frigid Man* 106). What is in play, for Morioka, is not ultimately a desire for intercourse (which would be dangerous enough). Instead, such men may be turned off or even "herbivore," with regard to actual sexual contact with members of the opposite sex (Morioka, "A Phenomenological Study" 2014). Rather, the desire is to take over, to swallow whole. It is "the desire to abandon my own body, transplant myself into her body, and manipulate this pretty body in accordance with my own will. But since this cannot actually be achieved, I have no choice but to settle for the fixation on the 'uniform' that so strongly evokes the image of 'brainwashing'" (Morioka, *Confessions of a Frigid Man* 81).

Even so, my thought here is not to endorse the broader framework that Morioka brings into play, one that links lolicon specifically to a narcissism theory in which adult men see a path not taken by themselves, one that might have been taken if their telos (like Kanecki's) had not somehow gone horribly wrong during adolescence. Rather, my thought is the simpler one that consumption is continuously in play, at multiple levels within manga of various different kinds. Not always, one hopes, in precisely the way that it is present in lolicon. But nonetheless, the substitution of violence and devouring for sex across a broader range of manga, including both *Tokyo Ghoul* and *Attack upon Titan*, is difficult to miss. On-screen controversy over the belated on-screen consummation of Kanecki and Touka's relationship may indicate that some fans preferred consumption to consummation. Self-consumption by Tokyo's ghouls also has its obvious counterpart.

By way of drawing these preliminaries to a close, my claim that the ghouls of the story are threatening, attractive, and monstrous may also benefit from a little clarification. *Threatening*, because it is *of the new*, a coming thing. They have what ordinary humans lack. But, at a deeper level they are especially threatening because theirs is a representation of community and not of isolated individuality. They are more Sawney Bean (with his cannibal tribe of wild Scotsmen) than Hannibal Lector. And this dimension of the social raises the specter of the political. Foucault (2003) notoriously associated the monstrous carnivorous masses in anti-Jacobin literature with the threatening devourers of the social body (Foucault 98). (The image is familiar. Buchner's *Death of Danton* [1835] gave us the line that the revolution is like Saturn; it devours its own children.) The image of the ravenous community cannibalizing society and devouring an old order of things is, in obvious ways, more threatening than the isolated carnivore, whether a charismatic psychopath, a desperate loner, or a seemingly ordinary man trusted by his neighbors. Carnivores too come in several flavors. As the story progresses through *Tokyo Ghoul: re*, we see that there is an emerging alignment with political critique in which the powers that be do not come out well.

Attractive, because of the demonic aspect of the characters rather than in spite of it. Those who have fully embraced their ghoul-being enjoy an apparent freedom from familiar moral constraints as well as physical ones. My assumption here is that monstrosity need not exclude the demonic, with its strange, devilish, attraction. In a one-to-one beauty comparison between the ghoul hunters of the CCG and the young ghouls at Anteiku, the former would not be winning many prizes. At least, not until we begin to encounter half-ghouls, bred specifically to seek out and destroy their more fully fledged ghoul counterparts. Here, we do see a simple inversion of what Morioka (among others) has written about. The cute bodies are those of the consumers, and not the consumed. Cute but also lethal. An exemplar being Rize, whose attack upon Ken Kanecki at the end of a date which otherwise was quite successful, opens the story. Ken does not date often or, it seems, well. Another cute female ghoul is the novelist within the novel, Sen Takatsuki, the prophet of a one-eyed king, part one thing, part another. More *kawaii*, and with the openly politicized goal of a transformed world. And then there is Touka, who is a perfect match, lacking the grand vision of Sen and the petty appetites of Rize.

Finally, these people are all *monstrous*, with clear similarities to (and differences from) vampires. More formally, a case can be made for a good matchup with familiar typologies of monstrosity, that is, the accidentally monstrous being whose telos has been altered, the morally terrible creature, and the hybrid. Some ghouls match up better with some of these characteristics than others. Kanecki, with the accidentally monstrous and hybrid, the ghouls of the Aogiri Tree with the morally terrible. Touka is merely hybrid, a less complicated ghoul next door. Any plausible account of the concept of monstrosity that did not fit ghouls, even the sympathetically portrayed ghouls, would be problematic.

The Monstrosity of Cannibalism

In the previous section, I have associated cannibalism with the monstrous. Kanecki is appalled by his own monstrosity, Touka is ashamed of hers. But is it really so monstrous, or merely so by virtue of circumstances under which humans must be killed or subjected to mutilation? Let us imagine that the surrounding events allow the ghouls at Anteiku to live out their lives with no ghoul hunters, no Aogiri Tree, and only the consumption of meat from suicides. (Of which there is a ready and uninterrupted supply.) We might even allow that the suicidal humans who provide their sustenance are aware of the likelihood of being consumed, and perhaps even opt for forests and cliffs where this is most likely to happen. Perhaps they might even wish for continuity in some form, or long to be desired, or crave a terrible and final humiliation as punishment for unspecified failures, and this might lead to something like tacit consent. Would we still be inclined to regard the cannibalism of Kanecki and the other ghouls in the same way, under such extremely favorable conditions? (Conditions more favorable even than those at Anteiku.)

My suspicion here is that we would; that any attempt to normalize the practice of cannibalism or even to take the rough edges off of it, would be misplaced. And my point here is conceptual. It is about that which is integral to the concept of cannibalism, to the way that the concept is used, and what it means *as we use it*. What is integral to the normative content of the concept is that matters of consent and the manner of death are not the problem. Faced with an instance of cannibalism, our first thought would not be "Was there prior agreement?" or "Is this opportunistic, or did the consumer also do something wrong?" Instead, the practice of cannibalism is judged wrong by being judged cannibalism.

We might, then, wonder why someone would even be tempted to pursue a softening option. There do, however, seem to be at least three plausible reasons that cannot simply be dismissed: a desire to narrow the moral gulf between meat-eating and cannibalism, as a way to strike at the former; a broader "each to their own" commitment to cultural relativism; and a special suspicion about the colonialist narratives in which the monstrosity of cannibalism has, historically, been embedded. For the moment, I will set the first of these aside, and return to it in the final section. At least some of the time, when the fearless thought that cannibalism is *nothing special* is set out, the other two reasons coalesce. That is how I will respond to them here, as different aspects of the same normalizing line of thought. This is how they first appear in the literary canon, in Montaigne's essay "On Cannibals" (1580), where he remarks that eating a man alive is worse than eating him dead, and the latter is not any worse than many of the practices of torture and punishment practiced between neighbors and fellow citizens under adverse conditions and "under the cloak of piety and religion." This, for Montaigne, was worse "than to roast and eat a man after he is dead" (Montaigne 113).

I will also admit that appeals to the monstrosity of cannibalism *were* used as part of long-running attempts to justify various forms of colonialism in order to bring civilization to supposed savages who would otherwise have continued to engage in such practices. The obvious example here is the narrative of Carib (*karibna*) cannibalism, during the Spanish conquest of the Americas (Whitehead 69). These cannibals were the bad Indians, by contrast with other groups, although the classification of cannibal and non-cannibal lined up suspiciously well with the division between those who resisted Spanish power and those whose resistance was overcome. Similarly, the pattern of convenient appeal was repeated in accusations of cannibalism by the British during the colonial period, and may be detected even as late at H. G. Wells's depiction of the Morlocks in *The Time Machine* (1895):

> Even now man is far less discriminating and exclusive in his good than he was— far less than any monkey. His prejudices against human flesh is no deep-seated instinct. And so these inhuman sons of men—! I tried to look at the thing in a

scientific spirit. After all, they were less human and more remote than our cannibal ancestors of three or four thousand years ago. (Wells 79)

The cannibalistic, but apparently industrious, subterranean Morlocks need to be conquered (killed) for the sake of civilization's future. The latter rested with the listless Eloi who themselves rested for most of the time and grazed meat-free. Entitlement to dominate had to be earned through a superiority of practice, eating practice as well as industry, but there was no question about where it was to be found. The image of the cannibalistic masses recurs. These are, respectively, the descendants of the working class (hence the industry) and of the wealthy (hence the idleness), with power relations inverted and the Morlocks on top. Yet the contrast of civilization and cannibal plays upon imperial power, vegetarian refinement, and tacitly, upon notions of manifest destiny.

Faced with this problem of entanglement in colonial narrative, some postcolonial narratives have tended to preserve a sense of cannibalism's monstrosity by introducing a note of skepticism about its occurrence, drawing upon the inaccuracy of reports and cases where the charge was little more than propaganda (Arens 184–5). However, an awareness of its historical standing has always tended to return. In some places, at some times, cannibalism was real. This still leaves open the rejection of colonialism's apologetics in more pragmatic terms, by appealing to the simple point that even if cannibalism was practiced in some places, the colonial system still did vastly more harm than good. But this may not appeal to those who wish to say that, even in its special abhorrence of cannibalism, the colonial system was wrong. A ready pathway here is the association of our abiding sense of its monstrosity with Western prejudice, and with an affective pattern geared for conquest.

There is something to this thought. After all, Montaigne had a point. If we are not deeply repelled by the killing of others in wars (even if we do not wish to engage in it ourselves), then why react so badly to the eating of enemies afterward? What is the greater harm? Surely the killing itself and not the aftermath. Perhaps, in cultures where shame plays a particularly strong role, matters might be different. Perhaps the misuse of the corpse of Hector by Achilles, and the latter's decision to tie it to a chariot and circle around the burial mound of his friend Patroclus, is understandably seen as the greater abomination in the *Iliad*. But that is not where we live. Yet we too seem to have a strong sense of bodily integrity which extends beyond life and into times when the body has become a corpse. The embeddedness of this bodily integrity is a familiar response. Utilitarian medics are not allowed to randomly harvest passersby on the pretext that while one individual has been harvested, several have been saved. We do not even permit them to harvest from the dead without something like prior consent and/or family consent. Nor, it seems, can we agree to just anything being done with our remains. Plastination, in the manner of Gunther von Hagens, is permissible for scientific, educational, and display purposes, consumption is not. Vegans cannot offer their bodies to meat eaters as a compromise future menu option. A strong sense of integrity, which rejects an absolute voluntarism about entitlements to dispose, pervades the liberal societies of the West. Abortion rights are endorsed on this basis, even in countries where the legacy of nineteenth-century Christianity, is heaviest. Its weight is not enough to outweigh our liberal sensibilities when it comes to such integrity.

But is this combined sense of bodily integrity, and the abhorrence of cannibalism which predates it, but with which it has coalesced, anything more than an accident of time and place? Within a certain kind of philosophical framework where intuitions are generally *mere* intuitions, the wrongness in question will be hard to place. Jeremy Wisnewski runs an argument along these lines, "not in defense of cannibalism so much as it is a defense of the rights of people to engage in practices crucial to their culture" (Wisnewski 265). In a slightly different vein, Mikel Burley has drawn upon the experience of the Wari of Western Brazil to argue that being seen as human (in a rich sense of the latter) does not exclude the possibility of being seen as food. His concern is with "explicating a range of ways of understanding human beings in which the possibility of a person's being something to eat is not excluded" (Burley 486). Here, I will register a certain kind of sympathy with Burley's position. We clearly *can* have a concept of human, and of a shared humanity, while still eating humans. This is both a conceptual point and an empirical one; that is, we have evidence that they are not strictly incompatible. And so, a certain attempt to make the idea of the human and the idea of food source mutually exclusive, a familiar argument from Cora Diamond (1978) that Burley is directly challenging, seems to have multiple exceptions.

Indeed, while it is true that we do not ordinarily think of humans as a food source, all that it takes to make this happen is for something (or several somethings) to go badly wrong before our patterns of response are liable to change in significant ways. What it is to have a particular concept should cover both circumstances, not just one, and it does seem to me that Diamond's approach suffers from this restriction. When the smooth running of the world breaks down, we see beings in a different way. In the present case, both as human and as meat. Shame about cannibalism is premised upon a grasp of this combination, a grasp that it really is a human who is being eaten. Diamond accepts the empirical evidence but disputes the conceptual point: "We do not eat our dead, even when they have died in automobile accidents or been struck by lightning, and their flesh might be first class. We do not eat them; or if we do, it is a matter of extreme need, there is very great reluctance" (467). My difference from Diamond here is simply an acceptance that the exceptional circumstances are also integral to the concept, that the concept has not ceased to function, or that we have lapsed into a deeper form of cognitive dissonance than usual. My difference from Burley, on the other hand, is greater. From the conceptual point that Diamond's position is overly restrictive in its understanding of the very idea of a human, he slips toward normalization and a position closer to Wisnewski's appeal to a reasonable cultural diversity, as a possible way of coping with death and bereavement. In other words, "There are many ways in which respect and piety can manifest, and cannibalism is one of them" (Burley 500). The fact of occasional instances of honorific human consumption is not in dispute. But accepting this is a long distance away from also accepting that there is nothing generally repellant about cannibalism, or that our revulsion at the prospect is a culturally skewed "yuck factor," rather than an affective response which viscerally embodies some manner of deep but unspoken knowledge, a "yuck factor" of a more defensible sort (Midgley 2000). It seems to me that Burley slides toward the latter when speaking of the possible ways of being human in apparently neutral terms. The terms in which one person might like frogs and another snails and a third may be fond of cannibalism (just so long as the form of life permits). This looks closer to a defense or quasi-defense of the practice.

We might, of course, dismiss this on methodological grounds, drawing upon a familiar point about responding to anomaly: while there are *some* radically counterintuitive "fearless thoughts" that turn out to be true (e.g., the Earth orbits the Sun and not vice versa), the fact that a thought falls into this class also gives us reasons to consider that any proof of its legitimacy might equally well be read as a *reductio*, an indication that one or more premise is wrong, or that the reasoning process has gone astray. This approach to anomaly is sufficiently widespread that Quine (an archetypal analytic philosopher) and Rai Gaita (who is anything but typical and whose interests here are of an entirely different sort) both subscribe to versions of it (Quine 14–19; Gaita 310). In the present case, I do find it persuasive. When someone proves that necrophilia, bestiality, or cannibalism is licit, I am inclined to assume that their moral framework is flawed, or the arguments that they deploy within it are skewed. What is striking about defenses of cannibalism's normality is that it reverses the regular assumptions about how to proceed by pointing to the lack of any clear-cut justification for the prohibition in Kantian terms, utilitarian terms, or virtue ethical terms. (The description is drawn directly from Wisnewski's approach.) The presupposition of such an approach is that the burden of demonstration rests with those who accept the regular norms by which human societies, and modern broadly liberal societies in particular, generally work, and not with the advocate of the fearless thought. In terms of methodology, this seems like an odd presupposition to make.

Even so, like other methodological points, the presupposition that the burden of demonstration rests with the normalizer of cannibalism is open to question. So, let us assume that when confronted with attempts to normalize cannibalism, there really is a case to answer. In its defense, this idea of cannibalism's normality also need not be set out in terms allied to a demythologizing, scientific frame of mind which points out that protein is protein, irrespective of its origins. The possibility of normalizing in various different ways may be clearer when we break down the apparent focus of the disgust associated with cannibalism. For example, if we read the tale of the Sakyamuni Buddha's previous lives in the *Jataka*, we will encounter a story where, as Prince Sattva, he gave up his body to be eaten by a starving tiger. We are not disgusted at the prospect of his human body being consumed, but impressed by the mythical level of sacrifice. Nor are we disgusted by sky burial in Tibet, when the human dead are cut up to be consumed by birds rather than accumulated in graveyards. Indeed, the latter has become something of a controversial (ghoulish) tourist attraction. It is not, then, the sheer prospect of the human body being consumed which provokes the reaction of disgust, but rather the *mixing* of living human and dead human. Realms which belong apart. And this looks suspiciously close to a kind of insecurity about *being*, an insecurity about our mortality transposed into fears about purity and projected onto the inoffensive corpse of another. The taboo, then, might seem to arise out of our evasion, out of our weakness and fragility, however the latter is understood. Like other forms of puritanism, and politically suspect forms of disgust, it may stand in need of a good critique.

Such an appeal to the relativity of cultural norms is, however, less telling than it may seem. Admittedly, all diets have prohibitions, and these prohibitions do not always fall in the same place. Where they fall is often a matter of accident and circumstance. However, any move toward normalization would find it difficult to attend sufficiently to the peculiar rarity of cannibalism. It would involve underestimating the prohibition. Most, perhaps all, human societies have shown few qualms about killing people, regularly and in appallingly large numbers. Curiously few of the victims anywhere have ever actually been eaten, even when liberal notions of bodily integrity have not been in place. Heads have been captured for presentation, teeth have been harvested for dentistry, fingers and breasts removed as souvenirs or out of morbid curiosity, scalps have been taken as proof of a kill or for the sake of bounty. Battlefield bones have been disinterred for fertilizer. Cannibalism has also (I think undeniably) occurred along with these things, but more in the shadows. Opportunistically, and like the cannibalism of Touka, often in shame, mostly for survival in dire circumstances, when wagon trains fail and planes crash. Even in the narrative of cannibalism by the Wari that Burley relies upon, those who eat the deceased group member must go through at least a show of reluctance. Not out of a sense of the finality of accepting their loss, but out of the realization that what they are being asked to consume is actually a corpse. In the exceptions, such as honorific consumption, as in cases of dire need, the action is not merely seen as one of respect, but simultaneously as something dreadful. All out cannibalism, of a sort where people were *reduced* to meat, really would be a circumstance in which the concept of a human was absent. The range of behaviors consistent with a grasp of the latter concept remains restricted, even if the lines cannot quite be drawn where Diamond once suggested.

It is also noteworthy that attempts to suggest that some people like frogs and others like snails, and that cannibalism may fit somewhere into this mix of dietary diversity, have themselves been implicated in Western colonialist narratives. Appropriately, in relation to Japan, with the suggestion that as Buddhism became marginalized and Shinto more evident during the militarism of the 1930s and 1940s, the way was paved for ritualized cannibalism. A linear connection has regularly, and without much more than a favorable timeline, been drawn with the incidents of cannibalism upon Allied airmen resulting as the bombing of Japan accelerated in 1944. Most recently (at the time of writing) the debate resurfaced several years ago around the film *Unbroken* (2014), starring Angelina Jolie, and based upon a text where "acts of ritual cannibalism" were claimed (Hillenbrand 322). There were calls for boycott of the film from Japan's political far right, with Shinto priest Mutsuhiro Takeuchi playing a prominent role. Note, the link requires the appeal to "ritual," rather than to the medicinal cannibalism (small amounts of livers of airmen) and nutritional cannibalism (meat from around the thighs) which figure in postwar confessions. The idea of ritual, and the appeal to a flaw in Shintoism, has tended to overshadow the testimony, and the appeal to the unchecked sadism of individuals which tends to be given a great deal of leeway under wider conditions of war and mutual atrocity.

This does look suspiciously like another Orientalizing narrative, moreover one which is overlaid with Western preferences for Buddhism over Shinto. A preference which, in this version, does little justice to either. We know very well, from other parts of the world, that Buddhism does not offer guarantees against the human flaws which become so evident in wartime. No religious practice does. And organized Buddhism's role, as a national religion, in both Rinzai and Soto variants, was far from unblemished. (I say this as someone with an abiding interest in the latter.) The targeting of Shinto then does an injustice of misrepresentation to Buddhism as well and obscures their complex entanglement. Japanese culture is obviously influenced by both, in deep ways, and in equally deep ways it treats cannibalism as abhorrent, as an impure and monstrous thing. One might even make a better case for a special abhorrence of cannibalism, and specifically of ritual cannibalism, based upon Shinto attitudes toward the impurity of the dead body and harmony between the dead and the living, evidenced in the notorious reluctance across Japan to consent to organ donation, or to be a party to transplants (Namahira 940-1). The Yasukuni Shrine, which has provided a resting place for Japan's fallen since the nineteenth century, enshrines only spirits and not corpses, not even those of an unknown soldier. The dire effects of Ken Kanecki's transplant, the life-saving operation, which transforms his telos and changes him into a ghoul, may itself be an attempt to play upon such an idea of exceptionalism and of a special culturally driven suspicion about the dead body and its contaminating threat.

But even this exceptionalist story about a special aversion and its possible roots in Shinto might be a little too convenient. In its own way, it too seems entangled with Orientalizing narratives. We have, after all, seen this kind of thing before, with a supposed link between the special animistic archaism of Shintoism and Japan's openness to technology. A mythology which has come to play a role, but a mythology, nonetheless. However, nothing so strong as a special abhorrence, beyond the ordinary familiar abhorrence, is required in order to discount the idea that a softer attitude toward cannibalism might somehow be found in Japan and might somehow show that the familiar abhorrence, which has coalesced with bodily autonomy in the West, is a cultural quirk. Japanese reactions to cannibalism look pretty much the same as almost everyone else's. And they would have to be in order for the storyline of *Tokyo Ghoul* to work. Indeed, it is tempting to think of the text as partly inspired by public fascination about the case of Issei Sagawa who, in 1981, after repeated failed attempts to get help for an obsession, murdered and consumed parts of a female student while studying in Paris. The French authorities deemed Sagawa insane, and promptly got him off their hands after only a limited incarceration. A string of Japanese doctors disagreed and insisted that he ought to have been imprisoned. Instead, Sagawa became a minor celebrity, in a sort of fascinating horror way, with an autobiographical account, *Kiri no Naka* (In the fog) (2002), becoming a best seller and the obvious antecedent to a number of manga, including both *Tokyo Ghoul* and *Attack on Titan*. There are, perhaps, echoes also of this case in Morioka's account of consumption and the young female body as well. Public fascination with Sagawa, like a curious viewer sympathy for the character of Hannibal Lector (who emerged in the immediate post-Sagawa aftermath), draws upon their unsettling danger, oddity, and unhomeliness. And a sense of the latter is bound up with the familiar taboo.

It is difficult to avoid the idea that Wells's *Time Traveller* was mistaken, even a little in denial of his own feelings, and that the taboo does go deep within our multiple understandings of what it is to be part of our moral community, *one of us*, or, in familiar terms, human. Deeper than cultural quirks and culinary localism. And, as a sort of heresy when social constructs can be found on all sides, the best explanation here may turn out to involve some naturalistic component. An attitude toward cannibalism as abhorrent may well be a very good candidate for an evolutionary account of the role of group selection, with the emergence of a stable practice of cannibalism carrying serious implications for population dynamics and survival. In which case, the kind of culturally shaped "yuck factor," which seems to place it as merely one local quirk among others, would instead involve a form of unarticulated knowledge, a matter of knowing how to get the social group through the times of extreme scarcity which have been all too common in human history, even if they bear little relation to how we (myself and likely readers) live now. From an evolutionary point of view, eating one another in times of pressure has never been a particularly good recipe for pulling through. Eating bodies which bear no threatening trace of illness poses a problem of supply most easily met with the Burke and Hare solution of making corpses out of the living.

Conclusion

I may, admittedly, be in danger at this point of showing a little too much. If the visceral disgust concerning cannibalism has such deep underpinnings, it could be difficult to explain early modern medicinal practices based around the mythical properties of powdered mummy, and powdered ex-people more generally. Yet, in such cases, what confronts us when we set aside special exceptions (comparable to the wartime case mentioned earlier) are practices which require transformation and sanitization. Something very different from honorific consumption of the recognizable body, or Ken Kanecki's longing to eat the corpse around the corner.

Yet, there may still remain a path to normalization in the future. Josh Milburn has recently appealed to the prospect of in vitro human meat within a strategy of the sort for which a promissory note was issued in the previous section: if the justifications of in vitro meat work in the case of animals (because it is harm free), then they may work equally well with human flesh. And so, a sense of the proximity between eating meat and eating people is triggered with the former coming out much worse than we might expect. (A theme that we have already actually encountered, in Wells, albeit jumbled together with some disreputable ideas of superiority and culture.) While not to everyone's taste, there might be something to this line of thought, where the seemingly harmless consumption of in vitro human flesh shows that the taboo on cannibalism has its problems. The approach might help us to carve apart cases where the "yuck factor" which is in place expresses a genuine kind of knowledge and cases where it does not, but is merely a product of historical inertia, a failure to move on under circumstances where the risks associated with a culture of human-meat-eating are no longer in place. Even so, I wonder about the sense in which this really would be cannibalism, especially if we regard the latter as I have done earlier, as a thick concept, with norms of prohibition and disapproval built in. Again, it seems odd to say, "John and Mary are a lovely couple. Cannibals, but they don't do anything wrong." And the thought here is not necessarily that the individuals in question might bludgeon strangers for their supper.

Rather, the thought is that what is problematic about cannibalism is not actually the eating of a certain kind of protein, however it might taste, but *the practice of eating human flesh*. And the latter is something much broader, broader even than the simple act of eating human flesh. Something which involves the vulnerabilities and relationships of an entire way of life. It poses a significantly different set of ethical problems from those associated with the consumption of flesh without history. Or, at least, without the kind of history that human flesh ordinarily has. In a sense, the eating of in vitro human meat would only be cannibalism in a very restricted way, if at all. The material would be biologically related to us, but it would never have been one of us.

This is not quite the same as saying that our familiar response to cannibalism is an attitude toward corpses, to the remains of actual humans. Curiously, it does seem broader than any such attitude toward a corpse and does seem to involve responses whose rationality might be hard to defend. Attempts by vegan activists, novelty chefs, and artists, to sell or distribute human milk products, human-sourced ice cream and cheese, have occurred in New York and London in recent years, and have generally been met with mixed reactions of interest, disgust, legal head-scratching, and polite requests from the powers-that-be to cease and desist. And flesh is not an issue here. No flesh is processed in the making of these products. They are, in much the same way as other forms of in vitro meat, harm free. The humans are obviously free range and not subject to the traumas which are ordinarily associated with dairy production. Yet, this *is* produce with history, but still not *a history of the right sort* to constitute anything like cannibalism in the familiar sense. We do not get down on all fours with Kanecki and Touka simply by consuming human-sourced ice cream.

But why have I repeatedly used their picture to help draw out the concept of cannibalism as a concept of something monstrous? Why not go for an even more sympathetic example based around honorific consumption? Here I want to say that our grasp of the concept is flexible enough to apply in multiple circumstances but is built around monstrous exemplars rather than honorific cases. We could, of course, shift the concept along, and there is nothing wrong with doing so when we have a suitable reason. When, for example, a concept ceases to play its traditional role in an effective way, or when we hope to extend its normative force onto some new practice.

But nothing of this sort holds here. Instead, and whatever else we want the very idea of cannibalism to do, we still need the concept to play its traditional role in relation to cases like Sagawa's. These are not likely to go away any time soon, and it would be very misleading to narrow the gulf between them and routine meat-eating, whatever the rights and wrongs of the latter. Overall, I am tempted to say that any practices of consumption that we might now consider as permissible ought not to be regarded as cannibalism in the regular sense, irrespective of whether or not the foods in question have a historic connection to a human body. Cannibalism is a concept that we need in order to pick out something far more monstrous, and to track a prohibition that runs far deeper than food regulations or notions of good taste.

References

Arens, William. *The Man-Eating Myth: Anthropology and Anthrophagy.* Oxford University Press, 1979.

Burley, Mikel. "Eating Human Beings: Varieties of Cannibalism and the Heterogeneity of Human Life." *Philosophy*, vol. 4, no. 91, 2016, pp. 483–501.

de Montaigne, Michel. *The Complete Essays of de Montaigne.* Translated by J. M. Cohen. Penguin, 1993.

Diamond, Cora. "Eating Meat and Eating People." *Philosophy*, vol. 53, no. 206, 1978, pp. 465–79.

Foucault, Michel. *Abnormal: Lectures at the Collège de France, 1974–1975.* Verso, 2003.

Gaita, Raimond. *Good and Evil: An Absolute Conception.* Routledge, 2004.

Hillenbrand, Laura. *Unbroken: Survival, Resilience.* Redemption, HarperCollins, 2002.

Ishida, Sui. *Tokyo Ghoul 1.* Viz Media, 2015.

Ishida, Sui. *Tokyo Ghoul 10.* Viz Media, 2016.

Midgley, Mary. "Biotechnology and Monstrosity: Why We Should Pay Attention to the 'Yuk Factor.'" *Hastings Center Report*, vol. 30, no. 5, 2000, pp. 7–15.

Morioka, Masahiro. *Confessions of a Frigid Man.* Tokyo Philosophy Project, 2017, http://www.philosophyoflife.org/tpp/frigid.pdf.

Morioka, Masahiro. "A Phenomenological Study of 'Herbivore Men.'" *The Review of Life Studies*, vol. 4, 2013, pp. 1–20.

Namahira, Emiko. "Shinto Concept Concerning the Dead Human Body." *Transplant Proceedings*, vol. 22, no. 3, 1990, pp. 940–1.

Quine, Willard Van Orman. *The Web of Belief.* Random House, 1978.

Wells, Herbert George. *The Time Machine & Other Works.* Wordsworth, 2017.

Whitehead, Neil L. "Carib Cannibalism. The Historical Evidence." *Journal de la Société des Américanistes*, vol. 70, 1984, pp. 69–87.

Wisnewski, Jeremy. "A Defense of Cannibalism." *Public Affairs Quarterly*, vol. 18, no. 3, 2004, pp. 265–72.

3

Monster and Victim

Melusine from the Fourteenth Century to the Age of *Homo Detritus*[*]

Jonathan Krell

Travelers who stop in the small town of Lusignan in western France, the birthplace of the Melusine myth, will be struck by the ubiquitous images of a mysterious serpent-woman. They will see copies of stunning medieval sculptures or illuminations. But they will also see postcards, coloring books, and trinkets—mostly aimed at children—disneyfying an ancient myth, transforming a noble and enigmatic mythological creature into a smiling little mermaid standing next to her handsome prince. Some might say that these frivolous souvenirs represent a degradation of myth into kitsch, and indeed, Melusine kitsch is everywhere in Lusignan. However, these Lusignan souvenirs are as much a part of the myth as the medieval iconography that preceded them by several centuries. They are also a testament to the persistence and longevity of Melusine, who has enchanted writers and artists since 1393. The great French ethnologist Claude Lévi-Strauss wrote that "we define the myth as consisting of all its versions. [...] There is no single 'true' version of which all the others are but copies or distortions. Every version belongs to the myth" (Lévi-Strauss, *Structural Anthropology* 217–18). So, it is in that spirit that I will be examining old and new versions of Melusine—monster and victim—in order to understand her remarkable longevity.

I will begin with a summary of the Melusine myth as it appears in the earliest prose version of 1393, by Jean d'Arras. Both Melusine and eight of her ten sons are monsters in some way, and so I will briefly discuss the double etymology—and the resulting ambivalence—of the word "monster." Ambivalence is also one of the most intriguing aspects of Melusine. I will summarize a few variants of the Melusine character in

---

[*] Parts of this chapter appeared previously in the following articles:

"Between Demon and Divinity: Mélusine Revisited." *Mythosphere: A Journal for Image, Myth, and Symbol*, vol. 2, no. 4, 2000, pp. 375–96.

"*Mélusine des détritus* ou les cris de la Terre." *Autour de Mélusine: Écriture et réécriture du merveilleux féerique*, Classiques Garnier, 2012, pp. 245–54.

I have used published English translations of French texts when available. Translations of Audeguy, Chawaf, Harf-Lancner, Louis-Combet, Maffesoli, Markale, and Monsaingeon are my own.

modern French literature, where her use as a metaphor varies widely according to the historical and literary moment in which she appears. She is both human and fairy, demon and divinity, man and woman, but always a figure of tragedy: a monstrous victim. Her tragic aspect is strikingly portrayed in a contemporary take on the myth, Chantal Chawaf's[1] 2002 novel *Mélusine des détritus*. Here the 600-year-old myth is inverted, upended by the current environmental crisis, created by humans and most disastrous for fairies.

The Myth

The Melusine myth has its origins in stories of hybrid female figures from ancient Greece and the Near East, the most common of which are bird-women and fish-women, as Misty Urban et al. explain: "Primordial goddesses and other munificent and terrible beings could assume a part-serpent, part-bird, or part piscine form" (Introduction, *Melusine's Footprint* 1). In her fairy form, Melusine is a serpent-woman. She descends from sirens[2] and hybrid female monsters like Scylla, Echidna, and Lamia of Greek mythology, and the Lilith of Hebrew and Mesopotamian mythologies (see Clier-Colombani 91–8, and Markale 173–250).[3] Her appeal may be due to, as Urban et al. suggest, the universality of the hybrid woman myth:

> The fascination with Melusine rests in large part on her parallels with other shape-shifting, water- or earth-associated females who have made persistent appearances in literature and legend worldwide. Women with ophidian, piscine, or other features reminiscent of dragon-kind slither through the foundational stories of any number of cultures, from the islands of Japan to the creation myths of the first peoples of the Americas. (Introduction, *Melusine's Footprint* 2)

In France, stories of mermaids and serpent-women—both written and oral—existed at least as early as the twelfth century, but the name Melusine was not given to the character until the late fourteenth century (Clier-Colombani 10). First composed in

---

[1] Chawaf published *Mélusine des detritus* under her adoptive name, Marie de la Montluel.
[2] Frederika Bain notes that there is no physical description of sirens in the *Odyssey*, where they first appear. However, "Early visual representations of them show varying combinations of bird and human, while later versions combine fishtails with human heads and torsos" (Bain 24). Bain quotes Misty Urban's *Monstrous Women in Middle English Romance* (Edwin Mellen, 2010, p. 60), where Urban states that "medieval artists often interchange the serpent-woman or mermaid and her close cousin the bird-woman or siren, sometimes even combining the two" (Bain 24).
[3] Scylla appears in the *Odyssey* (Book 12) as a monster with twelve feet and six heads, each of which bears three rows of teeth. In the *Aeneid* (III), Virgil describes her as part woman, part dragon. In Hesiod's *Theogony*, Echidna is part fair nymph, part giant snake, an eater of raw flesh. Echidna, like Melusine, is the mother of monstrous children: Cerberus, the Hydra of Lerna, Chimera, the Nemean lion, and Scylla. In the cabalistic tradition, Lilith was created from the same clay as Adam. She defied both Adam and God, sprouted wings and flew out of Eden to become the consort of Lucifer. She gave birth to many demons and was said to devour babies of women during childbirth.

prose by Jean d'Arras (1393) for the Duc de Berry, then in verse by Coudrette (1401) for the Sire of Parthenay, *Melusine* served to confer a semidivine origin upon the noble house of Lusignan, a prominent family in the Poitou region of western France since the tenth century. The illustrious Lusignan lineage included crusaders who became kings of Cyprus, Jerusalem, and Armenia.

The myth of Melusine, like many tales of fairies, recounts the making, then breaking of a pact between hero(s) and heroine(s), and the tragic consequences. Melusine was one of the three female triplets born to the king of Albanie (now Scotland) and his wife, a fairy named Pressine, who had married a mortal on the condition that he never see her during childbirth. He inadvertently broke his vow, causing Pressine and her three daughters to be exiled to the isle of Avalon, from which they could see and mourn their beloved Albanie. After fifteen unhappy years, Melusine, angered by her father's betrayal, finally gets revenge by trapping him inside a magic mountain in Northumberland. This in turn angers Pressine, who knew that Elinas had not betrayed her intentionally, and she curses Melusine to become a serpent from the waist down every Saturday. She would live eternally this way, unless she married a man who would agree to never see her on Saturday. If she found such a man, she would be allowed to die a natural death; moreover, she would become the matriarch of a great and noble lineage.

Melusine eventually crosses the Atlantic and wanders through France to the Poitou region. Raymondin, nephew of the count of Poitiers, has just accidentally killed his uncle during a boar hunt. Disconsolate, he wanders through the forest alone and chances upon the fair Melusine, sitting near a spring, for water is this fairy's element. Eventually, Melusine agrees to marry him on one condition: that he promise never to see her on Saturday. Raymondin does not know that on this day in her bath she assumes her hybrid fairy form, metamorphosing into a serpent from the waist down. Raymondin honors the pact, but after many years of a prosperous and happy marriage blessed by ten male children, his jealous brother spies on Melusine in her bath and reveals her secret to Raymondin. Raymondin eventually denounces his wife, blaming her—"sordid serpent!" (Jean d'Arras 597)—for the death of their son Fromont at the hands of his brother Geoffroy. Melusine vanishes, and the Lusignan family falls into decline. The departure of Melusine from Lusignan castle is one of the iconic images of the myth, beautifully illuminated in the *Les Très Riches Heures* of the Duc de Berry (c. 1440). In this scene Melusine is thrice a hybrid, "an unmistakable combination of the female, ophidian, and aerially equipped" (Urban et al., Introduction 4) as a dragon. She leaps from the Lusignan castle tower, her human footprint forever cast in the tower windowsill, and metamorphoses into a dragon. Jean d'Arras describes her flight:

> Heaving a pitiful sigh, she moaned plaintively and bounded into the air. Out the window she flew, soaring out over the orchard. 'Twas then that she changed into an enormous serpent of great girth, some fifteen feet in length. It must be said, too, that the stone upon which she stood in departing from the window is still there, and the imprint made upon it by her foot is still there. Great indeed was

the demonstration of grief by the whole assembly of barons, ladies, and maidens present there. (Jean d'Arras 609)

She flies around the castle three times, each time emitting a heartrending cry, and then disappears. These "cries of the Fairy" (*les cris de la Fée*) are evoked by Gérard de Nerval in his celebrated sonnet "El Desdichado" and by André Breton in *Arcanum 17*, and also lie at the heart of Chantal Chawaf's contemporary Melusine story.[4]

Melusine's monstrosity is inherited by her sons: all but the two youngest, Thierry and Raymonnet, have a curious physical deformity. Some go on to be heroes and kings. Urien, who will become king of Cyprus, has one red and one green eye. Guyon, with one eye higher than the other, will be crowned king of Armenia. Antoine has a lion's paw growing out of his cheek and Renaud has but one eye. Nevertheless, the former will become Duke of Luxembourg, and the latter king of Bohemia. Others are monstrous murderers. We have seen that Geoffroy—known as Geoffroy Big-Tooth, because his huge tooth resembles a boar's tusk—kills his brother Fromont. Cruel and hot tempered, Geoffroy especially despises monks. Furious when he learns that Fromont has joined the Abbey of Maillezais, he burns down the monastery, killing his brother with the rest of the monks. Son number eight, Horrible, is even more monstrous than Geoffroy. Huge and cruel, with three eyes, before age seven he had murdered "two of [Raymondin's] squires, and before he was three, had killed two of his nurses by biting their breasts" (Jean d'Arras 593).

Melusine's monstrous sons reflect the misogynistic belief common in the Middle Ages that normal children would resemble their father, while abnormal children were the fruit of their mother's dangerous imagination:

> A remarkable persistent line of thought argued that monstrous progeny resulted from the disorder of the maternal imagination. Instead of reproducing the father's image, as nature commands, the monstrous child bore witness to the violent desires that moved the mother at the time of conception or during pregnancy. [...] The monster thus erased paternity and proclaimed the dangerous power of the female imagination. (Huet 1)[5]

---

[4] Melusine's cry has also made its way into European folk tales: "Melusine's suffering, as a result of these multiple betrayals [by her mother, her father, and her husband], provides the narrative with a strong affective thread. A folkloric tradition found across Europe that attributes the haunting sound of a female cry produced by gusts of wind to the *cri de Mélusine*—documented in French and Czech territories if not others—testifies to this" (Urban et al., Introduction 5).

[5] The supposed monstrosity of the female imagination persisted even into the nineteenth century. Joseph Carey Merrick (1860–90) the so-called elephant man made famous by David Lynch's 1981 film, wrote a three-page autobiographical pamphlet in 1884, in which he claims that it was his mother's overactive imagination that directly caused his horrible disfigurement. The pamphlet begins as follows:

> I first saw the light on the 5th of August, 1860, I was born in Lee Street, Wharf Street, Leicester. The deformity which I am now exhibiting was caused by my mother being frightened by an Elephant; my mother was going along the street when a procession of Animals were passing by, there was a terrible crush of people to see them, and unfortunately she was pushed

Huet traces the association between mothers and monsters back to Aristotle's *On the Generation of Animals*, which situates females and monsters on the same plane of abnormality, degenerate because dissimilar from males. For if semen and menstrual fluids are analogous, the former is soul-giving while the latter is impure: "For the female is, as it were, a mutilated male, and the catamenia [menstrual fluids] are semen, only not pure; for there is only one thing they have not in them, the principle of soul" (Aristotle, *On the Generation of Animals*, Book II, 33). Like monsters, women are a "departure" from nature. Aristotle does admit, however, that there is an important difference between women and monsters. Women's deformities are necessary to produce future generations, whereas monsters are entirely useless. Male babies are proper and normal, but the female baby must be tolerated as a "natural necessity":

> For even he who does not resemble his parents is already in a certain sense a monstrosity; for in these cases Nature has in a way departed from the type. The first departure indeed is that the offspring should become female instead of male; this, however, is a natural necessity. (For the class of animals divided into sexes must be preserved, and as it is possible for the male sometimes not to prevail over the female in the mixture of the two elements, either through youth or age or some other such cause, it is necessary that animals should produce female young.) And the monstrosity, though not necessary in regard of a final cause and an end, yet is necessary accidentally. As for the origin of it, we must look at it in this way. If the generative secretion in the catamenia is properly concocted, the movement imparted by the male will make the form of the embryo in the likeness of itself. (Book IV, 76)

Ambivalence of the Monster

What exactly is this "monstrosity" shared by Melusine and her sons? There are two Latin etymons of the word "monster," *monstrare*, "to show," and *monere*, "to warn." *Monstrare* tells us that the monster is something to be shown, to be pointed out as a prodigy or a marvel. In Romance languages the connection is more obvious than in English. In French, "to show" is *montrer*, which in Middle French was written *monstrer*. The second etymon, *monere*, implies that pointing out the monster is a kind of warning or portent. However, what we are being warned about is not clear. It seems that the monster can be monstrously malevolent or monstrously marvelous. And that is its first ambivalence: the monster may be a sign from God or the work of Satan. The French Renaissance surgeon, Ambroise Paré, writes that while there may be

---

under the Elephant's feet, which frightened her very much; this occurring during a time of pregnancy was the cause of my deformity. (Merrick)

Stéphane Audeguy, in *Les Monstres: Si loin et si proches*, cites this text as a rare and moving example of monsters "in the first person" (Audeguy 114–17).

biological explanations for monstrous births, they may also bear witness to the "glory of God" or, on the contrary, prove the existence of "Demons and Devils" (Audeguy 34, quoting Paré, *On Monsters and Marvels* 3–4).[6] Much later, the French romantic writer Chateaubriand states in his *Genius of Christianity* (1802) that, regarding monsters in nature,

> some have pretended to derive from these irregularities an objection against Providence; but we consider them, on the contrary, as a manifest confirmation of that very Providence. In our opinion, God has permitted this distortion of matter expressly for the purpose of teaching us what the creation would be without Him. It is the shadow that gives greater effect to the light. (Audeguy 44, quoting Chateaubriand, Book 5, p. 144)

A second ambivalence of the monster is the question of where it exists in relation to us. Is the monster an outside object, a representation of some fearful alterity, perhaps linguistic, as the ancient Greeks considered anyone who could not speak Greek a babbling "barbarian," or perhaps geographical, as the Romans believed the inhabitants of Africa to be dog-headed cannibalistic savages?[7] Or is the monster also part of my subjective self, perhaps a creature of the Freudian Id or the Jungian shadow? To illustrate the monster as us, let us consider four authors who say just that. In *Les Monstres: Si loin et si proches* (Monsters: So far and so near) Stéphane Audeguy quotes Johnny Eck, a freak show performer who despite being born without legs or the bottom half of his torso had a successful career as an artist and musician. Eck, who appeared in the 1932 film *Freaks*, was a victim of what used to be called a "monstrous birth." Yet for him "normalcy"—or what we call normalcy—conceals monstrosity: he once said that "when I want to see monsters, I just look out the window" (Audeguy 1). The journalist Åsne Seierstad was struck by the "normalcy" of Anders Breivik, the Norwegian "monster" who murdered seventy-seven people—most of them teenagers at a youth camp—in July 2011. He was "born like one of us," she says, and so she titled her book about his trial *One of Us* ("Mind of a Terrorist"). Michel Tournier's *Gemini* is a novel about twins. One of the narrators claims that, except for twins like himself, all humans are murderers and monsters:

> Listen to this wonder, and consider its vast implication: every man has a twin originally. Every pregnant woman carries *two* children in her womb. But the

---

[6] Like Aristotle, Paré also believed in the monstrous power of the female imagination. "Monstrous children" may be the result of "the ardent and obstinate imagination (impression) that the mother might receive at the moment she conceived" (Paré 38). He cites the example of a woman who gave birth to "a girl as furry as a bear" because she "looked too intensely at the image of Saint John (the Baptist) dressed in skins, [. . .] while she was conceiving" (38).
[7] In ancient Greek, "barbaros" referred to the unintelligible speech of foreigners, thus related to "babbling" and "stammering." On the supposed cynocephalic inhabitants of Africa, see Krell, *The Ogre's Progress* 83, where I refer to Gilbert Durand's discussion of the myth of St. Christopher (Durand 197–9).

stronger will not tolerate the presence of a brother with whom he will have to share everything. He strangles him in his mother's belly and, having strangled him, he eats him, then comes into the world alone, stained with that original crime, doomed to solitariness and betrayed by the stigma of his monstrous size. Mankind is made up of ogres, strong men, yes, with stranglers' hands and cannibal teeth. And these ogres roam the world, in desperate loneliness and remorse, having by their original fratricide unleashed the torrent of crime and violence which we call history. (Tournier 142)[8]

Finally, Christiane Olivier is a psychoanalyst who studies family violence. She too believes that inside we all have an ogre that we must learn to control, lest we hurt others or ourselves. In *L'Ogre intérieur: De la violence personnelle et familiale* (The inner ogre: On personal and family violence) she describes the self-destructive behavior of anorexics and alcoholics as a psychic battle: the Id attacking the Ego (109). This image calls to mind the great 1956 science-fiction film *The Forbidden Planet*, in which an entire civilization (named the Krell) was wiped out by "the monsters from the Id," because all their base and aggressive instincts were given free reign.

Woman and snake, later a dragon, the hybrid Melusine fascinates by the ambivalence that she shares with the monster. The mirror with which she is often pictured symbolizes her double nature: Melusine is a fusion of dualities—human and mythical, evil and good, phallic and feminine. Three aspects of her ambivalence—three dualities in her character—stand out. First, her nature is both human and fairy; second, she has been condemned as demonic and commended as divine; third, possessing both female and male traits, she embodies the androgyny of the human creature.

Human/Fairy

Fairy of the forest, fairy of streams and rivers, Melusine is also part human: her father, King Elinas, is a mortal. When her mother, Pressine, curses Melusine for taking revenge—a human failing—against her father, she explains that the cause of Melusine's dilemma is that she had not learned the ways of nymphs and fairies, inheriting from her father a fatal attraction to humankind: "Your mortal descent from your father's side, without doubt, drew you and your sisters towards his human nature" (Jean d'Arras 71). Yet Melusine plays her human role well: soon she finds a husband and becomes a sort of businesswoman. All the while preserving her special relationship

---

[8] In Tournier's novel twins are superior beings, as they are in some cultures where, as symbols of fertility, they are said to have power over clouds and precious rain. In the narrator's grisly fantasy, only twins are exempt from humankind's monstrous nature. Aristotle, on the other hand, considers twins to be contrary to nature, and thus monstrous, in the same general category as creatures born with multiple heads or limbs. Twins are "portentous, because they are contrary to the general and customary rule." In monstrous births, "the cause why the parts may be multiplied contrary to Nature is the same as the cause of the birth of twins" (Aristotle, Book IV, 83).

to the earth and water, Melusine, like the fabulous head of a construction company, reveals an extraordinary talent for clearing forests and building castles and churches. In a few days, with the help of "a great number of landscape workers and woodcutters" (143) who mysteriously appear, she cuts down all the trees and raises up the walls and towers of the great fortress of Lusignan, a "strange and prodigious" (145) feat that leaves her entourage stupefied. This "wondrous" fairy,[9] by her choice to become human, distances herself from nature to bring culture and architecture to this forest-covered region. Moreover, through her ten sons, she founds, as her mother predicted, "a noble and powerful lineage who will accomplish great feats" (71). Her devotion to the human race, her building and child-bearing exploits are such that she becomes a female Prometheus, a mythic figure who expresses an optimistic vision in which humanity, thanks to hard work and innovation, will forever progress and move toward perfection.

Demon/Divinity

We have already seen Melusine's dubious ancestry. The serpent-woman descends from a host of monsters and demons from Greek, Mesopotamian, and Hebrew mythologies. Melusine, pictured as a winged serpent when she leaps from the heights of Lusignan castle, becomes linked not only to the evil Lilith but also to the winged Lucifer, the fallen angel, and the serpent of the Garden of Eden. This Satanization of the supernatural female figure characterizes most premedieval and medieval interpretations of the myth, before the fairy was ever christened "Melusine." Early versions describe her as assimilating the attributes of goddesses of love and sexuality like the Greek Aphrodite and the Roman Venus, with a twist of Christian moralizing. When pictured with her comb and mirror, she symbolizes vanity, sensuality, and lust, recalling the Prostitute of Babylon depicted on the famous Apocalypse Tapestry (1380), at the castle of Angers (Clier-Colombani 114 and illustration 69). She is the seductive siren who leads a Christian man down the path of evil. Early European legends describe a Melusine whose evil nature forces her to flee the church during the most sacred moments of the Catholic mass.[10] In the late nineteenth century, Émile Zola would exploit this dark side of Melusine in his novel *Nana*. Nana is a Parisian prostitute and actress, whose most celebrated role is as the fairy Melusine: she appears half naked in a watery grotto lit by shimmering diamonds and mirrors. Nana's animality petrifies men, and she is often compared to a horse, a lion, or the Beast of the Apocalypse. Nana was born poor,

---

[9] The name Melusine means "wondrous" or "wonder," according to Jean d'Arras (145). However, Laurence Harf-Lancner believes that "this explanation of Melusine's name remains enigmatic" (Coudrette 62, n. 18).

[10] As examples Frederika Bain cites two thirteenth-century English books: Walter Map's *De nugis curialium* (*Courtiers' Trifles*, c. 1200), and Gervase of Tilbury's *Otia imperialia* (*Recreation for an Emperor*, c. 1211). These are "the two most commonly cited early melusinian variants"; in both accounts "the supernatural or fairy woman is aligned with the demonic, unable to attend Mass or receive the Host" (Bain 21).

but she was fabulously wealthy by the end of her short life, having ruined some of the wealthiest men in Paris, just as Melusine ruined the Lusignan family by deserting them when Raymondin broke the pact.

Melusine was rehabilitated in the late fourteenth century by Jean d'Arras and Coudrette, who depict her as a good Christian, but in the end a victim of the circumstances of her birth and of human treachery. Upon meeting Raymondin, Melusine assures him that she is neither witch nor enchantress, but on the side of God: "I know indeed that you are imagining that my person and my words are only illusion and the work of the devil, but I swear to you that I am part of God's scheme, and that I believe everything that a good Catholic should believe" (Jean d'Arras 95, 97). She can thus merit the name "Melusine" or "Mère Lusigne," mother of the Lusignan family.

For André Breton, the leader of the French surrealist movement, Melusine is the "eternal feminine," first named in Goethe's *Faust*, the feminine sensibility that is humankind's only hope for survival during the dark days of the Second World War. Breton composed *Arcanum 17* while exiled on the Gaspé Peninsula in northern Quebec in 1944. He writes that "the time has come to value the ideas of woman at the expense of those of man, whose bankruptcy is coming to pass fairly tumultuously today, [...] to maximize the importance of everything that stands out in the feminine world view in contrast to the masculine, to build only on woman's resources" (61).

Breton is fascinated by Melusine at the moment when, betrayed by Raymondin, she jumps from Lusignan's castle tower and leaves the earth forever, a screaming half-human figure, at once terrible and pathetic. This scream, "buried for nine centuries under the ruins of the Château of Lusignan" (60), must ring out once more against war and injustice, a "great cry of warning and refusal" (60-1). Melusine's first scream represents "woman as she exists today, ... woman deprived of her human base [...] by the impatience and jealousy of man" (63). But then Breton describes her wild and dazzling beauty "at the instant of her second scream" (63), as the myth of Melusine converges on that of the child-woman, "that distinctive type that has always conquered poets *because time on her has no hold*" (64, emphasis in original). Rather than being eternally deprived of her humanity as in the medieval legend, Breton's Melusine is reborn.

She is "all womankind" (68), the feminine spirit pictured on the seventeenth major arcanum of the Tarot deck (The Star). This card depicts a young woman kneeling and emptying water from two urns into a stream. Above her, eight stars, the largest of which is Venus, the morning star, shine in the sky. The water from the two urns represents the masculine and feminine spirits united in this mediatrix between the perfect celestial world and the imperfect human world.

Card seventeen offers a ray of hope and redemption after the destructive forces of cards fifteen (The Devil) and sixteen (The Tower of Destruction). Like Melusine when Raymondin first sees her, this Star Woman is beside a stream. But for Breton, she transcends Melusine: "Beyond Melusine, [she] is Eve and now is all womankind" (*Arcanum 17* 68). Writing in Canada a few months after the Normandy invasion had finally brought hope to occupied France, Breton contends that Melusine, this spirit of the eternal feminine, is our sole hope for peace.

Androgynous Melusine

If for Breton Melusine represents "all womankind," most versions of the myth portray her as a hybrid creature with both female and male characteristics. Ana Pairet describes Melusine as having "three mixed bodies—the half-woman half-snake; the ambiguously gendered flying 'serpent(e)' that leaves behind a human footprint; and the motherly Dragon Maiden" (Pairet 43) who is said to return to Lusignan to nurse her two youngest sons. In Jean d'Arras's tale, she is medieval man's fantasy of the ideal woman: eternally young, beautiful, and fertile with male children. But we have also glimpsed some of her male traits. She clears forests and constructs churches and castles. Her serpent tail is an obvious phallic symbol, which, as we have seen, links her to Lilith. According to some versions of that legend, Lilith was an androgynous creature, fashioned by God—also androgynous—from the same clay and at the very same time as Adam, his equal in every way. Lilith and Adam formed one androgynous being, created in the image of their androgynous God.

A popular science writer in late nineteenth-century Germany named Wilhelm Bölsche was fascinated by the androgynous character of Melusine. In a book called *The Love Life in Nature*, he refers to the penis as the "Melusinean member":

> Certainly, a past lies in this [male] member. It is a Melusinean member. Here the human being makes its way back to the fish, from which he has come, albeit back in days now lost in purple haze. The eternal merman / mermaid (*Der ewige Nix*) stretches all the way forward to that member. But there is even more to it than that. Here we find the path that stretches all the way to the very crown of humanity. [. . .] A path of enlightenment, but also of doubt, errancy, and curse. (Bölsche 2: 265)

"Doubt, errancy, and curse"—three nouns that one could use to summarize the Melusine myth, which for Bölsche seems to be symbolic of sexual life in general. One is reminded of the Enlightenment philosopher Diderot for whom a monstrous birth is not an act of God or the devil: it is merely an accident of nature that our ignorance prevents us from understanding. Paradoxically, these accidents may be a normal occurrence in nature, explaining sexual difference. In *D'Alembert's Dream* he presents the notion—suggested by the initial resemblance of male and female organs in the fetus—that we are not preformed as male or female, but begin life as hermaphrodites: "Man may just be the monster of woman, or woman the monster of man" (Diderot, quoted in Audeguy 49 and Spangler 110).

All human beings must gaze into Melusine's "mirror of androgyny" (Markale 267), and either accept or reject their plural nature. Melusine overcomes binary oppositions, and stresses the plurality, rather than the duality, of human nature. The liquid syllables of her name express, in the words of Claude Louis-Combet, who was moved in the 1980s to rewrite the novel of Melusine, "obsessions that, long ago, gave rise to the image of Melusine and that compel this image to be ever vital in its unsettling intimacy" (Louis-Combet, back cover). And these obsessions are, perhaps, rooted in our double nature as human animals. Melusine transcends both the feminine and the human; she illustrates the hybridity of the human animal and is an appropriate symbol for the human condition. As the Melusine scholar Jean Markale declares,

> We are all the children of Melusine. Our double nature, animal and human, our desperate attempts to leave the earth, escape gravity and sprout wings to fly off into the sky, our inability to recognize ourselves as we are; all that makes us, in one way or another, like Melusine's sons, the good and the bad, the normal and the abnormal. (254)

Victim of *Homo Detritus*

Up to now we have seen Melusine in all her mythical glory, Satanized, Christianized, androgenized. We have not really addressed the tragic end of the myth. Melusine, because her husband has violated their pact, will never be allowed to die as a mortal woman. Betrayed by Raymondin, she flies off the Lusignan castle tower and circles it three times, each time "emit[ting] such a strange and mournful cry that all wept for pity" (Jean d'Arras 609). These cries, we saw, were central to Breton's analysis, representing women's protest against centuries of male aggression and domination, culminating in the catastrophe of the Second World War.

In *Mélusine des détritus*, published in 2002, Chantal Chawaf[11] proposes a new interpretation of the myth, in which the reader cannot help but question the wisdom of Melusine's desire to become human. For this novelist, the eleven centuries of Western civilization elapsed since the founding of the house of Lusignan mark a dystopian regression of humanity, rather than progress. Chawaf's protagonist, Melusine, is a young girl who has the misfortune to live in a small city in central France where two major highways intersect. She has contracted asthma after years of breathing in diesel fumes. To make matters worse, a nuclear power plant looms over her town, and fears about the unknown consequences of radiation terrify her and the other residents. This Melusine is fully human, but she does possess mysterious fairy-like qualities that recall her namesake: she is a kind of water spirit, most at home in or near the river that runs near her home; her best friends are dragonflies, ladybugs, and dewdrops, and she has the vague feeling that she has lived in her village for centuries. Her doctors fail to see the fairy in her: to them she is merely hysterical and depressive.

The symptoms of Melusine's illness are her desperate, choking cries during her asthma attacks. This modern Melusine is a metaphor for the earth; her anguished screams represent the illness of unbridled "progress" that is destroying the planet:

---

[11] Chantal Chawaf is the author of over thirty novels and essays. Chawaf is her husband's name, and *Mélusine des détritus* is the only book she has published under the name given to her by her adoptive parents: Marie de la Montluel.

She cries to the trees, she begs the nests to shelter her, to protect her from the trucks. She casts her lament upon the wind, she cries out the window to mourn the earth doomed to perdition. [. . .] Her cries were [. . .] the cries of her frustrated youth, the cries of her life and its broken, mad heartbeat, gasping in the indifference of a dead city. [. . .] She tries to empty her mucous membranes inflamed by the diesel fuel, to cough up the bottom of her throat and chest filled with gasoline fumes. (Chawaf 32, 40)

Her boyfriend Jean—a modern knight in shining armor—is stunned by Melusine's cry, which later in the novel evokes a condemnation of nuclear energy:

"Are you sick? Are you sick?" asks Jean.

Were you sick? Oh! The whole planet was sick in you, sick of its nuclear power plants, sick of its nuclear fuel reprocessing plants, sick of its weapons, its nuclear, chemical, biological weapons, sick of its uncertainty, sick of its choices, sick of everything you felt as imminent, unbalanced, obvious, sick of the cooling towers looming over us. (213–14)

Melusine grumbles about the current condition of the human race and visualizes a dark posthumanist future in which people will have degenerated into robot-like creatures. For her the earth's future is not that suggested by the French word *futur*, reassuring and predictable; rather it is an *avenir*—something to come that is uncertain, unpredictable, vaguely threatening:

Isn't humanity beautiful? Isn't it beautiful to want to cough up all your organs because you are so polluted, and you have so many allergies! Pitiful heap of guts! Money owns the world, not you! [. . .] Humanity is screwed! The planet no longer belongs to humans! They want to perfect us, they want robots. Go away, life! Into the garbage! Down with nature! Up with the end of the world! (41–2)

Our journey through this age of the Anthropocene, warns Chawaf, is headed "into the garbage." Her *Mélusine des détritus* is a fictional enactment of a very real worry that concerns ecologists today: *waste*, be it nontoxic, toxic, or radioactive. To describe the latest evolutionary avatar of Homo sapiens ("wise human"), a French environmental scientist has coined the term *Homo detritus* ("garbage human")—that would be us, the "negative mirror" of *Homo economicus*, the "economic human" of the age of industrial progress (Monsaingeon 18). At the top of the list of the follies of *Homo detritus* is radioactive waste. It lives up to the etymology of a French word for waste, *ordures*, which derives from the Latin *horridus*: something terrible that makes one shudder with fear; something monstrous (Monsaingeon 28). It is telling that Chawaf finished her novel shortly after the terrorist attacks of September 11, 2001. Her bleak outlook for Melusine's world includes the threat of terrorism through nuclear proliferation.

Jacques Derrida once said in an interview that "the future [*avenir*] is necessarily monstrous: the figure of the future, that is, that which can only be surprising, that for which we are not prepared, you see, is heralded by species of monsters. A future that would not be monstrous would not be a future" (*Points* 386–7). And the sociologist Michel Maffesoli maintains that a future-oriented society like ours, obsessed with growth and progress, tends to neglect the present, leading to a "disenchantment of the world" (Maffesoli 29). If we recall the two etymons of "monster," *monstrare* ("to show"; *montrer*) and *monere* ("to warn" of some imminent but unknown disaster), it is clear that Chawaf's contemporary Melusine corresponds to the second etymology. The guttural cry of this twenty-first-century fairy is a voice meant to reenchant the world, to save us from a sinister, portentous, monstrous *avenir*, to lead us instead back to our origins, in Chawaf's words, "to coolness, fertility, the source, the gift of life, the gift of living life" (*Le Corps et le verbe* 12).

References

Aristotle. *On the Generation of Animals.* 350 BCE. Translated by Arthur Platt, NetLibrary, 2000.
Audeguy, Stéphane. *Les monstres: Si loin et si proches.* Gallimard, 2007.
Bain, Frederika. "The Tail of Melusine: Hybridity, Mutability, and the Accessible Other." Urban, et al., pp. 17–35.
Bölsche, Wilhelm. *Das Liebesleben in der Natur* (Love life in nature), 3 vols. Eugen Diederichs Verlag, 1900–3.
Breton, André. *Arcanum 17.* Translated by Zack Rogow, Sun & Moon Press, 1994. Translation of *Arcane 17,* 1945. J.-J. Pauvert, 1971.
Chateaubriand, François-René de. *Genius of Christianity.* Translated by Charles I. White, John Murphy and Co., 1871. Translation of *Le Génie du Christianisme,* 1802.
Chawaf, Chantal. *Le Corps et le verbe: la langue en sens inverse.* Presses de la Renaissance, 1992.
Chawaf, Chantal [Marie de la Montluel]. *Mélusine des détritus.* Rocher, 2002.
Clier-Colombani, Françoise. *La Fée Mélusine au Moyen Age: Images, mythes et symboles.* Le Léopard d'or, 1991.
Coudrette. *Le Roman de Mélusine.* 1401. Translated by Laurence Harf-Lancner, Flammarion, 1993.
Derrida, Jacques. *Points…: Interviews 1974–1994.* Edited by Elisabeth Weber, translated by Peggy Kamuf et al., Stanford University Press, 1995. Translation of *Points de suspension: Entretiens,* Galilée, 1992.
Durand, Gilbert. *The Anthropological Structures of the Imaginary.* Translated by Margaret Sankey and Judith Hatten, Boombana Publications, 1999. Translation of *Les Structures anthropologiques de l'imaginaire,* 11th ed., Dunod, 1992.
Harf-Lancner, Laurence. *Les Fées au Moyen Age.* Honoré Champion, 1984.
Huet, Marie-Hélène. *Monstrous Imagination.* Harvard University Press, 1993.
Jean d'Arras. *A Bilingual Edition of Jean d'Arras's* Mélusine, *or,* L'histoire de Lusignan. Edited by Matthew W. Morris, Edwin Mellen Press, 2007. Translation of *Le Roman de Mélusine, ou l'Histoire des Lusignan,* 1393.

Krell, Jonathan. "Between Demon and Divinity: Mélusine Revisited." *Mythosphere: A Journal for Image, Myth, and Symbol*, vol. 2, no. 4, 2000, pp. 375–96.

Krell, Jonathan. *The Ogre's Progress*. University of Delaware Press, 2009.

Lévi-Strauss, Claude. *Structural Anthropology*. Translated by Claire Jacobson and Brooke Grundfest Schoepf, Basic Books, 1963. Translation of *Anthropologie structurale*, Plon, 1958.

Louis-Combet, Claude. *Le Roman de Mélusine*. Albin Michel, 1986.

Maffesoli, Michel. *Écosophie: Une écologie pour notre temps*. Les Éditions du Cerf, 2017.

Markale, Jean. *Mélusine*. 1983. Albin Michel, 1993.

Merrick, Joseph Carey. *The Autobiography of Joseph Carey Merrick*. 1884. publicdomainreview.org/the-autobiography-of-joseph-carey-merrick-1884/.

"Mind of a Terrorist" [Rebroadcast]. *To the Best of Our Knowledge*. Podcast, National Public Radio, July 21, 2018.

Monsaingeon, Baptiste. *Homo detritus: Critique de la société du déchet*. Seuil, 2017.

Olivier, Christiane. *L'Ogre intérieur: De la violence personnelle et familiale*. Fayard, 1998.

Pairet, Ana. "Polycorporality and Heteromorphia: Untangling Melusine's Mixed Bodies." Urban, et al., pp. 36–51.

Paré, Ambroise. *On Monsters and Marvels*. Translated by Janis L. Pallister, University of Chicago Press, 1982. Translation of *Des monstres et prodiges*, 1573.

Spangler, May. "L'hermaphrodisme monstrueux de Diderot." *Études françaises*, vol. 39, no. 2, 2003, pp. 109–21.

Tournier, Michel. *Gemini*. Translated by Anne Carter, Doubleday, 1981. Translation of *Les Météores*, Gallimard, 1975.

Urban, Misty, et al., editors. *Melusine's Footprint: Tracing the Legacy of a Medieval Myth*. Brill, 2017.

Urban, Misty, et al., editors. "Introduction." Urban, et al., pp. 1–13.

4

J. M. G. Le Clézio's Defense of the Human and Other-than-human Victims of the Derridean "Monstrosity of the Unrecognizable" in the Mauritian Saga *Alma*

Keith Moser

Introduction

Placing the biocentric theories developed by Jacques Derrida in his late philosophy into the context of the relatively established field of Monster Studies, this chapter explores J. M. G. Le Clézio's defense of the human and other-than-human victims in *Alma* who have fallen prey to what Derrida refers to as the "monstrosity of the unrecognizable" (*The Beast and the Sovereign vol. 2* 266). Given that a salient feature of his literary project has always been to give a voice to disenfranchised peoples in addition to expressing his disquieting ecological anxiety related to the dawn of the Anthropocene, Le Clézio covers some familiar ground in this polyphonic narrative. Nonetheless, he seamlessly blends the tragic tale of one of the most original protagonists that he has ever conceived "Dodo le héros" (Dodo the hero)[1] with the fate of the dodo bird (Le Clézio 180). Dominique Felsen nicknamed "Dodo" initially seems to be a rather improbable hero, since his face is so badly disfigured that he literally becomes a freak show spectacle. However, it is soon apparent that this "monster" who can touch his eyeballs with his tongue due to his facial deformities represents a sort of "ambassadeur" to all of the marginalized "ghosts" living on the periphery of modern civilization whose poignant suffering calls into question the dominant values undergirding neoliberal, consumer republics (Le Clézio 182). Specifically, the author demonstrates that the resin that binds this freak show artist with a bird viewed as "monstrueux" due to its large size and inability to fly is that they find themselves outside of "moral consideration," because they do not have a human face in Levinisian terms (Le Clézio 43; Preece 46). Similar to Derrida in *The Animal That Therefore I Am*, Le Clézio compels the reader to not turn away from the ethical summons extended by the gaze of the "wholly other"

---

[1] All translations are my own unless otherwise indicated.

that is capable of experiencing the searing pain that life entails in all of its divergent forms (Derrida, *The Animal* 11).

Monsters as a Product of Binary Logic in Derrida's Posthumous Thought

As Colin Milburn highlights in his analysis of Derridean notions of human and other-than-human monstrosity, Derrida and Monster Studies scholars such as Evelleen Richards, Mia Spiro, Terry Caesar, Iris Idelson-Shein, and Nadja Durbach decry the binary logic that lies at the heart of the formation of the social construct commonly referred to as a "monster." It is oppositional thinking that enables individuals to vilify, ostracize, and marginalize other-than-human entities and those who are considered to be lesser persons based upon simplistic dichotomies. In *The Animal That Therefore I Am* and *The Beast and the Sovereign* series, Derrida posits that binary codes justify the egregious violence that is often inflicted upon other sentient beings including *Homo sapiens* who do not fit so neatly into preexisting categories. In this regard, Colin Milburn underscores "the importance of monstrosity as an object of scientific inquiry and as a semiotics of radical alterity itself" throughout Derrida's philosophy (605). Milburn further clarifies, "Derrida's monsters are material and semiotic actors [. . .] symbolizing deconstruction and challenging the 'history of normality'" (606). The philosopher's concept of the "monstrosity of the unrecognizable" illustrates that "there is no crime against animality" to protect other species, nor is any ethical consideration given to people who exhibit atypical corporality that deviates from social norms (Derrida, *The Beast and the Sovereign vol. 1* 110).

In simple terms, compassion is only extended to those who are deemed to be our "fellow" (Derrida, *The Beast and the Sovereign vol. 1* 106). Dominique Felsen is utterly alienated from society owing to his "freakish," nonnormative body in *Alma*. The problem is that "many people do not recognize their fellow in certain humans" who "lack" the typical attributes of a person because of congenital abnormalities or disease (Derrida, *The Beast and the Sovereign vol. 1* 108). After he contracts a rather enigmatic kind of leprosy from a prostitute resulting in extreme facial anomalies, "dodo" is relegated to the status of a subaltern who is no longer "fully human" (Larsen and Haller 170). Without features that are clearly discernable as a human face, Le Clézio's protagonist "is a monster because he exists at the intersection between the most fundamental oppositions of experience. Not quite one thing, and yet not quite another" (Caesar 159). For all intents and purposes, "dodo" is denied full personhood and the ethical dignity that accompanies this recognition, since his deformed body defies any sort of easy compartmentalization into "binary pairs" predicated upon dichotomous thinking (Idelson-Shein 49). As the deeply unsettling scene in the cemetery in which Dominique is sadistically beaten with a cricket bat by a group of young men reveals in *Alma*, both Le Clézio and Derrida persuasively maintain that the creation of "monsters" allows people to absolve themselves of any moral responsibility whatsoever for the anguish felt by those who are perceived to be subhuman or somehow less than human. As this exploration of one of Le Clézio's most recent works of fiction will soon uncover, Dominique is the epitome of this "artificial monstrosity" in all of its various forms adversely affecting the human and other-than-human population adamantly denounced by Derrida in the aforementioned seminars published shortly after his death (Derrida, *The Beast and the Sovereign vol. 1* 25).

From an ecological perspective, the other "dodo" in the shape of the extinct bird itself in *Alma* is also an ideal Derridean metaphor for symbolizing how our socially constructed understandings of the world operate on an ideological level through the evocation of monsters. As numerous critics like Kelly Oliver, Ron Broglio, Andrea Hurst, Suzanne Guerlac, Gerald Bruns, and Patrick Llored have noted, "Deconstruction has always gestured towards the more-than-human" (Broglio 33). In particular, Derrida painstakingly and systematically undermines "the monstrosity of the general singular" that exemplifies the traditional distinction between "human and animal" revolving around binary logic (Hurst 122). In an effort to reexamine the relationship between our species and other life forms to which we are inextricably linked in an interconnected and interdependent biosphere from a more objective angle, the philosopher deconstructs "the age-old binary opposition between human and animal" in addition to "questioning the very category of 'the animal' itself" (Oliver 54). Appealing to scientific logic reflecting the discoveries of modern science, Derrida dissects the dichotomous thinking at the core of the human-animal divide. The philosopher challenges this radical separation by reminding the reader of the "immense multiplicity of other living things that cannot in any way be homogenized" (Derrida, *The Animal* 48). For Derrida, the catch-all concept of the "animal" defined in opposition to the human needs to be reproblematized. Not only is this kind of myopic thinking scientifically erroneous, but the philosopher also contends that it is fraught with peril because it removes the Cosmic Other[2] "from the sphere of law and ethics" (Kleinhaus 1). Convinced of our unique and superior essence in a chaotic, deterministic universe that does not respect the dichotomous existential hierarchies that we have conceived, the beast is a monstrous Other that we have bestowed upon ourselves the right to subjugate in the absence of any semblance of ethical reflection.

In his reevaluation of what renders human beings both strikingly similar and dissimilar to other organisms, which transcends the inherent limitations of binary thought paradigms that he provocatively labels "a sin against rigorous thinking," Derrida also takes aim at one of the basic tenets of Levinisian ethics (*The Animal* 48). According to Emmanuel Levinas, "The face-to-face encounter encapsulates, in essence, the responsibility of the subject for the Other" (Horner 236). Although Derrida also valorizes the force of the gaze that implores us to recognize and respect alterity, he strongly criticizes Levinas for his refusal to admit that other-than-human entities have a face at all. In this vein, "Derrida wants to contest the ethical relation described by

---

[2] This is a term that I coined in *J.M.G. Le Clézio: A Concerned Citizen of the Global Village* (2012). In this specific chapter, I am employing this expression in the same sense as Derrida's notion of the "wholly other."

Emmanuel Levinas [who] does not really think that animals have faces" (Bruns 409). Clearly articulating what is at stake in this moral debate, Derrida poses the following questions in the ninth session of *The Beast and the Sovereign* lecture series:

> Ok, the snake has eyes, it has a tongue, it has a head to some extent, does it have the face? What about the snake's face? [...] Does an ethics or a moral prescription obligate us only to those like us-you remember the question of the *semblable* [...] i.e. man, or does it obligate us with respect to anyone at all, any living being at all, and therefore with respect to the animal? (237-44)

In stark contrast to Levinas, Derrida reaches the conclusion that other organisms are also endowed with faces that are capable of interrogating us from an ethical standpoint.

It is in this sense that the philosopher's destabilizing and comical encounter in which he finds himself naked in front of his pet cat in the opening pages of *The Animal That Therefore I Am* should be understood. The realization that he *sees* and *is seen* by this domestic animal becomes a catalyst for philosophical reflection that will ultimately lead to the rejection of Levinas's position that only *Homo sapiens* have faces. As a direct consequence of this poignant, transformative experience, Derrida is able to go beyond the binary logic and willful blindness preventing him from reading the signs of sorrow that are written all over the faces of the other-than-human victims of our mistreatment of the planet. In *Alma*, Le Clézio also beckons us to imagine the torment endured by the dodo bird after the arrival of the first European settlers on the island of Mauritius epitomized by a face-to-face encounter in the literary space. Furthermore, it is the absence of certain features that are easily identifiable as a human face that will lower Dominique Felsen to the status of a monster that he shares with an extinct creature. As this investigation demonstrates, the monstrosity of both "dodos" is a symbolic reflection of *différance*[3] in Derridean terms.

From Metaphorical Ghosts and Apparitions to Overt Manifestations of Monstrosity in Le Clézio's Oeuvre

As I outline in a previous article entitled "J.M.G. Le Clézio's Urban Phantoms and the Paradox of Invisibility" (2011), the author often takes advantage of the literary device of monstrosity in order to "'rendre visible' les 'peuples invisibles'" (render "invisible people" "visible") and to "faire entendre la voix des sans voix" (make the voices of the voiceless heard) (Salles and Roussel-Gillet 11). Even if this technique

---

[3] I am using this terminology in a very general sense. For a more comprehensive explanation of this crucial concept throughout Derrida's philosophy that transcends the pragmatic limitations of the present study, see Simon Lumsden. "Hegel, Derrida and the Subject." *Cosmos and History*, vol. 3, nos. 2-3, 2007, pp. 32-50. In his analysis of the complex nuances of this Derridean notion, Lumsden notes that understanding *différance* is "to capture the instability and factures that are constitutive of our interpretative schema," thereby "collapsing the basis of these binaries" (36).

of unveiling "la présence de ces êtres en bordure de notre visibilité" (the presence of these beings on the edges of our visibility) is not entirely new in the Franco-Mauritian author's repertoire, Le Clézio engages more directly with conceptions of monstrosity in *Alma* (Ridon 39). In earlier canonical texts such as *Voyages de l'autre côté*, *Désert*, and *Poisson d'or* in addition to the obscure and aptly named novella *Fantômes dans la rue*, the Nobel laureate focuses on "the way the monstrous past [and present] has turned its victims, humans, into fractured, ghostly and ghastly-uncanny beings" representing the ugly underbelly of the modern world (Spiro 28). Although Le Clézio has been conjuring up apparitions for decades as a subversive act of solidarity in support of the disenfranchised, as evidenced by the fact that the mysterious protagonist Naja Naja in *Voyages de l'autre côté* appears to be a shape-shifter capable of assuming many different ontological forms, the writer presents more overt manifestations of monstrosity for the first time that are much less subtle in his latest Mauritian saga. By delving into what specialists in the field of Monster Studies describe as "the rhetoric of the freak show" and "discourses of freakery," Le Clézio continues to diversify his literary and humanistic project in a career that already spans more than half a century (Solomon 167; Durbach 56). In the highly original, captivating, and somber novel *Alma*, there is a noticeable progression from the depiction of metaphorical ghosts in the previously mentioned texts to the explicit portrayal of monstrous beings.

Even if the author's artistic choice of allowing the monster to take center stage represents a novel approach, he broaches many of the same subjects that have haunted him since the publication of his first work *Le Procès-verbal* in 1963. As Gilberte Favre affirms in her brief synopsis of *Alma*, "Ce roman qui remonte à l'histoire familiale de l'auteur nous interpelle sur notre planète et la justice dite 'humaine'" (This novel, which goes back to the author's family history, interrogates us about our planet and so-called human justice). Given that the reclusive writer has long been at the forefront of humanitarian advocacy as an unwavering proponent of social and climate justice in the Francophone world through his writings and the launching of the *Fondation pour l'interculturel et la paix*, Favre notes that *Alma* is still vintage Le Clézio. Not only does the writing style reflect the same kind of lyrical prose that characterizes the author's fiction but Le Clézio also seeks yet again to remove all of the skeletons from his own family's closet. Similar to the semiautobiographical sections of *Le Chercheur d'or* and *La Quarantaine* in which he reflects upon the complicity of his colonial ancestors in the debasement of the indigenous population of Mauritius, Le Clézio tries to grapple with these "fantômes du passé" (ghosts from the past) linked to crimes against humanity for which there is no moral justification (*Alma* 125). In one of the official press releases for *Alma*, published in the electronic version of *Le monde*, an unidentified author reveals that one of the narrators Jérémie Fersen is a "sorte de double de l'auteur, comme lui né à Nice mais lié familialement à l'île Maurice" (kind of double of the author, like him born in Nice but linked to Mauritius through his family) ("*Alma* – J.M.G. Le Clézio (Gallimard – 2017)"). This same anonymous publicist further elucidates that the initial impetus for Jérémie's voyage to Mauritius was the discovery of a list of names on a slave registry from 1814 of people whose suffering has been largely forgotten or erased by the sands of time ("*Alma* – J.M.G. Le Clézio (Gallimard – 2017)"). Explaining the humanistic motivations for his extended stay in Mauritius, the narrator confesses, "Je veux voir toutes les traces, remonter à la source de toutes les histoires. Ce n'est pas facile. Elles sont cachées, secrètes, des scandales de famille, des mensonges pieux, l'oubli a recouvert cette île" (I want to see all the traces, go back to the source of all the stories. It is not easy. They are hidden, secret, family scandals, pious lies, forgetfulness has covered this island) (Le Clézio 145). As this candid admission on the part of the narrator who bears an uncanny resemblance to the author himself suggests, *Alma* is above all a story about the ghosts and monsters lurking in the shadows of the past and present. During his time in Mauritius, Jérémie also realizes that the plight of the *oiseau fantôme* ("ghost bird") (i.e., dodo) is connected to how it was painted as a monster unworthy of compassion by the same colonial forces (Le Clézio 335).

The Ethical Gaze of the Other-than-human Face in *Alma*

Adopting a Derridean approach to soliciting empathy for the dodo bird and other nonhuman entities who currently find themselves in a precarious situation on the brink of extinction, Le Clézio invites us to catch a glimpse of what is behind the "looking glass [. . .] from the point of view of the animal" (Derrida, *The Animal* 8). In his attempts to preserve the faint traces of this vanished creature that remain, the author compels us to not turn away from this gaze that still haunts us from the grave. The ethical summons emanating from this reconstructed gaze in the literary realm sheds light on how this other-than-human victim is one of the many causalities of the social construct of monstrosity. Throughout this face-to-face encounter with an extinct organism in a different space, the reader is able to formulate a mental image of the anguish endured by the final members of this species during their last ephemeral moments on this earth. Incorporating information from fossil remains, historical archives, and legends, Le Clézio provides a snapshot of this "dernière danse" (last dance) (87). In the Derridean sense, this figurative confrontation with these other-than-human ghosts is an ethical imperative that forces us to look deep into the eyes of one of the many "monsters" that we have created and destroyed since the beginning of human civilization.

A close examination of the reconstituted face of the dodo from these bits and pieces offers one plausible explanation as to why Dutch sailors seemed to express little remorse for the extermination of this species. Owing to the fact that this flightless animal only bore a vague resemblance to other birds with which they were familiar, Dutch explorers wondered whether it was even a bird at all. As Derrida's rejection of Levinas's assertion that only *Homo sapiens* have a face based on pervasive anthropocentric logic that still reigns supreme in Western society illustrates, it is quite probable that these seafarers would not have thought twice about eliminating a more normal looking bird from existence either. Nevertheless, as Monster Studies research has proven, a person who possesses an unusual body is too often perceived to be less than human to the point of being monstrous. This basic principle is applicable to other organisms as well.

As the documented perceptions of these sailors in historical records highlight, they describe the dodo as a "freak of nature" or an evolutionary oddity (Pendell 3). In her discussion of "the framing structure of freak shows," Chih-Ping Chen reminds us that the "'What is it?' exhibitions staged by the famous showman Phineas Taylor Barnum" included human and other-than-human forms of entertainment (368, 368). This "gros oiseau de la taille d'un cygne, complètement dépourvu d'ailes, et qui se nourrit de pierres" (big bird the size of a swan, completely wingless, and which ate stones) did not fit into their simplistic conceptual categories centered around binary logic (Le Clézio 278). Given that the explorers were unable to answer the question "What is it?" about a life form that could not be so easily classified, the dodo was "unrecognizable" as anything. Hence, Le Clézio argues that it was destined to become part of "une collection de curiosités" (a collection of curiosities) alongside other monsters (Le Clézio 280). In the words of Jeffrey Jerome Cohen, since the gigantic dodo was "not quite" a bird, it embodied "difference made flesh, come to dwell among us" (7). Moreover, for these Dutch sailors who had never witnessed a bird like the dodo ingest gizzard stones, which aid in the digestive process,[4] this "ridicule" (ridiculous) and "oiseau géant" (gigantic bird) appeared to be capable of eating anything (Le Clézio 87, 44). The dodo's designation as a "oiseau monstrueux" (monstrous bird) was partially related to this dietary habit that was misunderstood by the first and only Europeans to observe the seemingly peculiar behavior of this bird (Le Clézio 43). Unaware of the biological function of gizzard stones, these explorers pondered whether an organism that eats rocks and pieces of metal could be considered living in the same manner as a human being, or even a so-called lesser animal.

The moving descriptions of the dodo bird's fate are reminiscent of the techniques employed by the author in other works such as "Pawana," "Villa Aurore," and "Orlamonde" to "renoncer l'anthropocentrisme occidental" (reject Western anthropocentrism) (Cadorel 88). Attempting to eliminate "les barrières entre l'animal et humain" (the barriers between the animal and human) erected on the basis of binary thinking (Roussel-Gillet 159), Le Clézio presents the dodo as a sentient being possessing many of the same vital faculties as *Homo sapiens*. This concerted effort to undermine "l'erreur de l'anthropocenrisme" (the mistake of anthropocentrism) is most evident in the harrowing scene in the novel in which the crew members of a vessel transporting one of the last living dodo birds kill this innocent creature before it arrives at its destination (Roussel-Gillet 136). Awestruck by the dodo's ability to ingest nearly any metallic object, linked to its aforementioned digestive process, the sailors take a game that they have created too far leading to the slow and excruciating demise of this other-than-human victim. At the beginning of this spectacle, thunderous applause erupts when the dodo eats scraps of metal, nails, and rocks that are being thrown in its general direction. However, this form of entertainment will soon turn deadly after an overzealous individual strikes the bird with a sharp object.

---

[4] See Fritz et al. (2011).

Reexamining the dominant anthropocentric discourse in Western civilization that portrays all other organisms as robotic automatons that are incapable of feeling pain or emotions like humans, Le Clézio promotes an ethics of compassion for the dodo and other nonhuman victims in *Alma*. In response to the disproven notion that all other-than-human vocalizations including screams of agony are the product of an internal machinery, the Franco-Mauritian author urges us to confront the scientific reality of other-than-human anguish. During this "pluie meurtrière" (deadly rain), the visibly distressed dodo begins to bleed profusely as it tries to dodge these sharp items (Le Clézio 290). As the narrator explains, "Alors naît la peur, mais il n'y a pas d'issue, pas de cachette. Et puis d'un seul coup vient un grand vide, un trou au fond du corps, le cœur ne bat plus, n'a plus la force de faire courir les pattes, de faire sonner les ailes sur les flancs, le bec est lourd, il tombe vers le sol" (So fear is born, but there is no way out, no hiding place. And then in a single blow comes a big void, a hole in the depths of the body, the heart no longer beats, no longer has the strength to control its legs, to make its wings flap on its sides, the beak is heavy, it falls to the ground) (Le Clézio 290). In this passage, Le Clézio strives to rehabilitate the image of a misunderstood bird that has become synonymous with idiocy, as the expression "[you're] such a dodo"[5] demonstrates (Le Clézio 17). Counterpointing the anthropocentric mentality that this metal-eating "freak" was a mindless robotic entity, the author directs our attention to the universal suffering of existence. He alludes to the established empirical fact that many other species are endowed with similar pain receptors as humans (Sneddon et al., Burma et al., and Watabiki et al.). Le Clézio implores us to imagine the other-than-human gaze of a gigantic extinct bird with a massive beak during its final agonizing moments on this earth. In addition to being placed into the problematic, homogeneous category of the "animal," the dodo resisted easy classification in general because of its physical appearance and dietary practices. Although all other-than-human entities inhabit a moral *no-man's-land* owing to the human-animal divide, the dodo was a monstrous object of curiosity that could not be recognized as anything. For this reason, no one would rush to the defense of this creature, thus allowing this senseless crime culminating in the death of another sentient being to continue unabated.

In his reevaluation of signs of other-than-human distress that are often dismissed as insignificant, reactive behavior, Le Clézio observes that other species express suffering and discomfort in many of the same ways as humans. In this regard, the author notes that many early explorers were taken aback by the human-like responses of dodos that cried, moaned, sighed, and sometimes refused to eat when held in captivity. In the context of historical documents that chronicle the last days of the dodo, Le Clézio indicates in a recent interview that this bird was described "à l'époque un peu comme un humain, un peu ridicule et en même temps touchant" (at the time a bit like a human, a little ridiculous and at the same time touching) (Demorand). The Nobel laureate reiterates, "quand on le capture il pleure, il se laisse mourir de faim si on l'enferme, il ne peut pas vivre sans sa compagne et il est condamné. [C'est] Une figure tragi-comique,

---

[5] Le Clézio writes this expression in English in the original.

qui correspond assez à l'idée qu'on peut se faire des humains" (when it is caught it cries, it lets itself die of hunger if it is locked up, it cannot live without its companion and it is condemned. [It's] a tragi-comic figure, which corresponds roughly to the idea that we have of humans) (Demorand). Given that numerous voyagers essentially paint the same portrait of an organism that appeared to feel both pain and emotions rather deeply, Le Clézio asserts that these accounts should be taken seriously. In an episode in the novel that was evidently inspired by these stories of the sorrow experienced by the dodo, the narrator recounts the trauma of the birds that were captured alive. As the narrator reveals, "Ils ont entendu les plaintes de ceux qui ont été capturés vivants et enfermés dans un enclose, et qui refusent de manger et pleurent en se laissant mourir de faim" (They heard the complaints of those who were captured alive and locked up in an enclosure, and who refused to eat and cried while starving themselves to death) (Le Clézio 87). Due to the amount of evidence in the form of scientific research and historical archives related to the dodo, Le Clézio's deconstructive method for presenting the point of view of the "wholly other" and compelling us to look into its gaze in *Alma* should not be labeled as a type of personification. Instead, the author's reflections about the dodo are indicative of an effort to extend the concept of personhood itself to the entire biotic community of life. As a testament to how the well-documented observations of the first settlers of Mauritius concerning the behavior of the dodo blur the traditional lines between human and animal in Western society, Le Clézio also emphasizes the monogamous relations between male and female dodos. In fact, several first-hand accounts mentioned earlier confirm that some dodos died when separated from their mates, as they were unable to cope with the trauma associated with the loss of their partner. Furthermore, many researchers in the hard sciences such as Chantelle Ferland, Laura Schrader, and Kurt Leroy Hoffman have now confirmed the veracity of these anecdotal claims in studies dedicated to the stress induced by the forced separation of mates in several monogamous species. In this section of the text, the author leaves us to ponder whether these "mariages" accompanied by ritualistic dancing were really that different from human matrimony (Le Clézio 88). Regardless of the answer to this lingering question that exposes the faulty nature of oppositional thinking, the Franco-Mauritian writer undoubtedly advocates in favor of a (re-)conceptualization of our anthropocentric moral systems that takes into account the certainty of other-than-human suffering. For the travelers who witnessed the torment of the dodo, the most troubling aspect of their observations is that they saw an all-too-familiar reflection staring back at them as opposed to a monster.

    In this vein, Le Clézio's promulgation of "a humanism without human beings at the center" coalesces with Derrida's biocentric reworking of environmental ethics (Gopnik 67). As Claudia Egerer underscores, the "shared vulnerability" of pain and death is what unites all sentient beings in Derrida's posthumous thought (443). By focusing on this "shared bodily mortal existence" in *The Animal That Therefore I Am* and in *The Beast and the Sovereign* series, Derrida engages in a "sincere anti-Cartesian advocacy of cross-species sympathy" (Oliver 67; Nash 58). It is through "compassion or love" that the philosopher "complexifies the limit between the animal and the human" (Slater 691). The "acknowledgement of the gaze" of the Cosmic Other in Derrida's lectures demystifies the Cartesian theory of "the animal-machine" (Slater 687; Derrida *The Animal* 101). Affirming that the recognition of the gaze of another sentient creature discredits the outmoded idea that only humans know what it is like to feel pain, Derrida insists that this "regard" serves to "awaken us to our responsibilities and our obligations vis-à-vis the living in general, and precisely to this fundamental compassion that, were we to take it seriously, would have to change the very cornerstone [. . .] of the philosophical problematic of the animal" (*The Animal* 27). Derrida explains that this ecocentric realization erodes the shaky foundation of the social construct of the monster. After we have been transformed by the power of the other-than-human gaze, "the refusal of alterity through non-recognition" is no longer possible (Wadiwel 15).

In his analysis of the origins of human violence inflicted upon other *Homo sapiens* and the remainder of the biosphere in *The Beast and the Sovereign*, Derrida reinforces his theory that the monster is someone or something that has no moral standing. As the philosopher argues, "The worst, the cruelest, the most human violence has been unleashed against living beings, beasts or humans, and humans in particular, who precisely were not accorded the dignity of being fellows" (*The Beast and the Sovereign vol. 1* 108). Proposing a new ethical model that would remove human and other-than-human monsters from the shadows into the light of moral considerability in philosophical terms, Derrida declares, "I am surreptitiously extending the similar, the fellow, to all forms of life, to all species. All animals qua living beings are my fellows" (*The Beast and the Sovereign vol. 1* 109). Derrida's questioning of absolute human ontological sovereignty, which has supposedly given us the right to "master" every last parcel of the universe for our exclusive benefit without feeling any guilt for the deleterious effects of our narcissistic destruction, recalls the ecological solidarity championed by other contemporary French thinkers like Michel Serres, Edgar Morin, and Michel Onfray. Given that the same bittersweet physical laws govern the fleeting existence of every mortal creature that tries to stave off the omnipresent forces of death for as long as possible, Derrida contends that "we owe to animals the debts of pity and compassion" (Nash 65). Additionally, instead of turning away from the gaze of the cosmic "wholly other," "we need to challenge ourselves to discern their faces" (Nash 65). For Le Clézio and Derrida, it is time to (re-)establish a meaningful bond, or a certain kind of kinship, with all of the billions of "fellows" with whom we share the most beautiful and tragic story ever told: existence. Both writers convincingly theorize that other organisms must be granted some semblance of moral consideration, if we are to find a way to end the "infinite violence" connected to a lack of compassion for the suffering of other sentient beings (Derrida, *The Animal* 89).

The Ecological Consequences of the Anthropocentric Social Construct of the "Monster"

As the enduring image of one of the final remaining dodos in *Alma* whose face falls to the earth from whence it came and to which everything returns suggests, "humans and other animals share not only the same ecology, but, moreover, the same destiny" (Lestel 174). In a world that is teetering on the edge of oblivion because of the ramifications of anthropogenic climate change, Derrida affirms that "humans [...] can only save themselves by saving the other animals" (Lestel 174). The ethical paradigm shift to a more biocentric worldview promoted by Derrida has become a necessity due to the gravity of the situation. In *The Animal That Therefore I Am* and *The Beast and the Sovereign*, the philosopher seeks to uproot the ideological underpinnings of monstrosity that continue to justify our unsustainable rapport with the cosmos in spite of stern warnings from the scientific community. In the "third session" of *The Beast and the Sovereign*, Derrida challenges the "economy of forgetting" in the shape of the thick layers of anthropocentric ideology that conceal our "cosmic *Dasein*, our earthly identity" in Morinian terms (Derrida, *The Beast and the Sovereign vol. 1* 82; Morin, *Homeland Earth* 79). Explaining how human civilization has always tried to rid itself of the very monsters that we have conceived, Derrida muses, "So many animal monsters, fantastic beasts, chimeras, and centaurs that the point, in chasing them, is to cause them to flee, to forget them, repress them [...] to domesticate them [...] to tame them" (*The Beast and the Sovereign vol. 1* 82). In a society in which this "human right to domination" is rarely questioned, the monstrous "wholly other" has no place (Lawlor 169). In reference to how the homogeneous category of the "animal," contested by Derrida with his neologism *animot*,[6] excises all other life forms from the human sphere, Patrick Llored decries "the figure of the animal based on and with a view toward a violence seldom achieved in the history of the West" (122). In his posthumous thought, Derrida hypothesizes that the subjugation of the savage "beast" has reached epic proportions to the alarming point of placing our own existence into jeopardy.

Although the sophistication of modern technology has enabled us to exert more control than ever before over the biosphere, the philosopher explains that this partial mastery is a pyrrhic victory that could turn out to be the ultimate defeat. The act of placing all of the nonhuman monsters upon which our existence depends out of sight and out of mind in the creation of our human-centered universe has induced a kind of *ecocidal* forgetting that could result in our disappearance. Echoing the sentiments of the French philosopher of science Michel Serres who defines our current, parasitic relationship with the biosphere as a "world war" in essays like *Le Contrat Naturel*, *La Guerre Mondiale*, and *Biogée*, Derrida denounces this "war without mercy against the animal" that he describes as "war to the death" (*The Animal* 102). It is in this sense in which Derrida's dystopian "tableau of a world after animality, after a sort of holocaust, a world from which animality, at first present to man, would have one day disappeared, destroyed or annihilated by man" should be understood (*The Animal* 80). Offering the grim reality of mass extinctions as a concrete example of the predictable end game of

---

[6] As Marie-Eve Morin explains, "It is in order to point to this conceptual homogenisation of all sorts of animals and animal societies that Derrida coined the portmanteau 'animot': 'animal' is a word or concept, it refers to how all these living beings that we call animal are taken up in human discourses" (166).

this "war to the death," Derrida laments, "The number of species endangered because of man [that] takes one's breath away" (*The Animal* 26). As David Wood highlights, Derrida is philosophically opposed to the term "Anthropocene" because it "implies a rupture or an instantaneous mutation [. . .] in order to name a transformation in progress" (Wood 320; Derrida, *The Animal* 24). Despite the perceived inadequacy and inaccurateness of the word "Anthropocene" itself from Derrida's point of view, the philosopher clearly articulates the seriousness of the predicament. He explains that the incessant pursuit of the self-proclaimed human sovereign to impose order upon the monstrous beast has forged a path of self-destruction.

Similar to "Pawana," labeled an "apocalyptic tale" by the Le Clézio scholar Bruno Thibault, *Alma* explores the same devastating ripple effects of unfettered human aggression outlined by Derrida (723). As opposed to conceiving members of other species as monsters-automatons to be subdued or destroyed, Le Clézio generates a biocentric countervision casting "fellow" sentient beings in a more positive light. If merely for the sake of self-preservation, the author contends that we desperately need to reinstitute a more symbiotic relationship with the proverbial hand that feeds. Developing ecological metaphors around the interrelated concepts of interdependency and irreversibility, Le Clézio demonstrates in *Alma* that the social construct of a monster itself is an unsustainable form of thinking preventing global society from taking action in defense of an imperiled planet. To be more precise, the dodo bird and many other species have been wiped out entirely because of the pervasiveness of an anthropocentric moral code that only applies to humans. In his ecologically engaged works of fiction including *Alma*, Le Clézio issues a reminder that life as we know it will cease to exist if too many threads in the web of life are torn. Maintaining the overall health of the biosphere, which is being further degraded by human activity with each passing day, is of the utmost importance, since our saga is interwoven into this same fabric of life.

In the accompanying introduction to the 2003 edition of "Pawana" published by Gallimard, the contemporary French poet Bruno Doucey provides the following overview of the ethics of compassion that pervades this seminal text: "Qu'il s'agisse de bisons ou de baleines, la problématique est la même. Nous aurions tort de croire que leur disparition n'affecte que le monde marin ou le règne animal. Toutes choses étant liées, l'extinction de diverses espèces de cétacés entraîne des déséquilibres écologiques qui menacent également les êtres humains" (Whether it is bison or whales, the problem is the same. We would be wrong to believe that their disappearance only affects the marine world or the animal kingdom. All things being connected, the extinction of various species of cetaceans leads to ecological imbalances that also threaten human beings) (114). The apocalyptic tone of the passages in *Alma* in which Le Clézio addresses the question of ecological interdependency is reminiscent of "Pawana." Specifically, the author incorporates the highly contested folkloric tradition linking the disappearance of the dodo bird to the "near extinction" of the Tambalacoque tree in Mauritius into a larger discussion about deforestation (Herhey 105). According to popular legends, the "gros oiseau sans ailes" (big bird without wings) was the only creature capable of breaking the "hard endocarp, or inner fruit wall" of the Tambalacoque fruit (Le Clézio 33; Herhey 105). In recent years, this unproven correlation has been largely debunked by scholars such as David Herhey, Mark Witmer, and Anthony Cheke. During his stay in Mauritius, Jérémie hears about this myth for the first time. As he is touring one of the only small pockets of endemic forest left on the island protected by the Mauritius Wildlife Fund with his guide Aditi by his side, this young girl with mystical tendencies shows the narrator a young Tambalacoque tree casting doubt on the theory that this organism cannot reproduce without the dodo. As Aditi reveals, "On a prétendu qu'après la mort du dodo les tambalacoques ne pourraient pas survivre, parce qu'il était le seul à pouvoir digérer l'écorce de la graine, à la briser avec sa pierre de gésier, mais regarde, celui-ci est tout jeune, il prouve que l'arbre va continuer à vivre" (It has been claimed that after the death of the dodo the Tambalacoque tree could not survive, because it was the only organism capable of digesting the bark of the seed, of breaking it with its gizzard stone, but look, this one is very young, which proves that the tree will continue to live) (Le Clézio 137). In Mauritian culture, the Tambalacoque tree is often cited as an example illustrating the catastrophic ecological impact of the loss of the dodo. It is possible that the disappearance of the dodo was indeed a contributing factor along with many others that have placed this tree at the verge of extinction. However, empirical evidence does not support this legendary association, as Le Clézio himself implies in this portion of the novel.

Even if the widespread belief that this tree could not reproduce without the dodo is problematic, the author draws attention to the issue of deforestation that has long been identified by numerous scientists as one of the most serious crises affecting the modern world. As Claire Devarrieux highlights in the context of the destruction of approximately 90 percent of the lush forest that once epitomized the Mauritian landscape upon the arrival of the first Europeans, "Tout disparaît. La forêt est désormais une enclave placée sous la protection d'une ONG, alors qu'elle couvrait '*les neuf dixièmes de l'île*' en 1796" (Everything disappears. The forest is now an enclave under the protection of a NGO, while it covered "nine tenths of the island" in 1796). One of Aditi's main responsibilities is to protect endangered species like the Tambalacoque tree that have been ravaged by rapacious human consumption and a lack of ethical reflection. In a passage in which he does not mince his words regarding this absence of compassion and inability to heed the ethical summons of the other-than-human gaze, the narrator confesses, "J'aime bien sa candeur, son travail volontaire pour sauver les pigeons roses [. . .] les crécerelles, les paille-en-queue, contre les déprédations de la vie moderne" (I like her candor, her volunteer work to save the pink pigeons [. . .] the kestrels, the tropicbirds, against the depredations of modern life) (Le Clézio 136). The dodo may be the poster child for the Anthropocene in the Mascarene region, but Le Clézio observes that it has plenty of company on an exponentially growing list of extinct or endangered species reflecting the "ever-growing consensus within the scientific community that we have entered into a sixth mass extinction" (Wagler 78). Looking into the eyes of the pink pigeon, the kestrel, and tropicbirds, in this tiny sliver of endemic forest, allows Jérémie to realize that many species are presently living the nightmare of the final days of the dodo. Although these birds have a more normal appearance in comparison to the dodo, their precarious status attests to the fact that the monstrosity of the human-animal divide has never been more pronounced or deadly.

Another ubiquitous form of monstrosity in *Alma* that is in keeping with the recurrent themes that permeate Le Clézio's fiction is the urban space itself. As the author explains throughout his diverse body of work, the problem of excessive urbanization is intertwined with the realities of deforestation. In a similar fashion as other contemporary writers analyzed by specialists in the field of Monster Studies such as China Miéville, Henry James, and Ian McEwan, Le Clézio "equates urban monstrosity with modern growth," or the continual expansion of megapolises (Lamperez and McGhee 9). Several researchers including Bruno Thibault, Nadine Dormoy, Gérard Fanchin, and Fredrik Westerlund have investigated the author's deep-seated concerns about the effects of urbanization on a global scale. For instance, Fredrik Westerlund discusses Le Clézio's palpable anxiety related to "la violence de la ville grandissante" (the violence of the expanding city) that is usually framed as a grotesque space replete with aggression, prostitution, and other forms of sexual exploitation, acute poverty, crime, and misery (77). Gérard Fanchin correctly notes that a long line of Le Clézio's protagonists from Adam Pollo in *Le Procès-Verbal* to Aditi in *Alma* instinctively flee "l'univers carcéral et stressant de la ville, voire le village global" (the prison-like and stressful world of the city, even the global village) (18). Moreover, outlining how the author explicitly utilizes various metaphors of monstrosity in *Les Géants* to contest the allegedly superior nature of urban life, Bruno Thibault affirms, "la ville apparaît terrifiante comme Méduse et invincible comme une Hydre à tête multiples. Hyperpolis symbolise la mégalopole" (the city appears to be terrifying like Medusa and invincible like a multiheaded Hydra. Hyperpolis symbolizes the megalopolis) (24).

Similar to the distress explored by Thibault in *Les Géants*, there is a profound sense of loss and disenchantment that reverberates throughout *Alma*. Le Clézio tries to bear witness[7] to the anguish felt by human and other-than-human entities who have been "effacés par l'urbanisation" (erased by urbanization) (146). For those who are familiar with Le Clézio's work, the enormous shopping center Mayaland brings to mind Hyperpolis that will eventually be burned down in a despondent act of rebellion in *Les Géants*. As he enters into Mayaland for the first time, Jérémie records these dystopian observations: "Le dôme en forme de lotus ou de nénuphar m'a paru encore plus *monstrueux* au soleil, ses bulbes enclos pareils à des bulles de savons tremblotaient dans l'air surchauffé. A l'intérieur, on suffoquait" (The dome in the shape of a lotus or water lily seemed to me even more *monstrous* in the sun, its bulbs like bubbles of soap trembling in the overheated air. Inside, we were suffocating') (Le Clézio 158, my emphasis). In a later scene, the narrator builds upon this description of the urban monstrosities that concretize modern life by indicating that this site is a metaphorical "terre des illusions" (land of illusions) peddling empty symbolic fantasies that have

---

[7] In his monograph *Le Clézio, témoin du monde*, the Le Clézio scholar Claude Cavallero reveals that the heart of the Franco-Mauritian author's literary project is to bear witness to the suffering experienced by those whose voices have been stifled.

no basis in reality[8] (Le Clézio 321). As the ironically named "Tranquilité"[9] discovers in *Les Géants*, Jérémie starts to wonder if there is no serenity to be found anywhere in the ever-expanding metropolises in which the majority of the human population now resides. As opposed to representing the pinnacle of civilization, or the crowning achievement of humanity, the urban space is a place of unfathomable horrors for many of Le Clézio's characters. The author suggests that the quotidian anguish experienced by millions of people around the world in urban areas is much more frightening than the imaginary monsters that we have created, whose only crime is that they do not conform to our binary worldview. Le Clézio implies that the *real* monsters emerge from the cover of darkness in large cities that he describes as a breeding ground for frustration, sorrow, and rage.

The Denial of Moral Status to Individuals Exemplifying Atypical Human Corporality

For those who deal with "the plight of being trapped in bodies that others find loathsome" like the human "Dodo" in *Alma*, there is no reprieve from hegemonic forces, even outside of the confines of the urban space (Lasch 117). Derrida's aforementioned denunciation of human and other-than-human violence directed against sentient beings who are "not accorded the dignity of being fellows" is a fitting description of the phenomenon of dehumanization resulting in the denial of moral status to individuals personifying atypical human corporality (*The Beast and the Sovereign vol. 1* 108). Irrespective of the country that he is in (i.e., Mauritius or France) and regardless of whether he is on the outskirts of a metropolis or in the countryside, Dominique Felsen is a pariah who rather gracefully shrugs off extreme reactions to his appearance, insults, and physical violence. All of the injustices and debasement from which "Dodo" suffers on a regular basis are emblematic of a "recognition of the monstrous as defective products of the human species" on the part of the Nobel laureate (Chen 370). Given that he is not considered to be a full-fledged human without a nose or cheeks and "deux trous pour les yeux sans paupières" (two holes for eyes without eyelids), some people who encounter "Dodo" believe that anything is permissible from an ethical perspective (Le Clézio 28). The Levinisian moral imperative that obligates us to respect and recognize the alterity of the Other through the power of the gaze is rendered problematic in Dominique's case, since he no longer has any features that are recognizable as a human face at all. Despite his repeated protestations that "Je ne suis pas un monstre!" (I am not a monster!), Dominique ceases to inhabit the "category of

---

[8] For a more systematic investigation of simulation and hyperreality in Le Clézio's fiction, see Keith Moser. "The Ubiquity of the Simulated Object That Has Consumed the Modern Subject: The Problematic Search for Happiness and Identity in a Globalized, Hyper-real World." *International Journal of Baudrillard Studies*, vol. 11, no. 1, 2014, www2.ubishops.ca/baudrillardstudies/vol11_1/v 11-1-moser.html. Accessed May 20, 2018.

[9] This is how the protagonist's name is spelled in *Les Géants*.

the human" after he contracts what appears to be a type of leprosy (Le Clézio 48; Still 133).

Many disturbing scenes in the novel give credence to Derrida's theories regarding "the worst, the cruelest, the most human violence" endured by people who find themselves outside of moral consideration (*The Beast and the Sovereign vol. 1* 108). However, one disconcerting episode in particular stands out as the embodiment of the brutality inflicted upon the monster. As he is in the cemetery at night, a group of six well-dressed young men wearing polo shirts viciously attack "Dodo" for no apparent reason. Deriving sadistic pleasure from this torture of a person that they judge to be subhuman,

> Ils commencèrent à rire, à jeter des coups de roche et de la terre sèche [. . .] Alors celui qui est grand, avec un joli visage et des yeux noirs, il vient avec une batte de cricket, peinte en rouge et blanc, et il me tape sur la tête [. . .] Il tape beaucoup, dix coups, vingt coups [. . .] Alors les garçons s'arrêtent, ils ouvrent leur braguette et ils pissent sur moi [They started laughing, throwing rocks and pieces of dirt [. . .] Then the tall one, with a pretty face and black eyes, he comes at me with a cricket bat, painted in red and white, and he hits me on the head [. . .] He strikes me a lot, ten blows, twenty blows [. . .] Then the boys stop, they open their zipper and they piss on me]. (Le Clézio 131)

The unconscionable behavior exhibited by these seemingly affluent young men is a reflection of the dominant values that undergird their society. As a monster that falls into the conceptual cracks, the doctrine of moral considerability does not apply. For this reason, when Dominique tries to introduce himself before this unprovoked assault, the delinquents "répètent: 'Pe'sonne! Pe'sonne!'"[10] (repeat: Nobody! Nobody!) (Le Clézio 130). "Dodo" is a faceless monster "who will never again be a full agent" in the eyes of many people who have been indoctrinated from birth to conceive the world in binary codes (Sztybel 244). Thus, these young men probably think that they have done nothing wrong.

Given that his appearance has placed him in the vulnerable position of being stripped of any sort of moral status, Dominique's only value is "as a form of entertainment as a public display for a bemused audience" (Idelson-Shein 174). In order to earn a little money, "Dodo" performs as the "homme-lézard" (lizard-man) at a fair (Le Clézio 245). According to the standard definition of a "Freak Show" provided by Guy Kirkwood referring to "the practices of displaying human difference for profit, particularly popular in America from the mid-nineteenth century until around the 1920s and 1930s," Dominique becomes a "freak" in the vocational sense of the term (5). Revealing that the word "freak" was "a technical designation for performers in the freakshows that became so popular at the end of the nineteenth century," Theodora Goss reminds us that monstrosity was once a common profession in Western society (149).

---

[10] Dominique and some other characters often speak in Mauritian creole.

Fully aware of his outsider status, Dominique declares, "Je suis Dodo, just a dodo.[11] Mais je peux faire rire les gens, c'est pour ça que je suis né" (I'm Dodo, just a dodo. But I can make people laugh, that's why I was born) in the chapter "Lézard" in which he recounts his experiences as a sideshow performer (Le Clézio 244). Following in a long tradition of famous "freaks" like the elephant man, the bearded lady, the three-legged man, and the camel girl, Dominique briefly decides to become a professional monster in *Alma*. Introducing him to the crowd as something far removed from the human realm that defies simple classification, the presenter proclaims, "Venez, m'sieurs-dames, approchez, approchez, l'homme-lézard le seul le vrai, m'sieurs-dames, capab'lécher son œil avec sa langue, les petits enfants n'ayez pas peur, l'homme-lézard ne fait pas de mal, il mange seulement les mouches et les moustiques" (Come, ladies and gentlemen, come on up, come on up, the lizard-man the only true one, ladies and gentlemen, capable of licking his eye with his tongue, little children do not be afraid, the lizard-man is harmless, he only eats flies and mosquitoes) (Le Clézio 245). In a profession in which "freakishness was marketed and packaged," the showman is clearly trying to sell a product (Kirkwood 6). Nevertheless, the transparency of his techniques illustrates that "Dodo" has been reduced to a "not quite" human commodity that is no longer recognized as any kind of a "fellow."

"Dodo": The Freakish Ambassador of the Marginalized

One of the only people who acknowledge Dominique's humanity in spite of his facial abnormalities is a nurse named Vicky. In an unlikely turn of events, this compassionate nurse develops a bond with a protagonist that most people want to avoid at all costs. During his hospitalization after the malicious assault mentioned earlier, Vicky convinces "Dodo" to enter an unorthodox competition. With Vicky's support, "Dodo" wins a trip to Paris as part of the "pari des grands dimounes"[12] (grand *dimounes* prize) contest (Le Clézio 163). Even though the details surrounding this competition are quite nebulous, it is sponsored by the Kestrel Company with the assistance of the Parisian priest "Père Antoine." As the winner of this prize, "Dodo" travels to Paris where he is expected to play the role of an "ambassadeur" creating a sense of solidarity within "la grande famille des SDF, des clochards sans frontières" (the big homeless family, bums without borders) (Le Clézio 182, 204).

The idea of an association called "Bums Without Borders" might seem comical, or perhaps even absurd, but Father Antoine appears to be a true humanist with pure intentions. Even if the success of this project is debatable in *Alma*, this Catholic priest works tirelessly to give a voice to the diverse, misunderstood homeless community comprised of former veterans, immigrants, ethnic and moral minorities, and individuals who have a mental health disorder. In an unconventional manner, Le

---

[11] As I suggest earlier, there is a considerable amount of code switching in the narrative.
[12] In Mauritian creole, the word "dimounes" means people.

Clézio evokes "the metaphor of the monster-the outcast, the stranger, the marginal being who lives in multiple worlds without delegation" (Richards 404). Dominique is a delegate who is charged with the task of reaching out to other ostracized people in order to bring their invisible suffering that is often discounted to light.

Not only does "Dodo représente les exclus" (Dodo represent the excluded) on several different levels in the novel, but he also symbolizes the multifaceted nature of the monster "embodying domination and resistance" (Rampazzo; Chen 380). In the middle of the night when most people are sleeping, "Dodo" walks for many miles through the hidden world of Parisian slums listening to the appalling stories of those who "croient qu'ils sont invisibles" (think that they are invisible) (Le Clézio 251). "Dodo's" efforts to place a spotlight on "les ombres humaines" (human shadows) are subversive, because he forces people to look at the homeless population differently and to not turn away from their haunting gaze. Like other Le Clézian protagonists, Dominique is a "témoin de la douleur du monde" (witness to the pain of the world) (Le Clézio 177).

As Chih-Ping Chen notes, monsters can be both voiceless ghosts and rebellious entities that challenge the status quo depending on the precise context in question. Without proposing a simplistic, reductionistic solution for the complex issue of homelessness, Le Clézio takes advantage of the metaphor of the monster and discourses of freakery to solicit empathy for the phantasmal beings residing on the margins of society. As numerous scholars like Christine Jocoy, Vincent Del Casino, John Belcher, and Bruce Deforge have underscored, binary distinctions such as "productive" and "unproductive" are antithetical to a genuine dialogue concerning the global pandemic of homelessness. In *Alma*, Dominique is an ambassador to all of the homeless freaks in Paris who personifies a kind of clandestine resistance in a society in which "Il n'y a pas de place pour un monstre" (there is no place for a monster) that is supposed "to remain as unobtrusive as possible" (Le Clézio 49; Lasch 122). The author subverts the social construct of the monster by placing the disenfranchised back into plain sight, thereby provoking an encounter with the Levinisian gaze. When ostracized individuals are reduced to the status of a ghost, it is easy to blame them for their own misfortune instead of addressing the systemic issues that made them imperceptible in the first place. Father Antoine's commitment to an ethics of compassion for the downtrodden in *Alma* is strikingly similar to these humanistic aspirations expressed by the narrator of *Fantômes dans la rue*: "Peut-être qu'un jour les êtres humains deviendront complètement, magnifiquement visibles [. . .] Peut-être qu'un jour l'amour sera partout, recouvrira chaque instant de la vie d'une poudre de diamant" (Maybe someday human beings will become completely, magnificently visible [. . .] Perhaps one day love will be everywhere, it will cover every moment of life with a diamond powder) (47–8). The mere gesture of recognizing that every marginalized person he meets has a unique story that cannot be placed into a tiny box is a counter-hegemonic form of subversion, because it erodes the category of the monster itself. As opposed to being vile monsters, the Parisian specters in *Alma* are "fellows" of flesh and blood whose anguish we have removed from public view in order to avoid ethical reflection altogether.

Conclusion

In conclusion, this Derridean interpretation of the trauma experienced by human and other-than-human entities in *Alma* reveals that monstrosity is really a question of how we see the world and our place in it. Moreover, both the philosopher and the Nobel laureate are astutely cognizant that monsters are the product of a fragmented human imagination predicated upon binary codes reflecting the essence of what it means to be a "human" or an "animal." For Derrida and Le Clézio, the social construct of the monster is above all a hegemonic mechanism permitting us to wash our hands clean of any moral responsibility toward the Other. The monsters that we conceive may be imaginary, but the deadly ramifications of dichotomous thinking are all too real. From an ecological perspective, the most destructive binary of all is the human-animal divide that appears to have set into motion a sixth mass extinction that could foreshadow the end of the human race at the advent of the Anthropocene. Furthermore, Derrida's philosophy, Le Clézio's fiction, and the field of Monster Studies are more relevant than ever in the contemporary political landscape in which the rhetoric of monstrosity reduces the intrinsic worth of a human being fleeing persecution, violence, and even genocide to an "alien." Instead of conjuring up monsters to denigrate, repress, and exclude certain humans and the cosmic "wholly other" from the ethical domain, Derrida and Le Clézio suggest that it is time to celebrate alterity. Given that the beasts that haunt our collective imagination are not innocent whatsoever, the only solution for uprooting the seeds of human and other-than-human aggression is to rid ourselves of the monsters that we have created once and for all.

References

"*Alma* – J.M.G. Le Clézio (Gallimard –2017)." *Les amis de la bibliothèque de Pléhédel*, Oct. 20, 2017, http://amisbiblioplehedel.fr/page/2/?cat=-1. Accessed May 20, 2018.

Belcher, John, and Bruce Deforge. "Social Stigma and Homelessness: The Limits of Social Change." *Journal of Human Behavior in the Social Environment*, vol. 22, 2002, pp. 929–46.

Broglio, Ron. "Interviewee: Lynn Turner. Interviewer: Ron Broglio." *Antennae: The Journal of Nature in Visual Culture*, vol. 38, 2016, pp. 30–6.

Bruns, Gerard. "Derrida's Cat (Who Am I?)." *Research in Phenomenology*, vol. 38, 2008, pp. 404–23.

Burma, Nicole, et al. "Animal Models of Chronic Pain: Advances and Challenges for Clinical Transition." *Journal of Neuroscience Research*, vol. 95, no. 6, 2017, pp. 1242–56.

Cadorel, Raymond. "Le Mexique dans l'œuvre de J.M.G. Le Clézio." *Récifs*, vol. 7, 1985, pp. 63–91.

Caesar, Terry. "'Beasts Vaulting among the Earthworks'; Monstrosity in *Gravity's Rainbow*." *Novel: A Forum on Fiction*, vol. 17, no. 3, 1984, pp. 286–8.

Chen, Chih-Ping. "'Am I a Monster?' Jane Eyre Among the Shadows of Freaks." *Studies in the Novel*, vol. 34, no. 4, 2002, pp. 364–84.

Demorand, Nicolas. "Jean-Marie Gustave Le Clézio: 'J'ai commencé ce livre il y a 30 ans, en lisant les listes de baptêmes d'esclaves.'" *FranceInter*, Oct. 5, 2017, www.franceinter.fr/e missions/l-invite-de-8h20/l-invite-de-8h20-05-octobre-2017. Accessed May 20, 2018.

Derrida, Jacques. *The Animal That Therefore I Am*. Translated by David Wills, Fordham University Press, 2008.

Derrida, Jacques. *The Beast and the Sovereign*. Translated by Geoffrey Bennington, vol. 1, Chicago UP, 2009.

Derrida, Jacques. *The Beast and the Sovereign*. Translated by Geoffrey Bennington, vol. 2, Chicago UP, 2011.

Devarrieux, Claire. "Le Clézio, dodo le héros." *Libération*, Oct. 6, 2017, next.liberation.fr/l ivres/2017/10/06/le-clezio-dodo-le-heros_1601422. Accessed May 20, 2018.

Dormoy, Nadine, and Liliane Lazar, eds. *A Chacun sa France*. Peter Lang, 1990.

Doucey, Bruno. "Lectures accompagnées." *Pawana*, by J. M. G. Le Clézio, Gallimard, 2003, pp. 4–23.

Durbach, Nadja. "'Skinless Wonders:' Body Worlds and the Victorian Freak Show." *Journal of the History of Medicine and Allied Sciences*, vol. 69, no. 1, 2012, pp. 38–67.

Egerer, Claudia. "The Speaking Animal Speaking the Animal: Three Turning Points in Thinking the Animal." *Turning Points: Concepts and Narratives of Change in Literature and Other Media*, edited by Ansgar Nünning and Kai Marcel Sicks, De Gruyter, 2012, pp. 437–52.

Fanchin, Gerard. "Le Discours Littéraire: Finalité Esthétique et Visée Pragmatique." *French Studies in Southern Africa*, vol. 31, 2002, pp. 16–26.

Favre, Gilberte. "Alma, Le Clézio, Au nom du père." *Les Blogs*, Oct. 26, 2017, http:// itineraires.blog.24heures.ch/archive/2017/10/25/le-clezio-au-nom-du-pere-864582. html. Accessed May 20, 2018.

Ferland, Chantelle. "Cage Mate Separation in Pair-Housed Male Rats Evokes an Acute Stress Corticosterone Response." *Neuroscience Letters*, vol. 489, no. 3, 2011, pp. 154–8.

Fritz, Julia et al. "Gizzard vs. Teeth, It's a Tie: Food-Processing Efficiency in Herbivorous Birds and Mammals and Implications for Dinosaur Feeding Strategies." *Paleobiology*, vol. 37, no. 4, 2011, pp. 577–86.

Gopnik, Adam. "The Habit of Voyaging." *Pen America: A Journal for Writers and Readers*, vol. 11, 2009, pp. 60–77.

Goss, Theodora. "Listening to Krao: What the Freak and Monster Tell Us." *Conjunctions*, vol. 59, 2012, pp. 149–55.

Guerlac, Suzanne. "Derrida and His Cat: The Most Important Question." *Contemporary French and Francophone Studies*, vol. 16, no. 5, 2012, pp. 695–702.

Herhey, David. "The Widespread Misconception that the Tambalacoque or Calvaria Tree Absolutely Required the Dodo Bird for Its Seeds to Germinate." *Plant Science Bulletin*, vol. 50, no. 4, 2004, pp. 105–8.

Hoffman, Kurt Leroy. *Modeling Neuropsychiatric Disorders in Laboratory Animals*. Woodhead Publishing, 2015.

Horner, Kierran. "The Equality of the Gaze: The Animal Stares Back in Chris Marker's Films." *Film-Philosophy*, vol. 20, nos. 2–3, 2016, pp. 235–49.

Hurst, Andrea. "This Auto-bio-graphical Animal That I Am." *Journal of Literary Studies*, vol. 23, no. 2, 2007, pp. 118–47.

Idelson-Shein, Iris. "Meditations on a Monkey-Face: Monsters, Transgressed Boundaries, and Contested Hierarchies in a Yiddish *Eulenspiegel*." *Jewish Quarterly Review*, vol. 108, no. 1, 2018, pp. 28–59.

Jocoy, Christine, and Vincent Del Casino. "Homelessness, Travel Behavior, and the Politics of Transportation Mobilities in Long Beach, California." *Environment and Planning A*, vol. 42, 2010, pp. 1943-63.

Kirkwood, Guy. "Freak Show Portraiture and the Disenchantement of the Extraordinary Body." *Australasian Journal of American Studies*, vol. 36, no. 1, 2017, pp. 3-42.

Kleinhaus, Belinda. "Posthuman Ethics, Violence, Creaturely Suffering and the (Other) Animal: Schnurre's Postwar Animal Stories." *Humanities*, vol. 5, 2016, pp. 1-19.

Lamperez, Joseph, and Alexandra McGhee. "On Minotaurs and Amazement; or, What Can the Urban Monster Do for You?" *Urban Monstrosities: Perversity and Upheaval in the Unreal City*, edited by Lamperez, Joseph, and Alexandra McGhee, Cambridge Scholars Publishing, 2017, pp. 1-12.

Larsen, Robin, and Beth Haller. "Freaks." *Journal of Popular Film and Television*, vol. 26, no. 2, 1998, pp. 164-72.

Lasch, Christopher. "The Last Freak Show." *Omni*, vol. 11, no. 1, 1988, pp. 116-22; pp. 175-6.

Lawlor, Leonard. "Animals Have No Hand." *The New Centennial Review*, vol. 7, no. 2, 2007, pp. 43-69.

Lumsden, Simon. "Hegel, Derrida and the Subject." *Cosmos and History*, vol. 3, nos. 2-3, 2007, pp. 32-50.

Le Clézio, J. M. G. *Alma*. Gallimard, 2017.

Le Clézio, J. M. G. *Fantômes dans la rue*. Elle, 2000.

Lestel, Dominique. "The Infinite Debt of the Human Towards the Animal." Translated by Matthew Chrulew, *Angelaki*, vol. 19, no. 3, 2014, pp. 171-81.

Llored, Patrick. "Zoopolitics." *SubStance*, vol. 43, no. 2, 2014, pp. 115-23.

Milburn, Colin. "Monsters in Eden: Darwin and Derrida." *Modern Language Notes*, vol. 118, no. 3, 2003, pp. 603-21.

Morin, Edgar. *Homeland Earth: A Manifesto for the New Millennium*. Translated by Sean M. Kelly and Roger LaPointe, Hampton Press, 1999.

Morin, Marie-Eve. "Worlds Apart: Conversations between Jacques Derrida & Jean-Luc Nancy." *Derrida Today*, vol. 9, no. 2, 2016, pp. 157-76.

Moser, Keith. *J.M.G. Le Clézio: A Concerned Citizen of the Global Village*. Lexington Books, 2012.

Moser, Keith. "The Ubiquity of the Simulated Object That Has Consumed the Modern Subject: The Problematic Search for Happiness and Identity in a Globalized, Hyperreal World." *International Journal of Baudrillard Studies*, vol. 11, no. 1, 2014, www2.ubishops.ca/baudrillardstudies/vol11_1/v11-1-moser.html. Accessed May 20, 2018.

Nash, Richard. "Joy and Pity: Reading Animal Bodies in Late Eighteenth-Century Culture." *The Eighteenth Century*, vol. 52, no. 1, 2011, pp. 47-67.

Oliver, Kelly. "Sexual Difference, Animal Difference: Derrida and Difference 'Worthy of Its Name.'" *Hypatia*, vol. 24, no. 2, 2009, pp. 54-76.

Pendell, Charles. "Exterminated by Man." *The Amateur Naturalist*, vol. 1, no. 1, 1904, pp. 1-4.

Preece, Rod. "Selfish Genes, Sociobiology and Animal Respect." *Animal Subjects: An Ethical Reader in a Posthuman World*, Edited by Jodey Castricano, Wilfrid Laurier UP, 2008, pp. 40-62.

Rampazzo, Théo. "*Alma* de Le Clézio, un nouvel hymne à l'amour de l'Île Maurice." *Le Figaro*, Oct. 15, 2007, www.lefigaro.fr/livres/2017/10/15/03005-20171015ARTFIG0

0006--alma-de-le-clezio-un-nouvel-hymne-a-l-amour-de-l-le-maurice.php. Accessed May 20, 2018.

Richards, Evelleen. "A Political Anatomy of Monsters, Hopeful and Otherwise." *Isis*, vol. 85, 1994, pp. 377–411.

Ridon, Jean-Xavier. "J.M.G. Le Clézio: Between Here and There, a Displacement in Memory." *World Literature Today*, vol. 71, no. 4, 1997, pp. 717–23.

Roussel-Gillet, Isabelle. *J.M.G. Le Clézio: Ecrivain de l'incertitude*. Ellipses, 2011.

Salles, Marina, and Isabelle Roussel-Gillet. "Introduction." *Le Clézio, passeur des arts et des cultures*, edited by Thierry Léger, Isabelle Roussel-Gillet, and Marina Salles, Presses Universitaires de Rennes, 2010.

Slater, Michelle. "Rethinking Human-Animal Ontological Differences: Derrida's 'Animot' and Cixous' 'FIPS.'" *Contemporary French and Francophone Studies*, vol. 16, no. 5, 2012, pp. 685–93.

Sneddon, Lynne, et al. "Defining and Assessing Animal Pain." *Animal Behaviour*, vol. 97, 2014, pp. 201–12.

Solomon, William. "The Rhetoric of the Freak Show in Welty's *A Curtain of Green*." *The Mississippi Quarterly*, vol. 68, nos. 1–2, 2015, pp. 167–87.

Spiro, Mia. "Uncanny Survivors and the Nazi Beast: Monstrous Imagination in *See Under: Love*." *Prooftexts*, vol. 35, 2015, pp. 25–36.

Still, Judith. *Derrida and Hospitality: Theory and Practice*. Edinburgh UP, 2010.

Sztybel, David. "Animals as Persons." *Animal Subjects: An Ethical Reader in a Posthuman World*, edited by Jodey Castricano, Wilfrid Laurier UP, 2008, pp. 241–57.

Thibault, Bruno. "'Awaité Pawana': J.M.G. Le Clézio's Vision of the Sacred (The Questing Fictions of J.M.G. Le Clézio)." *World Literature Today*, vol. 71, no. 4, 1997, pp. 723–9.

Thibault, Bruno. *J.M.G. Le Clézio et l.a métaphore exotique*. Amsterdam: Rodopi, 2009.

Wadiwel, Dinesh. "The Will for Self-Preservation: Locke and Derrida on Dominion, Property and Animals." *SubStance*, vol. 43, no. 2, 2014, pp. 148–61.

Wagler, Ron. "The Anthropocene Mass Extinction: An Emerging Curriculum Theme for Science Educators." *The American Biology Teacher*, vol. 73, 2011, pp. 78–83.

Watabiki, Tomonari. "Amelioration of Neuropathic Pain by Novel Transient Receptor Potential Vanilloid 1 Antagonist AS1928370 in Rats Without Hyperthermic Effect." *Journal of Pharmacology and Experimental Therapeutics*, vol. 336, no. 3, 2011, pp. 743–50.

Westerlund, Fredrik. "La vie urbaine-mort urbaine: La ronde et autres faits divers de Jean-Marie Gustave Le Clézio." *Moderna Språk*, vol. 92, no. 1, 1998, pp. 71–80.

Witmer, Mark, and Anthony Cheke. "The Dodo and the Tambalacoque Tree: An Obligate Mutualism Reconsidered." *Oikos*, vol. 61, no. 1, 1991, pp. 133–7.

Wood, David. "Derrida Vert?" *The Oxford Literary Review*, vol. 36, no. 2, 2014, pp. 319–22.

5

Strange Fish

Caliban's Sea-changes and the Problems of Classification

James Seth

When Trinculo sees Caliban for the first time in *The Tempest*, he cannot fully determine whether Caliban is human or animal, or whether the nebulous shape in front of him even belongs on land:

> What have we here, a man or a fish? Dead or alive?—A fish, he smells like a fish; a very ancient and fish-like smell; a kind of not-of-the-newest poor-john. A strange fish! Were I in England now, as once I was, and had but this fish painted, not a holiday-fool there but would give a piece of silver. There would this monster make a man. Any strange beast there makes a man. (2.2.24–30)

Trinculo attempts to use deductive reasoning, but his first question proves to be the most difficult. In England, Caliban would have been a sideshow performer begging for silver, but on the island, he is part of the environment. As Trinculo inspects Caliban, he becomes increasingly more confused, and as his language describing Caliban oscillates between human and animal: "man," "fish," "poor-john," "strange fish," and "monster." Trinculo's juxtaposing words suggest that Caliban inhabits all possibilities of species, and Shakespeare's language allows scholars to interpret Caliban as a creature belonging to either the human or animal world. But if the language describing Caliban is messy, does that, by extension, make him messy, as well? By merely existing, he demonstrates the ineffectualness of his masters' language to define himself in the world; neither Trinculo, Stephano, Prospero nor any other character settles on one clear delineation. In short, it is the blurring of categories that this play finds most disturbing, and Caliban's purpose seems to be to represent this dilemma.

Caliban remains a compelling figure because he invites so many interpretations of his "true" category.[1] As one critic explains, there is a "universality of the new Caliban

---

[1] Twentieth-century scholars made Caliban a sociopolitical symbol, both as "monster" and as victim. In the backdrop of the First World War, José Enrique Rodó's *Ariel* (1900) portrays Caliban as an oppressive symbol of the United States, representing the negative aspects of humanity: treachery,

metaphor" that invites many discussions of global relationships (Vaughan 261). Trinculo's first encounter with Caliban is, to some degree, a farce on the work of travel writers and natural historians, who began publishing their observations on native communities, plant life, and animal species at the time the play was produced in 1610. Pliny's *History of the World*, translated by Edward Topsell as *Historie of Foure-footed beasts* (1607), and Florio's translation of Montaigne's essay, *Of the Canibales* (1603), offer Shakespeare inspiration for the island setting, its species, and its culture.[2]

Of the terms Trinculo uses in his first encounter with Caliban, "monster" is easily the most nebulous and dehumanizing. At forty-six times, it is also one of the most prominently used words in the play. Stephano and Trinculo address Caliban exclusively as "monster," and with many different compound forms, including "servant-monster" (3.2.3), "man-monster" (12), and "bully-monster" (5.1.261). Yet, Shakespeare makes Caliban Trinculo's "strange bedfellow" during the storm. For Shakespeare's audience, this moment portrays the discomfort of the dominant race and species forming intimate relationships with "monsters." Caliban, the offspring of a "blue-eyed hag" (1.2.270), is, according to Prospero, "not honour'd with / A human shape" (284–5). Trinculo and Stephano's encounter with Caliban conveys European society's fears of native islanders, as well as the interbreeding of English travelers and indigenous peoples.

As the scholarly discourse on *The Tempest* moves beyond a postcolonial—or even post-postcolonial—reading, Caliban is increasingly regarded as a figure representing not only alternate races but alternate species as well. Posthumanist scholarship of the last several decades has allowed for a compelling interpretation of characters like Caliban, who defy traditional categories of the "human" by their animalistic behavior and appearance. While an argument on Caliban's racial status remains imperative to

---

materialism, and greed. In the mid-twentieth century, however, Caliban's image shifted as writers identified him not as oppressor, but as a member of the oppressed and enslaved populations under European colonialism. Octave Mannoni's *La psychologie de la colonization* and its 1956 translation, *Prospero and Caliban: The Psychology of Colonization*, reversed Rodó's representations of Prospero and Caliban by showing how the latter symbolizes the American and African slave populations, while Prospero the oppressive European colonizers. Caribbean writer George Lamming offered what is perhaps the most salient argument on Caliban's historical ancestry. Lamming identifies himself as Caliban, and Caliban as representative of indigenous and black slave populations in the Americas. Lamming's argument inspired a decades-long discourse on Caliban and Prospero as opposing symbols of colonial oppression. See George Lamming, *The Pleasures of Exile*. Ann Arbor: University of Michigan Press, 1992 and Fernández Retamar, *Caliban and Other Essays*, trans. Edward Baker. Minneapolis: University of Minnesota Press, 1989. Miranda's scorn for Caliban's "vile race" (1.2.359) has long inspired a reading of the play that figures Caliban as a native of Algerian ancestry oppressed by colonial rule. Thus, his animal names may be given to emphasize his racial and ethnic baseness.

[2] As Noel Cobb and Ania Loomba argue, Montaigne's essay is especially influential (Cobb 75; Loomba 165). Cobb reiterates, "It is quite possible that Shakespeare actually lifted much material from it," and this is confirmed by Loomba, who points to nearly identical passages by Montaigne and Gonzalo (75). Gonzalo conjures a vision of "commonwealth" where there is no "riches, poverty, / And use of service," nor "use of metal, corn, or wine, or oil" (2.1.156-9). This is also Montaigne's vision of the New World, a place with "no custom of servitude, no riches or poverty [...] no use of wine or wheat" (162, 153). Loomba argues, "If Gonzalo conjures up Montaigne's view, Caliban personifies the other, more common approach; he is, Prospero alleges, "a born devil, on whose nature / Nurture can never stick" (4.1.188-9). He is a "natural man who simply cannot be civilized or assimilated into culture" (163).

the discussion about his character, posthumanist critics suggest that there is another equally compelling argument that characters like Caliban represent alternative species. Michel Foucault, Cary Wolfe, and early modern posthumanist critics like Joseph Campana and Scott Maisano have considered, developed, and complicated the idea that "man" is an invention, and an ephemeral one.[3]

A critical trend of Shakespearean animal studies calls for a consideration of Animalia's coexistence with early modern society and culture. In *Man and the Natural World* (1983), Keith Thomas argues that in early modern England, "the official concept of the animal was a negative one, helping to define, by contrast, what was supposedly distinctive and admirable about the human species" (40). Shakespearean characters with animalistic behaviors like Caliban encourage comparisons with their rational, more civilized counterparts. Bruce Boehrer's work expands the discourse of early modern representations of anthropomorphism. He underscores the challenges anthropomorphism presents in an age of "anthropocentrism," or the general belief that humans are inherently superior to nature—and are given the liberty to use plant and animal life to their own purposes. Caliban is deemed "monster" because, Boehrer argues, he "refuses to conform to kind" (27). Boehrer suggests that a moralizing audience will (or should) accept Caliban's humanity and figure his actions within a postlapsarian world. Boehrer's argument does not clarify the source of Caliban's "degeneracy," whether it is nature, nurture, or a mixture of both. Boehrer recognizes the tension between anthropomorphism and anthropocentrism within *The Tempest* and identifies Caliban's animalism, but that is where his point ends. Shakespeare's language suggests that Caliban does not exist wholly in either the human or animal world, but this should not encourage scholars to view Caliban as simply a shapeless mass. Instead, Caliban is a hybrid character whose animalism can be understood through an image of hybridity that appears early in the play, what Ariel calls "sea-change."

In *The Tempest*, sea-change is the transformation that occurs when humans dwell in the ocean for long periods of time and become something "rich," "strange," and inhuman. In Act I, Ariel sings a song about the unusual effects of long-term submersion, describing the apparent "sea-change" of Ferdinand's drowned father:

Full fathom five thy father lies,
Of his bones are coral made,
Those are pearls that were his eyes
Nothing of him that doth fade,
But doth suffer a sea-change,
Into something rich and strange. (1.2.399–405)

---

[3] See Michel Foucault, *The Order of Things: An Archaeology of the Human Sciences*. New York: Pantheon, 1971 and Cary Wolfe, *What Is Posthumanism?* Minneapolis: University of Minnesota Press, 2010. Also see *Renaissance Posthumanism*, eds. Campana and Maisano. New York: Fordham University Press, 2016.

The lifeless body changes into something aquatic and inhuman once it has been in the ocean for so long that it has begun to adapt to its surroundings. The sea does not make Ferdinand's father dissolve into the sea ("Nothing of him that doth fade"), but rather, the sea mediates the metamorphosis so that the body becomes a part of the environment—bones become "coral" or coral-like, and eyes become "pearls," becoming "rich" and "strange." Death itself is a bodily change, and Shakespeare describes the nature of this transformation as a process that melds the body into its final environment, just as corpses become part of the earth after burial. Ariel's song is meant to arouse unrest in Ferdinand, but there is a metaphoric potential of "sea-change" beyond the physiological process postmortem. Sea-changed creatures are "rich" and "strange," and their close relationship with the ocean makes them monstrous. Shakespeare thus portrays Caliban as a physical representation of a similar kind of sea-change, a process that erases the characteristics that define a character as human. It is through this sea-change that we can better understand why Caliban adopts animalistic behaviors.

Transforming into something new because of the environment matters a great deal to this play, especially since Prospero defines Caliban as "a born devil, on whose nature / Nurture can never stick" (4.1.188–9). Prospero characterizes him as what Ania Loomba calls the "'natural' man' who simply cannot be civilized or assimilated into culture" (163). I believe that Caliban's animalism, or more precisely, his being sea-changed, resists this interpretation. Caliban's sea-creaturely aspects demonstrate that he is just as much a product of his environment as his intrinsic behavior. Throughout the play, characters question Caliban's humanity by treating him and describing him as the lowest forms of sea life, particularly creatures that reside on both land and water. Caliban then adopts these characterizations and replicates the behaviors and attitudes of sea creatures, reiterating his subhuman status. I will discuss Caliban's sea-change in two ways: first, I will discuss his connection with hard-shelled creatures like tortoises and crabs, and second, I will focus on Caliban's relation to amphibious creatures, particularly toads and frogs. Adapting to changes in his environment, Caliban assumes the behaviors and characteristics of these lower-ranking sea creatures. These sea creatures navigate the shoreline separating sea and land, just as Caliban embodies the nexus between human and animal.

Hard-shelled Caliban

In early modern culture, shelled sea creatures were known for their sedentariness and sloth, and tortoises in particular were associated with the phlegmatic humor (Paster 135). For example, the woodcuts and accompanying poems of Henry Peacham present an illustration of the phlegmatic man that also includes a tortoise (Peacham 129). In *The Tempest*, Prospero calls Caliban "tortoise" for being slow at bringing wood (1.2.318). Rather than simply calling him slow, Prospero gives Caliban the name "tortoise" to berate and dehumanize him while also asserting his dominance as human master over the animal-like slave. Once Caliban is named "tortoise" by Prospero in Act I, the play then enables and encourages this association. Immediately after Prospero calls

Caliban a tortoise, Ariel enters *"like a water nymph,"* to which Prospero approvingly remarks, "Fine apparition!" (1.2.319) Shakespeare forces a distinction between the watery creatures: the sluggish "tortoise" and the sprightly water nymph. In this early scene, Prospero establishes categories of good and bad servants via the language of sea creatures.

Language is one of the most crucial components to the Prospero-Caliban relationship, as it constantly reinforces existing power structures and categories. George Lamming argues that language becomes Caliban's "prison," and that the process of teaching language is "the first important achievement in the colonising process" (109). Those who have power over language (i.e., colonizers) have power over the concept of the "self" (109). But while postcolonial critics regard Prospero's imposition of language on Caliban as a violation, a posthumanist reading can show how language can also work to recategorize subjects from human to animal, or from human to subhuman creature.

This section will demonstrate how Caliban takes on (and is described as having) the behaviors and physiognomy of shelled sea creatures, primarily due to changes in his surroundings. At multiple points in the play after being called "tortoise," Caliban can be interpreted as tortoise-like—sluggish, slothful, hump-backed, or covered with some kind of protection. Prospero's word "tortoise" does not singularly change Caliban, but it does influence the way we read him; there are several points at which his environment gives him a hard shell, both in behavior and in appearance. From his descriptions of island, it is apparent that Caliban keeps to the coast like tortoises and crabs, and he frequently has to cover himself under various "shells" to defend from Prospero's punishment and nature's wrath.

During the second storm in Act II, Caliban covers himself with his gabardine to hide from Trinculo, who Caliban believes is another of Prospero's spirits sent to torment him in the guise of other animals. Prospero's spirits can change themselves to urchins, apes, hedgehogs, and adders, reiterating the play's focus on outward transformation. In fact, Caliban is worried about this creaturely punishment because of his tortoise-like sluggishness: "Here comes a spirit of his, and to torment me for bringing wood in slowly" (2.2.15–16). He then lies down and covers himself with the cloak. Ironically, he has changed himself into something resembling a sea creature; by making a temporary dwelling over his body, he physically changes into a kind of tortoise. This change in appearance affects how he is perceived and approached by other characters. Upon discovering him, Trinculo asks: "What have we here, a man or a fish? Dead or alive?—A fish, he smells like a fish; a very ancient and fish-like smell" (2.2.25–6). As Trinculo drunkenly deliberates the species of the covered creature, he notices that Caliban is "legged like a man, and his fins like arms!" (2.2.33–4). Slowly, he realizes that the creature is, in fact, human, though supposedly struck by a lightning bolt (36). When Trinculo realizes there is no other shelter, he crawls under the cloak with Caliban, metamorphosing him into something even more monstrous and inhuman.

The play both fears and entertains notions of hybridity, and no other scene plays on hybrid monstrosity to comic effect like the image of Caliban and Trinculo huddled under the gabardine "shell." Approaching, Stephano believes them to be "some monster of the isle with four legs" (2.2.65), and he tries to "keep him tame" by giving them liquor (69). When the "monster" calls out Stephano's name, the bewildered drunk believes it is a "devil," something more evil and sinister than a mere monster (97). Similar to the way that Prospero's word "tortoise" encourages associations between Caliban and the sea turtle, the uttering of "monster" by Trinculo and Stephano signals a similar set of associations that are materialized through the comical monster hybrid with "four legs and two voices" (89). A most delicate monster, indeed. The comic visual of Trinculo and Caliban transforming into a four-legged animal materializes the play's anxieties of interbreeding between Europeans and native islanders; after all, it is not simply the rape of Miranda that the play finds corrupt, but Caliban's desire to make more of himself (1.2.352-3). In this case, though, we have a comically perverse reimagining of the island spirits' human-to-animal transformation. Caliban inadvertently becomes the transformed (or sea-changed) creature he initially fears during the storm, and provokes the same fear in Stephano.

The play associates Caliban with the tortoise because of not only his sluggishness and appearance but also his constant burden and continual punishments. On several occasions, Caliban also exhibits the physical characteristics of tortoises by constantly carrying heavy objects at the direction of higher-ranking characters. For example, he enters Act II, Scene 2 carrying a "*burden of wood* [emphasis in original]," in the same scene that he is called "tortoise." Early modern culture would have been familiar with a Roman myth about turtles, which Topsell includes in *The History of Four-Footed Beasts and Serpents*. According to the myth, the origin of the tortoise's shell was punishment for arriving late to Jupiter's banquet or marriage celebration (Topsell 795). The image of Caliban carrying the "burden" of wood while being called "tortoise" reiterates his position as the island's slave and also emulates a punished tortoise forced to carry her home on her back. In Act IV, Stephano and Trinculo find a hoard of garments, and the stage direction indicates that they "*load Caliban with apparel* [emphasis in original]," which also comically portrays Caliban as a tortoise carrying his burden (4.1.253).

In addition to tortoises, recent scholarship on the play's description of "sea-change" has also put the similarities between Caliban and other hard-shelled sea creatures in sharp relief. Dan Brayton's chapter in *Shakespeare's Ocean*, "Consider the Crab," identifies Caliban as being like a sea-changed shellfish. Before making his case, Brayton identifies the reclamation of the phrase "sea change" by Sylvia Earle as a change that occurs to the ocean by human involvement, rather than a change to humans by the transformative power of the ocean (as Ariel's song conveys). Brayton argues, however, that Ariel's song "cannot help but evoke historical questions about the European ventures at sea in early modernity," and he thus analyzes the passage to point out the extent to which humans in *The Tempest* gain control or agency over nature, particularly colonizers like Prospero (54). Characters who represent "European ventures" are able to master not only nature but native species as well. Brayton poses the question: "Is [Caliban] a sea creature or a creature of the land? Perhaps, like a crab, he is something of both" (58). I would agree that Caliban's sea-creaturely forms offer the greatest insights on the sea as a transformative space. Ariel uses the language of "sea-change" to explain how the sea hardens the skin, makes human subhuman, and creates "strange[ness]," (1.2.404). Yet, I would go further in stating that it is other characters' vision of Caliban as lowly and sea-creaturely that also affects how we interpret him. Caliban has been hardened both by his natural environment and by the intrusion of Prospero and other European explorers. He has become, like his father, "crabbed" (3.1.8).

There are two references to crabs in *The Tempest*. The first describes crabs as part of the island ecosystem and Caliban's diet. The second, which closely follows the first, is used in a figure of speech wherein Ferdinand refers to Prospero as "crabbed" compared to "gentle" Miranda (3.1.8). Just as Caliban and Ariel are distinguished between tortoise and sea nymph, Ferdinand uses a similar sea-creature language to distinguish his love from his new master. The first reference to crabs indicates an important connection between Caliban and crustaceans; Caliban lives and works near them and is intimate with their habitat and behaviors. Caliban's knowledge of the flora and fauna of the island, coupled with his physiognomic traits that help him survive, all contribute to the play's goal, which is to portray Caliban as a hybrid of human and sea creature. Crabs, along with a menagerie of other wildlife, are what Caliban traps for food. He tells Trinculo and Stephano the various ways he catches these animals, as well as his talents for picking various nuts:

> I prithee, let me bring thee where crabs grow;
> And I with my long nails will dig thee pignuts;
> Show thee a jay's nest and instruct thee how
> To snare the nimble marmoset; I'll bring thee
> To clustering filberts and sometimes I'll get thee
> Young seamews from the rock. Wilt thou go with me? (2.2.166–71)

Caliban describes himself as a hunter-gatherer, but there are ambiguities in his description of fruits, nuts, and animals. For example, the Folio uses "scamel" instead of "seamew," or seagull, which editors of the Oxford Shakespeare have replaced for what may be a typesetter's error or an entirely different word (2.2.171). Regarding Caliban's "crabs," it is not explicit what kind of crab he is referring to, or whether or not these crabs are animals or fruit. As Brayton notes, "crabs" also refers to crabapples, or "the sour apples that were eaten roasted or boiled," and Shakespeare makes reference to both crustacean and sour fruit in his works (60). Shakespeare's use of the word "grow" rather than "breed" could indicate either kind of crab, but Caliban's crabby physical features, coupled with the word "crabbed" less than thirty lines after, seems to suggest the crustacean.

To expand on Brayton's point, Caliban is certainly a creature of both land and sea, but he does not simply appear as such. Rather, Caliban transforms into "something of both" through the play's use of sea-creaturely language, the directives of other characters, and the environment in which he is so familiar. However, Caliban also bears strong resemblances to poisonous sea creatures, ones that are reviled not for their sluggishness but for their hidden dangers.

The Witch's Familiar

Prospero's language depicts Caliban as satanic offspring, as well as a venomous creature. Among the venomous creatures that are also connected with satanic ritual and witchcraft, the toad was among the most common in early modern culture. Prospero summons Caliban by saying, "Thou poisonous slave, got by the devil himself / Upon thy wicked dam, come forth!" (1.2.321–2). Though Caliban is never called "toad," he displays a number of similar characterizations and replicates the toad's behavior, often in retaliation for Prospero's rule. In *The Tempest*, there is only one explicit reference to toads, wherein Caliban makes a list of witches' creaturely charms. In his speech to Prospero, Caliban conjures the memory of his mother and the life that he would have lived had not Prospero taken control of the island. He curses Prospero and wishes that he would have Sycorax's powers to plague the magician with toads:

> This island's mine by Sycorax, my mother
> Which thou tak'st from me [. . .]
> Cursed be I that did so! All the charms
> Of Sycorax, toads, beetles, bats, light on you,
> For I am all the subjects that you have. (1.2.333–43)

This speech is one of the most powerful in *The Tempest*, in that it presents the creaturely Caliban as a character capable of feeling and even worthy of sympathy, though much of this sympathy has been attributed to twentieth-century criticism. Caliban invokes his mother's memory by describing the frightening extent of her power, and he declares his right to rule after being forcibly demoted.[4] Caliban's obstructions to the throne are not merely the questions of his legitimacy as ruler, but even more generally, the question of his humanness. Any monster could make a man, but how could a "monster" ever make a ruler?

Caliban calls forth "all the charms" of Sycorax, specifically "toads, beetles, [and] bats." The toad is first in this list likely because it was one of the most characteristic of the witch's familiars. As Keith Thomas explains, the "witch's familiar" was the most unconventional pet: toads, flies, weasels, and monkeys; of these, toads were designed to provoke horror and disgust (40). Toads and frogs were some of the vilest creatures in English culture, to the extent that the English began calling the French "frog-eaters," shortened to "frogs," to express their disgust at the idea of eating them. Frogs and toads simply did not have a place in the English domestic sphere, as pets or in cuisine. They represented disease and filth. Even when toads were tamed or did not excrete poison,

---

[4] This is a common theme in Shakespeare's later plays, especially *King Lear*. Caliban shares connections to both the castoff son, Edgar, and the plotting, bastard son, Edmund. Edgar's statement, "Edgar I nothing am," (2.3.21) shares Caliban's feelings of emptiness, having been demoted to nothing; as Edgar is forced to live as "Poor Tom," Caliban is "cursed" to live as a slave. But like Edmund (and Richard III), Caliban seeks vengeance to restore what he believes he is owed. His instinct to seek revenge upon Prospero is also, ironically, an instinct which the play uses to dehumanize Caliban.

they were nonetheless regarded as abhorrent creatures and connected to witchcraft. When Caliban threatens to use the charms and animal familiars of Sycrorax, he believes that being her heir grants him this power. Though Caliban can neither use spells nor conjure beasts, I believe that the play presents him as something like an animal familiar, serving as a vehicle for satanic power.

Serpents, toads, and frogs were synonymous with witchcraft and satanic ritual in early modern culture, and thus part of many similar narratives about the powers of hell.[5] There were three texts produced in Shakespeare's time that provided scientific, religious, and cultural knowledge of toads and frogs: Edward Topsell's *History of Serpents* (1608), the Geneva Bible (and the King James Version in 1611), and King James's *Daemonologie* (1597), which is generally believed to have influenced *Macbeth* (1606). Topsell's entry on toads describes two kinds, "the one called *Rubeta palustris*, a Toad of the fens, or of the waters; the other *Rubeta terrestris*, a Toad of the earth" (730). After listing the characteristics of each, Topsell describes the cultural history of toads, noting with special interest how "the Women-witches of ancient time which killed by poysoning, did much use Toads in their confections" (730). Toads' poison is a powerful agent for practitioners of magic and medicine. In early modern representations of witchcraft, toads are boiled in pots for potions, and generally included in witches' magical properties. Topsell includes the following excerpt from Pliny's original work in his translation, *The History of Serpents*:

Occurrit Matrona potens, quae molle Calenum
Porrectura viro, miscet sitiente rubetam.
There came a rich Matron, who mixed Calen Wine,
With poyson of Toads to kill her Spouse, O deadly crime. (730)

Topsell's story demonstrates the cultural narratives of toads as accessories to murders of rich men. Toads carry out their witch-mothers' plans by secreting poison, served in wine. Many similar narratives in Shakespeare's time, as well as the occasion of the Scottish witch trials in the late sixteenth century, helped perpetuate the myth that toads were an integral part of vengeful plots that relied on the creatures' poison.

When Prospero declares Caliban a "poisonous slave, got by the devil himself / Upon thy wicked dam," he invokes early modern representations of poisonous witch's familiars. Supernatural narratives about toads pervaded early modern English culture and influenced the associations between toads and witchcraft.[6] King James I and VI

---

[5] The toad's connection to Satan is even more explicit in Milton's *Paradise Lost*, wherein the poet describes him as "squat like a Toad, close at the eare of Eve; / Assaying by his Devilish art to reach / The Organs of her Fancie" (IV.800–3). As Satan transforms into various animals, his most diabolical are the most venomous, and by positioning himself "like a Toad," he prepares to do his worst to poison Eve's imagination. Caliban is regarded as a similar influence on Miranda, attempting to rape her in hopes of producing offspring and reclaiming Prospero's paradise.

[6] Even early modern myths without witches describe toads as agents of supernatural power. Thomas Lupton explains one such myth in *A Thousand Notable Things of Sundry Sortes* (1579), informing readers that if they "put a Toad in a new earthen pot, and the same be covered in the ground in the

played a major role in first major Scottish witch hunt, an event which James Sharpe explains "resulted in mass trials and numerous executions in 1590–1" (48). These witches were accused of producing storms while the king and queen were at sea and engaged in satanic rituals. In *Daemonologie*, King James I describes the trial of one Agnis Tompson, who was reported to have hung a black toad "by the heeles, three daies, and collected and gathered the venome as it dropped and fell from it in an Oister shell, and kept the same venome close couered, vntill she should obtaine any parte or peece of foule linnen cloth" (95). Like the rich matron in Topsell's poem who killed her husband with poisoned Calen wine, Agnis uses toad poison in her ritual but keeps it secured in an oyster shell and "kept the same venome close couered" until securing cloth.

Shakespeare's witches also use toads prominently in their potions. Caliban lists "toads, beetles, [and] bats" (1.2.342) as vital creatures in Sycorax's collection, and *Macbeth* famously presents toads as vital ingredients in witches' brews. In what seems like a reenactment of James I's narrative in *Daemonologie*, the First Witch chants:

> In the poison'd entrails throw.
> Toad, that under cold stone
> Days and nights has thirty-one
> Swelter'd venom sleeping got,
> Boil thou first i' the charmed pot. (4.1.5–9)

It is important that toads are the first ingredient in the pot. In a sense, they act as a catalyst for the brew. In order for toads to be ready for the potion, they have to be "under cold stone" for a month, allowing its poison to eke out of its body. As Thomas Pennant explains, "Superstition gave [the toad] preternatural powers, and made it a principal ingredient in the incantations of nocturnal hags" (15). The witches dance while holding up the toad's "poison'd entrails" in a similar manner that Agnis Tompson holds up the toad "by the heeles" to allow its poison to ooze into the oyster shell. Caliban's description of his mother's creaturely magic corresponds to the foul rituals in *Macbeth* and *Daemonologie*. Sycorax relies on various animals and animal parts to enact her "mischiefs manifold and sorceries terrible" (1.2.265). Caliban mentions the "wicked dew" (1.2.323) brushed with "raven's feather" (324), as well as the "charms" of "toads, beetles, [and] bats" (341–2), which Sycorax uses to deadly effect. Caliban does not have power over these creatures as his mother or Prospero does, but he believes that he is an inheritor of this same kind of magic.

Shakespeare describes treacherous characters as "toads" in other plays as well, most notably in *Richard III*. Richard, hunchback and treacherous, is the butt of series of remarks personifying him as toady and treacherous. Anne remarks, "Never hung poison on a fouler toad" (1.2.147), Margaret calls Richard "poisonous bunch-backd

---

midst of a corn-field, there will be no hurtful tempests or storms there" (54). If toads could be held captive and controlled, they would be able to influence the generation of crops and deter turbulent weather.

toad" (1.3.244), and Elizabeth has a variant on Margaret's description, "foul bunch-backd toad" (4.4.81). Both Richard and Caliban display their evil by their misshapen outward form, and like Richard, Caliban is called "poisonous." Caliban also carries heavy objects at the direction of higher-ranking characters, emulating not only a tortoise but also a "bunch-backd toad." Also like Richard, Caliban is compared to the devil and deemed satanic offspring. Both Richard and Caliban have a toad-like physiognomy that, as Shakespeare's language suggests, is evident of satanic influence.

Caliban's connections to Satan and treachery coincide with the fact that the sea itself is a hell space surrounding the island in *The Tempest*. The concept of the sea as hell was a common trope for seafarers, and Robert Monro notably uses an adage conveying this idea in his travel journal (1637): "Betwixt the devill and the deep sea" (Topsell 728). Monro's quote speaks to the way that early modern English culture depicted the sea as a hellish space. Shakespeare characterizes the sea as a fierce hell space by staging the opening storm, and the connection between hell and the sea is made more explicit by characters' constant fear of drowning and the language they use to convey going deeper into "hell." Ariel recounts Ferdinand's cry, "'Hell is empty / And all the devils are here'" (1.2.215-16). Trinculo, believing that Stephano is drowned, believes the voices around him are those of "devils" (2.2.88). Stephano, seeing Trinculo and Caliban huddled together, exclaims: "This is / a devil, and no monster" (2.2.97). The seafaring courtiers are plagued with thoughts of being victims of swirling devils, as well as the ocean's wrath. The greatest fear is that they will plunge below the earth. The sea itself is a gaping, monstrous mouth leading to hell, and those who are sea-swallowed are changed into a coral reef, like Ferdinand's father.

If the sea is a hell space that instigates a monstrous "sea-change," it makes sense that Caliban is modeled after one of sea's most vengeful creatures. Prospero famously describes Caliban as

a devil, a born devil, on whose nature
Nurture can never stick; on whom my pains,
Humanely taken, all, all lost, quite lost;
And as with age his body uglier grows,
So his mind cankers. (4.1.188–92)

Prospero insists that all of his "pains" were lost on Caliban, the "born devil," shifting the blame on Caliban's evil from nurture to nature. To Prospero, Caliban functions as an inept Satan within the garden he has planted, literally and figuratively. Caliban is unable to conceive or appreciate his master's work, his mind "canker[ed]," or infected, with hate. Shakespeare's representation of Caliban as satanic offspring coincides with Caliban's creaturely and subhuman characteristics. Caliban is the malefactor in Prospero's utopian kingdom, a serpent in creation that influences two ignorant humans (Prospero and Trinculo) to violate law and order and thus defy the Creator. Just as Satan's body is able to change to suit his desire, so too does Caliban's "body uglier grows." This description emulates the depiction of the drowned body of Ferdinand's father; yet, while Ferdinand's father's body grows richer (literally, as his eyes becomes pearls), Caliban's body becomes more monstrous and ugly.

Symbolically, Caliban-as-toad emerges from sea to land, hell to creation, and witch's womb to Edenic Island. Caliban's multiple associations with the term "poisonous" (as toad-like, vengeful, plotting, and satanic) also allow for a much more clearer understanding of the way Shakespeare incorporates biblical allegory within the play's anxieties of the New World. The representation of frogs as devils or agents of wickedness has a well-known history in biblical narrative. Frogs and toads have long been implicated in the work of Satan and the punishment of humankind. In Exod. 8:1, frogs are part of God's plague, infesting homes and coming into their beds. In Revelation, frogs are one of the Devil's disguises: "And I saw three unclean spirits like frogs come out of the mouth of the dragon, and out of the mouth of the beast, and out of the mouth of the false prophet" (Rev. 16:13-14). The image of frogs swarming out of the dragon's mouth like "unclean spirits" characterizes them as eternally impure. No matter the practitioner, toads were the common ingredient in the plot against humanity.

Natural histories and travel writing contain descriptions of toads that resemble biblical narratives. Topsell discusses the behavioral characteristics of toads in the Americas while including stories of the amphibians' plague-like residence among the native communities. Toads are so prevalent in the New World that they intervene in women's birthing processes:

> In the *New World* there is a Province called *Dariene*, the air whereof is wonderful unwholesome, because all the Countrey standeth upon rotten marishes. It is there observed [. . .] that women conceiving with childe, have likewise conceived at the same time a Frog, or a Toad, or a Lizard, and therefore *Platearius* saith, that those things which are medicines to provoke the menstruous course of women, do also bring forth the Secondines. (Topsell 728)

Topsell goes on to discuss women who, in one example, "[bring] forth four little living creatures like Frogs" instead of children (728). If we place *The Tempest* in a historically representative region not unlike Darien, it is possible to imagine a similar scenario; rather than producing a child, Sycorax gives birth to a toad, or a half-human, half-toad. Topsell also explains how the native women abort their amphibious children with herbal medicines (728). In many ways, Caliban is described and treated like these mutant offspring from the New World. Prospero claims that Caliban was "got by the devil himself / Upon thy wicked dam" (1.2.321–2), proposing that his very existence is a mistake of nature, or an omen signifying the devil's work.

Shakespeare's portrayal of Caliban as one of the basest sea creatures, one who grows uglier and more poisonous, reiterates the connections between amphibious witch's familiars and the hell space of the ocean in early modern English culture. Caliban's toady behavior, and particularly the language that Prospero uses to identify it, reiterates a number of cultural myths on the degeneracy of toady creatures and their susceptibility to Satan. Caliban's "sea-changes" into tortoise-like, crab-like, and toad-like creatures evidence the changes in his environment and his adaptability to them. Like Ariel's image of Ferdinand's father, these changes make him a richer, stranger character. Caliban's multifaceted animalism also makes him Shakespeare's most fluid character, one who reveals the expansiveness of human existence by representing the blurry threshold of human and animal.

References

Boehrer, Bruce. *Shakespeare and the Animals: Nature and Society in the Drama of Early Modern England*. Palgrave, 2002.
Brayton, Dan. *Shakespeare's Ocean*. University of Virginia Press, 2012.
Cobb, Noel. *Prospero's Island*. Coventure, 1984.
de Montaigne, Michel. *Of Cannibals*. In *Montaigne's Essays in Three Books: With Notes and Quotations. And an Account of the Author's Life. With a Short Character of the Author and Translator by the late Marquis of Halifax*, 6th ed., Translated by Charles Cotton and B. Barker, 1743.
James I, King. *Daemonologie, In Forme of a Dialogie Diuided into Three Bookes*. Robert Walde-graue, 1597.
Lamming, George. *The Pleasures of Exile*. University of Michigan Press, 1992.
Loomba, Ania. *Shakespeare, Race, and Colonialism*. Oxford UP, 2002.
Lupton, Thomas. *A Thousand Notable Things*. Walker, Edwards, and Reynolds, 1815.
Milton, John. *Paradise Lost*. Edited by Barbara K. Lewalski. Blackwell, 2007.
Paster, Gail Kern. *Humoring the Body: Emotions and the Shakespearean Stage*. University of Chicago Press, 2004.
Peacham, Henry. *Minerva Britanna*. W. Dight, 1612.
Pennant, Thomas. *British Zoology*, Vol. III. Benj White, 1776.
Retamar, Fernández. *Caliban and Other Essays*. Translated by Edward Baker. University of Minnesota Press, 1989.
Shakespeare, William. *The Oxford Shakespeare*. Edited by Gary Taylor and Stanley Wells. Oxford UP, 2005.
Sharpe, James. *Instruments of Darkness: Witchcraft in Early Modern England*. University of Pennsylvania Press, 1996.
Thomas, Keith. *Man and the Natural World*. Penguin Books, 1983.
Topsell, Edward. *The History of Four-Footed Beasts and Serpents*. E. Cotes, 1658.
Vaughan, Alden T. "Caliban in the 'Third World': Shakespeare's Savage as Sociopolitical Symbol." *Critical Essays on The Tempest*, edited by Virginia Mason Vaughan and Alden T. Vaughan, G.K. Hall and Co., 1998, pp. 247–66.

6

Monster of Vacancy, Ghost of Culture, Instrument of Clarity

Cultural and Textual Analysis of the Function of the Sonoran Desert as Monster in Luis Alberto Urrea's *The Devil's Highway*

Mindy Adams

"Your lungs, now, are leaking moisture to the vampire air," writes Luis Alberto Urrea as he guides his reader through the stages of death by hyperthermia in the most gruesome and terrifying stretch of *The Devil's Highway* (122). Throughout the text, he suffuses the Sonoran landscape with demonic, monstrous, and occult forces. Devils spit insults from beneath rocks. La Llorona, Chupacabras, La Mujer Azul, and dozens of other phantoms and hoodoos wander the "ghost roads" of the desert. The demonic black head laughs from time to time. Cabeza Prieta is the name of the *place*; this is the Cabeza Prieta:

> Out of the small hole rose a black human head. It glistened, either wet or made of coal, some black crystal. Its eyes were burning white. Its teeth were also white. Its face was narrow and it sported a sharp beard on its chin. It rose until just the tops of its shoulders were visible. It cast a shadow. And it turned as it watched the traveler pass. It was laughing at him. (14)

In *The Devil's Highway*, Urrea makes the Sonoran landscape itself into a monster for us to read. In this narrative, monsters do indeed make strange and frightening mirrors. In "Monster Culture (Seven Theses)," Jeffrey Cohen offers guidelines for understanding what monsters tell us about the cultures that create them. This chapter applies Cohen's "Monster Theory" to Urrea's demonic landscape in order to explore how his monster functions both as a cultural signifier and as a textual feature. I contend that this representation of the natural world as a "monster" is a dangerous conceit, even if the author employs it with the ultimate purpose of exposing the cultural forces that create the "monster." In this regard, this investigation also considers how this literary device of the demonization of the landscape can at once counter and *repeat* the cultural and social ills that underpin the "horrors" of the US-Mexico border. Those horrors are nonfictional, just as the text itself is a work of nonfiction. The monster is a fictional apparatus, which is utilized for a variety of nonfictional purposes. In other words, monsters in the literal sense of the word do not really exist. The real terrors for which Urrea's desert monster stands in, however, might be too brutal and vicious for a reader to confront without the distance of the trope and the thrill of the horror.

The Monster as a Mirror of Culture

Cohen writes, "Every monster is [. . .] a double narrative, two living stories: one that describes how the monster came to be and another, its testimony, detailing what cultural use the monster serves" (13). If the desert becomes the monster in Urrea's text, then we must question its creation in order to understand it more fully. Nevertheless, we cannot simply ask how *a desert* comes to exist. A desert just is; it is a part of the natural world, a part of "creation." The desert can only become a monster when social circumstances force people into it who do not know how to be there, who do not respect its power. What creates the monster of the Cabeza Prieta is a lack of culture. In this context, I am referring to people who do not understand or care to learn their places. Modern Americans should feel a deep anxiety over living on a land where they have no idea how to live from a cultural standpoint. Urrea gives us a monster that speaks to such an anxiety. The author fittingly invokes, among the ghosts that haunt the place, traditional peoples whose religions and lifestyles he claims mirrored, reflected, and respected the austerity of the landscape: the Yaqui, Hohokam, Papago, and Anasazi. He writes, "Footprints of long-dead cowboys are still there [. . .] beneath these the prints of the phantom Hohokam themselves" (7). The phantom Hohokam are ghosts of placed culture, people with cultural knowledge of how to live in the desert. We can infer that the destruction of these peoples and their cultures is one of the larger forces that helped to create the desert monster in the first place.

Regardless, a monster cannot exist without victims; they are also necessary to its creation, or in Cohen's words, "how it [comes] to be" (13). Let us recall that the black head laughs at a passing traveler. The desert only becomes a monster when culturally unprepared people *actually go there*, either by necessity (perhaps seeking American cash-money) or for recreation (perhaps to dune buggy). The monster does not discriminate. However, the author's distinction between these two types of desert deaths makes a profound comment on the kind of society that is capable of transforming its landscape into a monster. Urrea reminds us that the former class of desert traveler is a product of the pairing of Mexico's political and economic failings with Americans' taste for cheap Mexican labor to do the great bulk of the physical work in our society:

> May through July [. . .] is known as "death season." It is when the lettuce, tomatoes, cucumbers, oranges, strawberries are all ready to be picked. The cows are waiting in Iowa and Nebraska to be ground into hamburger, and grills are ready in

McDonald's and Burger King and Wendy's and Taco Bell for the ground meat to be cooked. KFC is waiting for its Mexican-plucked, Mexican-slaughtered chickens to be fried by Mexicans. And the western desert is waiting too. (34)

Urrea marks the contrast he will draw with the other kind of desert traveler by reminding his reader that "not only Mexicans die in the desert" (117). He goes on to recount the tragic death of Lisa Scala and Martin Myer, a thrill-seeking tourist couple, when the steering column breaks on their dune buggy. He describes them as a couple for whom "the desert [is] their playground" (118). The desert monster is particularly hungry and greedy in the instance of the dune buggy breakdown. Urrea offers the following description of Myer's demise: "The land tried to hide him and keep him for itself" (118). By situating the desert's monstrosity at both ends of the social spectrum, he invites the reader to consider how our social structure and its inherent inequalities contribute to the monster's existence. The victims from both poles of society are alienated from and foreign to the landscape, highlighting the cultural ills at both ends of the social spectrum. There is desperation on one side, and frivolity on the other. This juxtaposition suggests that the social disparity that these distinct sets of victims represent plays a role in the monster's coming into existence. While the victims are equalized in death, the specific lack that has driven each into the monster's clutches is certainly class-bound.

If we take Cohen's claim that the "monstrous body" is "pure culture" seriously, then what we find in Urrea's monster is a pure *lack* of culture that symbolizes the absence (destruction) of the placed culture that came before (4). This is where we might find what Cohen calls "its testimony" (13). Urrea's monster is passive and lazy: it merely consumes. As opposed to tracking people down, it simply sucks the water out of victims who unwittingly come to it. It is an ironic mirror to hold up to a culture that is depleting the groundwater of its arid regions, quite literally sucking the land dry. At the same time, the dominant economic and cultural paradigm casts aside its subaltern underclass of willing victims after using them up like disposable commodities. The desert monster is a testament not only to America's rapacious history but also to our hideous, contemporary cultural attitude toward both land and work. In essence, its "cultural use" is to expose our cultural failings.

The landscape-as-monster metaphor, however, is not entirely new. One could even argue that other historical representations of the landscape as monster may be partially to blame for the cultural attitudes toward the land that we carry with us into places like the Sonora. Explaining that several accounts from the early stages of colonization describe the American landscape as monstrous, Catherine Alber reveals,

> In Richard Hakluyt's *Portable Voyages* of the late 1600s, Slotkin notes, the word monstrous constantly recurs and comes to seem the most characteristic adjective applied to the New World. In addition to "monstrous" glaciers and "monstrous mountains [...] the natives, like their land are also monstrous." (9)

According to Alber, this passage is indicative of an instinct to classify Native American peoples as monstrous in order to efface their alterity and to assert cultural superiority over them. This is true and disturbing enough in and of itself, but there is a fundamental difference between relegating the human Other to the status of a monster and placing a monstrous label upon a glacier or mountain. How do we account for the latter? I argue once again that such monster-making reflects a different kind of anxiety, not simply a fear of the human Other, but a deep sense of not belonging in or understanding a place. The immigrants and pleasure-seekers in the Sonoran Desert are alike in neither belonging to nor understanding the landscape. While Urrea explicitly and implicitly critiques the kind of culture and cultural practices that would transform a landscape into a monster, he still participates in the rhetoric of his fifteenth-century forebears. Despite his evident predilection to engage in critical thought, he accepts the land-as-monster metaphor. He thus reinforces the ubiquitous attitude that lets us off the hook for ever having to consider that it could be otherwise, for ever having to entertain the notion of learning to live in place. Urrea's language of monstrosity, to some extent, allows us to place the problem beyond the realm of human control and culpability. Like the early colonists, he conceives a monster that renders places off-limits, beyond the scope of human comprehension and the restraint inherent in the "ghost culture" that actually could live respectfully within a landscape. This recalls Cohen's fifth thesis: "The monster polices the border of the possible" (12).

Sandra Cox offers a different interpretation of the monstrous landscape in *The Devil's Highway*. She sees it as a "representation of sameness that links reader and migrant through the mutual terror of death and bodily destruction" (21). In support of her reading, Cox cites Urrea's line "in the desert, we are all illegal aliens" (qtd. in Cox 22). Her article focuses on the epideictic impulses of *The Devil's Highway*, asserting that it "implicitly call[s] for judgments about the people and events it describes" (13). She maintains that the desert is the antagonist through her assertion that this element of the work has an epideictic purpose as well. Cox suggests that Urrea intends for the reader to culturally interpret and make meaning of "the hot arid openness" (22). Cox elucidates that the author is leading the reader to the conclusion that "the economic systems that push [the immigrants] to brave the dangers of the desert are as real and deadly as a summer afternoon in the rural wastes of Yuma County, Arizona" (22). Cox lauds the work as a radical text that forces its readers to examine and evaluate aspects of their own culture, a text that "preempts a dissociative response that might allow Americans to shift blame or avoid collusion" (24). Indeed, it seems probable that this is Urrea's ultimate goal. Nevertheless, does repeating the language and mindset of early colonialists like Hakluyt and demonizing the landscape to achieve his ends not constitute (or at least invite) a subtle shifting of blame? Doesn't the inclusion of a nonhuman culprit make space for a degree of dissociation? At the very moment when the reader is prepared to examine the cultural consequences of his or her own aversion to work and dependence on immigrant labor for his or her daily needs, does the comfortable repetition of the notion that the landscape itself is the "antagonist" not represent a slight deviation from the real issue? Do the cultural consequences of this repetition counterpoint Urrea's cultural critique, or can these two aspects of the text somehow work together?

One way of looking at Urrea's desert monster that might reconcile its simultaneous critique and repetition of destructive cultural values is to consider it to be a rhetorical place holder. Ironically, throughout a large portion of the text, the monster conceals rather than exposes the root cultural problem(s) that create it. In this vein, its literary function is to propel the narrative. The monster also invokes all of the "comfortable discomfort" of the language and structure of the horror genre that lulls the reader into *not* engaging with essential cultural questions. This paradoxical phenomenon grants the writer just enough time to paint a rending portrait of the conflicting, cultural forces that we have conveniently and dissociatively enshrined as "the horrors of the border." Examining how the monster functions textually, I hope to resolve the irony of its simultaneous exposure and concealment of its own "double narrative" in Cohen's terms (13).

Horror Genre as Textual Device

In his sixth thesis, which stipulates that "Fear of the Monster Is Really a Kind of Desire," Cohen discusses the pleasure and delight that a reader takes in the monster story. He claims that there is an escapist enchantment inherent in the social inversions of the monster story. Cohen posits that the reader feels satisfaction from confronting monsters in "a temporary place" (17). As he theorizes,

> The story on the page before us may horrify (whether it appears in the *The New York Times* news section or Stephen King's latest novel matters little) so long as we are safe in the knowledge of its nearing end (the number of pages in our right hand dwindling) and our liberation from it. [. . .] The audience knows how the genre works. (17)

One implication of this theory for Urrea's monster is that it enables the reader to digest the *truly* horrifying section of the book in which the author describes the slow and painful deaths of the Yuma 14 in gruesome detail from a safe and fantastical enough distance. He gives his reader, for lack of a better word, a break. The monster narrative temporarily keeps the reader from having to look at the situation in light of the full complexity of border issues that the work has brought up. The monster can stand in temporarily for a litany of interrelated cultural problems. The reader can take a breather and just watch the grotesque and suspenseful details unfold, as the "monster" begins consuming its victims. In this section of the book, Urrea abandons his journalistic adherence to objective facts and complicated relationships, thereby allowing his audience to indulge in the cathartic and paradoxical pleasure of the horror genre. Katerina Bantinaki offers an explanation of the "paradox of pleasure" (391) that people find in horror, suggesting that we seek it out "primarily in hope of the intense positive emotional experience it affords us" (391) even though it generates emotions we would avoid in real life. In short, Urrea is throwing us a literary bone: fantasy, suspense, gore, and horror-genre narration.

Some scholars such as Mary Vásquez and Sandra Cox have analyzed *The Devil's Highway* as a hybrid text. Mary Vásquez declares, "It is a hybrid text, part story, part essay [that] moves on both sides of a line that, like the U.S.-Mexico border, is often arbitrary" (187). Proposing a similar reading, Sandra Cox also asserts that *The Devil's Highway* is a hybrid narrative, citing the author's "[ability] to couple objective journalistic techniques with narrative intentionality," thus allowing for shifts between "reporting and narration" (19, 19). It is noteworthy that Cox focuses her analysis of this hybridity on the same "10 horrific pages [in which] Urrea describes the symptoms of mortal hypothermia" that I underscored in the previous paragraph as those that most closely correspond to the horror genre (21). This disquieting portion of the story is by far the most gory, gruesome, suspenseful, and fear-inducing part of the book. In her detailed reading, Cox seems to be quite drawn to this part of the narrative.

While she focuses her analysis on how Urrea manages to "press the readers into the subject position of the dying men," thus engendering sympathy, she also recognizes that this section of the book is compelling, cohesive, and evocative (21). I posit that what makes it so persuasive, coherent, and redolent is precisely these elements of horror. There is something perversely and paradoxically satisfying in these pages that aligns with Bantinaki's explanation of how the pleasure that we find in horror arises from the emotions we would avoid in reality. Cox and Vásquez call it a hybrid text that mixes narrative and journalistic prose. I propose that it is a hybrid genre, which mingles horror and realism, wherein terror sometimes takes the reigns.[1] Aside from the aforementioned ten pages detailing the stages of death by hyperthermia, elements of horror also find prominence at two other important moments in the book.

In the first chapter, "The Rules of the Game," Urrea introduces the desert in terms of its ghosts and horrors, interweaving this terror with tales of and allusions to the desert's history. As a textual device, this monsterization minimizes the complexity of the region's dark history, offering the thrilling notion that it has always been a monstrous and scary place. These "desert spirits of a dark and mysterious nature [who] have always traveled these trails" provide a compelling, but not necessarily satisfactory explanation for all of the "red shadows" (Urrea 5, 6). By mixing historiography and horror, Urrea exposes the complexity of that history more fully, albeit less precisely. Poetic language and mysterious images *do* hold a reader's attention. In addition, having enmeshed the history of the region with these macabre elements from the very beginning, the ugly story of greed and genocide in the American Southwest is subtly evoked each time that the monster emerges. The monster operates as a stand-in that comes to substitute for a bloody past.

Supernatural fears and dread assume the place of this complexity once again in chapter eight. This section represents a fatal turning point in the men's journey during which the "mystery lights" cause them to lose their way. Adopting a journalistic style, Urrea offers a slew of possibilities for explaining the origin of these lights. Each

---

[1] Using a fantastical genre for political purposes is not unique to Urrea. Roberto Bolaño's *2666*, which also documents atrocities at the US-Mexico border, relies on a similar genre hybridization. In contemporary film, Apichatpong Weerasethakul's *Uncle Boonmee Who Can Recall His Past Lives*, Nicolas Klotz's *Low Life*, Pedro Costa's *Cavalo Dinhiero*, and others make radical use of fantastical elements to accommodate complicated political realities.

suggestion reflects a problematic and poorly understood force in the very real tragedy of border politics (e.g., aggressive border patrol tactics, coyotes, fellow immigrants-migrants, and headlights that emerge seemingly from nowhere). All of these textual elements form an interrelated and convoluted web that is too complex to recall during this critical juncture of the narrative. Enter the desert monster. Let the supernatural "mystery lights" take over and snare your prey. The desert monster reinforces the uncertainty related to all of the possible sources of these lights. Moreover, it enables the full complexity of border issues and all of the players involved to remain. Finally, it allows the question of culpability to stay open. In a sense, the desert monster is a scapegoat, but only if we remember that biblical scapegoats were *literally* loaded down with people's *actual* sins and destined to atone for them. If the desert monster is a stand-in, it is a heavily laden one![2]

In light of the idea of a symbolic scapegoat standing in for something more complex, let's return to the previously cited quote from "Monster Culture" about the reader's comfortable familiarity with how the horror "genre works" (17). If the analysis from Cohen about the safety of dwindling pages is true of the horror genre generally, it is not applicable to *The Devil's Highway* at all. The audience does not know how *this* genre works. Urrea's monster abandons the reader with nearly one hundred pages left to go. In the aptly named Part Four, "Aftermath," this "stand-in for complexity," or sacrificial substitute (i.e., the desert monster) in the Girardian sense, disappears. What emerges is the absurdity of all the real people who cannot confront or even grasp the complexity of the situation at the US-Mexico border. In simple terms, they need a monster. In the final section of the book, numerous characters begin fabricating the various monsters that suit their own ingrained narratives about the border. Rooster Boy Mendez, the *guia*, fits the bill as a monster for most citizens in the historical context of this real-life story. He can be thrown in jail as a sacrificial scapegoat for those who want to slay the beast. The reader of the book, however, is not so satisfied with this simplification. We know that Mendez is not the monster. In place of the scapegoating tendencies of the media[3] and an outraged public clamoring for solutions, we are left with what Cox calls "a psychic friction" that prevents "easily trac[ing] blame for the brutal conditions and eventual deaths that the migrants face to a single agent" (24).

> Expounding upon this idea, Sandra Cox reveals, the texts implicate Mexicans and Americans at all levels: the Pressures of NAFTA on corporations, the indebtedness of the Mexican government to the US, the consumption habits of even the most conscientious American consumer. All of these factors confluently

---

[2] For a more comprehensive discussion of the sacrificial role assumed by scapegoats throughout much of recorded human history that transcends the pragmatic limitations of this particular study, see René Girard's *The Scapegoat* and *Violence and the Sacred*.

[3] Building upon the ideas of his longtime friend and colleague René Girard, Michel Serres often decries the symbolic catharsis provided by the corporate mainstream media in the contemporary landscape. See chapter one "The Dawning of the Age of Information" in Keith Moser's book *The Encyclopedic Philosophy of Michel Serres: Writing the Modern World and Anticipating the Future* (2016).

produce the necessary conditions under which the people in Urrea's narrative suffer and die. (24)

In these lines, Cox gives her own complex reading of the desert monster, confirming Cohen's assertion that monsters always return to "ask us how we have misrepresented what we attempted to place [and] ask us to reevaluate our critical and cultural assumptions" (20). As a textual and rhetorical device, Urrea's monster has succeeded in its task. It holds a place for complexity until the reader is both emotionally invested and informed enough to ask the question himself: What is this monster, really?

Conclusion/Alternative Vision

The Sonoran Desert and its harsh landscape make a fitting monster for contemporary American culture. Most Americans, living in the luxury of insulation from all discomforts of the natural world, do not know how to sustain themselves *anywhere* on this stolen continent, much less in its harshest regions. The monster speaks to and reflects the deep anxiety of Urrea's readership, whom I imagine sitting in air-conditioned buildings, sipping coffee, or reading *The Times* while someone else, somewhere else, provides the backbreaking manual labor that sustains their existence. Moreover, this readership, with limited awareness of its own luxury, might hardly comprehend that many of the world's poor and disenfranchised would walk across a continent for the privilege of serving them, even risking death along the way. In addition to highlighting this unsettling social disparity, the Sonora-as-monster metaphor also serves the text well as a placeholder for political complexity. As the author deems necessary, he can use the monster to conceal or expose the various forces in the multifarious complex of social, economic, and political values and relationships that *actually* devour immigrants (and suck the land dry). The question remains as to whether Urrea's ends justify his rhetorical means. The land-as-monster conceit reinforces and perpetuates the unspoken attitudes and assumptions that lie at the root of the actual social ills that create our border horrors. If we are to survive the Anthropocene epoch, we have to change how we live and work on this earth. This urgent paradigm shift has to begin with seeing the earth as habitable and nurturing, as opposed to being a monster that must be conquered or slain in the Cartesian sense. Language matters: if we lose the metaphor, then maybe in the process we can rid ourselves of the monstrosities of our own creation.

In the service of deconstructing the cultural mindset that would make a monster of the desert, or any landscape for that matter, we might look to Jim Corbett who actually lives in the Sonoran Desert. Corbett contends that "the home of a peaceful people must be in places others consider wastelands" (48). He has devoted a considerable amount of his life to walking political refugees from CIA-instigated Central American civil wars through the *exact* same stretch of desert depicted in *The Devil's Highway*. Leaving metaphorical scapegoats behind, Corbett has even brought along his real goat herd during these treacherous journeys. His caravans of refugees have made it safely across the desert time and time again. They are able to survive with the nourishment provided by these goats, in addition to vitamin C tablets during certain seasons, for ten or more days in the Organ Pipe or Cabeza Prieta, if necessary. He speaks of the desert as a place of mystical vision, but without the romantic bent of a nature writer. From a cultural perspective, he writes:

> To be at home in desert solitudes, peaceful peoples must enter into partnership with other highly adapted life that allows them to walk gently over a land that is ruthless to misfits. To be at home in deserts, a gentle, peaceful people must also be ruthless. Sentimentalism is a luxury of the rich and violent. (48)

Jim Corbett's manifesto *Goatwalking* is the perfect complement to *The Devil's Highway* for anyone who dares to consider genuine cultural solutions to multifaceted issues that haunt the modern world. These kinds of real solutions begin with seeing the land as an ally in rectifying our social and cultural ills, rather than as an adversary onto which we might subtly shift the blame.

References

Alber, Catherine. "Monster Bodies, Monster Space: Cormac McCarthy's Blood Meridian and the Demythologization of the American Frontier." *Southwestern American Literature*, vol. 40, no. 2, Spring 2015, pp. 7–18.

Bantinaki, Katerina. "The Paradox of Horror: Fear as a Positive Emotion." *Journal of Aesthetics & Art Criticism*, vol. 70, no. 4, Fall 2012, pp. 383–92.

Cohen, Jeffrey. "Monster Culture (Seven Theses)." *Monster Theory: Reading Culture*, edited by Jeffrey Cohen, University of Minnesota Press, 1996, pp. 3–26.

Corbett, Jim. *Goatwalking: A Guide to Wildland Living, a Quest for the Peaceable Kingdom*. Viking Penguin, 1991.

Cox, Sandra. "Crossing the Divide: Geography, Subjectivity, and Transnationalism in Luis Alberto Urrea's the Devil's Highway." *Southwestern American Literature*, vol. 38, no. 1, 2012, pp. 8–26.

Urrea, Luis Alberto. *The Devil's Highway: A True Story*. Bay Back, 2004.

Vásquez, Mary S. "Food for the Journey: Walking the Border with Rubén Martínez and Luis Alberto Urrea." *Monographic Review/Revista Monográfica*, vol. 21, 2005, pp. 180–93.

Part II

Transgressive, Monstrous Gender and Corporality

7

Transgressive and Sovereign Authority in the Valois Court*

Touba Ghadessi

The multiplicity of definitions that accompany the term "monster" for centuries is one that lends itself to perplexity, certainly, but also to nuanced interpretations. It is through these gradations of meanings that latent knowledge can surface, revealing ideas that push interpretations farther. In line with a history of difference that encompasses the monster as a wide category, the figures discussed here allow for engaging epistemological paths to emerge. The intent of the present analysis is not to challenge previous interpretations of known historical figures and their representations, but rather to offer an additional reading that provides an approach for deeper contextualization. More precisely, what can be monstrous, when, and to whom elucidates the reasons for iconographical and textual choices tied to certain regal portraits. When Michel Foucault discussed the notion of the human monster in his lectures at the Collège de France in 1975, he stated that this notion was juridical. Essentially,

> What defines the monster is the fact that its existence and form is not only a violation of the laws of society but also a violation of the laws of nature. Its very existence is a breach of the law at both levels. [...] [The monster] violates the law while leaving it with nothing to say. It traps the law while breaching it. (Foucault 55–6)

However, this juridical and natural transgression faded when the human monster *was* the law, when the human monster was the sovereign figure embodying its own just legal expression. Because extraordinary bodies are meant to deviate from norms established by a culturally dominant group, the bodies discussed in this chapter problematize that

---

* Without Keith Moser's kind invitation, diligence, and patience, this chapter would not be. I am thankful to him and to the many colleagues who, along the way, have allowed me to see that a book emerging from these few pages might be a feasible endeavor. In particular, I am grateful to Nadja Aksamija, Cristelle Baskins, Katie Chenoweth, Edwin Duval, Samuel Garcia, Marina Leslie, Kathleen Long, Tara Nummedal, and Laurie Nussdorfer whose generous thoughts I look forward to incorporating in my lengthier project.

very notion since they are, inherently, at the head of that norm-defining hierarchy.[1] As long as the iconographical control remained in the hands of the ruling authority, the human monster endured as a wondrous figure. Once the public reclaimed its agency as a provider of cultural meaning, then the trope died and the human monster became once more an anomaly, unable to rule. From François I (1494–1547) to Catherine de' Medici Valois (1519–89), and to Henri III (1551–89), the body of the ruler swayed from supernatural and mighty to unstable and nefarious. Chosen as fertile paradigms to note the variability of meanings embedded and embodied, these figures allow for further dialogue on the malleability of transgression.

Deciding to categorize the ruling body as monstrous is charged and deliberate, particularly in the early modern period. Because this analysis uses a portrait of François I as a point of entry to understand the notion of hermaphroditism at court and beyond, a statement on natural philosophy, the understanding of monsters, and how hermaphrodites fit into this discourse is crucial.

Often, bodies were deemed monstrous because they deviated from canonical norms promoted by newly published anatomical treatises, ideas put forth by natural philosophers, and the subsequent courtly ideals that publicly displayed the results of such discourses. Monsters engendered both admiration and horror on the part of early modern audiences who sought to understand and question God and Nature.[2] The term "monster" thus respects an early modern rhetoric, as well as an etymological history. This history shows that systematic methods of inquiry used to understand monsters as phenomena outside the normal course of Nature co-existed with the theological understanding of monsters as signs of divine wrath or omens.[3] The curious and the marvelous animated the imagination of natural philosophers and anatomists who used centuries of created knowledge to shape their conception of the world. For instance and in spite of his extensive surgical experience, Ambroise Paré (1510–90) did not let his medical assertions shatter his belief that monsters were a divine mark placed on Nature or that they might represent what happened to those who faced God's wrath (Paré 1030). One interpretation did not subsume the other and he allowed both to find expressions in his treatises. To support this oscillating dichotomy, Paré recasts the etymological origins of the term "monster" to underline the theological premise that monsters were visible signs meant to be shown. The origin of the word "monster" is found in the Latin *mostrare* (to show), and Paré himself discussed the monster as "a being that one shows" (Smith 270).[4] Display remained at the ontological basis of

---

[1] I here gesture toward Rosemarie Garland Thomson (1997) and the strong theoretical model she provides for the intellectual nomenclature attached to physical disability.
[2] Jean Céard (1996) discusses the use of terms such as "monster" and "marvel" by contextualizing them within a discourse of natural philosophy; he also warns the reader against an anachronistic understanding of the term "monster," which omits the multivalent emotional and intellectual responses audiences gave to deformed beings. By doing so, Céard also allows for monsters and marvels to become mutually inclusive categories.
[3] See pp. 173–214 from Lorraine Daston and Katharine Park's *Wonders and the Order of Nature 1150-1750* in particular for the different perceptions of monsters.
[4] As Paré affirms, "un être que l'on monstre" (1020).

the monster's being but, in the case of monstrous bodies associated with rulers, also intrinsically necessary. In a sense, the spectacle of Nature could only be made visible through the ruling spectacle deployed by the sovereigns who used these inquiries for their own benefit. Frequently, the examples of Nature's deviation chosen by rulers were meant to provide the exceptions needed to reinforce the structure of a new canon, their canon.

Deviations from canonical norms could occur at many levels—number of limbs, size of anatomical parts, and of course sexual differentiation. The binary division of male and female sex imposed by the church was officially and publicly sanctioned by ruling authorities. As a remnant of medieval concepts, this rigid division problematized the inability to sit within an easily categorized set as the breaking of established bounds could presage the downfall of an entire systemic structure.[5] The social norms attached to these respective biological determinants therefore regulated their behavioral manifestations, at least through public performance. According to this simplistic but widely endorsed ideal, the concept of a being who could not fit either of these sexual categories could be classified as monstrous, since it would push the boundaries of the norms that were supposed to delineate it. Notably, though, strict divisional understandings of sex were in actuality much more nuanced and permeable.[6] In fact, as Kathleen Long (2016) has beautifully demonstrated, sophisticated and layered knowledge about ambiguous sexual bodies are central epistemological tools for understanding the Renaissance through a full and interdisciplinary lens.[7] Hermaphrodites, as *neither* but also as *both* sexes would therefore fit into the category of the monstrous, but also be apposite examples of extraordinary bodies.[8] Interest in hermaphrodites was neither new nor groundbreaking in early modern France; the revival of classical texts and the Neoplatonic view debated and adopted alternately by scholars and rulers made the figure of the hermaphrodite a fraught site for reflection.

As for the medical interests in hermaphrodites, it followed an early modern drive to understand and categorize the world through observation and the production of

---

[5] As Leah Devun posits, "Medieval texts emphasize the problematic nature of individuals who do not fit easily into binary sex categories. Despite the continuum of sex difference proposed by the Hippocratic/Galenic model, Pseudo-Albert, Peter of Poitiers, and Peter the Chanter limited the transgressive potential of a hermaphrodite by establishing him/her firmly within either one of two genders—he/she cannot be neither or both in social contexts. [...] hermaphrodites were a source of confusion and even suspicion to their contemporaries, necessitating their division into binary gender categories of male and female, and conveying the extent to which neitherness and bothness had the potential to threaten social and natural norms" (198).

[6] The pervasive and problematic discussions of Thomas Laqueur (1990) still shape many thoughts on the one-sex model and its implications for understanding difference in the early modern period. In this case, however, it is interesting to apply it to external signs of sexual difference. See pp. 22 and 52–70.

[7] This is first stated on p. 4 and reiterated throughout the book.

[8] Rosemarie Garland Thomson provides a strong theoretical model for the intellectual nomenclature attached to physical difference. In doing so, she allows for a discourse that frames bodies of individuals whose physical features did not conform to the visible norm determined by a dominant cultural group. This is evidently problematized in the case of a ruler whose body oscillates between said public norms. See *Extraordinary Bodies: Figuring Physical Disability in American Culture and Literature*.

epistemological paradigms. But, just as teratological writings did not forego theological explanations for scientific ones, the explanation of hermaphrodites' sexual difference played on both mythological and medical planes. The theory of the seven-chambered uterus was used since the Middle Ages to explain hermaphroditism. This theory purported that three of the chambers produced males, three produced females, and the last produced hermaphrodites (Walton, Fineman, and Walton 8). This view blended in the collective imaginary with the alchemical concept of hermaphrodites as holy beings who restored order on material chaos by trampling over the four elements (Riolan 26, 67–8).[9] Even through an alchemical lens, hermaphrodites, because of their rarity and their unusual place in a divided sexual binary, kept their status as anomalous humans. To reinforce this notion, natural scientists and anatomists played with epistemological categories to bolster this teleology. For instance, Jean Riolan in his 1614 *Discours sur les hermaphrodits* argued that hermaphrodites were not wonders since they did not possess full reproductive organs from both genders, but rather a defective version of each. Realdo Colombo explored the anatomical anomalies of otherwise normative human beings in Book Fifteen of *De re anatomica*, published posthumously in 1559. Colombo adopted a medically guided approach to the study of abnormal bodies, one grounded in his anatomical professorship and his immersion in medical expertise.[10] Thus, Colombo never mentioned monsters as portentous signs; he did not attack those who had treated them as such, but he purposefully omitted any reference to their prophetic dimension. Colombo's treatise, by virtue of its deliberate exclusion, was one of the few and first teratological treatises to deal with monsters as pathological anomalies *only*, placing them in the realm of medicine (Carlino 143).[11] By dissecting a hermaphrodite and writing descriptively about it, Colombo turned his readers into witnesses who could see the wondrous secrets revealed by anatomizing extraordinary bodies (Colombo 268).

The importance of medical discourse in determining the status of hermaphrodites transcended the theoretical realm and served to establish their status as full juridical entities. The most famous trial recounting the legal tribulations of a hermaphrodite in the early modern period is undoubtedly that of Marie/Marin le Marcis. In his 1612 *Traité des hermaphrodits*, Jacques Duval devotes twenty chapters to the story of this *fille-homme*.[12] He recounts how he met her, and his subsequent finding of her

---

[9] This view was particularly developed by Paracelsus. See Walton, Fineman, and Walton 35.
[10] See Robert J. Moes and C. D. O'Malley's translation (1960), p. 508. Colombo replaced Vesalius temporarily as the chair of surgery and anatomy on January 19, 1543, and permanently in 1544.
[11] I am indebted to Andrea Carlino who generously shared this article and discussed his research with me. As Carlino reveals, "During the Renaissance they were perceived and understood in many different ways: monsters were prodigies and natural wonders, monsters were signs of future catastrophes, they were used for religious and political propaganda. At the same time, they started to be conceived and studied into a medical framework. [. . .] My claim is that Colombo's approach to monstrous subjects through anatomical dissections induced him to conceive their morphological 'differences' as anatomical abnormalities. This approach signifies inscribing monstrosity in pathology, therefore evacuating the merely teratological and superstitious conception still operating in texts produced by other doctors and anatomists such as Ambroise Paré" (143).
[12] The case of le Marcis is discussed from chapters 60 to 80.

"membre viril," in spite of opposing opinions from other physicians. The impossibility of reaching a consensus about his or her gendered position eventually led to the release of Marie/Marin and his lover Jeanne. He was, however, forbidden to dress as a man or have any sexual relations until he reached the age of twenty-five (Daston and Park 3).[13] The civic life of hermaphrodites thus appears to have depended very largely on medical assessment. Paolo Zacchia, in his *Quaestonium medico legalium* (begun in 1621), studied the medico-juridical case of hermaphrodites and eunuchs at length. In doing so, he summarized thoughts that anchored centuries of exchanges regarding pathologized bodies and their judicial positions. Zacchia directly addressed these questions in books three through sixteen by examining the medico-legal status of eunuchs and hermaphrodites (Zacchia 223). He also returned to that issue in his section on monsters in book seven (Zacchia 76); ultimately for Zacchia, juridical personhood for hermaphrodites, eunuchs, and *spadones* boiled down to their ability to reproduce.[14] This is no surprise since Zacchia's legal commentaries were inspired by the Pandects—a compendium of civil laws—written by the Emperor Justinian in the 530s, where the seminal powers of a man often determined his legal status. Therefore, if a hermaphrodite or a eunuch (who suffered a partial penectomy rather than an orchiectomy) was able to reproduce, he retained the right to marry, have an heir, and transmit possessions, and thus to possess material goods in his or her name. This kind of direct link underlines many issues inherent in intertwining theological law with juridical assessment of personhood (Figure 7.1).

In almost all aspects, hermaphrodites were nebulous and contested bodies. It is therefore quite fascinating that a ruler often associated with a great level of control regarding the equation of image and power would tolerate, much less welcome, a portrait of himself as a monster. The portrait in question shows François I as a composite Roman divinity, accompanied by a poem extolling his many virtues. Commissioned by his older sister Marguerite de Navarre, this portrait is intriguing for many reasons—its complex iconography, the references latent in its poem, and its relation to defining legal moments for France.

A small gouache painting on vellum affixed to oak (124mm × 134 mm), this portrait is held in the Reserve, Cabinet des estampes, in the Bibliothèque nationale in Paris. Its dating is approximate and varies between 1536 and 1552. Its authorship is also questioned and attributed to Nicolò Belin da Modena, Nicolò dell'Abbate, or the Maître des Heures de Henri II. Barbara Hochstetler Meyer's formal analysis gives an elegant visualization of this portrait:

> The king stands in slight contrapposto. On his head is a parade helmet with a greyish-purple head piece, a gold crest inset with white plumes, and a scalloped and pierced, raised, gold visor painted to resemble a damascened finish. The thin drapery swirling about his torso and hanging in vertical pleats over his thighs is

---

[13] Ten years after his release, Marin was actually living as a man and was employed as a tailor.
[14] Spadones is the general term for eunuch, though spadones are not always castrated; they simply do not have the ability to reproduce and are usually impotent.

Figure 7.1 Artist unknown (attributed to Nicolò Belin da Modena, Nicolò dell'Abbate, or to the Maître des Heures de Henri II), *François Ier, c.* 1536–52.

red in color. It is partially gathered on his right shoulder under a gold lion mask pauldron while short pleats fall on both sides of a gold apotropaic head of Medusa, the Gorgoneion, centered on his chest. The upper portion of the robe, which has a turned-back gold band at the top, billows out below the abdomen, its underside a pale blue. Here it is caught up in a greenish-yellow sash from which a curved, gold-rimmed, blue hunting horn is suspended. The sash crosses the chest diagonally under the Gorgoneion and over a fold of cloth and the bare left shoulder to support a long grey quiver embossed with an intricate, gold spiral pattern; a sheath of gold arrows protrudes from its top behind the left arm. The lower red pleats are trimmed with gold fringe. Underneath, reaching to mid-calf, is a skirt which is faded blue over the right leg, pale blue-green over the left and edged with a complex gold design. The tip of a tall, unstrung, gold bow rests against the king's left hip while a gold caduceus with entwined snakes in gold, purple, and grey is held in front of his bare left arm. His right arm, bent slightly and encased in grey vambrances and cowter, holds a weapon that resembles northern Italian thrusting sword with a short purple blade edged in gold, gold quillions terminating in upturned volutes, and a grey hilt with a pointed gold pommel. On his feet are brown sandals with large gold wings at the heels. Each leg from mid-calf to ankle has a brown greave-like covering with a bow attached at the top from which ribbons are vertically linked to the sandals. The index finger of the king's left hand points down to the dedication. Its letters, in Roman book hand, are brownish-gold on a pale ground that seems suspended as if it were a carved plaque in front of a gold cartouche with profile grotesque masks inset at each side and a frontal, winged, bald head on the bottom. (Meyer 291–3)

Gender polysemy and the attribution of feminized characteristics to male courtiers were not uncommon and were done for very specific reasons including metaphorical love. Because of courtly and scholarly passions for texts such as Ovid's and Plato's, the figure of the mythological Hermaphroditus and that of the androgyne became frequent tropes for a humanistic ideal that combined all qualities in one being.[15] Marguerite de Navarre, as a well versed and learned mind, knew these conceits and could use them with ease. She also knew her brother well and, as any French courtier would, was familiar with his triumphs and his claims to victory. In this vein, Raymond Waddington suggests that the iconography, as well as the poem, may in fact point to actual accounts of François I in battle, and some recounting may be couched in a satirical frame addressing the king's eccentricities.[16]

A reading seems to be missing, one that does not negate previous analyses, but rather adds a layer to a portrait that can only make sense in a court that reveled in multiple embedded meanings. The body of the hermaphrodite lends itself well to different epistemological approaches, from history of science to literature. In the case of this portrait, the body of François I functions effectively not as that of a monster but as that of a perfected being, a hermetic hermaphrodite. As such, additional power can be inscribed onto the legal and corporeal authority the king held.

Kings, princes, cardinals, and sovereigns of many kins understood that collecting objects and displaying them amounted to demonstrating that they possessed the

---

[15] See p. 305 from Meyer in particular.
[16] See especially pp. 123 and 125 from Waddington.

knowledge these objects held.[17] This assertion of authority found various articulations and evolved with the interests and the political needs of rulers. Among one of the most coveted ways to demonstrate one's mastery of nature, grasp of philosophical endeavors, and ultimately devotion to faith was alchemy. Tara Nummedal has superbly demonstrated the importance of alchemy at court and its centrality for "state formation, court culture, natural knowledge, and social identities" (Nummedal 11). The French court was no stranger to alchemical discourse and practice—this pervasive interest finds resonance at many levels and quite beautifully in the intellectual organizations given by Rebecca Zorach's study of the French Renaissance. Her divisions (Blood, Milk, Ink, Gold) mirror and "align with the four colors of physical matter of the numerologically organized cosmologies of alchemists and natural philosophers. [. . .] As with the system of the elements and humors, the four substances also transform, physically and metaphorically, into one another" (Zorach 27).[18]

While alchemical understandings shifted over time, certain main grounding principles remained. The transmutation of base metals to nobler ones provided the intellectual framework on which metaphorical expansions could attach. From antiquity to the Renaissance, alchemical propositions varied but revolved around the central axis of transformation. Often, for this transformation to occur, union was necessary. In particular and during the early modern period, an emphasis was placed on the "*conjunction* of male and female, the union of spiritual and physical, as necessary for the perfection of matter" (Long 110, emphasis in original). This meant that the "hermaphrodite, an increasingly important figure in alchemical works, was the symbol of this necessary but complex *conjunction* and balancing of male and female" (Long 111). As for the actual process, "Alchemy was perceived as a process of purification; but at the same time, this process [was] dependent upon the fusion of the spiritual and material realms. [. . .] Most alchemical treatises thus revolve[d] around an obsession with the human body as well as with metals" (Long 111). That body oscillated between a metaphorical site and a tangible one—it was at once both genders, both elements, and in their conjunction, neither. This turned the hermaphrodite into a contested figure since it was an emblem of perfection attained, but it was also associated with pathological sexual transgression.[19]

All of these elements played into the complex understanding of the hermetic body in the early modern period, and these intertwined notions were made manifest through the vellum portrait of François I. A brief iconographical reading identifies him to Minerva through the Gorgon, the plumed helmet, and the diaphanous robe, while

---

[17] For a full discussion on the relationships between possessing, knowing, and socially defining oneself, see pp. 17–47 from Paula Findlen as an overview.

[18] Zorach reiterates this point throughout the book.

[19] Discussing this tense dichotomy, Devun states, "Because the alchemical hermaphrodite was a symbol and not a person capable of illicit behaviors, it carried with it few of the negative connotations associated with intersex humans, who were classified as 'monsters' in moral and medical texts, and who were treated with equal parts curiosity and disapprobation. But the alchemical hermaphrodite depended upon understandings of intersex people in medieval society, and it therefore shared in some of the transgressive elements of intersex" (195).

the bow, the quiver, and the hunting horn tie him to Diana. Mercury's tropes are the king's caduceus and his winged sandals, and François I's sword and armor link him to Mars. His martial and regal power is seen in the lion armor and, in the case of this poem, Amor is not Cupid, but Eros, ennobling his soul.

A superficial and incomplete nod to salic law may lead viewers to question the feminine associations of the French king with female attributes. However, the court of François I was known for the use of imagery revolving around the female body, and this intentional choice was intended to symbolically express abundance (Zorach 9).[20] And indeed, the body of the king is in abundance, both visually and textually. The text of the poem supporting the depiction of François I reads:

> Francoys en guerre est un Mars furieux
> En paix Minerve et Diane a la chasse
> A bien parler Mercure copieux
> A bien aymer vray Amour plein de grace
> O france heureuse honore donc la face
> De ton grand Roy qui surpasse Nature
> Car l'honorant tu seres en mesme place
> Minerve, Mars, Diane, Amour, Mercure.
>
> François in war is a furious Mars
> In peace Minerva and Diana of the hunt
> A well-spoken, copious Mercury
> A much-loving, true Amor full of grace
> O fortunate France honor this face
> Of your great king who surpasses Nature
> For there you will have honored in the same
> Minerva, Mars, Diana, Amor, Mercury. (Waddington 99–132)

While Platonic humanistic ideals of the universal man serving as an allegory for the French king are apposite for this reading, the poem may hold an additional dimension. And to see it, a gesture toward Katie Chenoweth's impeccable argument about the importance of language, sovereignty, law, and language as law in the Edict of Villers-Cotterêts is paramount. This edict intended to institutionalize French as the central and unique language for justice, law, and state administration in France. The 192 articles in the edict were to centralize and reinforce political authority in France. Two articles in particular affirmed the French language not merely as an expression of ruling authority but, in fact, *as* justice, law, and administration.[21] Articles 110 and 111 declare:

---

[20] See chapter 2 in particular.
[21] As Chenoweth indicates, "*1539* and *Villers-Cotterêts* now signify above all a turning point in the history of the French language, namely, the institution of French as the uniquely recognized language of justice, law, and state administration in France. [. . .] Widely recognized as the first state

110. And so that there should be no cause to doubt whether the aforementioned legal decisions have been understood, we wish and order that they should be made and written so clearly that there neither is nor could be any room for ambiguity or uncertainty, nor cause to ask for interpretation [interpretation: interpretation or translation].

111. And because such things have often occurred regarding the understanding of Latin words contained in legal decisions, we wish that, henceforth, all decision and other procedures, pertaining to our sovereign courts or other lower or inferior courts, whether they be registers, inquiries, contracts, commissions, sentences, wills, or any other acts and writs of justice [. . .] should be pronounced, recorded, and delivered to parties in the French mother tongue [en langage maternel françois], and not otherwise ("Ordonnance").[22]

According to the edict, all documents had to be written in the "langage maternel françoys, et non autrement." A notable juxtaposition—*françois* and *maternel*—leads to the gendering of François I as the father and mother of language, and hence as the authoritative parent of justice and state administration. This intentional and powerful hermaphroditic gendering of the king made him both the "Père des lettres," allowing French vernacular to hold cultural authority, as well as the one who upheld the *mother* tongue "la langue maternelle," the nurturing aspect of what France provided for her subjects.

As such, François I became the embodiment of a perfected alchemical hermaphrodite, able to generate, regenerate, and reproduce without the need for a queen. He was the father and the mother of France. These generative powers were expressed visually through a painted body clearly marking both attributes of ideal male and female sexes, rather than ambiguous attributes that might belong to both or neither categories. The text reinforced the importance of having both sexes and their signifiers in one being, "en mesme place." Their conjunction mattered, as it did in an alchemical discourse. Additionally, the text tied the adjective "copious" to Mercury, as an evident reference to alchemical generation and reproduction. Indeed, in the hermaphroditic figure of Mercury the human body and the metal, as two separate realms, became united. Mercury symbolized the dual divinity from whom all planets and seven metals emerged

---

language policy in Europe, Villers- Cotterêts and 1539 also stand for a wider- reaching, modern formation of sovereignty in language—and of sovereignty *as* language" (67–8).

[22] English translation adapted by Chenoweth from Lodge, p. 126: "110. Et affin quil ny ayt cause de doubter sur l'intelligence desdits arreztz, nous voulons et ordonnons qu'ilz soient faitz et escriptz si clairement, quil ny ait ni puisse avoir aucune ambiguite ou incertitude ne lieu a en demander interpretation." "111. Et pource que telles choses sont souventeffois advenues sur l'intelligence des motz latins contenuz esdictz arreztz, nous voulons que doresenavant tous arretz ensemble toutes autres procédeures, soyent de noz cours souveraines ou autres subalterns et inférieures, soyent de registres, enquestes, contractz, commissions, sentences, testamens et autres quelzconques actes et exploictz de justice, ou qui en dépendent, soyent prononcez, enregistrez et délivrez aux parties en langage maternel françois, et non autrement" ("Ordonnance") (Chenoweth 83, fn1).

and was also, essentially, the element able to effectuate alchemical transformations.[23] Beyond its direct ties to the alchemical process—to its sixth step, in particular, that of conjunction—Mercury, and by extension the hermaphroditic figure it created, was also in dialogue with Christian theology (Federmann 25).[24] Transcending its monstrous qualifiers as a transgressive, uncategorizable, and abnormal, the hermetic and chemical hermaphrodite acquired a status that linked its embodiment to the figure of the *Rebis* not only as the dual bodied and purified form of renewal but also as a metaphor for Christian dogma. Leah Devun has successfully argued that "alchemical texts played upon the metaphorical parallelism of the philosophers' stone and Jesus Christ to claim Christ him/herself as a hermaphrodite, the perfect combination of contraries— masculine and feminine, human and divine—in one body" (195). From the feminine humanity of Christ given to him through the body of the Virgin Mary, to the creation of Eve from Adam's rib as a statement of both sexes embodied in one, biblical narratives and interpretations made intertwined alchemical and Christian narratives facile archways.[25] Every element—pun intended—in François I's portrait thus aligned with an intentional representation of the king of France as a hermaphrodite. One gendered identity was not be subsumed by the other and the maintaining of opposites gave the figure its power. In order to hold authority and to assert the importance of sovereignty, François I had to be both male and female, an ideal hermaphrodite, a copious being, in abundance of everything, a Christian figure at once divine and human, perfectly balancing his dual nature, and embodying France which he could shape to his image. François was the paradigmatic *françois*, generating the state and her children/subjects without needing another body—his was not only sufficient but also plentiful.

The presentation of the king in such a nuanced, yet strong visualization of power, functioned effectively only as long as the iconography remained meaningful for the viewer and the rhetoric was controlled by the sovereign authority designing its intent. When Marguerite de Navarre commissioned a portrait of her brother, her intent paralleled that of the king. When François I's daughter-in-law, Catherine de' Medici Valois, came to the court of France, her circumstances differed greatly from that of an already acknowledged and accepted ruler. Her foreignness was salient, and it escaped the realm she could control. The perception of her difference was manipulated to

---

[23] As Long reveals, "From Mercury can be generated Jupiter (tin), Mars (iron), Venus (copper), Saturn (lead), Luna (silver), and Sol (gold)" (111).

[24] As noted in Long, "During the 2nd and 3rd centuries a secret Hermes Gnostic cult also flourished. Hermes was worshipped as the All-Spirit, as the demiurge who created the material world and permeates it as Logos. He is identified with the Savior, the mediator between God and the world, which he saves from the planets' destructive influence" (111, fn 9).

[25] As Devun explains, "The human and divine natures within Christ create a hermaphroditic union facilitated by the impregnated body of the Virgin Mary. Although this understanding of Christ is not identical to that of the Book, it is clear that by the fifteenth century a number of texts were circulating that identified Jesus as a feminine or hermaphroditic figure while noting the role of the Virgin in furnishing Jesus with his humanity. [...] The production of Eve from Adam's rib may also have suggested the embodiment of the female within the male at the moment of creation, indicating that hermaphroditism should be a part of alchemical creation as well" (212).

thwart her political efforts during tumultuous times, and her body became a vexed site onto which conflicts were ascribed.

François I and Pope Clement VII (1475–1534) decided that Catherine was to be wedded to Henri d'Orléans (1519–59), future Henri II of France and shortly thereafter, the French court administration recorded all her possessions. Among these, a dwarf, Jehan de Nano, was listed as a "vallet de chambre."[26] This inventory of goods was continually updated through the years, and inevitably, Jehan de Nano appeared repeatedly as Catherine de' Medici's "vallet de chambre."[27] This dwarf was not the only dwarf who was with Catherine when she came to France, and he was certainly not the only one she possessed through her rulership. As perfected miniature bodies, dwarves were commonly used foils for rulers who used these flawed bodies surrounding them to reinforce the rigid standards of their courts. Unlike courtiers who were to abide by the court's mandates and emulate the ruler's behavior, dwarves mitigated those regulations and allowed for a heterogenous vocabulary of difference to enter these, sometimes suffocating, spheres. They functioned as practical monsters that alleviated pressure for both courtiers and ruling figures. It was expected that the future Queen of France would adopt courtly tropes that were familiar and common. Less expected, but no less monstrous, was the family of hirsutes brought to the court of France and, eventually, placed under the protection of the queen of France.

In 1547, a hirsute boy was brought to Henri II de France as a gift for his coronation. When the conquest of Tenerife in 1495 marked the end of independence of the Canary Islands and the beginning of their attachment to the Spanish kingdom, the fate of a hirsute boy should have followed those of his fellow native Guanches. However, because his body was monstrous and rare in its monstrosity, he was instead offered as a gift upon the conquerors' return to the mainland.[28] A few years later, Francesco Cappello, Venetian ambassador to the Iberian Peninsula, returned to the Venice with several gifts including colorful parrots and a strange savage boy—Pierre Gonsalvus.[29] Eventually, on March 31, 1547, as one of many diplomatic gifts bestowed upon the future king of France, Pierre Gonsalvus at the age of ten found his way to the French court.[30] For forty-two years, Petrus Gonsalvus lived in Paris as part of Henri II's court, where he received military training and a literary education including Latin—an

---

[26] Bibliothèque nationale de France (BNF). Garde Robe (GR). Manuscrit français (MF) 2952 (215), n.a. 9189, dated 1530, 15v.

[27] The above manuscript continues with dates every year, and Jehan de Nano is found on pages 25v, 51r, 65r [...].

[28] See pp. 6, 37, and 40 from Felipe Fernández-Armesto.

[29] See pp. 91, 105, 107, 109–12, and 115–16 from Symcox, Rabitti, and Diehl.

[30] In a letter dated April 18, 1547, to the Duke of Ferrara, Ercole II d'Este (1508–59), his Ambassador Giulio Alvarotto described the gifts given to the future Henri II, including a ten-year-old boy covered in hair: "È stato donato al re un putto de circa X anni portato dalle Indie, molto bello, ma tutto piloso il volto et tutta la vita, come appunto si dipingono gl'humani silvatici. I pelli sonno longhi circa cinque dita. Sonna rari molto, tanto che si vedeno tutti i lineamenti deall fazza. Sonno di colore tané chiaro et molto sottili et fini più che'l pello di zebelino, et sanno de buon. Lui parla spagnuolo et va vestito come è l'ordinario d'ognuno. Però su per la vita ha il pello frusto. Non si chi l'habbi donato a Sua Maestà." Roberto Zapperi's transcription corrects the previously published one by C. Occhipinti, which contained several mistakes. See p. 158 from Zapperi.

accomplishment that made him unusual, even among French courtiers (Waquet 273). During those years, Pierre Gonsalvus married a glabrous woman named Catherine, with whom he eventually had seven children (Zapperi 65).[31]

Records indicate Pierre Gonsalvus and his family stayed in Paris until 1589—the year of Catherine de' Medici Valois's death. Given the succession of Valois kings who followed Henri II's death, it is not unlikely that the Queen Mother was the only constant parameter in the lives of the Gonsalvuses and the main protection for the family once sheltered by her late husband. When Catherine de' Medici Valois died and her son Henri III was assassinated, the Gonsalvus family found itself without protection and because of various political alliances, moved to Parma.[32] These tumultuous times crystallize why Catherine de' Medici Valois's protection of this hirsute family is particularly relevant. Owning the Gonsalvus family did not afford Catherine an easily identifiable noble status. Hirsutes were understood as neither civilized enough to be part of a human society nor beastly enough to be entirely relegated to the animal world. Henri II and Catherine may have viewed the Gonsalvuses as having acquired civilized manners, but succeeding monarchs and courts probably did not share in this unusual opinion. Catherine's gesture to protect the Gonsalvus family referred to her husband's desire to educate and shelter the hirsute family, and to her own desire to protect the family her husband had supported. Through the kingships of her sons Charles IX and Henri III, Catherine did not falter in her pledge to the Gonsalvus family, and by extension, to her late husband, in spite of the implication of savagery and foreignness associated with hirsutes in the collective imaginary. These notions would have been even more amplified for Catherine whose own body was already the site of monstrous transgression. Hirsutes did not function as imperfect mirrors of perfect royal bodies in the same way that dwarves did. The bodies of the Gonsalvuses were so distant from the civilized and normative self promoted at court that their wildness could only, remotely, serve to mitigate Catherine's foreignness. No known portrait of the queen exists alongside members of the Gonsalvus family—a close visual and recorded association would have been equivalent to admitting that Catherine's detractors, in their attempts at demonstrating that the queen's body was inherently monstrous in its affection for power, were in fact validated. While the protection of the hirsutes was real—records of payment to the Gonsalvuses for instance—the public presentation of the association of Catherine with the hirsutes was purposefully erased, leaving meaning in this intentional void, as well as a statement about not only a monstrous hierarchy but also and mostly about controlling the kinds of transgressions associated with sovereign bodies.

Inherently, Catherine's body as a queen and then as a regent was unsettled because she was a woman. Appropriating and adapting gender roles to her ambitions allowed

---

[31] The names of the children were Madeleine (born c. 1575, hirsute), Paul (born c. 1577), Henri (born c. 1580, hirsute), Françoise (born c. 1582, hirsute), Antoinette (born c. 1588, hirsute), Horace (born 1592, hirsute), Hercule (born 1595).

[32] The travels of the Gonsalvus family members are well documented, textually and visually, and they found their ways through and to many different courts.

Catherine to control her position at first, but eventually and through many years, her body became a conflicted site that she had difficulties reversing. Catherine's marriage to Henri II was her access to the court of France in many, if not all, ways. As his wife, Catherine knew to perform a role that played on her status as a woman, but she also asserted her rights through what could at times be a fraught status. Complicated and tenuous, the position of queen meant that she was at the center of the court, regardless of her husband's interests in other women and one in particular—Diane de Poitiers. During Henri II's reign, Catherine's discretion in this matter was praised because she not only shielded her husband but also protected him and handled difficult situations with unusual poise.[33] Once her husband died, she performed her duties as widow beyond what was expected of her, though she promptly commissioned works that reaffirmed her position as the *only* widow of the deceased king. As Sheila ffolliott (1989) has established, Catherine cast Diane de Poitiers aside and confirmed her widow and regent roles through intricate and powerful iconographies. These visual statements of social preeminence acquired a meaning that escaped the control of the widow and regent as her children came to power, particularly when Henri III accessed the throne.[34] Catherine's motherhood and what it meant for France and royal assertions, combined with her son's perceived lack of involvement led to the public decrying her virility and his effeminacy.

The mastery Catherine had shown in using her body—and all that it entailed—was a feat, but one that was arduous to maintain. Indeed, "Whereas a good woman was obedient, deferential, and dependent, a good politician was commanding, aggressive, and independent" (Crawford 673). The difficulty of maintaining a balanced dichotomy was not lost on courtiers and ambassadors who were noting the strong hand held by Catherine, and consequently the insubstantial one presented by her son. In 1579, the English ambassador to France stated that "it is easy to see that the Queen Mother is king and queen of this country and has lost none of her authority" (qtd. in Walker and Dickerman 260). The strength she showed was intended to solidify France and to do so through Valois kingship. In order to show that strength and have room to practice effective politics, Catherine had to play her role as a widow, as a Queen Mother, and as a woman with agile dexterity and with much controlled ambiguity. But that ambiguity was difficult to circumscribe—it soon escaped her and became a detrimental social weapon against her son. The body of the king became monstrous in its incapacity to manage this tight balance and the ambiguity turned into an unmanageable gender shifting, particularly since this play with gender was not one intended by the king. The form it took, it was neither initiated nor approved by him. Increasingly, in the pamphlets written during and after the reign of Henri III, gender shifting and hermaphroditism

---

[33] This is stated by Venetian ambassador Giovanni Capello (qtd. in Albèri, ser. 1, 2:284). As cited in Crawford 655.

[34] The intent of this chapter is to give a point of entry and final note to the reader—hence its opening with François I and its jump to Henri III as a closing figure. The book project from which this chapter is inspired will examine each of the Valois kings following François I and will use that chronology to reinforce some of the readings briefly addressed in this chapter.

Figure 7.2 Rebus-image of *La politique*, engraving from Catholic League broadsheet "Le Pourtraict et description du Politique de ce temps, extraict de l'Escriture Saincte," 1589.

became associated with deviance and weakness. His predecessors had been able to commission images of themselves as androgynous figures, and members of his family had essentially cross-dressed for specific representations.[35] But for Henri III, gender transgression became a disgraceful manifestation of his deviance (Figure 7.2).

The public perception of their sovereign's monstrous body was made clear in many pamphlets circulated during Henri III's reign. For instance, the personification of *La politique* is a quote from a Beaujoyeulx balet comique character, but here, she is subduing the king to her will. To the upper right, Venus, Mars, and Cupid are meant to deride the "Italianate" taste of the king, rather than exude his many qualities. At the bottom, Turkish turbans point to Islam as a lascivious and despicable "other" and also refer to Henri's "Turkish arrogance." Linked to this image is the satirical portrait of Henri III as a grotesque and monstrous female body meant to point to Henri III's Machiavellian ruling and his transgression of nature (Figure 7.3).

The accompanying text only serves to reinforce his deviance:

> Les mamelles de femme qui sont audessous marquent que ce prince efféminé a confondu la nature mesme estant pour ainsi dire hermaphrodite dans ses excès. Ils ont aussi voulu faire entendre par ce prodige qu'il grossit ses mamelles du sang de

---

[35] Described in *Recueil des choses notables qui on este faites a Bayonne* (1566), as cited in Zorach 220.

Figure 7.3 Satirical portrait of Henri III de France, engraving, late sixteenth to early seventeenth century.

son people pour nourrir des sang-sues, c'est à dire qu'il remplit ses coffres de l'argent de ses sujets pour entretenir d'indignes favoris qui le sucent continuellement et l'engagent aux plus folles depenses. Les Aisles, et la queue du dragon font voir qu'ayant fait pacte avec le diable par ses sorcelleries, et pratiques de Magie, il en a pris la forme dès qu'il s'est donné à lui.[36]

Using the dissatisfaction Henri III's display of lavish spectacle engendered, many decried every aspect of the court's ostentatiousness as an expression of the king's vile character. From the mignons—Henri III's effeminate entourage and showered with gifts by the king—who surrounded him, to the *Balet Comique* and their accompanying engravings, everything fueled the fire that had started years before Henri III became king. The court that Henri III inherited was not a peaceful or a welcoming one. Between the violent factions of the Catholic League and the Protestants, a middle road of politique seemed least threatening. But in Henri's hands, it became a deeply flawed path—it was seen as the remnant of his mother's Italianate style of ruling, one that was feeble and unable to steer people toward an actual decision. Its diplomatic importance as a compromise tool was entirely lost for Henri III. Used by both factions against him, his weak rulership found articulation through his body, losing sovereign authority one excessive celebration after another. As popular sensibilities saw the indulgences of the Valois court grow, history noted Henri III and by extension his body as an un-enviable and uncontrollable kind of monster. He became seen as the reason France was at war, in debt, and broken. Like François I, his body was a personification of France and as such, the monstrous representations of the king also spoke to the dire state of the polity he was leading. It is therefore apposite that his satirical portrait as *La politique* encompassed all these aspects. The parallel with the mythological composite of François I is at best amusing, in truth absolutely condemnatory. Henri is here "visualized as monstrous figure derived from personifications of France and Nature, his substance sucked dry by leeches rather than productively feeding his people" (Zorach 235). As much as François I's body was abundant and generous, Henri III's is depleted and lacking. His excess was one that ruined France, while François's excess was to generate a more capacious France (Figure 7.4).

Posthumously and very tellingly, the monstrous body of Henri III was the center of satirical texts and images of the well-known *L'isle des hermaphrodites*. Published in 1605 and immensely popular through the reign of the beloved Henri IV, the *Isle des hermaphrodites* did not present the hermaphroditic body as generative or plentiful. This anti-utopia was about gender transformation, about the desire of the male ruler

---

[36] The woman's breasts beneath [the head] show that this effeminate prince has confounded Nature herself being, so to speak, a hermaphrodite in his excesses. They also wanted to show by this marvel that he fattens his breasts with the people's blood to nourish leeches, that is that he fills his coffers with his subjects' money to keep unworthy favorites who suck on him continually and commit him to the most foolish expenditures. The wings and the dragon's talk show that, having made a pact with Satan through his sorcery and magical practices, he took the devil's form from the moment he gave himself to him.
Translation courtesy of Keith Cameron, qtd. in Zorach 233.

Figure 7.4 Artus Thomas (?), François de Lacour (?), Etienne Tabourot (?), Jacques Davy du Perron (?), *L'isle des hermaphrodites*..., first published in 1605.

to become female, and about the instability that such effeminacy could bring to power. Rather than the actual body of the ruler, it was external affects that served as gendered signs, and they did not only cover but also change what this ruling body should have been and should have done. The opulence of excess became aberrant and the acquisition of both genders was shown as transgressive rather than bounteous. These associations were enhanced by the reality of the Valois court at the time and the combination fed the public's hatred of him and, effectively, Henri III lost active agency in the construction of his image. In fact, even his attempts at royal spectacle played against him. His body escaped him and became the recipient of his subjects' animosity—metaphorically at first, and physically eventually through his assassination. Because of this, all of the alchemical associations of power and generation found in the body of François I were lost. The hermaphrodite became a parody of what a unified, abundant, strong state should be. The hermaphroditic body politic of Henri III was divided, unreconciled, feminized, caricaturized, and it destroyed the state that the Valois dynasty had taken care to construct. While François I was a perfected alchemical being who surpassed nature, Henri III became a deviant being whose body was outside of the normal course of nature. Instead of François I's plentiful body, having both genders and becoming generative for himself and, by extension, for the state, the body of Henri III was neither male nor female, and this ambiguity, this unnatural transgression, only made him more sinful, more draining on his people.

These paradigmatic, yet incredibly particular, figures complicate the variances found in the collective imaginary and allow us to examine the heterogeneous paths through which history writes itself—they essentially shed light on the dialogue between a monarch's political intentions and the public's changing perception of authority. These various monstrous and transgressive bodies allowed for alternate governing epistemologies to occur. Through visual and textual productions, they became manifestations of political transformations and as meanings shifted, the definition of monstrous became porous.

Whether monstrosity was used as a wondrous quality aligned with structural power or whether monstrosity became a projected deformity meant to condemn fallibility, these bodies transgressed norms, and it is through their transgressions that they demonstrate how sovereigns manipulated imagery and public perception to their advantage—until the intellectual corporeal weapons they created turned against them.

References

Albèri, Eugenio, editor. *Relazioni degli ambasciatori veneti as Senato durante il secolo decimosesto*, 15 vols. Società editrice Fiorentina, 1839–63.
Alvarotto, Giulio. Letter to the Duke of Ferrara, Ercole II d'Este (1508–59). 18 April 1547. Archivio di Stato di Modena, Archivio segreto estense, Cancelleria ducale, Sezione estero, Carteggio ambasciatori, Francia, b. 24.
Bibliothèque nationale de France (BNF). Garde Robe (GR). Manuscrit français (MF) 2952 (215), n.a. 9189, dated 1530, 15v.
Carlino, Andrea. "Strani corpi. Come farsi une ragione dei mostri nel XVI secolo." *Phantastische Lebensräume, Phantome und Phantasmen*, edited by H. K. Schmutz, Basilisken-Press, 1997, pp. 143–59.
Céard, Jean. *La nature et les prodiges: l'insolite au XVIe siècle, en France*. Droz, 1996.
Chenoweth, Katie. "The Force of a Law: Derrida, Montaigne, and the Edict of Villers-Cotterêts (1539)." *The Comparatist*, vol. 36, May 2012, pp. 67–85.
Crawford, Katherine. "Catherine de Medicis and the Performance of Political Motherhood." *The Sixteenth Century Journal*, vol. 31, no. 3, Autumn 2000, pp. 643–73.
Colombo, Realdo. *De re anatomica – Libri XV*. Nicholas Bevilacqua, 1559.

Daston, Lorraine, and Katharine Park, "Hermaphrodite in Renaissance France." *Critical Matrix*, vol. 1, no. 5, 1985, pp. 1–19.

Daston, Lorraine, and Katharine Park. *Wonders and the Order of Nature 1150–1750*. Zone Books, 1998.

Devun, Leah. "The Jesus Hermaphrodite: Science and Sex Difference in Premodern Europe." *Journal of the History of Ideas*, vol. 69 no. 2, 2018, pp. 193–219.

Duval, Jacques. *Traité des hermaphrodits – Parties genitals, accouchemens des femmes, etc. Où sont expliquez la figure des laboureurs & verger du genre humain, signes de pucelag, defloration, conception, & la belle industrie don't use Nature en la promotion du concept & plante prolifique*. 1612. Isidore Lisieux, 1880.

Federmann, Reinhard. *The Royal Art of Alchemy*. Chilton, 1969.

Fernández-Armesto, Felipe. *The Canary Islands after the Conquest: The Making of a Colonial Society in the Early Sixteenth Century*. Oxford University Press, 1982.

Ffolliott, Sheila. "Casting a Rival into the Shade: Catherine de'Medici and Diane de Poitiers." *Art Journal*, vol. 48, no. 2, Summer 1989, pp. 138–43.

Findlen, Paula. *Possessing Nature – Museums, Collecting, and Scientific Culture in Early Modern Italy*. University of California Press, 1994.

Foucault, Michel. *Abnormal*. Edited by Valerio Marchetti and Antonella Salomoni. Translated by Graham Burchell, Picador, 1999.

Laqueur, Thomas. *Making Sex: Body and Gender from the Greeks to Freud*. Harvard University Press, 1990.

Lodge, R. Anthony. *French: From Dialect to Standard*. Routledge, 1993.

Long, Kathleen. *Hermaphrodites in Renaissance Europe*. Routledge, 2016.

Meyer, Barbara Hochstetler. "Marguerite de Navarre and the Androgynous Portrait of François Ier." *Renaissance Quarterly*, vol. 48, no. 2, Summer 1995, pp. 287–325.

Moes, Robert J., and C. D. O'Malley. "Realdo Colombo: 'On Those Things Rarely Found in Anatomy' an Annotated Translation from the De Re Anatomica (1559)." *Bulletin of the History of Medicine*, vol. 34, no. 6, 1960, pp. 508–28.

Nummedal, Tara. *Alchemy and Authority in the Holy Roman Empire*. The University of Chicago Press, 2007.

Paré, Ambroise. *Des monstres et prodiges*. Gabriel Buon, 1585.

Riolan, Jean. *Discours sur les hermaphrodits où il est demonstré contre l'opinion commune, qu'il n'y a point de vrays hermaphrodits*. Pierre Ramier, 1614.

Smith, Norman R. "Portentous Births and the Monstrous Imagination in Renaissance Culture." *Marvels, Monsters, and Miracles – Studies in the Medieval and Early Modern Imaginations*, edited by Timothy S. Jones and David A. Sprunger, Medieval Institute Publications, 2002, pp. 267–83.

Symcox, Geoffrey Giovanna Rabitti, and Peter D. Diehl, editors. *Italian Reports on America 1493–1522 – Letters, Dispatches, and Papal Bulls*. Repertorium Colombianum X. Brepols Publishers, 2001.

Tallett, Frank and D. J. B. Trim, editors. *European Warfare, 1350–1750*. Cambridge UP, 2010.

Thomson, Rosemarie Garland. *Extraordinary Bodies: Figuring Physical Disability in American Culture and Literature*. Columbia University Press, 1997.

Waddington, Raymond B. "The Bisexual Portrait of Francis I: Fontainebleau, Castiglione, and the tone of Courtly Mythology." *Playing with Gender: A Renaissance Pursuit*, edited by Jean Brink, Maryann C. Horowitz, and Allison P. Coudert, University of Illinois Press, 1991, pp. 99–132.

Walker, Anita M., and Edmund H. Dickerman, "The King Who Would Be Man: Henri III, Gender Identity and the Murder at Blois, 1588." *Historical Reflections/Réflexions historiques*, vol. 24, no. 2, Summer 1998, pp. 253–81.

Walton, Michael T., Robert Fineman, and Phyllis J. Walton. "Of Monsters and Prodigies: The Interpretation of Birth Defects in the Sixteenth Century." *American Journal of Medical Genetics*, vol. 47, no. 1, 1993, pp. 7–13.

Waquet, Françoise. *Le latin ou l'empire d'un signe – XVIe-XXe siècle*. Albin Michel, 1998.

Zacchia Romanu, Pauli, totius status ecclesiastici proto-medici generalis. *Quaestionum medico-legalium, tomi tres. Editio prima Veneta, Lugdunensi & Noribergensi, quae passim soedis scatebant erroribus multò emendiator: Accedunt Interpolationes, & Auctaria ex novis Inventis & Observationibus Recentiorum Auctorum. Curà Joannis Danielis Horstii, Diversorum S.R.I. Principum Archiatri, & Collegii Medici Moeno-Francofurtani Senioris. Opus omnibus medicinae et juris utriusque peritis, Necnon Tribunalium (Ecclesiastici, Civilis) Assessoribus maximè necessarium*. Bonifacii Viezzeri, 1737.

Zapperi, Roberto. *Il selvaggio gentiluomo – L'incredibile storia di Pedro Gonzalez e dei suoi figli*. Donzelli Editore, 2005.

Zorach, Rebecca. *Blood, Milk, Ink, Gold – Abundance and Excess in the French Renaissance*. The University of Chicago Press, 2005.

8

"Maybe Something I Never Wanted Will Be Born"

Etgar Keret's Monstrous Dream of Motherhood

Elisa Carandina

"*My imagination, unbidden, possessed and guided me, gifting the successive images that arose in my mind.*"

Mary Shelley, *Introduction to Frankenstein*

"*Tu sei giovane, Issione, ma sei nato sotto il vecchio destino. Per te non esistono mostri ma soltanto compagni.*"

Cesare Pavese, *Dialoghi con Leucò*[1]

"*We are all Frankensteins, or monsters.*"

Fred Botting, Limits *of Horror: Technology, Bodies, Gothic*[2]

Introduction

Inspired by Mary Shelley's *Frankenstein*, Chloe Dewe Mathews has recently developed an artistic project titled *In Search of Frankenstein – Mary Shelley's Nightmare*.[3] In the exhibition and in the photo book, the so-called Geneva notebook by Mary Shelley is reproduced together with Mathews's photographs of a location in the Swiss Alps not far from the place where the reverie of Shelley became *Frankenstein* the novel during the summer of 1816.[4] Upon her discovery of the story of the summer of 1816 (the "year

---

[1] "You are young, Issione, but you were born under the old destiny. For you there are no monsters but only companions." Cesare Pavese. *Dialoghi con Leucò*. Einaudi, 2014.
[2] Fred Botting. *Making Monstrous: Frankenstein, Criticism, Theory*. Manchester University Press, 1991.
[3] Under the same title there is an exhibition and a photo book published by Kodoji Press in 2018: http://www.chloedewemathews.com/in-search-of-frankenstein/.
[4] Regarding the circumstances and the landscape in which Mary Shelley wrote and set *Frankenstein*, see Hitchcock 15–73 and Randel.

without summer" that kept Mary Shelley and the rest of the famous group of people to which she also belonged inside a villa on the Geneva lake), Matthews explains in the introduction to her book that she took a trip to the Giétroz glacier and to the nuclear bunkers around Verbier. The geographical context surrounding Frankenstein, the book as well as the creature who is often wrongly referred to by this same name, became a way for the photographer to reengage with "human folly and hubris of the (mis)use of knowledge (science) to control and dominate nature," as stated by Paul Goodwin (177). However, Mathews's project also tells the story of another form of "(mis)use of knowledge": another illegitimate appropriation with some additional precisions. The reproduction of the first of the two manuscripts conserved at the Bodleian Library and, more precisely, the one written between August and early December 1816, clearly shows Percy Shelley's revisions. Even if this appropriation of Mary Shelley's text was authorized by her, a look at her future husband's editing immediately evokes the idea of manipulation and appropriation. As highlighted by Anne K. Mellor in a summary of her research findings, in his attempt at editing the text "Percy Shelley on several occasions distorted the meaning of his wife's text" (14).[5] This betrayal of Mary Shelley's words as a (legitimized) form of a manipulation is especially relevant in the context of a text that problematizes the human and, more precisely, the male use of science. It is also an appropriate introduction to my reading of what I consider a postmodern rewriting of Mary Shelley's *Frankenstein* in contemporary Hebrew literature.

Frankenstein and the "Circumvention of the Maternal"

The tension between female authorship, on the one hand, and procreation by a man alone, on the other hand, has been fully developed in the feminist literary approaches to *Frankenstein* exploring the process leading to the creation of the monster as a violation of boundaries (regardless of whether these borders are metaphorical or not).[6] Following Mary Shelley's definition of her revised novel as a "hideous progeny,"[7] particular emphasis has been put on the opposition between creation and procreation. Among the different approaches, the text has also been read through the lens of what Margaret Homans defines as Shelley's protest against the circumvention of the maternal, namely "the circumvention of the maternal creation of new beings by the narcissistic creations of male desire" (114).[8] In the novel *Frankenstein*, the circumvention of the maternal leads to a double violation of boundaries due to the fact that Victor Frankenstein uses his scientific knowledge to create life, thus taking the place both of the gods and of

---

[5] Mellor (2003). See also Mellor (1988), Shelley, and Robinson (2016).
[6] For a feminist reading of *Frankenstein*, see Botting; Brooks; Covi; Cronan Rose; Gilbert and Gubar 213–47; Hodges; Hoeveler (1998); Hoeveler (2003); Homans; Jacobus; Johnson; Knoepflmacher; London; Mellor (2003); Mellor (1998); Moers; Mously; Mulvey Roberts; Poovey; Sherwin; and Spivak.
[7] I am citing appendix C from the 1831 edition of the text.
[8] See also the chapter "Usurping the Female" in Mellor (1998), pp. 115–26.

the woman in a Promethean act of hubris. In this respect, Mary Shelley's critique of science and of "the dangers inherent in the use of [. . .] gendered metaphors in the seventeenth-century scientific revolution" (Mellor 89) has been more specifically approached from the perspective of what Homans defines as Adam's desire in Milton and Shelley. According to Homans,

> Created to the specification of Adam's desire [...], Eve is, like Frankenstein's demon, the product of imaginative desire. Milton appropriates the maternal by excluding any actual mother from the scene of creation. Eve is the form that Adam's desire takes once actual motherhood has been eliminated; and in much the same way, the demon is the form taken by Frankenstein's desire once his mother and Elizabeth as mother have been circumvented. These new creations in the image of the self are substitutes for the powerful creating mother and place creation under the control of the son. (105)

This male imaginative desire belongs to "the recurring fantasy of a child born from man alone," in the words of Rosi Braidotti (87). From this perspective, the monster is the result of an attempt at the reproduction of the same, at the reflection of the self. Moreover, the circumvention of the maternal affects the moment that has been historically considered the necessary starting point of teratology as discipline: its origin. As underscored by Georges Canguilhem,[9] when the scientific discourse about monsters became a discipline, the conception of monsters became the main issue. In the history of teratology, the question is always how such monstrous creatures can be conceived.[10]

Etgar Keret's "Horsie"

In order to explore some aspects of the unauthorized appropriation of the creation/procreation process mentioned earlier, I will address the question of the monster's origin and nature through the lens of a short story written by the Israeli author Etgar Keret (1967–) "Horsie," originally published in 2002 and translated by Miriam Shlesinger and Sondra Silverston in 2005 in the collection titled in English *The Nimrod Flipout*. Keret is a major figure in the literary canon of contemporary Hebrew literature. He is internationally renowned not only for his short stories but also for his graphic novels in addition to his scriptwriting for television and film. His reception is summarized as follows by Yigal Schwartz (2017b): "In a short time, Etgar Keret became an Israeli cultural hero and is considered someone who expresses in a sharp and colorful way the mood of his generation and the next" (427).[11] The critical approach to Keret's

---

[9] See Canguilhem.
[10] Regarding the notion of monster, the works that are relevant for the present contribution are as follows: Causi; Charlier; Cohen; Gaster; Hensel-Mittman; Marchesini; and Palese.
[11] For a full list of his works, excerpts and some additional bibliographical references, see these websites: http://www.etgarkeret.com (his page on the website of the Institute for the Translation

literary production, and especially to his short stories, has been mainly developed with respect to its contribution to postmodern literature and, in particular, to the possibility of a "true" Hebrew postmodern and post-Zionist literature.[12] In this respect, Keret is considered one of the leading voices of the postmodern wave in Hebrew literature, at least among the scholars who consider this possibility.

Like Mary Shelley's *Frankenstein*, Keret's "Horsie" explores the monstrous consequences of trying to control the procreation process from a male point of view. Not only is the theme of the creation/procreation of the monster as circumvention of the maternal at the core of "Horsie," but I would also suggest reading this short story as a postmodern rewriting of Mary Shelley's *Frankenstein*. In order to describe Keret's postmodern variation of the fantasy of a child born from man alone, I will start from the end. After evaluating the successfulness of this attempt, I will then explore in detail the literary strategies employed in the short story. Assuming that the father is conducting an experiment whose goal is the procreation of a son as the "product of imaginative desire," I will first address his opinion about the results of this process in an effort to assess if he was ultimately satisfied with these outcomes from the point of view of the father-creator. In a private moment shared with his son before putting him to sleep, every night the anonymous father remarks: "Too bad [. . .] too bad Mom couldn't dream a dream that might've come true, too" (Keret, *The Nimrod Flipout* 104).[13] These few words allow the son to be defined as the successful fulfillment of the father's dream. Some regrets notwithstanding, the son is defined as the concretization of the father's fantasies as opposed to the mother's wishes. The latter are defined as not being powerful enough to affect the newborn. From the father's perspective, the mother could not dream a dream that is able to shape the baby. By defining the son as belonging exclusively to the paternal side, the father can assume and claim for himself the role of Victor Frankenstein, speculating like him about the fact that his offspring will consider him as its creator and source because the creature owes its being only and exclusively to him. Given that the process of circumvention of the maternal has been successfully achieved, it is then the process itself and its outcome that need to be analyzed.

In "Horsie," the creation of a son that belongs to the father starts with the fear of what has been considered another form of monstrosity: the mother's body. Due to the fact that it is a body that does not provide a fixed bodily form, Rosi Braidotti defines it as "morphologically dubious" (Braidotti 80). This perspective emphasizes the in-betweenness associated with the maternal body at the core of the speculations regarding the notion of abjection and the consistent approach to maternal bodies and powers. In this respect, monstrosity is clearly associated with the in-betweenness as

---

of Hebrew Literature) http://www.ithl.org.il/page_13212 (the website of the Bio-Bibliographical Lexicon of Modern Hebrew Literature) https://library.osu.edu/projects/hebrew-lexicon/00226.php.

[12] Regarding postmodernism in Keret, see Abadi; Balaban; Bejerano; Chodnovsky; Gurevich 287–304; Katsman 2005a, b, 71–97, 2013; Mendelson-Maoz (1996); Mendelson-Maoz (2018); Mendelson-Maoz (1997); Peleg 64–9; Shklovsky; Schwartz; Taub 9–21, 137–47; and Tzivoni.

[13] See p. 72 from the original Hebrew text.

a violation of boundaries, both by excess and by lack in Braidotti's words: "Woman/mother is monstrous by excess; she transcends established norms and transgresses boundaries. She is monstrous by lack: woman/mother does not possess the substantive unity of the masculine subject" (Braidotti 83).[14]

Keret's analysis of the fear triggered by the mother's body is expressed by the boyfriend's reactions to his girlfriend's pregnancy. More precisely, it is what is perceived from the boyfriend's point of view as the unbalance between them that is immediately put forward, as shown by the following conversation between the anonymous couple:

> "You're freaking out." She laughed. "Look how you're sweating." "Sure I'm freaking out," he said, trying to laugh too. "It's easy for you, you have a uterus, but me, you know me, I get uptight even when there's no reason and now that there is." "I'm scared too," she said, wrapping herself around him. "Forget it," he said, and hugged her. "It'll all work out in the end, you'll see. If it's a boy, I'll teach him how to play soccer, and if it's a girl—you know what, it wouldn't hurt her either." Then she cried a little and he comforted her, and then she fell asleep and he didn't. Far back, deep inside him, he could feel his hemorrhoids opening one by one like flowers in springtime. (Keret, *The Nimrod Flipout* 101–2)[15]

The fear of the mother's powers and body takes the form of a uterus envy. However, in the English translation, the two words that the boyfriend uses to address his girlfriend at the beginning of their conversation are left out: *yah zonah*, "yo bitch." The original Hebrew text clearly illustrates the aggressive and insulting verbal reaction to the hybridity of the pregnant girlfriend's body. This body excites and frustrates the father's imagination because he can only speculate about the outcomes of a process that he feels is completely beyond his control. As the following passage clarifies,

> At first, when there was no belly yet, he tried not to think about it, not that it helped, but at least it gave him something to aim for. Later, when she started to show a little, he began to imagine it sitting there in her stomach, a pocket-size little asshole in a shiny three-piece suit. And really, how could he know that it wouldn't be born a little shit because kids, they're like Russian roulette, you never know in advance what you'll end up with. (Keret, *The Nimrod Flipout* 102)[16]

The biggest fear of the main character is that something he never wanted will be born. Lost in his fears, he resolves to ask the advice of his great-grandmother who seems to be the only one up to the task in his opinion. Surrounded by maternal figures who know better than him how to manage the situation, the father-to-be desperately needs a way to claim a role in the whole process and to avoid the birth of something that

---

[14] See Braidotti; Kristeva, and Leitao 48.
[15] See p. 69 in the original Hebrew text.
[16] See pp. 69–70 in the original Hebrew text.

might not be what he wants. In this regard, it is indeed from his great-grandmother that he finds a solution to his problems:

> "At night, wait till she falls asleep, and then lie with your head right up against her belly, so that all your dreams move straight into it." He nodded, even though he didn't really understand, but the great-grandmother explained, "A dream is nothing but a strong wish. So strong that you can't even put it into words. Now, the fetus, which is in her belly, has no opinions about anything, so he'll sop it right up. Whatever you dream, that's exactly what will be." (Keret, *The Nimrod Flipout* 103)[17]

It is only through his imagination that he can control his girlfriend's pregnancy and affect the outcome, directing the development of the fetus using his imaginative powers. The well-known dichotomy between a biological, bodily, and maternal birth and a figurative second birth that is intellectual, spiritual, and fatherly becomes a paradoxical variation on Frankenstein's theme in Keret's short story. The boyfriend's claim on his fatherhood can be indeed likened to Victor Frankenstein's aforementioned desire to create a "new species" that will see in him a creator, a source and a father. The allusion to the scientist's attempt to circumvent the maternal by using his knowledge and imagination is confirmed by a small detail in Keret's short story. The great-grandmother gives the main character the critical piece of advice while she is watching an episode of a television series. To be more precise, she is watching a scene where a character named "Victor" confesses to a woman wrapped in a towel that he is her "real" father. This little hint of the character's name reinforcing the looming presence of Shelley's novel is thus hidden in this soap opera version of *Mater semper certa est, pater numquam*.

Through the great-grandmother's voice, a genealogy of women gives the father a way to take control of the situation. The idea of controlling the development of the fetus through dreams, of making the newborn an expression or, more correctly, a reflection of the father's wishes, gives the father's character all the power he needs to realize the flight from the feminine, and particularly from the "monstrous power of the maternal imagination and desire [that] lies at the heart of the recurring fantasy of a child born from man alone" (Braidotti 87). It is precisely this combination of the father's imagination and desire that is used to control the development of the fetus, emphasizing the circumvention of the maternal as brainization of the procreation process, as in the birth of Athena form Zeus's brain.

Reassured by the great-grandmother's trick, the father-to-be finally calms down. Even if he does not remember his dreams, he is confident that the outcome will be precisely what he wants excluding from the process the woman who in the meantime has become his wife. As the following passage demonstrates,

> After that, he slept every night with his head right next to her belly, which was getting bigger all the time. He didn't remember the dreams, but he was willing

---

[17] See p. 71 in the original Hebrew text.

to swear they were good ones. And he couldn't remember a time in his life when he'd slept that way, so peacefully, he didn't even get up to pee. His wife didn't really understand that funny position she found him in every morning but was happy to see him relaxed again and he stayed relaxed the whole way, right to the delivery room. (Keret, *The Nimrod Flipout* 103)

What could possibly go wrong? As a figure emanating from his imagination, the soon-to-be-born baby can only be the fulfillment of his wishes, or the perfect accomplishment of his desires. However, a little surprise awaits the two parents:

> In the end, they had a little horse. More accurately, a pony. They called him Hemi, after a successful industrialist whose glitzy TV appearances had impressed the great-grandmother, and they raised him with lots of love. On Saturdays, they rode him to the park and played all kinds of games with him, mainly cowboys and Indians. The truth is that after the birth, she was depressed for a long time, and even though they never talked about it, he knew that no matter how much she loved Hemi, deep in her heart, she wanted something different. (Keret, *The Nimrod Flipout* 103–4)[18]

A pony. That's what the father wanted and what the father gets—but not what the mother nor the perplexed obstetrician, nurses, and the doctor expected. He gets his "hideous progeny," a horse born from a woman. Actually, it is not really even a horse. It is a pony that his wife calls a midget, after consulting with a great deal of specialists who said that it would never really grow.

This is a double violation, just like the one committed by Victor Frankenstein, because it destroys nature in the attempt to circumvent the maternal. First of all, there is the violation of the mother's body and desire, the illegitimate appropriation of her space. Consequently, there is the violation of nature and the birth of a de-humanized offspring as a consequence of the satisfaction of male desire. Moreover, the pony as a reflection of the self can also be considered in the context of what Yigal Schwartz defines as the Yom Kippur literary generation to which Keret belongs (215–34). Schwartz employs this expression to describe the group of authors born in the 1950s whose literary production shares many of the same stylistic and thematic elements. These authors also share many common foundational experiences:

> Childhood in the first and/or second decade of a young, pioneering, and optimistic country, on the one hand, and life against the background of Holocaust trauma, on the other. [. . .] Other foundational experiences are the Six-Day War, which broke out in the transitional period between their childhood and adolescence (for a large part of this group, this war overlapped with their bar or bat mitzvah ceremonies), and the Yom Kippur War, which comprised a transitional link between their adolescence and maturity. (Schwartz, "Our Shadows and Ourselves" 3)

---

[18] See p. 71 from the original Hebrew text.

According to Schwartz, one of the characteristics of the literary production of the Yom Kippur generation is the "dark twin/light twin syndrome." This is namely the fictional presence of a double, a child, or a boy, considered as the real or imagined brother of the main character. This brother can either be a "light twin," the chosen one, the favorite, or the "dark one," the one who is abandoned: an outcast.

From this perspective, Keret's protagonist dreams of a companion to play with. In a world where monsters no longer exist because they are merely companions (as Pavese's quote suggests), the monster is a harmless boy's dream come true. The sleep that produces monsters is no longer the sleep of reason; it is simply a normal sleep that produces the remedy to the boy's loneliness. And all this is somehow perfectly normal.

Etgar Keret's Grotesque

The paternity theme in Keret's works has already been approached with respect to the representation of masculinity and to the role of the artist, which sometimes involves the personal experiences of Keret as a father.[19] However, it is not my intention to develop this topic from a sociocultural perspective, nor to address its implications in terms of ars poetica. Instead, I intend to focus on the literary strategies displayed in "Horsie" in order to explore the creation of the monster theme from the point of view of both the postmodern grotesque and the postmodern rewriting of Shelley's *Frankenstein*. According to Orley K. Marron's explanation of Keret's fantastic reality, we should consider it as belonging to Eric Rabkin's definition of fantasy, namely the presence of a violation of the laws of nature governing the world as we know it incorporated into the context of a story (Marron 87). This use of fantasy is precisely what defines the grotesque as a dynamic that needs to take place in the world as we know it in order to create its disorientating effect that comes from the confusion between real and unreal, as noted by Philip Thomson.[20] Exploring the use of the grotesque in Keret's works, Adia Mendelson-Maoz suggests reading them as a form of "the literature of extreme situations," as defined by Reuven Tzur (Mendelson-Maoz, "Extreme Situation" 269–72). According to Mendelson-Maoz, Tzur combines Robert Denoon Cumming's and Jean-Paul Sartre's approaches and defines this literature as the combination of three elements: the description of extreme situations on the plot level, a contradictory vision on the structural level (e.g., the usage of incompatible perspectives), and an emotional reaction of anguish and discomfort in the minds of readers confronted with the two elements mentioned earlier. From a critical point of view, these kinds of works are often characterized by their irreducibility to a single, noncontradictory interpretative line. Taking examples from the first two collections of short stories published by Keret

---

[19] See Kubovy; Marron; Mendelson-Maoz (2018), and Shemtov.
[20] For a more comprehensive definition of the grotesque, see Bakhtin; Bloom; Edwards and Graulund; Kayser, and Thomson.

in 1992 and 1994, Mendelson-Maoz shows how in his works the horrendous and the grotesque are to be considered as belonging to the literature of extreme situations.

This usage of the grotesque changes radically in the collection of short stories *The Nimrod Flipout*, which I consider to be a major step in the literary production of the Israeli author toward the postmodern grotesque. As already pointed out by Miri Kubovy regarding the topic of madness, *The Nimrod Flipout* is a major turning point compared to Keret's earlier works: what previously was the individual uncanny answer to reality becomes then the norm. Keret's readers are used to his protagonists being regularly confronted with a system that they systematically defy by breaking its rules. However, for the first time, they witness what Kubovy interprets as follows: "Rather than breaking the ordinary by a strange, or a seemingly insane act, by injecting to it life and originality, victory and heroism are achieved by turning the crazy, and the insane into ordinary norms, creating a new standard of ordinariness and normalcy; normalizing lunacy for the sake of emotional and cognitive survival" (Kubovy 107). Keret's use of the grotesque in this collection is consistently postmodern in its creation of a world where "the freak is the norm" in the words of Angela Carter (Carter 111). The grotesque element that previously—with respect both to Keret's literary production and to its non-postmodern use—was a tool to stress the violation of norms thus becomes the norm reconfiguring its usual dynamic. From this perspective, Wolfgang Kayser's description of the grotesque's effect as the loss of the reliability of the world instilling a "fear of life" (Kayser 184) becomes the description of the "normal," or the everyday. This postmodern normalization of the grotesque problematizes the dichotomy between nature and culture, the acceptable and unacceptable, the appropriate and inappropriate. With respect to the specific context of Israel, this same issue has been approached from the perspective of the realism found in the works of another Israeli author frequently associated with Etgar Keret in descriptions of the debated postmodern wave in Hebrew literature. Effectively summarizing this view, Todd Hasak-Lowy ponders, "This time Orly Castel-Bloom writes in a realist fashion, or is it that our reality has become Castel-Bloomian?" (100). However, instead of focusing on the socio-literary dimension of the grotesque dynamic and its relevance with respect to the postmodern grotesque, I will further explore the normalcy of the monster in Keret's world with the aim of developing some remarks concerning the consequences of this vision of the postmodern grotesque related to the nature of the monster.

What Is Monstrous in Keret's Monster?

The monster as well as the grotesque have been defined according to their incongruity and hybridity. However, in Keret's "Horsie," the monster not only is no longer characterized by hybridity but is also made "normal" by the postmodern grotesque. The pony is not monstrous in and of itself: it becomes monstrous only if it is considered to be born from a woman. Its birth is not monstrous in itself; it is the intervention of the father that makes it monstrous. It is thus the father's desire that is monstrous. The problem is not his desire in itself (the father himself ignores what he dreams about every night), but rather his claim to an exclusive parenthood that excludes the mother from the process. A monstrous desire of reflection of the self dehumanizes the newborn, making the birth both inhuman and illegitimate. At the same time, it is the perfect fulfillment of a father's dream, a manifestation and concretization of a male desire that is entirely autoreferential and parodically literal. According to John Ruskin's definition, it is the true grotesque because it comes from the father's creative imagination. As Ruskin theorizes,

> Now observe how in all this, through every separate part and action of the creature, the imagination is *always* right. It evidently *cannot* err. [. . .] So it is throughout art, and in all that the imagination does; if anything be wrong it is not the imagination's fault, but some inferior faculty's, which would have its foolish say in the matter, and meddled with the imagination. (105)

Hemi is a grotesque monster not in itself, but only if put into a context. The postmodern grotesque is part of a postmodern rewriting of Shelley's *Frankenstein*. Thus, the veritable force of its parody can only be appreciated if it is read in respect to Victor Frankenstein's attempt to circumvent the maternal. More precisely, it has to be considered alongside Lynda Hutcheon's notion of repetition with difference in the context of postmodern literature. In the world of texts in which postmodernist literature places both its ironic rupture and connection with the past, "We can only 'know' (as opposed to 'experience') the world through our narratives (past and present) of it, or so postmodernism argues" (Hutcheon, *A Poetics of Postmodernism* 128). Only a reading of "Horsie" as a parodical version of Shelley's *Frankenstein* allows us to access Hemi's monstrous nature. In this vein, a comparison with another classic monster myth will clarify the postmodern nature of Hemi's monstrosity.

According to one of the numerous versions of the Centauri myth, their race originates from the transgressive desires of Ixion who attacked and tried to rape Hera. Hera's husband, Zeus, formed a figure of Hera out of a cloud and sent it to him. Lying with the cloud, Ixion conceived the so-called Centaurs. In one version of the story, they are shaped like men. In another variation of the myth, Centaurs are human-horse hybrids.[21] The context in which the Centaurs are born is defined by Ixion's desire and attempted rape, a desire that manifests itself as completely autoreferential to the point that the real object of desire (i.e., Hera) is replaced by a cloud, something that could be imagined as assuming any shape or form. A cloud can take the desired shape, similar to Keret's fetus. The outcome, or the offspring, is monstrous in both cases. Nonetheless, there is a major difference. In the story of the Centaurs, the monstrous is a classical half-man, half-horse hybrid that thus defies traditional boundaries. In Keret's fiction, the monster is no longer a hybrid; it is fully something else and this is somehow "normal." The father considers him his son and takes care of him exactly as he would have done

---

[21] See Angelino and Salvaneschi; Dubois; Dumézil; Gallé; Gendrat-Claudel; Gourmelen; Padgett; and Scobie.

with a son. Once the freak is the norm, the grotesque then becomes part of a daily routine. In this postmodern version of *Frankenstein*, the monster is normalized both regarding his "nature" and in the manner in which he is treated. Keret's monster loses his hybridity, and his unique vision of the grotesque makes the uncanny something ordinary.

Conclusion

The fear of the monstrosity associated with the mother, with her body, and with her power as a desiring agent thus becomes the monstrosity of the father's desire to bypass it or deny it entirely. The father strives to make the newborn his and only his, to leave his mark on him, and to shape him as only he sees fit. It is precisely the attempt to avoid the birth of something that the protagonist might not want that generates the monster. Moreover, it is the fear of the hybridity that creates something terrifying in its belonging exclusively and absolutely to someone and to something, or more precisely, resembling too closely to someone and to someone's desire. Being the result of the protagonist's solipsistic desire, Hemi belongs neither to two species nor to two parents. He is just a "normal" pony sleeping on the hay on the floor of the nursery shaking his head from side to side as if he were listening to someone talking to him. Every once in a while, he even whines because of an especially funny dream (Keret, *The Nimrod Flipout* 104). The flight from maternal monstrosity and hybridity generates yet again a hideous progeny, a progeny that paradoxically and parodically belongs to the category of the monster due to its non-hybridity. It is a monstrous reflection of a narcissistic creation conceived by male desire. As in the myth of the Centaurs, what the hybrid monster represents by its refusal to belong to only one dimension is made explicit by Keret's pony belonging clearly and exclusively to only one world, the realm of the father's desire. Taking control of the monster as a hybrid produces the monster as a reflection of the father's deepest desire, as a reflection of the self aiming only at reproducing himself. The main character of Keret's "Horsie" creates in his image, concretizes his wishes, has a dream that frightfully as well as comically comes true—this is consistent with the notion of the grotesque defined as an unresolved conflict between a comic element and a terrifying one. And what does he really want? A pony.

References

Abadi, Adina. "Nonsense in the Works of Etgar Keret and Orly Castel-Bloom and Its Expression in Language [Hebrew]." *Helqat lashon*, vol. 40, 2009, pp. 55–72.
Angelino, Carlo, and Enrica Salvaneschi, editors. *Il Centauro (II), Synkrisis*. Il melangolo, 1986.
Bakhtin, Mikhail. *Rabelais and His World*. MIT Press, 1968.
Balaban, Abraham. *A New Wave in Hebrew Fiction: Postmodern Hebrew Fiction* [Hebrew]. Keter, 1995.

Bejerano, Ana Maria. "Etgar Keret: inhalaciones de normalidad en forma de Ventolin literario postmodernista." *Estudis Hebreus i Arameus*, vol. 24–5, 2002, pp. 43–8.
Bloom, Harold, editor. *The Grotesque*. Bloom's Literary Criticism, 2009.
Botting, Fred. *Making Monstrous: Frankenstein, Criticism, Theory*. Manchester University Press, 1991.
Braidotti, Rosi. *Nomadic Subjects: Embodiment and Sexual Difference in Contemporary Feminist Theory*. Columbia University Press, 1994.
Brooks, Peter. *Body Work: Objects of Desire in Modern Narrative*. Harvard University Press, 1993.
Canguilhem, Georges. *The Normal and the Pathological*. Translated by Carolyn R. Fawcett in collaboration with Robert S. Cohen, Zone Books, 1991.
Carter, Angela. *The Infernal Desire Machines of Doctor Hoffman*. Penguin, 1982.
Causi, Pietro Li. "Generazione di ibridi, generazione di donne. Costruzioni dell'umano in Aristotele e Galeno (e Palefato)." *Storia delle donne*, vol. 1, 2005, pp. 89–114.
Charlier, Philippe. *Les monstres humains dans l'Antiquité: analyse paléopathologique*. Fayard, 2008.
Chodnovsky, Liza. "Do Black Holes Exist? On Parody in the Short Stories of Orly Castel-Bloom and Etgar Keret [Hebrew]." *Iton 77*, vol. 48, 1998, pp. 24–9.
Cohen, Jeffrey Jerome, editor. *Monster Theory: Reading Culture*. University of Minnesota Press, 1996.
Covi, Giovanna. "The Matrushka Monster of Feminist Criticism." *Textus*, vol. 2, 1989, pp. 217–36.
Cronan Rose, E. "Custody Battles: Reproducing Knowledge about Frankenstein." *New Literary History*, vol. 26, 1995, pp. 800–32.
DuBois, Page. *Centaurs and Amazons: Women and the Pre-History of the Great Chain of Being*. University of Michigan Press, 1982.
Dumézil, Georges. *Le problème des centaures: étude de mythologie comparée indo-européenne*. P. Geuthner, 1929.
Edwards, Justin D., and Rune Graulund. *Grotesque*. Routledge, 2013.
Gallé, Hélène. "Avatars des Centaures: du Mythe à la Fantasy." *Strenæ*, vol. 8, 2015, http://journals.openedition.org/strenae/1364.
Gaster, Theodor H. "Monsters." *Encyclopedia of Religion*, edited by Lindsay Jones, Macmillan Reference USA, 2005, pp. 6163–6.
Gendrat-Claudel, Aurélie. "Dès le commencement ils furent une race noble et forte: Généalogies et métamorphoses des Centaures dans la littérature italienne." *Cahiers d'études romanes*, vol. 27, 2013, pp. 83–114.
Gilbert, Sandra M., and Susan Gubar. *The Madwoman in the Attic: The Woman Writer and the Nineteenth-Century Literary Imagination*. Yale University Press, 1979.
Goodwin, Paul. "In Search of Frankenstein; Or the Contemporary Prometheus." *In Search of Frankenstein. Mary Shelley's Nightmare*, edited by Chloe Dewe Mathews, Kodoji Press, 2018, pp. 177–82.
Gurevich, David. *Postmodernism, Culture, and the Literature at the End of the Twentieth Century*. (Hebrew). Dvir, 1997.
Hasak-Lowy, Todd. "Postzionism and Its Aftermath in Hebrew Literature: The Case of Orly Castel-Bloom." *Jewish Social Studies*, vol. 14, no. 2, 2008, pp. 86–112.
Hensel, Marcus, and Asa Simon Mittman, editors. *Classic Readings on Monster Theory Demonstrare, Volume One*. Project Muse Arc Humanities Press, 2018.
Hitchcock, Susan Tyler. *Frankenstein: A Cultural History*. W.W. Norton, 2007.

Hodges, Devon. "Frankenstein and the Feminine Subversion of the Novel." *Tulsa Studies in Women's Literature*, vol. 2, no. 2, 1983, pp. 155–64.
Hoeveler, Diane Long. "Frankenstein, Feminism, and Literary Theory." *The Cambridge Companion to Mary Shelley*, edited by Esther H. Schor, Cambridge University Press, 2003, pp. 45–62.
Hoeveler, Diane Long. *Gothic Feminism: The Professionalization of Gender from Charlotte Smith to the Brontës*. Pennsylvania State University Press, 1998.
Homans, Margaret. "Bearing Demons: Frankenstein's Circumvention of the Maternal." *Bearing the Word: Language and Female Experience in Nineteenth-Century Women's Writing*, edited by Margaret Homans, University of Chicago Press, 1986, pp. 100–19.
Hutcheon, Linda. *A Poetics of Postmodernism: History, Theory, Fiction*. Routledge, 1988.
Jacobus, Mary. "Is There a Woman in this Text?" *New Literary History*, vol. 14, no. 1, 1982, pp. 117–41.
Johnson, Barbara. "My Monster/My Self." *Diacritics*, vol. 12, 1982, pp. 2–10.
Katsman, Roman. "Etgar Keret: The Minimal Metaphysical Origin." *Symposium: A Quarterly Journal in Modern Literatures*, vol. 67, no. 4, 2013, pp. 189–204.
Katsman, Roman. "Nostalgia for the Myth: Personality, Ethics and Ideology in the Etgar Keret's Postmodern Mythopoiesis [Hebrew]." *Mikan*, vol. 4, 2005, pp. 20–41.
Katsman, Roman. *Poetics of Becoming: Dynamic Processes of Mythopoesis in Modern and Postmodern Hebrew and Slavic Literature*. Lang, 2005.
Kayser, Wolfgang Johannes. *The Grotesque in Art and Literature*. Indiana University Press, 1963.
Keret, Etgar. *Anihu*. Zmora Bitan, 2002.
Keret, Etgar. *The Nimrod Flipout*. Chatto & Windus, 2005.
Knoepflmacher, Ulrich Camillus "Thoughts on the Aggression of Daughters." *The Endurance of Frankenstein: Essays on Mary Shelley's Novel*, edited by George Lewis Levine and U.C. Knoepflmacher, University of California Press, 1979, pp. 88–119.
Kristeva, Julia. *Powers of Horror: An Essay on Abjection*. Columbia University Press, 1982.
Kubovy, Miri. "Make the Familiar Strange, and the Strange Familiar: Fatso and Other Compromises of Etgar Keret." *Tre generazioni di scrittori a confront*, edited by Yigal Schwartz and Gabriella Moscati Steindler, Editoriale Scientifica, pp. 99–110.
Laurent, Gourmelen. "Imposture ou dualité: que faut-il penser de la naissance d'un centaure? Sur un curieux passage du Banquet des Sept Sages (Plutarque, Moralia, 149 C-F)." *L'imposture dans la littérature: Cahier XXXIV*, edited by Arlette Bouloumié, Presses Universitaires de Rennes, 2011, pp. 217–34.
Leitao, David D. *The Pregnant Male as Myth and Metaphor in Classical Greek Literature*. Cambridge University Press, 2012.
London, Bette. "Mary Shelley, Frankenstein, and the Spectacle of Masculinity." *Publications of the Modern Language Association of America*, vol. 108, no. 2, 1993, pp. 253–67.
Marchesini, Roberto. *Post-human: verso nuovi modelli di esistenza*. Bollati Boringhieri, 2002.
Marron, Orley K. "Etgar Keret's Fantastic Reality." *With Both Feet on the Clouds: Fantasy in Israeli Literature*, edited by Danielle Gurevitch et al., Academic Studies Press, 2013, pp. 87–111.
Mathews, Chloe Dewe. *In Search of Frankenstein-Mary Shelley's Nightmare*. Kodoji Press, 2018.

Mellor, K. Anne. "'Making a Monster': An Introduction to Frankenstein." *The Cambridge Companion to Mary Shelley*, edited by Esther H. Schor, Cambridge University Press, 2003, pp. 9–25.

Mellor, K. Anne. *Mary Shelley, Her Life, Her Fiction, Her Monsters*. Methuen, 1988.

Mendelson-Maoz, Adia. "Extreme Situation—Horrendous and Grotesque—in the Works of Castel-Bloom and Keret [Hebrew]." *Dapim: Research in Literature*, vol. 11, 1997, pp. 269–95.

Mendelson-Maoz, Adia. "Keret's 'Living-Dead' and the Sacrifice of Israeli Masculinity." *BGU Review- A Journal of Israeli Culture*, Winter 2018, https://in.bgu.ac.il/en/hekshe rim/Pages/bgur2018.aspx. Accessed Mar. 20, 2019.

Mendelson-Maoz, Adia. "Possible Worlds in the Works of Orly Castel-Bloom and Etgar Keret [Hebrew]." *Alei Siah*, vol. 38, 1996, pp. 39–64.

Moers, Ellen. *Literary Women*. Doubleday, 1976.

Mously, Andy. "The Posthuman." *The Cambridge Companion to Frankenstein*, edited by Andrew Smith, Cambridge University Press, 2016, pp. 158–72.

Mulvey Roberts, Marie. "The Corpse in the Corpus: Frankenstein, Rewriting Wollestonecraft and the Abject." *Mary Shelley's Fictions: From Frankenstein to Falkner*, edited by Michael Eberle-Sinatra, St. Martin's Press, 2000, pp. 197–210.

Padgett, Michael J., editor. *The Centaur's Smile: The Human Animal in Early Greek Art*. Princeton University Art Museum, 2003.

Palese, Emma. *Mostri, draghi e vampiri: dal meraviglioso totalizzante alla naturalizzazione delle differenze*. Mimesis, 2012.

Peleg, Yaron. *Israeli Culture between the Two Intifadas: A Brief Romance*. University of Texas Press, 2008.

Poovey, Mary. *The Proper Lady and the Woman Writer: Ideology as Style in the Works of Mary Wollstonecraft, Mary Shelley, and Jane Austen*. University of Chicago Press, 1984.

Randel, Fred V. "'Frankenstein,' Feminism, and the Intertextuality of Mountains." *Studies in Romanticism*, vol. 23, no. 4, 1984, pp. 515–32.

Robinson, Charles E. "Frankenstein. Its Composition and Publication." *The Cambridge Companion to Frankenstein*, edited by Andrew Smith, Cambridge University Press, 2016, pp. 13–25.

Ruskin, John. *The Complete Works of John Ruskin*, vol. III *Modern Painters*. Kelmscott Society, 1900.

Schwartz, Yigal. "'Our Shadows and Ourselves': The 'Yom Kippur Generation' in Israeli Fiction." *BGU Review- A Journal of Israeli Culture*, 2017a, https://in.bgu.ac.il/en/hekshe rim/Pages/2017.aspx. Accessed Mar. 20, 2019.

Schwartz, Yigal. "'A Story or a Bullet between the Eyes': Etgar Keret: Repetitiveness, Morality and Postmodernism." *Hebrew Studies*, vol. 58, 2017b, pp. 425–44.

Schwartz, Yigal. *Vantage Point: Issues in the Historiography of Modern Hebrew Literature* [Hebrew]. Kinneret-Zmorah Bitan-Dvir, 2005.

Scobie, Alex. "The Origins of 'Centaurs.'" *Folklore*, vol. 89, no. 2, 1978, pp. 142–7.

Shelley, Mary Wollstonecraft. *Frankenstein, or, The Modern Prometheus: The Original Two-volume Novel of 1816-1817 from the Bodleian Library Manuscripts*. Bodleian Library, 2008.

Shelley, Mary Wollstonecraft, and Charles E. Robinson, editors. *The Frankenstein Notebooks*. Garland Pub., 1996.

Shemtov, K. Vered. "A Sense of No Ending, Part 2: Etgar Keret and the Changing Concept of Time." *Dibur*, vol. 6, 2018, pp. 57–64.

Sherwin, Paul. "Frankenstein: Creation as Catastrophe." *PMLA*, vol. 96, no. 5, 1981, pp. 883–903.

Shklovsky, Rahel. "Happiness is a Stolen, Passing Moment [Hebrew]." *Iton*, vol. 77, no. 268, 2002, p. 6.

Spivak, Gayatri Chakravorty. "Three Women's Texts and a Critique of Imperialism." *Critical Inquiry*, vol. 12, no. 1, 1985, pp. 243–61.

Taub, Gadi. *A Dispirited Rebellion: Essays on Contemporary Israeli Culture* [Hebrew]. Hakibbutz Hameuchad, 1997.

Thomson, Philip J. *The Grotesque*. Methuen, 1972.

Tzivoni, Idan. "Some Comments on the Comics Literature of Etgar Keret [Hebrew]." *Iton 77*, vol. 234–5, 1999, pp. 24–6, 45.

Part III

Teaching Monstrosity in the (Post-)Modern World

9

Reading Monsters

How Mary Shelley Teaches Incels to Read *Paradise Lost*

Neil Barrett

The incel community has already been fairly censored and satirized by now, but incel extremists who have drawn popular attention in the past five years by committing acts of mass violence have still served many purposes. First, they drew attention to a community of misogynists that had been relatively hidden among online forums. Second, they served as a symbol for that community, to be either celebrated or demonized. Finally, they also served as a reminder that the rhetoric of misogyny is alive and well. By attacking a sorority at the University of Santa Barbara, 22-year-old Elliot Rodger became a symbol of incel violence, invading academia to kill women. With so many school shootings in America, alarms to arm teachers or drill students are often sounded. Without commenting directly on the efficacy of such initiatives, I would argue that universities and high schools should also reevaluate the misogyny that lies on so many of our bookshelves in plain sight. Although this is a pragmatic consideration above all, it is indeed an arduous task because close, meticulous readings demand patience.

I have been enamored with John Milton's poetry since I was an undergraduate student. My penchant for Milton has survived college and I teach him now whenever I can. This academically informed predilection for Milton has admittedly blinded me toward what is most problematic in his poetry. My understanding of the threat that misogynist language poses, even when it is in the sublime or the canonical, has been challenged by watching Elliot Rodger in the wake of his murders and realizing that he used language recognizable in such classical texts as *Paradise Lost* and *Frankenstein*. Both texts are important to me, and I have long argued for the beauty of their language and the insight they offer to the human condition. Yet, in light of the violent misogyny that Elliot Rodger has become a symbol for, I have had to reevaluate exactly *how* I teach these texts. What I have learned is that Mary Shelley was able to do what I had not been able to accomplish. Specifically, she appreciated the beauty in *Paradise Lost* while doing justice to the appalling misogyny present in Milton's poem. The incel killings are emblematic of this horror that has long inflicted humanity.

When read with the violent nature of Elliot Rodger in mind, the horror of the canon's use of misogyny is reanimated. Mary Shelley performed a similar act of resuscitation in her gothic novel *Frankenstein*. By reading *Frankenstein* carefully, we not only understand the misogyny that is dormant in *Paradise Lost* but are also reminded that we must still read contemporary acts of violence against women as monstrous. The novel *Frankenstein* thereby offers a vantage point toward understanding misogyny (even as it is expressed by Rodgers in his own manifesto). What could be productive for modern classrooms is how Mary Shelley's novel becomes a space for feminism and misogyny to interact, thereby fostering a dialogue that contests fundamental misogynistic claims and hegemonic devices. This conversation could also enable students with radically divergent worldviews to share in the experience of the Other. The horror of Elliot Rodger's actions must be remembered and the violence of Frankenstein's monster must be acknowledged if modern readers are to appreciate the warning leveled by Mary Shelley regarding misogynist rhetoric, however eloquent it may be. If successfully implemented, a monster might recognize itself as monstrous in her novel.

Monster Rhetoric

Frankenstein is about a man failing to recognize what is monstrous within himself. The emotions that are personified in Victor Frankenstein's double, the creature, are his own monster. Those emotions are so compellingly voiced that the novel's having been written by a woman should challenge any young man who sympathizes with the rhetoric of the monster, which ranges from pathetic and reflective to violently misogynistic. Mary Shelley's monster, at its most evil, finds itself situated between traditional misogyny and contemporary hate speech. Specifically, a line can be drawn from *Paradise Lost*, through *Frankenstein*, to Elliot Rodger's incel manifesto. Elliot Rodger and the incel movement are reminders of the horrors that Mary Shelley captured in her novel's popular monster. Arguably, Shelley's use of the monster's rhetoric is strategic. Despite caricaturing misogyny so well, it points to the unheard voices of female characters not only in her own novel but also to those in *Paradise Lost*. Young men still struggle with a language of misogyny that is as old as *Paradise Lost*. Frankenstein's monster offers toxic masculinity an opportunity to hear itself spoken eloquently and with an invitation to take seriously the monster's victims, the monster's literary influences, and the monster's author herself.

In order for this humanistic project to bear fruit, we have to be horrified at a creature that strangles women without remorse. Unfortunately, Mary Shelley's monster has been turned into a cartoon. There are countless representations of this creature, ranging from Hollywood film villains to children's television characters. Most of these take for granted the true horror intended by Shelley. What makes Frankenstein's monster horrific is akin to what should horrify us regarding contemporary killers. These are individuals who make a conscious decision to make others suffer, and Frankenstein's monster elucidates the reasoning behind this decision clearly.

There is nothing cartoonish or funny in Mary Shelley's novel, but rather there is a macabre aesthetic that can be traced to a history of reading books by her mother's grave (Gilbert 50). *Frankenstein* centers on an obsessive young college student who, after his own mother's death, finds a way to animate lifeless matter with electricity. Bent on creating a living creature from the dead, he digs through cemeteries and charnel houses, ultimately constructing a creature so hideous that he leaves it mumbling to itself on the operating table. After being abandoned by its maker, Frankenstein's creature then wanders the streets, only to be attacked by frightened villagers and rejected by the humans whose acceptance he despondently craves. The creature eventually stumbles upon a family of immigrants who sing to each other, read to each other, and demonstrate a kind of "domestic affection" that Mary Shelley develops as a theme in her work (Shelley xiv). When the family shelters an Arab refugee and teaches her to read, the creature follows along and becomes competent enough to not only speak fluently but also read such classical texts as *Plutarch's Lives*, *The Trials of Young Werter*, and *Paradise Lost*. After being rejected by the De Laneys, the creature demands a bride so that it can actualize a state of peace reminiscent of the De Laneys or of Adam and Eve in the Garden of Eden. When Victor refuses, the monster commits itself to a life of revenge on the maker who created it to live its life alone.

In the final chapter of the novel, Frankenstein's monster stands over the dead body of Victor and justifies its life of murder to Robert Walton, our narrator. Although the monster appears sad, Walton accuses the monster of Victor's death, arguing that any remorse the creature feels is superfluous. "If you had listened to the voice of conscience and heeded the strings of remorse before you had urged your diabolical vengeance to this extremity," Walton argues, "Frankenstein would yet have lived" (208, 208). The names of the monster's other victims should also be included in Walton's reprimand. The creature is responsible at this point for the deaths of William Frankenstein, Justine (both children), Henry Clerval, Frankenstein's father, and Elizabeth Larenza. The monster's rebuttal is compelling enough for Robert Walton to sympathize with it and is worth quoting at length:

> After the murder of Clerval I returned to Switzerland, heart-broken and overcome. I pitied Frankenstein, my pity amounted to horror; I abhorred myself. But when I discovered that he, the author at once of my existence and its unspeakable torments, dared to hope for happiness, that while he accumulated wretchedness and despair upon me he sought his own indulgence of which I was forever barred, then impotent envy and bitter indignation filled me with an insatiable thirst for vengeance. I recollected my threat and resolved that it should be accomplished. I knew that I was preparing for myself a deadly torture, but I was the slave, not the master, of an impulse which I detested yet could not disobey. Yet when she died! Nay, then I was not miserable. I had cast off all feeling, subdued all anguish, to riot in the excess of my despair. Evil thenceforth became my good. Urged thus far, I had no choice but to adapt my nature to an element which I had willingly chosen. The completion of my demoniacal design became an insatiable passion. And now it is ended; there is my last victim! (209)

The monster then announces that it will leave to die, allowing the elements to kill it slowly. This final speech admits to a self-pity and envy which lead to its "thirst for vengeance." This is the same progression of feeling charted in Elliot Rodger's manifesto. Being envious is common, even human. However, at some point, both the creature and Elliot Rodger commit themselves to a logic that justifies there "demoniacal design(s)." These kinds of justifications are what truly make them monsters.

Elliot Rodger made plenty of similar speeches. He maintained a YouTube blog and wrote a manifesto which he published online, both of which were pored over by police after he stabbed three college students to death, shot and killed two more in front of the Alpha Phi sorority house at the University of California, Santa Barbara, and wreaked more havoc from his car before ultimately killing himself. Besides the six killed by Rodger, thirteen were injured on what he himself termed his "Day of Retribution." While the final pages of Elliot's manifesto titled "My Twisted World" were picked apart and widely reported on in the wake of the San Bernardino shootings, the buildup that details (exhaustively) his coming of age and the onset of puberty are worth considering, especially for teachers. These are the pages before Elliot was a killer, or an ideologue. His experience is not unlike countless other boys' that I have taught. The son of a successful father, a child of divorce, and a strange kid who was often bullied, Rodger's upbringing does not deviate from that of countless other young men who grow up seeking affirmation and love. He enjoys watching *Star Wars*, skateboarding, trading Pokémon cards, and playing video games. He starts using social media at its founding in chat rooms and on AOL Instant Messenger (AIM). He experiences porn at a young age via the internet. His experiences with girls are riddled with insecurity and doubt. It is not in the setting of Elliot's life that we find anything strange so much as his extreme language. Elliot sought "Retribution" for his loneliness.

For example, when Elliot is embarrassed in front of girls, he describes it as being "traumatized [. . .] to no end" (Rodger 32). Puberty, for Elliot, is a "void," after which "does the true brutality of human nature show its face" (Rodger 25). Rodger's reaction to puberty, which is "the start of hell" for him, manifests the beginning of his violent rhetoric (Rodger 47). Elliot desires sexual companionship and finds that it is out of reach because the female sex as a whole finds him unattractive for reasons that he cannot explain. "I don't know why you girls aren't attracted to me, but I will punish you all for it," he declares (qtd. in Nagle 67). He reiterates, "I'm the perfect guy and yet you throw yourselves at these obnoxious men instead of me, the supreme gentleman" (qtd. in Nagle 67). People who have sex become a source of contention for Rodger, and he ultimately blames sexually active people for his misery. Of course, this logic is extreme. His rhetoric follows suit. Elliot's sexual frustration culminates in horrific violence. He writes:

> My whole world twisted even deeper into darkness and despair as my depressing life continued on. My hatred for people who have sex festered inside me like a plague. [. . .] It was the worst torture ever to see them making out and being intimate. My life, if you can call it a life, was living hell. (Rodger 57)

Rodger fantasizes about boiling people alive, pulling the skin off of their flesh, and massacring a humanity that has left him out: "All I ever wanted was to fit in and live a happy life amongst humanity, but I was cast out and rejected, forced to endure an existence of loneliness and insignificance, all because the females of the human species were incapable of seeing the value in me" (Rodger 1). This language, with its hyperbolic phrasing and its detachment from the "human species," is strikingly parallel to the creature who tells Victor, upon being rejected by the De Lacey family, "I, like the archfiend, bore a hell within me, and finding myself unsympathized with, wished to tear up the trees, spread havoc and destruction around me, and then to have sat down and enjoyed the ruin" (Shelley 130). Learning that Victor intends to marry Elizabeth drives the creature's need for revenge even further, and it demands that Victor make a creature-bride or else it will visit Victor on his wedding night. This is also Elliot Rodger's reasoning.

Alongside their language, a poignant parallel between Frankenstein's monster and Elliot Rodger is their lack of empathy toward women. The creature lacks remorse at having strangled Elizabeth. Elliot not only blames women for rejecting him but also resolves this tension in the most misogynist and violent terms: "I will arm myself with deadly weapons and wage a war against *all women and the men they are attracted to.* And I will slaughter them like the animals they are" (Rodger 101; emphasis in original). Sadly, this is the rhetoric that made Elliot Rodger famous. What remains horrifying about Mary Shelley's monster to this day is that it adopts a logic whereby women are something to be made for it, that a woman is a thing created to appease the monster's loneliness. The misogyny that the monster learns makes it horrifying, and Shelley's novel is meant to be disquieting.

Not everyone understands the horror of incel monsters either. While most were horrified by Elliot Rodger's actions, he became a revered symbol among incel communities online. "Incel" is an abbreviation of "involuntarily celibate." Like Rodger, incel forums and communities which congregate on PUAhate or incel subreddits tend to blame society (or women) for their celibacy, and Rodger's rhetoric found an audience in the more violently inclined of that community. The logic of this community endorses a hierarchy of masculinity whereby "alpha" males are attractive to women and are allowed to procreate while "beta" men are left at the mercy of ruthless competition. The anger that is fostered in these online echo chambers can be extreme. Angela Nagle, for example, in a piece for *The Baffler*, reports on some of the most disconcerting behavior being shared by a group of such "betas" on 4chan. The worst was posted by a man named David Michael Kalac, showing a picture of his strangled, naked girlfriend and jokingly captioning "Turns out it's way harder to strangle someone to death than it looks in the movies" (Nagle 67). Such perverse humor could only find refuge in depraved minds. There is nothing funny about it. It is horrific, but the incel community has entertained psychopaths and idolized mass killers. Furthermore, it is also harrowing to consider that those who harbor this sickness walk among us. They remain unrecognized until public events like the mass killings which have been deemed the "Incel Rebellion."

After the San Bernardino killings, images of Elliot Rodger adorned with Byzantine iconography, as if he were a Christian saint, were circulated online. T-shirts were sold, and the depravity of this twisted hero-worship finally led to another mass killing when Alek Minassian drove a van into a crowd of people in Toronto, killing ten (predominantly women) and injuring sixteen. Minassian also announced his killing spree online prior to the act, hailing Elliot Rodger by name as "The Supreme Gentleman" on Facebook ("Alek Minassian"). The incel community has since been banned from reddit, though some subgroups have reappeared that foster non-misogynistic incels like r/IncelsWithoutHate. Online communities have also found groups committed to exposing, ridiculing, or advising incels (r/IncelTears, r/IncelsinAction, r/IncelAdvice). Though there has been a reaction to incels in the wake of Rodger and Minassian, it is still terrifying that their images became memes and icons. Rather than treating them as monsters, the incel killers were treated as either jokes or "Supreme Gentlemen." These depictions fail to do justice to those who suffered at their hand.

This reaction to monsters ought to be horrifying enough, but how is it possible to become so insensitive to murder? At the end of *Frankenstein*, the monster claims that it *was* horrified at itself until it had decided to "cast off all feeling" and "riot in the excess of [its] despair." The monster notes its lack of remorse over having killed Elizabeth, Victor's bride and arguably the most noble character in the novel. In a sense, the monster claims that strangling her was easy. Perhaps, this is their most horrifying influence; monsters make murder look easy, even to those who do not take the lives of others.

Monster Allegory

The monster's lack of remorse and its unflinching resolve mirror the character of Satan in John Milton's *Paradise Lost*. The creature recounts its reading *Paradise Lost* and its identification with both Adam and Satan. Satan wins out. "Many times I considered Satan as the fitter emblem of my condition," the monster recounts, "for often, like him, when I viewed the bliss of my protectors, the bitter gall of envy rose within me" (Milton 124). Satan's example certainly fails to ward the creature away from following in his evil footsteps, which is precisely what those who teach *Frankenstein* might hope for in their own (hypothetically troubled) audience. At least for the creature, *Paradise Lost* fails to convey the horror of choosing the Satanic path adequately. This may follow from Milton's reliance on allegory to depict violence and horror. When Milton uses allegory to depict violence on a female body in his poem, he lightens the blow that such violence should have on the reader. Basically, in a poem resplendent in natural imagery and psychologically complex depiction of human emotion, Milton turns sexism into a rather horrific cartoon.

Having taught *Paradise Lost* for three years to high school seniors, when confronted by a student about the sexism inherent in the story of Adam and Eve, I have dodged the issue. I admit. I certainly encouraged feminist readings of any text we examine (or thought I did). Nevertheless, owing to my attachment to Milton's poetry, I kept looking for justifications in his biography or in the ambivalent interpretations of problematic lines. *Frankenstein* demonstrates the hazards of casually propping up a misogynistic tradition, challenging the age-old deflection of writers who do. I would postulate, "But doesn't he write beautifully?" And Milton does. This is part of the problem.

Teaching in the American South, or "the Bible-Belt" as it is affectionately termed, I have also observed that Sunday School has already taught many of the students in my classroom who the primary characters in Milton's epic are. Christian ideology informs even those who are not traditionally well read. This is one reason why I enjoy teaching *Paradise Lost*. All of the characters are familiar: Eve, Adam, Satan, God, and Christ. When students have general notions about these characters, Milton gains an opportunity to challenge static conceptions of those characters in his readership. The most tantalizing aspect of *Paradise Lost* to the romantic poets, for example, was the complexity given to Satan. A traditional symbol for evil became a heroic champion of individual liberty. Even more ambitious is Milton's task of challenging a traditional concept of God.

What Milton proposes to do in Book I of his epic poem is to "Assert Eternal Providence, / And Justify the ways of God to men" (I.26-7). Literary critics over time have interpreted this as Milton's way of putting the Christian God on trial (Empson 94). In other words, how does the Christian God hold up against the literary and philosophical treatises that humans have offered against it? Milton takes the question seriously, and his sincerity is one reason *Paradise Lost* is still so enshrined in the Western literary canon.

Milton is also protected because of his style and his willingness to challenge authority. Milton wrote pamphlets that challenged censorship and defended divorce when neither opinion was popular. In this regard, he even went so far as to defend regicide during a time when English civil war was brewing and there was still a sitting king. It should be noted that the parliamentary state that *did* decapitate King Charles I in broad daylight turned into another totalitarian regime under Oliver Cromwell, only to fail and restore King Charles II to the throne. It is a testament to his immense literary talent that John Milton was not tortured and killed for his inflammatory rhetoric during this tumultuous time period. A popular explanation for Milton's amnesty has long been chalked up to his reputation as a poet. In the classroom, the style with which Milton challenges authority should be an opportunity for readers to also challenge traditional understandings of the human condition. Questions that ask who is responsible for the fall of man can turn into questioning whether Eve is truly to blame for issuing Sin and Death into the world (or whether God is). Milton himself even becomes an authority that ought to be challenged when the justification of God's ways is packaged with sexist ideology.

One of Milton's most reputable critics was Mary Shelley's mother, Mary Wollestonecraft, one of England's earliest published feminists. She and generations of feminists since have reasonably found fault with the depiction of Eve as "less equal" than Adam in the divinely sanctioned hierarchy of the Garden of Eden. When Satan first spies upon the pair, he notes that they are "not equal, as their sex not equal seemed; / For contemplation he and valour formed, / For softness she and sweet attractive grace, / He for God only, she for God in him" (IV. 296-9). Historically, Eve is blamed for the fall of man because she was curious enough to eat from the Tree of the Knowledge of Good and Evil. However, just as Satan is celebrated for his defiance in the face of authoritarian rule, Eve's curiosity has also been read as a strength rather than a weakness. William Empson claims that Eve is blameworthy not for the fall of man but of trusting "goodness rather than God" (180). This makes her a metaphysical believer par excellence rather than a "weaker vessel." Dr. E. M. W. Tillyard once even commented that, were Milton to find himself in the Garden of Eden, he would have eaten the fruit immediately and written a pamphlet explaining how it was his duty to do so (qtd. in Empson 172). Milton's defense of free will is much of what makes him so special to the canon, and Eve certainly has that.

Still, even if Milton's characterization of Eve can be defended, there is one looming allegorical monster that complicates any defense of his style: Sin herself. Anna K. Juhnke posits in "Remnants of Misogyny in *Paradise Lost*" that Milton's version of Eve is not all that bad, given the history of medieval caricatures of Eve as an evil snake woman in league with Satan who should be blamed for eating the fruit. However, by nonetheless preserving the stock image of a snake woman conspiring with Satan, Milton employs a "ready made allegorical figure of sin" that "embodies twenty centuries of misogyny" (Juhnke 53, 55). Milton, according to Juhnke, did not do away with the misogynistic caricature. He simply transformed it. Even if Eve is off the hook, sin is still being personified as a woman.

When Satan first runs into Sin as he is escaping Hell in Book II, he does not even recognize her. While born a beautiful woman from Satan's flaming head when he became envious of the Son of God in heaven, Satan finds Sin disfigured in Hell. Recounting her horrific story, we learn that Sin became pregnant with Death after having slept with Satan in heaven. Death is born after they all fall into Hell, ruining the mother's body. Death tortures and rapes Sin routinely as they both stand guard at the gate of Hell. To make matters worse, Death's progeny is a pack of Cerberean dogs who repeatedly chew themselves out of Sin's womb as part of her torturous schedule. Sin's depiction as a woman who is tortured and raped ad nauseam is grotesque, though Timothy O'Keeffe points out that Milton's depiction is only "slightly less gruesome" than Hesiod's or Ovid's version of the same type (O'Keeffe 75). Interestingly, this is as "gruesome" as Milton's poem gets. It is not characteristic of his otherwise sublime style, begging the question as to whether the scene belongs in this poem at all.

Sin's character is obviously faulty to feminist readings of the text, but it also fails as an allegory for aesthetic reasons. According to Samuel Johnson, "Milton's allegory of sin and death is, undoubtedly, faulty" (184). Johnson picks apart the allegory because it stretches what realism is offered by Milton to understand the cosmology of the poem. Johnson finds Sin and Death's construction of a bridge between Hell and Earth to be "a work too bulky for ideal architects" and concludes: "This unskillful allegory appears to me one of the greatest faults of the poem; and to this there was no temptation but the author's opinion of its beauty" (184–5). According to Johnson, Milton's inclusion of the Sin and Death allegory is included simply because Milton thought the image of them building a bridge out of Chaos was beautiful. Johnson also notes the original stages of Milton's magnum opus and details how it was initially drafted as a Mystery. Mysteries were dramas peopled by allegorical characters with abstract names such as "Justice, Mercy, [and] Faith" (138). Such dramas were usually heavy-handed morality plays that were meant to instruct their audience to avoid sin and pursue virtue. Of further interest is that Sin is not a character listed by Johnson in Milton's initial plans. She was apparently added later in the writing process. This significant detail reveals that Milton revised his heavily allegorical dialogue into a much more sophisticated narrative, filled with nuance and character development, but insisted upon using a stock, sexist image of Sin that has become contentious with readers over time.

When asked about whether *Paradise Lost* is sexist, I can simply point to Sin. Milton is a valuable poet to read and *Paradise Lost* offers much to think about, but Milton's allegory of Sin needs to be corrected. It relies on a traditional disfigurement of a sexualized female body in order to warn readers not to be tempted by sin. What is needed is a text that addresses *Paradise Lost*'s major themes yet responds to the inherent sexism thoughtfully, and this is precisely what Mary Shelley brings to the table with her novel *Frankenstein*, making it an even more necessary read for potential incels. The productive irony of *Frankenstein* is that the monster does not identify with the allegorical monster in *Paradise Lost*.

Milton only calls certain characters by the term "monster" in *Paradise Lost*. Of his use of the term or its derivatives, fourteen in all, six apply to devils in Hell, sea monsters, Chaos, or Hell itself. He refers to Satan twice, but more than any other individual character, Death is named as the monster. Death has only a vague, shadowy form. Besides the lance that it carries, Death is practically devoid of substance. This is appropriate, as one of the scariest aspects of Death is that we rarely see it coming. The troubling irony of this is that Death's victim, Sin, is the most graphically punished character in the entire poem. Her punishment, just by being associated with Satan, is worse than any other demon in Hell. The effect of using such a monstrous allegory is that we see Death not by its own monstrous characteristics. We see Death by the toll it takes on Sin. This vital distinction applies to Satan's monstrosity as well. Satan is a motivational speaker on a hero's journey until we see his mistress being punished so vividly on account of his rebellion. Satan rebelled, but Sin bears the image of monster.

The reality this allegory masks is the horrific punishment God inflicts on Eve's physical body. When Christ announces that Eve will serve her husband and will suffer the pains of childbirth, the implication is that she will be subject to Adam's sexual desire and that her body will be mutilated by her offspring. Sin foreshadows Eve. When we consider how Eve was created by God for Adam in the Garden of Eden to be subservient to him, we can piece together the logic that incels use to defend their misogynistic views. If we read any Christian account of human origins as written by men as a "true history," then the discontent of involuntarily celibate men is given credence. Part of their so-called punishment for the Fall is being allowed to prey on women's bodies. This is precisely how Frankenstein's monster reads *Paradise Lost*.

Monster Interpretations

Milton could have done without the allegorical, misogynist representation of Sin as a woman. The story could easily be told without these phallocratic elements. According to many scholars, this is exactly what Mary Shelley did. Sandra Gilbert calls *Frankenstein* a "mock *Paradise Lost*" (56). Leslie Tannenbaum refers to *Frankenstein* as a "filthy type of *Paradise Lost*" (113). There is an emphasis in the scholarship on the intertextual relationship between these two works that highlights how characters in *Frankenstein* mirror or relate to characters in *Paradise Lost*.

Specifically, Frankenstein's creature becomes a proper monster after identifying with *Paradise Lost* as any reader might be inclined to do. Mary Shelley did not choose *Paradise Lost* as the creature's textbook on humanity without cause. Part of its import is the fact that this creature fails to see any characters in the story who look like it does. If Adam is privileged, Eve is subservient, and there are no creatures who look like Frankenstein's monster to be found in the Garden (at least until Sin and Death arrive). John Lamb, in "Mary Shelley's *Frankenstein* and Milton's Monstrous Myth," succinctly explains Shelley's project and the creature's dilemma:

> Milton bequeathed to the world a text on which were inscribed the cultural commandments of being, and Mary Shelley set out to break those stone tablets and to expose the illusory nature of bourgeois individualism. *Frankenstein* is, then, about authorship, about creating a space in nineteenth-century culture to frame a different answer to the question "What was I?" and to add another voice to the discourse of identity. But such a clearing of cultural space required, if not a clear cutting, at least an undermining of the persuasiveness of *Paradise Lost* and Milton's monstrous myth. (306)

Lamb further explains that by failing to see itself in the limited voices of *Paradise Lost*, the monster experiences a sort of "cultural schizophrenia that could be described as a disruption of the self's relation with the world and with itself" (307). In a similar vein, Robert Ryan writes that Milton's Christian faith is espoused ironically by a "homicidal freak" and that the "ineffectual, baffled Christian faith of the monster [. . .] is used by Mary Shelley to call into question both Christianity itself and the ideology that Godwin and [Percy] Shelley were offering as an alternative to it" (150–1). Christianity just may be the monster in question.

According to these interpretations, Mary Shelley seems dead set at exposing how Christian ideology has assigned strict roles to humans, male and female. Anyone who does not fall into the Adam or Eve categories as defined by Milton and Milton's God is left out. It is not as if everybody read *Paradise Lost* as a history textbook in Mary Shelley's time, but the ideology that is espoused in *Paradise Lost* permeated the culture enough that Shelley made it the monster of her novel. On the one hand, Mary Shelley preserves the epic poem by alluding to it in a work that (could she have known?) would itself be preserved as a staple of Western Culture. On the other hand, Shelley revises the allegory in Milton's poem by making a male humanoid the grotesque symbol of evil in her novel. It is as if Mary Shelley's response to John Milton was, "You've made Sin a deformed woman? Very well, I will make a deformed man the villain of my novel, and he'll get all of his worst ideas from *your* book no less."

Nonetheless, Mary Shelley did appreciate *Paradise Lost* as a literary masterpiece. She even once said that despite Christianity's eventual loss of membership (a shortsighted critique of the religion shared by her famously atheist husband, Percy), "Milton's poem alone will give permanency to the remembrance of its absurdities" (qtd. in Ryan 154). Critics have thoroughly pointed out that if Shelley is not criticizing Milton himself, she certainly mocks such "absurdities" as his treatment of Eve.

According to Sandra M. Gilbert, Frankenstein's monster reads *Paradise Lost* only to learn that this world was not made for it. The creature has no origin myth, no history, and therefore no community. It would be a Christian were there any space for something like it to participate in. In a culture whose history is so patriarchal, this marginalization applies not only to Eve but also to Mary Shelley. Many therefore take Frankenstein's monster as a voice for the subjugated, those marginalized by the patriarchal order that *Paradise Lost* represents. According to this reading, the monster raging at the system is a mouthpiece for Mary Shelley. Clearly espousing this point of view, Robert Ryan muses,

> Why did Mary Shelley create this religious monster, this disconnected Christian whose faith can bring no hope? The question requires particular interest in light of the growing critical consensus that the reader's sympathetic response to the monster is an effect of the author's own identification with him, "Beneath the contorted visage of Frankenstein's creature," wrote U.C. Knoepflmacher, "lurks a timorous yet determined female face." (112)

Sandra M. Gilbert makes a similar claim after noting the superficial absence of an Eve parallel in *Frankenstein:* "Frankenstein is ultimately a mock *Paradise Lost* in which both Victor and his monster, together with a number of secondary characters, play all the neoBiblical parts over and over again—all except, it seems at first, the part of Eve" (56-7). Gilbert explains how both Victor and his monster perform characteristics of Adam and Satan as if they were children "trying on costumes" and blames the inability of the male characters to identify with Eve for their relative falls. Though the creature ought to identify most with Eve (or her double, Sin), "one of the most notable facts about the monster's ceaselessly anxious study of *Paradise Lost* is his failure even to mention Eve" (Gilbert 64). What makes Gilbert's reading so interesting is how it traces Eve's subtle influence on all of the characters in *Frankenstein*.

What any English teacher who finishes *Frankenstein* must feel is a poignant regret that the monster pursued a life of murder instead of simply reading more. The reader-response approach to *Paradise Lost* that Stanley Fish ushered into Milton studies would concur. Fish claims that sympathy for the devil is a sign of immature reading, one that falls for traps of ambiguity Milton leaves as a challenge to his audience. A haphazard reading glorifies Satan, but a careful and discerning reader finds the grace of God preferable as Milton did. Certainly, *Paradise Lost* begs repeated readings, and *Frankenstein* encourages its readers to do this. In a way, *Frankenstein* is a rereading of *Paradise Lost*. Satan's sin is founded in his envy, and he seeks to spread suffering. Eve's sin is to seek knowledge, to see the world as God sees it. If Frankenstein's creature has to fall, it is a shame he did not choose Eve as his model. Fewer people would have died, thereby giving those allegories Sin and Death that much less to feed on.

Monster Metaphor

If for no other reason, the Elliot Rodgers of the world should read *Frankenstein* as an introduction to Misogyny 101. It captures well the mentality that still exists in some men: either I have a woman to pacify my lesser, violent urges or I will wreak havoc on mankind. This is the logic that compels incel killers like Elliot Rodger and Alek Minassian to commit mass murder. Feminists have been fighting this idea of marriage epitomized by the mentality that women are property transactions for centuries. The monster does not consider the hypothetical female monster's desires or wishes but only wants a companion that will love and take care of it. Despite this introduction, it is unlikely that Elliot Rodger read *Frankenstein*.

Although Elliot Rodger recounts with ease the video games that he played as a child (*Donkey Kong, Banjo Kazoo, Goldeneye, World of Warcraft*, etc.), his reading list as an eighteen-year-old is described with much less specificity. This is ironic for two reasons. By eighteen, Rodger had taken to hanging out in Barnes & Noble hoping some beautiful woman would notice his presence. Additionally, his misogynistic and fascist ideologies began to take shape at this age. In his manifesto/autobiography, Rodger does recall reading the *Game of Thrones* and the *Hunger Games* series. He also mentions Joseph Murphy's *Power of Your Subconscious Mind* as a catalyst for his attempts at envisioning success with the lottery. Despite claiming that "Knowledge is Power" and spending "hours reading books that ranged from biographies of powerful leaders, histories of significant periods, self-help books, philosophy and psychology texts, and historical fiction novels," none seemed to make enough of an impact for him to cite directly (Rodger). As his testimony and the vocabulary in his manifesto suggest, Elliot Rodger was a reader, but how he read must be called into question.

It is easy enough to imagine Elliot Rodger picking up a copy of *Frankenstein* and renouncing his own life of vengeance in pursuit of nobler aims. Such a claim is simply make-believe, I admit. However, it is worth examining *how* the monster in *Frankenstein* reads, given that Elliot Rodger's reading led to similar rhetorical ends. Frankenstein's monster identified with characters in the books he read, and it sought nothing further from what it immediately considered the "true history" of its condition. If violently inclined readers feel emboldened by the texts they read enough to kill, they simply ought to read more. I would also argue that it is important that those who teach young people how to read remember patience as a critical aspect of the reading process. Complex canonical works require patience in their reading. This inherent complexity is one of the main reasons why these texts are included in the canon in the first place.

This expectation for patience with a difficult text is what literary scholar Jonathan Culler identifies as the *hyper-protected cooperative principle* (25). It is a mouthful, but the idea is that certain books which have been deemed masterpieces by literary communities over time should be protected by a canon. The canon serves as a stamp of approval saying, "These books are worth your time and effort. Trust us." What the cooperative principle asks readers of a canonical work to put forth is the effort necessary to share in the author's experience of the world. Seeing the world as Satan sees it, or Frankenstein's monster for that matter, is easy enough. Seeing the world as John Milton or Mary Shelley did is entirely different. The latter is immediately available with even a cursory read of these texts. The latter requires cooperation on the reader's part. Otherwise, reading becomes as pointless of an exercise as trying to look intelligent and sexy in a bookstore. Reading is much like falling in love in this way. It requires patience. Nothing accounts for a reader being patient with a text more than that reader writing another text that grapples with its ideas.

I do not want to simplify Mary Shelley's novel even by suggesting it is only a reimagining of another work. Of course, it is interesting that Shelley's otherwise sympathetic creature becomes the villain of her story *after* reading *Paradise Lost*. It is also difficult not to associate her mother's critique of Milton with Mary Shelley's novel. Yet, we should ourselves be careful. Mary Shelley warns her readers of such moralizing, of privileging various philosophical interpretations, in her preface to the novel. All Shelley claims to do is depict universal virtues and human emotions as best she can. This is why it is such a crime to make a cartoon of her monster, whose force as a warning hinges on this very humanity in her depiction of it. Unlike Sin, Shelley's monster is no simple allegory. She has shown us a type of reader, a monstrous reader that misreads *Paradise Lost* as a "true history" of its own condition (Shelley 124). The monster misreads *Paradise Lost* in two ways. First, the monster becomes a creationist after reading the poem and demands its own fair share of the fairer sex. Evidently, this type of reading leads to incel behavior. The other reading may be more sincere, though equally misguided. Practically, the monster does not seem to finish reading the poem at all and thereby fails to appreciate Milton's central use of metaphor, that of the Fall.

Part of the incel vocabulary is the characters "Chad" and "Stacy." Chad is the nickname given to "alpha" males who are athletic, charismatic womanizers. Accordingly, these men do not deserve the happiness that incels associate with sexual intimacy. Stacy, similarly, is a nickname for promiscuous females who throw themselves at the feet of Chads. Countless memes and jokes can be found on incel forums that both ridicule and demonize the sexually active. Within the intertextual context established in the chapter thus far, a fair way of characterizing the incel community is as a poorly constructed monster, seething with envy at the happiness Adam and Eve experience in the Garden of Eden. Not only does Frankenstein's monster fail to appreciate Eve's role in the poem, but it takes for granted that Adam and Eve are themselves cast out of the Garden after transgressing their creator. An incel might go even further, thinking that Adam and Eve are just another Chad and Stacy who deserve to be punished for their sexual bliss. What the monster and the incel take for granted is that *all* of humanity is fallen and that all consequently suffer (even Adam and Eve).

We see Adam and Eve's characters develop drastically after God has punished them for their transgression of his laws and for indulging in lustful behavior. Christ as God's messenger visits the Garden to find them naked and ashamed. Death is promised, and then the two are left alone to think about their fate. Adam, for his part, finally adopts the language of misogyny that would make incels proud. Adam rants, "Out of my sight, thou serpent, that name best / Befits thee with him leagued, thyself as false / And hateful; nothing wants, but that thy shape, / Like his, and color serpentine may show / Thy inward fraud, to warn all creatures from thee" (X. 867–71). Eve then begs for Adam's forgiveness. She does take the blame:

> On me exercise not / Thy hatred for this misery befallen, / On me already lost, me than thyself / More miserable; both have sinned, but thou / Against God only, I against God and thee, / And to the place of judgement will return, / There with my cries importune heaven, that all / The sentence from thy head removed may light / On me, sole cause to thee of all this woe, / Me me only just object of his ire. (X. 927–36)

And while an incel might imagine as ideal a beautiful woman, begging for the opportunity to serve him better, they would be taking for granted completely the humility that Adam learns from Eve's example. Adam is moved and mirrors her selflessness (though still adhering, of course, to the patriarchal hierarchy):

> If prayers / Could alter high decrees, I to that place / Would speed before thee, and be the louder heard, / That on my head all might be visited, / Thy frailty and infirmer sex forgiven, / To me committed and by me exposed. / But rise, let us no more contend, nor blame / Each other, blamed enough elsewhere, but strive / In offices of love, how we might lighten / Each others burden in our share of woe. (X. 952–61)

This exchange, when Adam and Eve choose to share in each other's suffering, marks the choice that stands in direct contrast to Satan deciding that "evil will be his good."

Satan convinces himself that his fall is a testament to his individual will, but his character does not appreciate the gravity of his fall on others. To weigh the consequences of Satan's actions, modern readers must consider every horrific crime committed after him, crimes that Adam appreciated all too late when Michael shows him the violence of mankind from Cain and Abel to Christ's crucifixion. That violent history does not end with Elliot Rodger but is perpetuated by him and every other misogynist. Satan's defense rests in his not knowing that someone like Elliot Rodger could emulate his example in such a harrowing manner. Satan, who has been romanticized by generations of readers, acts more on his own personal rage than on the bloodlust that follows the Fall. Such a reading is only possible if we ignore the fact that he looked directly at the bloody and devoured form of his daughter, his lover, molested in Hell by his own thoughtless progeny before stepping out into his quest for revenge. Satan is an attractive shape-shifter. Frankenstein's monster and Elliot Rodger are not. Frankenstein's monster becomes convinced that he cannot change without realizing how much Satan's rhetoric has already changed him. Elliot Rodger gives up on society, growth, friendship, or love to pursue revenge against an enemy that was not real. What distinguishes these two misogynists from Eve, all of whom succumbed to Satan's rhetorical guile, is that Eve fell for the promise of divinity. Misogyny settles for rage.

Satan stands in as a symbol for free will by claiming that "a mind is its own place, and in itself / Can make a heaven of hell, a hell of heaven" (Milton I. 254–5). To those who suffer at the hands of violent misogynists like Elliot Rodger, Hell is more than just a state of mind. Hell is the world of violence that scares Adam and Eve enough to consider celibacy, or suicide. The world is their hell. Mary Shelley understood this pessimism and made it the setting of her novel. Leslie Tannenbaum claims that Shelley's godless setting was a "Miltonic Hell" (112). Man and his creatures are depraved without any hope of divine grace swooping in and saving the day. Because Elliot Rodger appreciates only a figurative understanding of hell when he claims that puberty "was a hell for him," he would have a lot to learn from Shelley's novel. Hell is the state of falling alone. We do not have to fall alone. It is a choice, and a monstrous one at that, which cannot be easy.

It is naive to argue that Milton is to blame for Frankenstein's monster becoming a poetry quoting killer. If anything, the monster is guilty of making the nuanced and challenging *Paradise Lost* look like an easy text to read. The monster misses most of what Milton might have offered it. Similarly, I cannot suggest that reading more canonical works would have kept Elliot Rodger from becoming a murderer. I still cannot help but think of *Frankenstein* as critically important. Observing the parallels between Elliot Rodger and Frankenstein's creature reminds me to scrutinize the texts that I teach in my classes and to pay attention to how adolescents relate to the characters within them. Mary Shelley's novel caused me to reexamine my own predilections for Milton's poem and realize that I was giving him undue leniency when it came to Sin and Eve. While the possibility that a young man with Elliot Rodger's hate and rhetoric may be sitting in a classroom of mine, the reality is that young women who have to face the misogyny he represents certainly do. They need teachers who can admit that Milton's language, which makes evil animals of women in order to make a point, is not fair. It is easy to hope that arming teachers with guns or amplifying security measures in schools will keep students safe, but without acknowledging the misogyny on our bookshelves, these efforts are short sighted. Rather than worship the genius of old men, young people need to hear that Mary Shelley, who wrote her first novel as a teenager, ferociously grappled with the same daunting questions that haunted Milton centuries before. Elliot Rodger ponders the "very fabric of reality" in his manifesto at various points. He asks many fundamental existential questions such as "*Why did this all exist? How did life come to be? What was the nature of reality? What was my place in all of it?*" (Rodger 109; emphasis in original). Anyone who poses such questions should seek company in the minds of Milton and Shelley, rather than the fashion, cars, and fortunes that Rodger imagined would have helped him lose his virginity. Honest suffering, like the anguish Elliot Rodger claims to feel, can find honest company in good books.

References

"Alek Minassian Toronto Van Attack Suspect Praised 'Incel' Killer." *BBC News*, BBC, Apr. 25, 2018, www.bbc.com/news/world-us-canada-43883052.

Culler, Jonathan. *Literary Theory: A Very Short Introduction*. Oxford University Press, 1997.

Empson, William. *Milton's God*. Cambridge University Press, 1981.

Gilbert, Sandra M. "Horror's Twin: Mary Shelley's Monstrous Eve." *Feminist Studies*, vol. 4, no. 2, 1978, pp. 48–73. JSTOR, www.jstor.org/stable/3177447.

Johnson, Samuel. *Lives of the Most Eminent English Poets with Critical Observations on their Works, Volume I*. Philadelphia; Claxton, Remsen & Haffelfinger. 1868. Google Books. https://books.google.com/books?id=nk5CAQAAIAAJ&printsec=frontcover&source=gbs_ge_summary_r&cad=0#v=onepage&q&f=false. May 21, 2019.

Juhnke, Anna K. "Remnants of Misogyny in *Paradise Lost*." *Milton Quarterly*, vol. 22, no. 2, 1988, pp. 50–8. JSTOR, www.jstor.org/stable/24464584.

Lamb, John B. "Mary Shelley's Frankenstein and Milton's Monstrous Myth." *Nineteenth-Century Literature*, vol. 47, no. 3, 1992, pp. 303–19. JSTOR. www.jstor.org/stable/2933709.

Milton, John. *Paradise Lost. John Milton: The Major Works*. Oxford University Press, 2003.

Nagle, Angela. "The New Man of 4chan." *The Baffler*, no. 30, 2016, pp. 64–76, www.jstor.org/stable/43959201.

O'Keeffe, Timothy J. "An Analogue to Milton's 'Sin' and More on the Tradition." *Milton Quarterly*, vol. 5, no. 4, 1971, pp. 74–7. JSTOR, www.jstor.org/stable/24462807.

Rodger, Elliot. "'My Twisted World: The Story of Elliot Rodger.'" documentcloud.org, 2014, https://www.documentcloud.org/documents/1173808-elliot-rodger-manifesto.html.

Ryan, Robert M. "Mary Shelley's Christian Monster." *The Wordsworth Circle*, vol. 19, no. 3, 1988, pp. 150–5. JSTOR, www.jstor.org/stable/24042395.

Shelley, Mary. *Frankenstein: Or, The Modern Prometheus*. New American Library: A Signet Classic. New York, 1965.

10

"We Live in a Time of Monsters"

Teaching Composition through the Representations of Monsters and Monstrosity in Literature

Devon Pizzino

Writing instruction does not have to be monstrous, but the ideas created from it should be. I teach several types of composition courses, and the one that I find the most challenging in guiding students through is my English 201: Introduction to Literature course that serves as a continuation of their English 101: Composition I course and is typically taken during the spring semester. In the English 201: Introduction to Literature course, students are expected to practice and develop academic reading and writing skills—these skills were mainly introduced to them in English 101. However, the second required composition course focuses primarily on poetry, fiction, and plays. Students are also introduced to literary criticism and must acquire basic knowledge necessary for textual analysis such as literary terms and critical theory. Essentially, I often struggle to make such a course accessible, interesting, and functional because many of my students come from diverse and nontraditional backgrounds. For instance, I teach many first-generation college students, socioeconomically disadvantaged learners, students from largely African and Asian countries whose native language is not English, older students, and mothers with full-time jobs. In fact, many of them are learning intensive compositional skills in-depth for the first time in their English 101 course offered at the Manhattan-based community college where I teach. The academic discourse community that my classroom ultimately ends up reflecting is not one representing "the most powerful people in the community," who Patricia Bizzell asserts have "usually been male, European American, and middle or upper class" (1). Instead, many of my students are what academics, myself included, would call "under-prepared" (Hebb 22) yet eager and hardworking once they are interested and supported.

When a second semester Introduction to Literature course is an extension to an English Composition class, for example, by asking that classes center around developing critical reading, critical thinking, independent research, and writing skills through literature, it is then that the panic for me and many writing instructors sets in. How do we keep nontraditional students who are mostly *not* English majors engaged in material that requires them to closely read works of fiction while also improving their argumentative writing skills? I want them to read the assigned texts without googling summaries or looking up the electronic, modern versions of CliffsNotes. I want them to believe in their own abilities to understand a short story, poem, play, or essay. I want them to create arguments with complex thesis statements formed from synthesizing texts instead of relying on simplistic, formulaic ones. Recently, I attempted to address and resolve this conundrum by creating a themed writing course primarily focused on monsters and monstrosity. The goal of this course is to encourage students to see how texts—even ones that seem quite different—connect so that they confidently develop strong writing and rhetoric skills. The course's primary text, "Monster Culture" by Jeffery Cohen, situates the rest of the course's reading and assignment focus within the boundaries of monstrosity.

Cohen's essay is the first chapter in his edited collection *Monster Theory: Reading Culture*. This seminal text serves as a useful foundation for evaluating and examining the traditional works of classic authors and thinkers. What is interesting is that these authors are actually reflecting what Cohen argues: that various cultures create the monstrous from their own ontological desires, fears, misunderstandings, anxiety, conquests, struggles with difference, self-imposed boundaries, and search for order. Such texts, when viewed through Cohen's main ideas about how monstrous and cultural bodies are related, can provoke unsettling questions about society and guide students toward more analytical and research-based writing as they progress through college and across the curriculum.

I have noticed that my students are unsure of themselves and their ability to succeed, especially in intensive reading and writing courses where they are asked to engage with topics they may not typically think about. In their minds, they have not been able to navigate the academic community in a way that makes them feel that they are or will ever be good writers and readers. It is often because they have a different way of communicating when outside of the classroom that they do not realize what is actually functional and useful in the classroom. Some students have been warned that college is a much different world than the one to which they are accustomed, while others have not been prepared for the leap from previous academic experiences. As Jacqueline Jones Royster points out in her comparison of academic and nonacademic language, the notion of a single intellectual discourse community does not help this transition:

> There is *the* language, *the* discourse of academe and there are *other* languages and discourses that are not academe. We distill variations that we otherwise specify and use general terms in ways that suggest sameness, tacit understanding, and static, non-contentious representations, not just of language or discourse but also of *goodness*. Despite our occasional intent to suggest otherwise, such habits of distillation have engendered in our field hierarchies of power, privilege, and value, and they have continually reified notions of insider/outside, center/margin, us/other, and also notions of good/suspect. (24, emphasis in original)

In my urban, community college setting, my students feel like they are outsiders, and there is only one standard of *good* writing by which their reading and writing skills will be measured. By using "Monster Culture" as the main text for English 201, the class becomes a safe, intellectually challenging space, where students from diverse backgrounds can discuss the impact of these notions and hierarchies that Royster mentions on themselves and their communities.

The Purpose of Introductory Literature Courses and Assigned Texts

Introductory literature courses are intended to prepare students not just for analytic and research-based writing but also for additional and upper-level literature courses. To accomplish this objective, they must include well-known authors that are part of the canon and those whom the students will potentially revisit. I take advantage of online syllabi in addition to pedagogical materials shared with me by colleagues in order to supplement my course reading list. I have discovered that the vast majority of colleagues deem the same authors and texts to be crucial components of an introductory literature course. Just open any well-known publisher's *Introduction to Literature* textbook and there they all are: "The Yellow Wallpaper," "A Perfect Day for Bananafish," "A Very Old Man with Enormous Wings," "Hamlet," "Her Kind," "The Thing in the Forest," "A Rose for Emily," "My Last Duchess," "Good Country People," and so on. Even if we carefully select texts for a more personalized survey course, the authors are most certainly shared: Rushdie, Momaday, Brooks, Faulkner, Plath, Joyce, Marquez, Browning, Chopin, Woolf, Roy, Ellison, Sexton, Salinger, Ginsberg, Baraka, Frost. These writers are indeed household names to any English instructor. Just as familiar to us are our students' paper topics, thesis statements, and use of literary devices through which they prove that Seymour Glass probably has post-traumatic stress disorder and that Gilman's narrator's tragic mental breakdown is the product of a society that ignores the needs and desires of women. Even when we organically guide students to these analytic epiphanies, they are still following a formula that instructors instinctively set up for them in order to get them to an almost universally accepted reading of a particular text. This is more ominous to me than the monsters themselves waiting to be revealed in many of these same texts.

Cohen's Influence on Traditional Literary Interpretation

I find there is significant value in directing students to a more creative, though clearly supported, interpretation of these texts. And to inspire and pull forth such interpretations from our students, we need to explore methods that get them to come up with their own ideas based on the relationships between bodies of texts in the same way Cohen sees relationships between monstrous and cultural bodies. Cohen's third thesis observes in the monster's rejection of categorization that "the monstrous offers an escape from its hermetic path, an invitation to explore new spirals, new and interconnected methods of perceiving the world" (7). In acknowledging that the monster "always escapes" (Cohen 6), writers and thinkers (our students) must revisit traditional definitions of what is acceptable and what is not in society or rethink how a particular culture sets limits or understands various laws of nature.

If we adopt a similar mode for the interpretation of texts as instructors, we will ultimately encourage our students to rethink analysis and argument. We show them that it is acceptable to violate textual boundaries in order to create original arguments about what they think is actually happening in the text. For example, one of my assignments helps students come up with a unique topic guided by their own understanding of Cohen's text that they have thoroughly read and worked through together. Regarding the primary fictional texts we use for the first essay, we tend to start with Gabriel García Márquez's short story "A Very Old Man with Enormous Wings" and either "The Burning" or "December 29, 1890" by Momaday. On the surface, neither of Momaday's poems have explicit monsters. In fact, my students tend to be struck by oppositional forms in each—"The Burning" is steeped in cosmological and abstract imagery, or "strange upheavals" (3) that move the reader from some magnificent happening "no one understood" (3) to flickering figures in a forest setting. "December 29th, 1890" takes solid, tangible objects—"In the shine of photographs/are the slain, frozen and black" (1-2)—and with the reader's imagination transforms the photographs into a collection of stories, fluid points in time, which the poet has memorialized through sensory language. In Marquez's "A Very Old Man with Enormous Wings," there is a monstrous character with "a few faded hairs left on his bald skull and very few teeth in his mouth [. . .] huge buzzard wings, dirty and half-plucked" who speaks "in an incomprehensible dialect" (Marquez). Nonetheless, most of my students accept that the old man who has miraculously arrived into the town is more of a benevolent "angel" rather than ominous beast by the story's end. However, the goal of the first essay assignment is to guide my students' analyses so that they can identify the sinister, monstrous characters and ideas within these texts. In this regard, I can be sure they are unable to find another reading close to theirs online and be tempted to write someone else's interpretation into their own.

In an effort to realize this objective, I initially adapted an assignment from Professor Gita DasBender[1] who tends to avoid specific essay prompts that students could simply rewrite into a not-so-original thesis and ultimately dull essay. For her assignments, she uses phrases such as "in this essay I expect you to explore an interesting idea about" some particular focus of what her assigned texts have in common and then follows up with the statement, "so that your readers can understand something new and different about" her class unit. However, assignments like these are not just difficult for students, but they are also challenging for the instructor to execute well. These phrases are vague and seemingly overwhelming to explain, much less to incorporate into an essay

---

[1] DasBender and I used to work together at Seton Hall University, and she often shared her assignments and pedagogical strategies with the English Department faculty.

response. They start to become clearer when my students can view multiple literary texts through an essay like Cohen's "Monster Culture."

"Monster Culture" is doing more than simply showing how texts connect; it functions as a type of lens through which to find meaning in other texts and helps reveal ideas the reader would have otherwise not thought about had she not read it. Cohen's monsters become for my students the texts themselves. Cohen argues in his first thesis that "the monster exists only to be read: the [word] *monstrum* [he explains] is etymologically 'that which reveals,' 'that which warns,' a glyph that seeks a hierophant" (4). The task is to examine a selection of texts and point toward a particular reading of the text so that there becomes an identifiable monster and then figure out what message the reader must heed. The language in "The Burning" reveals and warns that "the monstrous nature of language itself . . . [—]the thing that speaks us, as speaking subjects—is inherently inhuman" (qtd. in Cohen x). Words and phrases such as "numb, numberless," (Momaday, "The Burning" 1) "disasters," (Momaday 2) "far planes of the planet buckled and burned," (Momaday 5) "scorched sky, clusters of clouds and eclipse" (Momaday 7) in "The Burning" are "stripped of all humanistic categories" (Clark 40). They are other-worldly, consuming, distant, and greater than the human imagination—the world created by Momaday is monstrous and terrifying. These abstract images are in response to our attempt to decode and understand our cosmology—both religious and scientific. Destruction and death, our own making, are imminent for the speaker and reader observing the "shapes in the shadows approaching/Always, and always alien and alike," which when they finally arrive will cause "fields [to be] fixed in fire, /And . . . flames flowered in our flesh" (Momaday, "The Burning" 13–16). It is a violent cosmogonic narrative that reveals human nature seeking to annihilate its own species for land and dominance.

The monster demands analysis and is meant to elucidate a "certain cultural moment—of a time, a feeling, and a place" (Cohen 4). Students must see in their texts how monsters are constructed from social misgivings, ignorance, fear and that monsters change depending on who the writer is, where the writer resides, and when the writer composed her or his piece. Moreover, they have to understand that texts are born from prior texts in addition to past experiences and problems. For Cohen, "Like a letter on the page, the monster signifies something other than itself; it is always a displacement always inhabits the gap between the time of upheaval that created it and the moment into which it is received, to be born again" (4). This concept of monstrosity has made me reconsider the rhetorical situation in writing with a monstrous twist. The time of upheaval Cohen mentions is the exigence; it is the "situation that both calls for discourse and might be resolved by discourse" (Grant-Davies 266). But something happens once that response is received by a reader or listener: it is reborn. Using a course theme of monsters and monstrosity, students can first find the monster based on the cultural moment examined in the narrative, and through synthesis—both textual and experiential—find meaning in what the monster signifies and how the author is responding to or attempting to resolve a particular situation.

The rebirth of student responses takes many poignant forms in my monster class. Through the lens of "Monster Culture," Momaday's poem "December 29, 1890" and

Marquez's short story reveal and portend counter-hegemonic forms of resistance. This kind of a textual reading becomes frightening and fascinating, and the students are part of this transformative experience. Students engage in "a method of reading cultures from the monsters they engender" (Cohen 3). In particular, they read the "resistant Other known only through process and movement" (Cohen x): The process is their analysis, and the movement is their writing. When my students examine "December 29, 1890," they are "read[ing] backward from the present, in a 'progression' that makes a problem of temporality rather than simply reinscribes it" (qtd. in Cohen x). As part of our close-reading process in order to bridge the gap between form and monstrosity, I first ask students to identify the speaker and action within the poem. Once the students acknowledge that the poem is about someone looking at photographs, we look at both the title and description that comes after the title—similar to descriptions of places and times written on the back of or beneath photographs.

Photos are taken to preserve memories and events, and by stating "Wounded Knee" immediately after the title, which is a date, students connect this moment of reflection to some version of the historical past. The speaker of this poem begins with the present moment of looking at photographs that are the only lasting indicators of an existence of a culture mostly exterminated at a real place and time in the past—Wounded Knee. After expounding upon this point, I ask students to look at the movement within the poem from palpable pictures to an almost cinematic flashback:

> Women and children dancing
> old men prancing, making fun.
> In autumn there were songs, long
> since muted in the blizzard.
> In summer the wild buckwheat
> shone like fox fur and quillwork. (Momaday, "December 29, 1890" 5–10)

The photographs "image ceremony" (4); in other words, they recreate the phantoms of the past—the women, children, and old men—who will always exist in the present. Each time the poem is read, these specters are "the slain, frozen and black / on a simple field of snow" (2–3). Typically, my students are struck by the word "image" being used as a verb but they also see a connection between this word and "photographs."

The question students have next usually centers around who murdered these women, children, and old men and why. I use this time to give them a brief synopsis of Wounded Knee and show them a couple online images of the true victims of this massacre. Then we talk about the tension between colonized and colonizer and how "Native Americans were presented as unredeemable savages so that the powerful political machine of Manifest Destiny could push westward with disregard" (Cohen 8). In other words, the conversation shows how Native Americans were seen as monsters so that there could be a justification for conquering and killing them. The Native American bodies in the photographs in the poem are even described using both mythic and dark imagery: they are "frozen and black / on a simple field of snow" (Momaday 2–3). The contrast between black and white functions as a counter-hegemonic tool highlighting the otherness of the bodies but also their innocence. At the end of the poem, the "dead in glossy / death are drawn in ancient light" (14). Even in death, the frozen and monstrous figures of Native Americans remain part of some other-worldly past that is beyond material comprehension. The poem asks the reader to conceptualize culture by analyzing the photographs like the speaker does. Thus, the photos referenced in this poem were probably taken by the colonizer who has eradicated this same culture in an attempt to colonize. My students now begin to understand that "the monster's body quite literally incorporates fear, desire, anxiety, and fantasy, giving them life and uncanny independence" (Cohen, "Monster Culture" 4). The colonizer cannot help but see the Native Americans as monsters even while the reader acknowledges that they are far from that in their dancing, singing, farming, and creating.

Finally, we see with "A Very Old Man with Enormous Wings" an actual monstrous body instead of an interpreted one: it is frail, old, human-like but also part animal. The reader is introduced to Marquez's monster through the eyes and ears of Pelayo who struggled "to see what it was that was moving and groaning in the rear of the courtyard. He had to get very close to see that it was an old man, a very old man, lying face down in the mud [. . .] impeded by his enormous wings" (Marquez). Pelayo then runs off frightened by this "disturbing [hybrid][2] whose externally incoherent bod[y] resist[s] attempts to include [him] in any systematic structuration. And so the monster is dangerous, a form suspended between forms that threatens to smash distinctions" (Cohen 6). The next few sections of the short story involve the townspeople's attempt to understand what the old man is and why he is there in their town as well as to determine whether they should kill him or simply imprison him for their own safety. While trying to make sense of this foreign body, they finally settle on the label of angel even though he defies the religious definition of one according to the town's Catholic priest, Father Gonzaga. It should be noted that many of my students would later question the validity of this label.

Without bringing "Monster Culture" into our discussion of this text, despite the misgivings my students might have about interpreting the old man as angel, they tend to accept this reading when working on their journal responses about this text prior to class on their own. During our class discussion, I ask them once again to take out the essay by Cohen and attempt to categorize the old man themselves. I ask them why they think he is an angel without any real evidence of his divine origin other than having wings and only the narrator's declaration that the "neighbor woman who knew everything about life and death" was the first to refer to him as an "angel" (Marquez). To help them come up with perhaps a different interpretation of what he may represent instead, I have them do a character analysis of the old man. We talk about what he looks like, sounds like, what he eats, how he behaves, and what motivates him to act in addition to investigating his relationships to the other characters. I ask if he changes over time and how, and whether anyone is transformed on account of his or her initial

---

[2] In the original quoted material Cohen uses the plural "hybrids."

interaction with the angel. Next, I have the students identify a thesis from "Monster Culture" that might apply to the old man the most if we were to agree that he is a monster based merely on his physical appearance.

Most of my students discover that Cohen's third thesis "The Monster Is the Harbinger of Category Crisis" (6) serves as a convenient critique since they note the old man's hybrid nature. The old man, "by refusing an easy compartmentalization" of his character's identity, "[he] demand[s] a radical rethinking of boundary and normality" (6). These connections move our discussion into the magical realism of Marquez's short story because the townspeople do not question his hybridity, but rather they simply want to know what the old man is in clear terms. This phenomenon reveals to the reader that the problem is not that this type of monstrosity exists, but that it cannot be explained easily by scientific laws or human logic. In other words, the "monster's body [. . .] demands instead a 'system' allowing polyphony, mixed response (difference in sameness, repulsion in attraction), and resistance to integration—a 'deeper play of differences, a non-binary polymorphism at the "base" of human nature'" (qtd. in Cohen 7). It is human nature to want to make clear (albeit arbitrary) distinctions in terms of how we perceive the world, each other, and ourselves. What Momaday and Marquez accomplish through monstrous language, otherness, and resistance shows that culture is more complex than traditional dichotomous thinking suggests. For this reason, society struggles with understanding differences as they exist between cultures and within them.

Moving Beyond Interpretation and into the Writing Process with Cohen

Cohen's essay "Monster Culture" serves as the introductory argument that influences how students respond to and construct arguments. By having his text be the first argument they read, and one that can be used as a lens to view the world or other texts, students will understand that philosophical and ideological positions do not exist in a vacuum. When we construct arguments, we are always thinking about some other ideas that came before the ones we now have. Before my students write any of their MLA-formatted, standard English, rhetorically situated, thesis-driven, multi-paragraphed essays with a clear introduction, body, and conclusion, I have them submit a weekly literature response on that particular week's readings. I call it a literature response because the only expectations I have for such assignments are that they read the assigned texts and use quotes to support any points they make about the texts. Otherwise, they have the option of making the response personal, linking ideas to things they have seen or read outside of our classroom, and to comment on whatever about the texts they are most interested in unraveling and questioning. Included here are some excerpted literature responses that my students have submitted:[3]

---

[3] For many reasons including authenticity, which I will systematically highlight later in the chapter, I have chosen to copy and paste student responses verbatim without correcting what are generally perceived to be grammatical errors in the so-called prestige dialect.

Student Sample Response #1: In his fourth thesis, Cohen says, "The monster is an incorporation of the outside, the beyond—of all those loci that are rhetorically placed as distant and distinct but originate within." (7). Although the monsters represent a form of our curiosity of the unknown, the monster inevitably is a reflection of ourselves because it is created or "originates" from us. In the short story, "A Very Old Man with Enormous Wings," Father Gonzaga ironically doubts if the supernatural creature is an angel the most. He even brings up the devil to make the villagers see the supernatural creature in a monstrous way. Marquez writes, "He reminded them that the devil had the bad habit of making use of carnival tricks in order to confuse the unwary. He argued that if wings were not the essential element in determining the difference between a hawk and an airplane, they were even less so in the recognition of angels." (2). Father Gonzaga decided to associate the supernatural creature with the devil within moments of meeting him. Perhaps, Father Gonzaga was fearful that he was, in fact, meeting an angel and this angel defied the beliefs of what an angel should be like. This fear of the supernatural creature actually being an angel is a reflection of Father Gonzaga's insecurity in his own religious faith.

Student Sample Response #2: "A Very Old Man with Enormous Wings" by Gabriel García Márquez connects to ideas about social construction within societies and reactions to anything that differs from the norm. As the news began to spread across the town, people became intrigued and curious with this new mystical and "angelic" being. However, what stood out to me the most was that everyone who came across the creature wanted to categorize it (Cohen) or use it for their own benefits. One example of categorizing would be the repetition of the word "angel". Even though it wasn't a self proclaimed name or titled, it was what Pelayo's "wise" neighbor could relate the very old man with enormous wings to. This reflects the naivety of the people within the town, and how easily people are able to accept a label based off of another's ideology without question.

In addition to analysis and close reading (and as a tool of assessing whether my students have read for the week), the literature responses also get them comfortable using certain compositional skills; one in particular is quote framing. Because my students are using quotes in their responses, these informal assignments reinforce that quotes must be introduced, explained, and related back to the initial guiding idea that made them choose the particular quote (which should later transition into connecting the quote to the thesis statement in the formal essay). These responses help develop their main essay, given that my formal writing assignments tend not to have a specific question. Instead, I encourage students to build on the ideas they formulated in their literature responses to help them hone their thesis statements.

Another function of these literature responses is to get students to relate better to material that they otherwise would not pick up on their own outside of the classroom. I ask students to point out in their responses what moves them or what they think about that may relate to a larger picture concerning how humans relate to each other and understand their world. In this way, I hope that the literary texts become more accessible and have real-world connections despite being pieces of fiction. The following are some student responses where the writers question the text, point out something striking, or relate it to a larger human problem:

> **Student Sample Response #3:** So why is it consider a monster [in Toby Litt's, "The Monster"] if is not harming nobody? In my understanding is consider a monster because it doesn't know his identity and neither where to go. In a human perspective could be considering a monster a person that doesn't know their true identity and doesn't have goals in life. To conclude Litt states, "the monster had no story, unless being a monster is story enough."
>
> **Student Sample Response #4:** Litt refers to the monster as "our monster". I find it interesting that the author decided to say "our" instead of "the" when describing the mental and physical pain the monster endures. I originally perceived the monster as innocent and childlike because it is always "rediscovering" things and how it lacks a form of self awareness, however, I noticed that the monster seems to be frustrated with its inability to remember anything. Referring to the monster the story states, "Waking, the fact of waking and the quality of it, was invariably a disappointment" (Litt 136) and "This was probably, apart from the moments just after a headbash, when our monster came closest to happiness." (Litt 137). I find the monsters frustration for its lack of knowledge and the result of it being inflicted pain to be extremely significant to why it will never go on a quest for its true identity.
>
> **Student Sample Response #5:** The monster in Toby Litt's short story represents an ideology of people who are deemed "different" in the society. The story appeals to our sense of emotion by explaining to us how people of a different nature view themselves when they are in a minority and are not accepted for who they are by society. As Toby Litt puts it, "There were other monsters in creation, or the monster assumed they were other monsters (it did not philosophize on the nature of monstrosity—all could be monsters, without norm from which to deviate)" (Litt 135). This explains the nature of the monster. They were all monsters with similar features. Because the monster in question was different in its way of life it was keen to associate itself with the other monsters. For example before people of color were given somewhat equal opportunities after slavery, they were the "monsters". People of color were misunderstood and victimized based on the color of their skin. In those days, this affected the lives of people of color in a physical and emotional way, thereby generating hate for their oppressors. In Toby Litt's monster, the monster is trying to figure out his true identity.

The literature responses vary in their sophistication, but despite the level of my students, they all are developing as readers and writers by even attempting to make connections or question the texts. I tell them at the beginning of the semester that many if not all of them will read texts that will bore, upset, delight, and confuse them. However, by making their best effort to complete these responses, they come to class being able to take part in a meaningful discussion. These assignments help keep the course moving in addition to preparing students to use their ideas from the readings in structuring their essay arguments.

As evidenced by the samples I included here, some of the writing styles and structure are choppy or somewhat awkward, yet it is clear that these students are attempting to pull meaning from unfamiliar texts. They are also creating what I would argue is good writing, especially because it will develop the more they practice. Like Paul Kei Matsuda, who discusses the relationship between the quality of a nontraditional student's work and misinformed perceptions of their work in "Alternative Discourses: A Synthesis," I find that

> students who come from other linguistic, cultural, and educational backgrounds sometimes compose texts that seem to lack coherence in the eyes of readers who are accustomed only to dominant varieties of English [. . .] the apparent lack of coherence is not necessarily an indication of the lack of intelligence (Kaplan 1966; Connor 1996); instead, it may come from differing definitions of what constitutes "good writing" (Li 1996). (193)

Student Sample #3, because of errors in language usage, first appears to be written by a lower-level student; however, this student actually ended up receiving high grades on each formal essay and an A for the course. She is not a native English speaker and may have put forth the most effort out of all of my students throughout the semester. Her question about why the character of the monster in "The Monster" by Toby Litt was seen as monstrous despite its outwardly gentle behaviors is quite complex in terms of human existence and identity. In fact, this question of what it means to have an identity versus the tragedy of no identity is deeply fascinating and relates well to both how writing instructors view the type of discourses our students create because of their unique identities and how identity functions in our own society. This initial question guided the focus of her first essay, although she used a different literary text. Here is an excerpt from the introduction of her first essay:

> The lack of difference in a culture makes people reject those that are different in terms of their gender identity. Everyone wants to be accepted the way they are because there are people who are born with a certain sex, but within the years they start exploring their true identity; this exploration sometimes leads to rejection by their family and culture. The main character of "Lusus Naturae" by Atwood represents an identity transformation, which lead her family to believe that it was better for all pretending she was dead. The exploration of gender identity is seen as monstrous in families, individuals in this transformation are discouraged by the society.

This four-page essay incorporated Cohen's text, Atwood's short story, and a poem as evidence.

I not only incorporated literature responses into the course but also sequenced assignments that help to focus the drafting process for each formal essay. One of the assignments asks students to pull quotes from each reading they are going to use for their essays to help teach synthesis using literature. I have students extract only quotes, one from each text that appears to relate in some way to the main text (e.g., Cohen's). I model this assignment for them by first taking the quote about female "'Deviant' sexual identity" (Cohen 9) from the main essay "Monster Culture" in which Cohen discusses the woman as Other: "The woman who oversteps the boundaries of her gender role risks becoming a Scylla, Weird Sister, Lilith ('die erste Eva,' 'la mère obscuré' [sic]), Bertha Mason, or Gorgon" (9). This selection from Cohen should help students develop a relationship between one additional literary narrative such as a poem or short story, monsters, and female identity. I then ask students to pull out a quote from each text that they can relate to Cohen's text in some way. For example, I use this quote from a poem by Sexton in which the female speaker describes her detachment from what is expected of women: "I have gone out a possessed witch [...] a woman like that is not a woman quite/I have been her kind" (Sexton 1–7). I then extract one from the short story "Lusus Naturae" by Margaret Atwood in which the narrator also emphasizes the detached relationship she has with social expectations of women:

> I saw something, but that something was not myself: it looked nothing like the innocent, pretty girl I knew myself to be, at heart [...] I'm sorry to say I lost control. I laid my red-nailed hands on him. I bit him on the neck. Was it lust or hunger? How could I tell the difference? He woke up, he saw my pink teeth, my yellow eyes. (Atwood)

At this juncture, I underscore the connections between these texts and Cohen's quote in my own words, thereby demonstrating the relationship between gender roles and monstrosity. Cohen's text emphasizes the deviation from traditional gender roles and its monstrous transformative impact on women. This is in keeping with his overall idea of monstrous difference and the social reception of this difference. Sexton and Atwood perpetuate it in their literary narratives about female sexuality or mental illness: women who rejected or rebelled against social stereotypes of them were no longer quite women. They are mad, deformed, and even animal-like.

If students can identify relatable quotes and explain why they relate to them, they can start to use these same texts as evidence to strengthen an argument—usually unique and personalized—they uncover from these connected quotes. As previously mentioned, these assignments do not have a required form. I direct students to make charts, or structure it in the easiest way to pull meaning and weave connections between texts. Table 10.1 shows some of the different ways my students have completed this assignment.

Table 10.1 Student Sample Quote Assignment #1

Quote from Cohen, "Monster Culture"	Quote from chosen poem or short story	Explanation on how/why these two quotes are related
"This refusal to participate in the classificatory 'order of things' is true of monsters generally: they are disturbing hybrids whose externally incoherent bodies resist attempts to include them in any systematic structuration. And so the monster is dangerous, a form suspended between forms that threatens to smash distinctions" (Cohen, 6).	"I have ridden in your cart, driver, waved my nude arms at villages going by, learning the last bright routes, survivor where your flames still bite my thigh and my ribs crack where your wheels wind. A woman like that is not ashamed to die. I have been her kind" (Sexton 15–21).	Sexton is speaking about this supposed witch that is free at night, and it unclear if Sexton herself is saying it or it's just narration of a outsider, who's part of society ironically, looking in on what she has been exempt from, "I have been her kind." When Cohen speaks about this monster" that threatens to smash distinctions," (Cohen 6, 11) it could be said about Sexton's witch who is a female at night in those days showing skin, breaking rules, and tasting freedom. A man can do this and call it a regular night; cracking a cold one with the boys. But a woman who threatens the patriarchy and systematic structuralization by being free, at night, waving her naked arms, feeling bites from the flames (sounds of the witch trials in salem) is a dangerous woman, "not a woman quite," not afraid to die this way, a monster of category crisis.

Student Sample Quote Assignment #2

Quote from Cohen Monster Theory: "Curiosity is more often punished than rewarded, that one is better off safely contained within one's own domestic sphere than aboard, away from the watchful eyes of the state" (12).

Quote from "The Yellow Wall-Paper": "I see her on that long road under the trees, creeping along, and when a carriage comes she hides under the blackberry vines. I don't blame her a bit. It must be very humiliating to be caught creeping by daylight!" (654).

Explanation on how/why these two quotes are related: Both quotes are related because they describe how curiosity is substandard. It's not a good thing to step out of one's boundaries because your inquiring mind can lead you to make decisions that eventually can result in painful and unpleasant outcomes. Which goes back to what Cohen said: "curiosity is more often punished than rewarded." (12) As the speaker from "The Yellow Wall-Paper" indicated it's embarrassing to be spying on others, but humiliating to be caught.

Student Sample Quote Assignment #3

Quote from "Monster Culture" by Jeffery Jerome Cohen: "The Monster prevents mobility (intellectual, geographic, or sexual), delimiting the social spaces through which private bodies may move. To step outside this official geography is to risk attack by some monstrous border patrol or (worse) become monstrous oneself" ("Monster Culture," 12. Cohen).

Quote from "Mirror" by Sylvia Plath: "A woman bends over me, Searching my reaches for what she really is. Then she turns to those liars, the candles or the moon. I see her back, and reflect it faithfully. She rewards me with tears and an agitation of hands."

Explanation on why the two quotes are related: The mirror in the poem "Mirror" by Sylvie Plath is bringing light to the fact that in society, people must look a certain way, even if the person doesn't look anything like society wants them to. This causes the person, instead of being who they are, to put on a facade for society and essentially be a completely different person. If a person were to go against this society will lash back at them and judge them negatively. The quote from Jeffery Jerome Cohen represents why the woman in the poem "Mirror" keeps abiding by societies rules even though she doesn't like them because she's afraid of being judged and treated like a "monster" (ugly).

Through this type of assignment, students are able to conceive original ideas about what these texts mean when read side by side. They each focus on gender issues within a culture and how the dominant, male-centered culture controls or limits the nondominant female gender within the same culture in different ways. This particular assignment ended up informing the direction of many of their second essays which revealed the oppressive nature of a patriarchal culture and its lasting effects on women. If I had asked students to write a paragraph that shows how the two texts relate, I would typically receive generalizations about the texts without direct quoting.

By asking students to focus on the quoted text and working slightly backward, they can more easily see the relationship and learn how to put texts into conversation with each other—which is one of the main goals of the research essay writing process. In these examples, the students are offering sophisticated analysis but using "hybrid discourse," what Judith Hebb refers to in her essay on "Mixed Forms of Academic Discourse: A Continuum of Language" as "a mix of home and school languages" (21). Ultimately, the students are processing information in a way that demonstrates deep textual engagement and developing aspects of the writing process. I could have simply asked students what they know about gender oppression. Instead, I had them find instances of it without being specific and perhaps limiting in my expectations. The aforementioned examples come from two female students of color, and a white, male student, yet they are engaging in a type of unified, progressive discussion about how the poems and short story reveal the consequences of gender oppression.

Both the literature responses and quote charts are not formal writing assignments and do not require that students follow any fixed form when they complete them; however, their function is to have students practice basic writing skills in less intimidating pieces in order to prepare for drafting argumentative essays because, as Matsuda cautions, "to encourage students to construct alternative discourses without providing them with an accurate understanding of the dominant discourse practices would be irresponsible because [. . .] students and newcomers to academic discourses are not granted the kind of authority that established scholars have" (195). How we understand and develop student writing practices is one of the reasons I chose Cohen's text as the foundational text of my writing course. Students can see what a scholarly text looks like as they attempt to engage with it and analyze it. In addition, they must be able to construct a guiding argument or thesis statement for their formal essays inspired by Cohen's essay, effectively integrate quotes from it, use it to connect with other texts assigned in the course as a way to understand and improve upon synthesis before finally including it in their works cited page to show they are using another source to support their arguments.

Although my course is an introductory literature class, we do not spend the entire semester only searching for meaning in the assigned literary texts. I review the skills they were taught in English 101: Composition I. Their essays are not traditional literary analyses; instead, I want them to continue to formulate an argument about the ideas they come up with after making connections with the assigned texts. They have to create an argumentative thesis statement around a particular idea that struck them from a single literary text, and while it can include a particular literary device they want to examine, it does not need to in order to be complete. They also must support their argument with evidence just as they did in English 101. While they are allowed to incorporate personal experience or other things they have seen and read, they must use the assigned texts (e.g., Cohen and other literary texts) as their additional sources in support of their arguments. In this vein, they are not simply learning a new writing genre. I am reinforcing the structure of a familiar genre from a previous course—the academic research argument. For example, these are some of the student-created thesis statements from our first assigned essay (#1–2) and final essay (#3–5):

Student Thesis #1: In "Monster Culture," by Jefferey Jerome Cohen, the third thesis spoke to me the most as I connected it to the world and human history. Thesis three is about how monsters represent the new and different entering a culture. A culture tends to label it as monstrous due to it being beyond category. This exact idea is demonstrated in the short story, "A Very Old Man with Enormous Wings," by Gabriel García Márquez and the poem "The Burning," by N. Scott Momaday. When a being is unfathomable, people label it as monstrous, then shun or exploit the entity.

Student Thesis #2: Monsters are widely represented as ugly and scary creatures; creatures that look like a deformed humanoid. People with disabilities are often perceived as such creatures even in the evolved societies of today that remain egocentric and fearful.

Student Thesis #3: Is it not enough. It's been years since the black society been lying to repeatedly, like even in today's society they still be lying to us and keeping the true hided a way like it's some secret from god. In fact, *Dutchman* by Amiri Baraka and *Get Out* by Jordan Peele use the character of Lula and Rose to demonstrate the hypocritical way the black community is treated.

Student Thesis #4: The monster comes out at night, the monster doesn't prey during the day. Amiri Baraka's play *Dutchman* and Jordan Peele's *Get Out* use stereotypes to illustrate the oppressive nature of racism by redefining both the black and white aesthetics. Though both *Dutchman* and *Get Out's* uses of stereotyping fetishize the black body, *Dutchman's* use of stereotyping speaks on the control and exploitation of the black race.

Student Thesis #5: The racial identity problems many groups deal with is Who am I really? Is it okay for me to be black, Spanish, Asian or any group outside of the white population just to fit in? After watching *Get Out* by Jordan Peele and the Play *Dutchman* by Amiri Baraka, the racial identity for black people in white communities shows that it is not okay to blend and mix into these communities without societies negative insight. The results of this negative response on young minority trying to fit in with white society have shown to be fatal and dangerous.

For their essay topics, they use literature, but they are not necessarily analyzing a single text from the standpoint of a particular literary device. While I do give students the option of taking advantage of literary devices in their essays, because many of them are uncomfortable with literary analysis, we slowly move to including devices in their thesis statements for the second and third essays. I encourage students to adopt this approach after they become comfortable using literary texts to support arguments. They can always decide to not include literary devices, but we practice using them in smaller in-class writing and group activities so they at least gain an understanding of the most common literary devices. My main goal is that they leave my class understanding, creating, and supporting their argumentative essay writing. They should also be able to apply these skills across disciplines. At the same time, if they do take literature classes at our institution or when they transfer to the senior college level, they can also analyze literature. The aforementioned examples once again represent different student levels, but they each demonstrate how "inviting under-prepared writers to cross the bridge of hybrid discourse, thereby entering the conversation of the university, will serve to empower them" (Hebb 28). The reason I chose these particular thesis statement examples out of many is that the students in question were not comfortable entering into the conversation when they first sat down in my English 201 class. Some of these students complained that I assigned too much reading and they do not like to read. Others were balancing a job then attending evening classes, such as mine that started at 7:30 p.m. Another had been told in high school that her ideas were not clear and that she could not coherently analyze literature. Another self-identified as bipolar and just did not "get literature" in his words. Nevertheless, we have manageable thesis statements and strongly supported paragraphs that allowed these students to pass my class, some with above average grades.

Implementing More Open-ended Assignments

Such assignments open up boundless possibilities for our students to uncover that "interesting idea" which then leads to "something new and different." For example, the term "difference" comes up often in *Monster Theory*: monsters are "best understood as an embodiment of difference [. . .] difference made flesh, come to dwell among us" (Cohen, "Preface" x), and "monstrous difference tends to be cultural, political, racial, economic, sexual" (Cohen, "Monster Culture" 7). These categories are primarily explored in the collection of literary texts we assign to our students, except we typically do not assign them as texts that have monsters in them, or that are monstrous in content. We instead might underscore the gender problems and oppression with which authors like De Beauvoir, Gilman, Plath, Sexton, Chopin, Atwood, Di Prima, Olds, Frost, and Faulkner grapple. Or, we focus on race when we teach Brooks, Baraka, Addison, and Leila Chatti. Or, we highlight mental illness when we teach Salinger, Ginsberg, and Foucault. These ideas are undoubtedly present in the works of these authors, but they can be conveyed to our students if we use the theme of monsters and the monstrous along with Cohen's essay in new and exciting ways.

To help students make these connections with some guidance, it is important to situate our formal essays within the context of assignments that build up to the eventual main focus. Deriving inspiration from DasBender, I require for each essay that students use one poem, one short story, and one critical essay. When we eventually get to drama, they must choose either a poem or short story and essay. Gender and sexuality come up in many of the traditional literary texts, given that they resonate especially when we consider current events in the light of the #MeToo movement. Hence, I like to show how women are transformed into a monstrous *Other* even in texts that seem on the surface simply just to be a reflection on the female gender. The essay "Monstrous Sexuality: Variations on Vagina Dentata" by Sarah Allison Miller follows how female genitalia pose a problem depending on the particular culture or time period. She posits that monstrous sexuality is its own study and "examines several incarnations of the vagina dentata [. . .] and some of which borrow elements from this paradigmatic monster by reference, metaphor, or association" (32). She further clarifies that this study "aims to analyze what these instances communicate about the monstrosity inherent in sexuality and the sexuality inherent in monstrosity, and to consider how these examples are shaped by the particular desires and fears of the cultures that produce them" (Miller 33). Similarly, Cohen cites several well-known female monsters that are metaphorical illustrations of cultural anxiety about gender identity. According to him, they are examples of women who defiantly transgress gender boundaries (Cohen, "Monster Culture" 9).

These sexually "abnormal" women change through time and culture, and they are reimagined in texts from De Beauvoir, Plath, Gilman, and Sexton. For example, in chapter three of *The Second Sex* by De Beauvoir, the woman is seen as *Other* and defined by incompatible binaries: she is the Praying Mantis, the Mandrake, or the Demon while simultaneously called the Muse, the Mother, the Goddess, and the Beatrice (267). She wavers between angelic girl and perverse virgin—or she becomes Miller's virgin with teeth imbedded in her vagina. A sexual ideal is suddenly no longer an ideal, but rather it is emblematic of a fear or the inability to make sense of the woman who thwarts male seduction, ultimately rejecting herself as a child-bearer. The deviant woman is also reflected in Sexton's "Her Kind," which shows what happens when women reject traditional gender roles like that of a mother who is always mentally sound and sexually "pure." These maverick women become monstrous others; they are the "possessed witch[es]/haunting the black air, braver at night" (Sexton 1–2), or the house wives imprisoned in "warm caves in the woods/filled with skillets, carvings, shelves" (Sexton 8–9) where their husband-worms and child-elves remain "whining, rearranging the disaligned" (Sexton 11–12), or the sexually liberated women who "waved [their] nude arms at villages going by" (Sexton 16) and who are "not ashamed to die" (Sexton 20). In simple terms, such women cannot exist in a world that refuses to allow the celebration of their sexuality. For Plath, the so-called abnormal woman is the older woman in "Mirror" who looks into a lake that reflects back her aging face as a "terrible fish" (Plath 18). The poem is critical of a youth obsessed culture that renders aging women invisible or monstrous.

"Monster Culture" and Traditional Literary Texts

While Cohen's text works extremely well with traditional literary narratives that infer a type of monstrosity such as an illness (mental or physical), depravity, desire, behavior, deformity, or unnatural/unfamiliar appearances, it also works with texts that do not have anything that seems obviously monstrous—at least at first glance. Let us consider Charlotte Perkin Gilman's "The Yellow Wallpaper." Her narrator's behaviors become progressively unsettling as the narrative unfolds. Moreover, the impression of the large vacation home is one haunted by the ghosts of its previous owners through the narrator's imagination and leftover wallpaper reminiscent of a nursery (Gilman 131–3). Her mental breakdown and loss of a clear gender role render her monstrous as is conveyed by her husband's horror at discovering her crawling around on the floor at the end of the story (Gilman 147). In addition, the character Seymour Glass from "A Perfect Day for Bananafish" is another example of a protagonist who is initially deemed monstrous because of the violence that erupts at the end of the story (Salinger 25). Many students insist that he must be a pedophile owing to his fixation on his prepubescent girl-child companion's feet (Salinger 23). Evidently, there is also the title, which readers presumably perceive as something sexually perverted. Yet his monstrosity stems not from his own desires, but rather from what the characters around him believe which through narrative form the reader tends to accept as well.

Students see him through the eyes of others: to Muriel's mother, Seymour is a "raving maniac [. . .] who may lose control" (Salinger 21–2), and while Muriel is "not afraid of Seymour" (Salinger 23), she admits that he appears "pale" and sickly (Salinger 22). Seymour fascinates Sybil who seeks him out on the beach but later leaves him "without regret" (Salinger 25). However, the woman in the elevator judges this same character to be unstable, which is evident in the manner in which she asks the elevator operator to let her out of this confined space that she briefly shares with Seymour (Salinger 25). All of these responses to Seymour's behavior in addition to the reader's own discomfort toward him allow his character to be seen as "the scapegoat monster" who is "ritually destroyed in the course of some official narrative, purging the community by eliminating its sins. The monster's eradication functions as an exorcism" (Cohen 18). To the people around Glass and Gilman's narrator, both of them are in a way eradicated, thereby liberating society of their burden. Students see that the expectations placed on people with mental illness—which is to ignore their symptoms and the desire for them to reintegrate into society simply by willing it—leave these sufferers no choice but to either kill themselves or succumb to a mental breakdown that divests them of their humanity. After discussing how these types of monstrosity are actually reflections of the society around them, students not only adopt common interpretations about these texts but also conceive original theses.

Conclusion

As long as students actively engage with the course, they will ultimately be successful. For those who find confidence in their ability, they will create writing that will be above average, landing them perhaps their first A or B in a writing course that they may have initially enrolled in with dread. While I am concerned about basic writing form that meets my department's course requirements outlined in the syllabus that all writing teachers must distribute at the start of the semester, I am much more drawn to this affirmation from Carmen Kynard in her essay "New Life in This Dormant Creature": "THE[4] language of the university" lacks—a focus on "interrogation [. . .] of social consciousness and change," not "just form over substance" (35). Kynard is right in her desire to encourage students to "[read] and [write] at the site of their own sociopolitical realities instead of from a hyper-Westernized, bourgeois, literary imposition (the de facto curriculum of freshman core courses)" (36). Through my course, I hope to show my students how to direct and support an argument and have the freedom to do that in a way that highlights the diverse backgrounds from which they come. I also hope such a course gives them the tools to comment on the sociopolitical realities of our world that currently hold the disenfranchised back, including some of my students who fall into this category. This is why I steadfastly maintain that the theme of monsters and monstrosities for my English 201 course and the use of Cohen's text is helpful and successful in teaching writing.

Most of my students are what Hebb refers to as "college students in the margins for whom English is a second language and for under-prepared basic writers, whose discourse is measured for correctness against 'traditional' academic discourse, whatever that may be" (22). Consequently, they struggle initially with academic

---

[4] This word is capitalized in the essay itself.

writing, often feeling like they cannot access it, let alone imitate it. One of my goals for my composition courses is to convince students of their own individual intellectual brilliance regardless of their background. I want my students to stop thinking that they cannot contribute meaningfully to academic discourse because they view it as more difficult to understand than to what they are accustomed.

When author Zadie Smith temporarily allowed herself to cross borders and speak in the language of her youth and that of the academe by "adding a new kind of knowledge to a different kind [she] already had [. . .] [she] felt a sort of wonder at the flexibility of the thing. Like being alive twice" (Smith). I have seen this change in my students who have been encouraged to add to their voices instead of allowing them to be stifled. Specifically, they participate more, they assist fellow students, they submit better work, they even share with me at the end of the semester their own realization that their relationship with reading and writing was strengthened by my unwavering belief in them through assignments and texts that asked them to confront their beliefs, values, and knowledge about the world and their place in it.

Smith describes the person who is "between worlds, ideas, cultures, voices," like many of my students, as "tragically split" (Smith). Smith ponders, "Whatever will become of them?" (Smith). We have an answer: they will be valued and will affect social change in ways that monolithic discourse no longer can. If, as Smith points out, "most of us have complicated back stories, messy histories, multiple narratives," then the world (work) we create should reflect this. The writings of my students, who are a part of the academic discourse community since they are already in the academe, similarly should be reflective of their education and diverse backgrounds that brought them together in my English 201 core writing classes. Let us consider the impact that these students who successfully complete college will have on our often "single-voiced" (Smith) nation that fears those who understand that "the voice that speaks with such freedom, thus unburdened by dogma and personal bias, thus flooded with empathy, might make" (Smith) a good writer, leader, and academician. Or, perhaps these students will move the academe more clearly toward that intellectual progress we claim to be seeking. Let our academic culture reflect our diverse population so our students begin to see people similar to themselves in front of university classrooms in addition to seeing similar sounding names attached to scholarly articles.

In "Monster Culture," Cohen views history as "composed of a multitude of fragments" (3). He refers to his own essay, which is a collection of these fragments, as an "unassimilated hybrid, a monstrous body" (3). Yet, we would accept his work as a scholarly argument for "understanding cultures through the monsters they bear" (Cohen 4). It thus stands to reason that we should be able to see the value in our own student work, even if their writing may seem monstrous to the dominant group that has shaped the particular discourse they are attempting to enter. Monsters and monstrous writing are meant to challenge and transform the status quo. Cohen's essay further supports the interest in and value of hybrid discourse. It also enables our students to access and produce deeply engaging intellectual work that just might even "radically undermine" a rigid system that still works to deny them entry (Cohen 6).

I find Cohen's "Monster Culture" to be a strong foundational text through its focus on difference, its examination of monster types in various social contexts, and due to the creative lens through which students can view other texts. We use this seminal work all semester. Students annotate it, and we consistently refer back to it with each literary text we read or idea we discuss so they learn to think about literary texts in conversation with Cohen's. They have to define many of his terms and be able to identify what makes the text sometimes difficult or initially inaccessible in order for it to become less "monstrous" on its own over time.

The course theme also encourages reflection on the realities of genuine monsters in current society. These could include those who commit violence against women and the continued emphasis on the Other when we think about immigrants, especially those the media and government often refer to as "illegals" or "aliens." These marginalized individuals are often given monstrous characteristics in the contemporary political and social landscape. These aforementioned texts on monsters and monstrosity help students locate these stories or commentaries in real life. These pervasive attitudes are vestiges of the past that have not yet been abandoned, even in our tireless pursuit for social justice.

A new monster emerges to take the place of an old one that was thought to be vanquished or driven out. Moreover, some monsters simply vanish over time as they are eventually understood and accepted as full-fledged humans. Finally, the most obvious value of using a text like Cohen's is that students *must* rely on their own knowledge to create arguments instead of simply googling what a text is about or regurgitating standard literary interpretations. Writers cannot imitate something that has not been done before, and this is one way we can move students toward more original thought.

References

Atwood, Margaret. "Lusus Naturae." *The Australian*, Aug. 30, 2014. *Nexis Uni*. https://advance.lexis.com/api/document?collection=news&id=urn:contentItem:5D29-0D51-F0JP-W0KD-00000-00&context=1516831. Accessed Jan. 3, 2019.

Bizzell, Patricia. "The Intellectual Work of 'Mixed' Forms of Academic Discourses." *Alt Dis: Alternative Discourses and the Academy*, edited by Christopher Schroeder, et al., Heinemann, 2002, pp. 1–10.

Clark, David L. "Monstrosity, Illegibility, Denegation: de Man, Nichol, and the Resistance to Postmodernism." *Monster Theory: Reading Culture*, edited by Jeffrey Jerome Cohen. University of Minnesota Press, 1996, pp. 40–71. *ProQuest*, https://ebookcentral.proquest.com/lib/stfranciscollege-ebooks/detail.action?docID=310376. Accessed Jan. 3, 2019.

Cohen, Jeffery Jerome. "Monster Culture." *Monster Theory: Reading Culture*, edited by Jeffrey Jerome Cohen, University of Minnesota Press, 1996. *ProQuest*, https://ebookcentral.proquest.com/lib/stfranciscollege-ebooks/detail.action?docID=310376. Accessed Jan. 3, 2019.

Cohen, Jeffery Jerome. "Preface: In a Time of Monsters." *Monster Theory: Reading Culture*, edited by Jeffrey Jerome Cohen, University of Minnesota Press, 1996. *ProQuest*, https:/

/ebookcentral.proquest.com/lib/stfranciscollege-ebooks/detail.action?docID=310376. Accessed Jan. 3, 2019.

De Beauvoir, Simone. *The Second Sex*. Translated by Constance Borde and Sheila Malovany-Chevallie, Vintage Books, 2011.

Gilman, Charlotte Perkins. "The Yellow Wallpaper." *Story of the Week*, Library of America, May 31, 2013, storyoftheweek.loa.org/2013/05/the-yellow-wall-paper.html. Accessed Jan. 31, 2019.

Grant-Davie, Keith. "Rhetorical Situations and Their Constituents." *Rhetoric Review*, vol. 15, no. 2, 1997, pp. 264–79. *JSTOR*, www.jstor.org/stable/465644.

Hebb, Judith. "Mixed Forms of Academic Discourse: A Continuum of Language Possibility." *Journal of Basic Writing*, vol. 21, no. 2, 2002, pp. 21–36.

Kynard, Carmen. "'New Life in This Dormant Creature': Notes on Social Consciousness, Language, and Learning in a College Classroom." *Alt Dis: Alternative Discourses and the Academy*, edited by Christopher Schroeder, et al., Heinemann, 2002, pp. 31–44.

Litt, Toby. *The Book of Other People*. Penguin Books, 2008.

Márquez, Gabriel García. "A Very Old Man with Enormous Wings." *Gene Therapy*, NDSU Centers, www.ndsu.edu/pubweb/~cinichol/CreativeWriting/323/MarquezManwithWings.htm. Accessed Jan. 3, 2019.

Matsuda, Paul Kei. "Alternative Discourses: A Synthesis." *Alt Dis: Alternative Discourses and the Academy*, edited by Christopher Schroeder, et al., Heinemann, 2002, pp. 191–6.

Miller, Sarah Allison. "Monstrous Sexuality: Variations on the *Vagina Dentata*." *The Ashgate Research Companion to Monsters and the Monstrous*, edited by Asa Simon Mittman and Peter J. Dendle, Ashgate Publishing Limited, 2012, pp. 311–28.

Momaday, N. Scott. "The Burning." *Gris-Gris: An Online Journal of Literature, Culture, and the Arts*, Nicholls State University, Mar. 6, 2018, www.nicholls.edu/gris-gris/issue-1/the-burning/. Accessed Jan. 3, 2019.

Momaday, N. Scott. "December 29, 1890." *In the Presence of the Sun: Stories and Poems*, St. Martin's Press, 1993, p. 139.

Plath, Sylvia. "Mirror." *The Collected Poems*, edited by Ted Hughes, Harper & Row, 1981, p. 173.

Royster, Jacqueline Jones. "Academic Discourses or Small Boats on a Big Sea." *Alt Dis: Alternative Discourses and the Academy*, edited by Christopher Schroeder, et al., Heinemann, 2002, pp. 23–30.

Salinger, J. D.. "A Perfect Day for Bananafish." *The New Yorker Digital Edition: Jul 13, 1963, Condé Nas*, Jan. 31, 1948, archives.newyorker.com/?i=1948-01-31#folio=CV1.

Sexton, Anne. "Her Kind." *Poets.org*, Academy of American Poets, Mar. 5, 2018, www.poets.org/poetsorg/poem/her-kind. Accessed Jan. 3, 2019.

Smith, Zadie. "Speaking in Tongues." *The New York Review of Books*, Feb. 26, 2009, nybooks.com/articles/2009/02/26/speaking-in-tongues-2. Accessed Apr. 20, 2019.

Part IV

Monstrosity in World Literature

11

Vamping It Up

Identity Performance and Intoxicated Bloodlust in the Poetry of Eduardo Haro Ibars

Alyssa Holan

Nadie sabe comerse como yo fotogramas,
excretar hologramas en un mundo vacío.
(Nobody knows how to swallow frames like me,
excrete holograms in an empty world)
    —Eduardo Haro Ibars, "El sueño en los cristales, imagen de la tarde." (*En rojo*,
Ediciones libertarias)

Allí en otras planicies
allí residen monstruos y vestigios
y allí mostramos dulce nuestro rostro
porque morir es dulce
y es todavía más dulce dar la muerte.

(Over there in other plains
over there reside monsters and vestiges
and over there we reveal as sweet our face
because to die is sweet
and it is even sweeter to provoke death).
    —Eduardo Haro Ibars, "Alamedas de cristal" (*Sex Fiction*)[1]

In Iván Zulueta's *Arrebato* (1979), José, an enthused filmmaker, is lured further into the intangible world of cinematography by the memory of his deceased friend, Pedro. The latter's echoing voice along with his vampiric image eternalized in the film negatives he leaves behind incessantly haunt the protagonist. While piecing together Pedro's last

---

[1] All translations are my own unless otherwise indicated.

film, José searches for a possible portal to the nonspace of ecstatic *unbeing* in which Pedro the vampire now resides, what Teresa A. Vilarós describes as "el punto de lo que está y de lo que no está, [. . .] el único punto en que el arrebato puede tener lugar" (the meeting point of what is and what is not, [. . .] the only point where rapture can take place) (206). Ultimately, heroine enables José to penetrate the aforementioned ontological divide represented in the film by the red still frame. Similar to that of Pedro, José's own transgressive journey extends beyond corporeal disembodiment though chemical intoxication and physical emaciation to encompass homosexual experiences and the inevitable arrival to eternalized nonexistence. In other words, he too falls prey to the camera lens, thus becoming a vampire.

In a similar vein, writing and publishing during Spain's early transition from dictatorship to democracy, Madrilean poet Eduardo Haro Ibars (1948–88) also reconceptualizes the allure of the vampire-blurring bestial comportment with homosexual desire and chemical intoxication. Along with intertextual references to Bram Stoker's *Dracula*, cinematographic metaphors—such as *la pantalla* (screen), *la ventana* (window), *el cine* (cinema), and *cintas verdes* (green tapes)—create a meta-cinematographic effect that emphasizes the initial (dis)placement of Haro's poetic subject outside of the fantastic scene being observed. Nonetheless, unlike the viewer who represses into his or her unconscious such immoral desires embodied by the bloodsucking anomaly from a psychoanalytic perspective, Haro's poetic subject, like Zulueta's José, allows them to surface. The male's initial visual connection with the monstrous being escalates into his personal appropriation of an alternative subjectivity that hinges on insatiable, collective corporeal defiance. Becoming one and the same with the vampire beast, he destabilizes any voyeur (male)/object (female) dynamic as outlined by Laura Mulvey in "Visual Pleasure and Narrative Cinema."

Historically speaking, the vampire as a bloodsucking, overtly subversive sexual being has long been associated with the female gender. Haro Ibars's representation of male same-sex desire through the *vampiric*, "the queer in its lesbian mode" (Case 388), magnifies the monstrous to an orgy-like masquerade of collective corporeal wounding and sadistic weeping. The chiaroscuro of the cinema enables the meshing of realities and the blurring of fleshes. Within the previously mentioned space of manipulated light and darkness, the physical divide of *la pantalla* paradoxically serves as the bridge by which the male subject *crosses into* the realm of the fantastical and correlatively, *over* to a traditionally deviant female embodiment. With respect to cultural appropriation of imagery and the potential of its resignification, Renée C. Hoogland asserts that such reconfiguration is exemplary of the nature of a consumer culture overall (168–9). Hence, a logical connection can be drawn between the poet's parodic performance of the flesh-craving vampire (via his poetic subject) and Spain's socioeconomic reality during the post-Franco era—namely, the country's evolution as a consumer society.

Contextualized within the urban space of the Spanish capital during the mid-1970s through the mid-1980s, Teresa M. Vilarós understands this desire "to hear the body speak" as characteristic of the *movida madrileña*, the underground countercultural movement in which Haro Ibars lives, writes, and publishes. With the death of Franco and the weakening of relegated gendered norms, Spanish youths gluttonously indulge in subversive corporeal expression. They consume and create alternative subjectivities through artistic creativity (as androgynous punk rockers, artists, and writers), alcohol and drug intoxication, and sexual experimentation—activities that challenge the singularity of identity. As exemplified by the popular celebratory saying "Madrid me mata" (Madrid is killing me), the transgression of bodily inhibitions often taunts the youths' own personal demise. Overall, such ownership of death correlates with the soaring popularity of horror films throughout Europe in the 1970s, with Spain being one of the major film centers for the production of vampire movies (Murphy xi).[2]

A key protagonist of *la movida*, Nacho Canut recalls the influence of Spanish horror films on the music of his band, the Pegamoides: "Películas de terror españolas [. . .] como una en que sale Tina Sainz en bragas y haciendo de vampira. Esa temática nos influía" (Spanish horror films like the one in which Tina Sainz comes out in panties and acting like a vampire. That theme influenced us) (qtd. in Cervera 149). Similarly, the horror genre impacts Haro Ibars's writing, lending form to his four poetic anthologies: *Pérdidas blancas* (1978), *Empalador* (1980) *Sex Fiction* (1981), and *En rojo* (1985). While *Empalador* immediately reveals the vampire intertextuality that defines it (its title being an overt reference to Vlad Tepes the Impaler, the fifteenth-century historical figure that inspires Stoker's *Dracula*), the Madrilean's other works also present a poetic subject that self-destructively embraces transformative undeath through performances of intoxicating forbidden pleasures that sadistically mark Spain's transformation into a fatherless state. In *Vision Machines*, Paul Julian Smith interprets this embracing of "the ugliest of the ugly" as "fatal strategies" in the sense of inevitability and mortality. According to Smith, through the exploitation of the undesirable, contemporary Spanish narrative writers (including Haro Ibars, author of *Intersecciones*) reconcile with death and at the same time "propose a new ethics of sexual relations and of artistic representation" (104). This study contends that Haro Ibars's fatal strategies extend into his poetic work and encompass a reconceptualization of "masculine" subjectivity based on transcendent corporeal ambiguity—the arrival to a defiant nonspace of boundaryless being that conceptually resembles the red still frame of *Arrebato*. Such monstrous showcasing of colliding planes of existence, replete with vampiric intertextuality and cinematographic references and metaphors, subversively underscores the transformative potential of material intelligibility. Furthermore, by penetrating the big screen and embodying alternative renditions of the spectacle of being, Haro Ibars's poetic subject metaphorically exposes an invisible collectivity, blood hungry for the corporeal freedoms implicit to the arrival of democracy to Spain.

---

[2] Carlos Losilla notes in *El cine de terror*: "El cine de terror clásico fue objeto entre los años 70 y 80 del siglo XX de una reivindicación que alcanzó tanto a los niveles más populares del público como a los más sesudos de la crítica cinematográfica" (In the 1970s and 1980s, classic horror films were the object of vindication at both the highest level of popular culture and in the most intellectual circles of film criticism) (13).

Penetrating the Big Screen

junto a la pantalla en la plata y el encaje de una sombra
brillan escudos de cartón piedra los soldados no podrán
con toda esa avalancha de carne y sentimiento mineral el poder
se expresa en caricias muchas veces y la estación abierta a toda noche.

(Next to the screen in silver and the lace of a shadow
cardboard shields shine down upon soldiers [who] will not be able
with all that avalanche of flesh and mineral to feel the power
that is expressed in caresses many times and in the station that is open all night
long). ("Wanderlust [Los vampiros de Léon]" 1–4)

A poem that recalls the nighttime, cannibalistic comportment of a pack of vampire soldiers "Wanderlust (Los vampiros de León)" (*Emplador*), immediately transports the reader to the realm of a movie theater, a space marked by the big screen, and manipulated light and shadow. Regarding the latter, the chiaroscuro of the environment intensifies the defiant allure of what the poetic subject observes, and the overall ambiguity of what he observes—whether or not the communal consumption being described is contained within the realm of the fantastical, that of cinematography, remains uncertain. Emotive intoxication as suggested by the presence of minerals, and gluttonous sexual innuendos as depicted by an "avalanche of flesh" and a sodomitic, never-closing station further confound corporeal boundaries and their corresponding significance. In this regard, the monstrous consumption of flesh becomes indistinguishable from a psychedelic trip and homoeroticism. Nevertheless, the power that antithetically qualifies the "caress" of the protagonists' hands as bloodsuckers, bearers of the syringe, and/or handlers of the male sex organ magnifies their subversive agency and the deconstructive impact of their overlooked presence. Propagandized notions of being burned beneath the flames of their forbidden corporeal pleasures, the scorched and fragmented remains masking spilled fluids left behind in the familiar space of an old bar: "[la estación abierta a toda noche] flamea carteles desgarrados ::: sus fragmentos / cubren despojos de café con leche en aquel bar tan viejo" ([the station (that is) open all night] burns torn posters ::: their fragments / cover spillages of coffee with milk in that really old bar over there) (5–6).

After initially sighting the vampires, the poetic subject names himself one of the carnivorous crew through his declaration of their shared possession of "marble." Paradoxically symbolic of both life/the desired phallus and death/the space of the cemetery, the unyielding material concretizes the perpetual presence of an anomalous collectivity whose biggest adversary is the light of day. Powerless before the sun, their alternative expressions of being reliant upon the veiling power of nocturnal hours or the imposed darkness of the fantastical realm of the movie theater: "el mármol era y es y siempre será nuestro / Yo no detengo al sol no puedo hacer / que no atraviese el pesado damasco las cortinas ciegas" (the marble was and is and always will be ours / I cannot prevent it [the sun] / from going through the heavy demask of the blind curtains) (7-9). Throughout the rest of the poem, the subject continues to identify with the vampire clan, and once again, corporeal deviance and the monstrous go hand in hand. "Fresh tombs" allude to the resting grounds of the undead as well as to their unhealed wounds from recent material indulgences. Leaving the burial sites behind, the collectivity hunts hungrily for nourishment in the shadowed crevices of existence. Nevertheless, the arrival of a new day and the need to shun its inherent clarity temporarily cut short their bloodthirsty quest. For the sake of self-preservation, the collectivity returns to the seclusion of their graves:

> nuestros soldados desertaron ya sus tumbas frescas
> buscan esos resquicios que los hombres llaman vida
> pero transcurre el tiempo engalanado las cintas verdes de los árboles
> se hacen dolorosamente nítidas y hay que volver al claustro
> Dejar las calles regresar al polvo.

> (Our soldiers already deserted their fresh tombs
> they look for those gaps that men call life
> but the adorned time passes the green tapes of the trees
> becoming painfully clear that we have to return to the cloister
> Leave the streets and return to dust). (15-19)

In the concluding stanza of "Wanderlust (Los vampiros de León)," the poetic subject's repetitive language underscores the unoriginality of the monstrousness that he and his cohort perform. His sighting of a distant castle reminiscent of the dwelling of Count Dracula himself attests to the long-standing presence of corporeal anomalies, as does his acknowledgment of the familiarity of the bloodsucking creatures' flight patterns between planes of existence. Regardless, the male imagines the impact of his own unbound presence; he envisions his collectivity's steps of transcendent dance reverberating incessantly through earthly boundaries of space and time, sensorially marking their personal bestial legacy:

> No hemos inventado el castillo allá lejos
> no hemos inventado nuevos pasos de baile entre el cielo y su sueño
> pero quedará siempre
> un recuerdo entre paredes viejas entre harapos de siglos.

> (We haven't invented the castle way over there
> we haven't invented new dance steps between the heavens and its dream
> but a memory will always remain
> between old walls among tatters of centuries). (20-3)

Similarly entitled, "Se suicida una mano [Wanderlust]" (*Pérdidas blancas*) opens with the poetic subject's description of a neighborhood cinema, its ringing bells placing the reader within a gothic scenario that problematizes temporal divides. Old cloaks heighten the mysterious and dated nature of the setting while metonymically representing the vampire, who, as the poem progresses, continuously transgresses planes of existence through corporeal flight. Recalling Jonathon Harker's commentary on the count's fingers in Stoker's work, the poetic subject's observation of the pearly nails of a moviegoer implicates the physical presence of a Dracula figure[3] within the movie theater itself—a historically sound notion. As visually represented by used condoms in Haro Ibars's "Tezcatlipocä" (*En rojo*),[4] movie houses often served as havens for transgressive sexual behavior: "El Cine Galáctico está lleno de condones usados y evolturas / de chicle y caramelos y bombones helados" (The Galactic Cinema is full of used condoms and wrappers / from chewing gum and candies and chocolate-covered ice cream bites) (72–3). The imagery of "Se suicida una mano (Wanderlust)" captures a similar sensation of sticky, sweet forbidden debaucheries, remnants of indulgent consumption marking the hands of the anomalous pleasure seeker. The presence of multiple "plumes" blurs collective monstrous flight with same-sex male desire and needles of addiction: "campanadas de un cine de barrio viejas capas de plumas / entre los dedos escudos de caramelo las uñas / nacaradas cubren despojos de una tarde" (Chimes of a neighborhood cinema old plume capes / between the fingers candy shields the pearly / nails covering spoils from an afternoon) (1–3).

In his annotated edition of *Dracula*, Leonard Wolf draws attention to the sexually deviant implications of the physical characteristics of Stoker's Dracula. He cites the American boys' entrapment game "in which one boy says 'If you masturbate, you'll grow hair on your palms,' and watches to see which of his listeners looks guiltily down at his hands," along with the standard nineteenth-century image of the masturbator as a "thin, pale, cadaverous-looking being, possessing cold hands, and maintaining irregular sleeping habits" (22–3). Wolf's observations strengthen the connection between the canonical figure and Haro Ibars's hybrid: the hand resurfaces as a leitmotif throughout the Madrilean's poetic corpus, marking not only the vampire's physical presence but also his existence as a sexual being. In "Se suicida una mano (Wanderlust)," the sighting of a "rare, hairy bird" hovering above the bell tower blurs a monstrous earthly presence with a pending masturbatory act. However, the vampire clan's ability to transgress time through "cintas verdes" implies their mere existence within the fantastical. Inevitably, the showering of white powder—metonymically symbolic of both male sexual gratification and drug intoxication—concretizes the subversive physical presence within the real, equating the notion of flight to a corporeally destructive petite mort: "y el polvo blanco el famoso polvo blanco / llueve peces y piernas y caricias y retorna de otro tiempo" (And the white powder the famous white powder / rains fish and legs and caresses as it returns to another time) (11–12).

As previously seen in "Wanderlust [Los vampiros de Leon]," the poetic subject's use of the collective voice in "Se suicida una mano (Wanderlust)" reveals his penetration

---

[3] In Stoker's *Dracula*, the nails of count become the focal point of Jonathan Harker's observation of the physical makeup of his host's hands.
[4] As suggested by its epigraphic citation of Roland Villeneuve, "Tezcatlipocä" pays homage to the "protector of vampires" (Haro Ibars 245).

of the big screen, or transformation from passive observer of the monstrous into a corporeally hungry hybrid beast. Once again, vampirism, homoeroticism, and drug intoxication appear analogous, with subversive corporeal penetration being the means through which the collectivity, marked by their piercing teeth and claws of mercury, searches for a sense of self conceptualization: "agonizamos despacio / en busca del sabor que prometía / aquel gesto en la plaza Nos buscamos / con los dientes y garras de mercurio hasta mañana por lo menos" (We slowly die / looking for the flavor/ promised by that gesture in the plaza / We search for ourselves / with teeth and claws of mercury until tomorrow at least) (14–17). Inevitably, the final stanza of the poem grounds the male subject back into the role of spectator. Casting his gaze upon the ruins of an abbey, the male subject makes an omniscient commentary about a lurking vampire boy who is eager for nightfall: "la abadía está en ruinas / pero bajo su suelo / un muchacho muy pálido espera que atardezca" (The abbey is in ruins / but under its ground / a very pale boy waits for the sun to set) (26–8). These last few verses further substantiate Haro Ibars's own consumptive habits, as they clearly allude to the scene at the abbey in *Dracula* in which the count violates his first victim, Mina, in front of her companion, Lucy:

> I could see the ruins of the Abbey coming into view; and as the edge of a narrow band of light as sharp as a sword-cut move along, the church and the churchyard became gradually visible. Whatever my expectation was, it was not disappointed, for there, on our favourite seat, the silver light of the moon struck a half-reclining figure, snowy white. The coming of the cloud as too quick for me to see much, for shadow shut down on light almost immediately; but it seemed to me as though something dark stood behind the seat where the white figure shone, and bent over it. What is was, whether man or beast, I could not tell. (Stoker 93)

"Diario de Jonathan Harker" (*Empalador*) playfully interacts with Stoker's work through its title and description of a communal trip to an unfamiliar land. In the case of the horror classic, the mysterious trip initially described in Harker's journal is revealed to be the Englishman's journey to Bistriz to meet Count Dracula himself. Here, however, the specific destination of those travelling and the motivation behind the corporeal displacement remain unclear. The convergence of the brilliant bus metaphorically fueled by drug consumption and the fog-filled surroundings visually concretizes colliding planes of reality and the ambiguous overtone of the poem in general. Nonetheless, the ability of the personified smoked crystal to "humiliate" its passengers and determine their final destination reveals the vulnerability of those who have chosen to embark on the intoxicating journey. The consumed substance's impurity heightens the reader's wariness of an unpleasant trip:

> Brillante autobús relacionado con bruma
> y sabia tierra Humillar
> es privilegio de las débiles fogatas en cristal de silicio tratado ya no puro
> Ellas confiesan el cómo y el por qué allá.

(Brilliant bus associated with fog
and wise earth to Humiliate
is a privilege of the weak fires in silicon crystal treated as no longer pure
They confess the how and the why over there). (5–8)

Structurally speaking, the poetic subject's impersonal commentary throughout the first half of "Diario de Jonathan Harker" has a paradoxical effect: while it locates the poetic subject outside of the fantastical as spectator/moviegoer, it also suggests his appropriation of Harker's voice (as suggested by the title of the poem) as stranger/voyeur in a foreign land within the realm of cinematography itself. The convoluted manner in which the male initially describes the protagonists of the trip belies the possibility of him "being" Harker: he perceives the passengers as "bland, sun consuming animals" (1–2), presumably in contrast with the moon worshipping and/or sun-fearing vampire. This transposition of the monstrous/unnatural with the human/natural as that which defines reality underscores Haro Ibars's *fatalist strategies* or exploitation of the ugly as a means to expose an alternative understanding of masculine subjectivity. Discursively allied with the vampire beast, the poetic subject is seemingly Dracula himself.

Throughout the rest of the poem, the poet's playful cinematographic intertextualities continue to blur the ontological planes of the real and the fantastic, of voyeurism with monstrous corporeal indulgences. The *pantalla* and the vampiric presence it metonymically represents surface as a time-defying mechanism through which the poetic subject, upon identifying with the anomalous being, transgresses temporal spaces. While homoerotically implicit, the declaration of a "received message" from an "impure voice" thrusts the male back into Stoker's tale as a subject other than Dracula himself.[5] Conversely, the viewing of film stills in a sperm-saturated cafe intermittently returning the poetic subject to an external position in which sadistic sexual deviance and the viewing of the horrific continually intertwine. Both are masked by permanent darkness:

Desviaciones astrales indican
un giro de cien siglos en la pantalla turbia
Recibido el mensaje recibida
la impura voz en superficie cándida
olor a semen viejo en el café donde las voces sufren
....

---

[5] The poetic subject's declaration of a message received from an impure voice recalls Jonathan's recollection of Count Dracula's welcoming letter in Stoker's masterpiece:

> My Friend.—Welcome to the Carpathians. I am
> anxiously expecting you. Sleep well to-night. At three
> tomorrow the diligence will start for Bukovina;
> a place on it is kept for you. At Borgo Pass my carriage will
> await you and will bring you to me. I trust that your journey from
> London has been a happy one, and that you will enjoy your stay in my
> beautiful land.
>   Your friend
>   Dracula   (Stoker 4)

enriquecedores hilos tenues,
amplían microfotogramas en el espacio
oscuro permanece el aura congelada por dos.

(Astral deviations indicate
a turn of one hundred centuries on the murky screen
Received the message received
the impure voice on a candid surface
smell of old semen in the café where the voices suffer
....
enriching soft threads,
enlarge microframes in space
dark remains the aura frozen by two). (11–15, 19–21)

The synesthetic image of "dark aura frozen by two" captures a temporal gap within the continuum of being similar to that depicted by the red still frame of *Arrebato*. Heroine as the metaphoric vehicle of transport marks an additional commonality between the two works. Also known as *caballo*, the drug manifests as the unruly beast that either fatally ends its users' travels or facilitates their profane experience of corporeal transcendence. Regarding the latter, unhinged shards of materiality and self-erasure attest to the experience of unbound euphoria. The release of a single sigh signals the safe return of the traveler after a voyage of chemically provoked, fleeting bliss:

De un viaje permanece solo el suspiro
y quien no ha muerto
con su caballo gris desprende esquirlas
produce profecías y se eclipsa—por la ladera en tanto
se arrastran cintas verdes y milagros.

(From a trip remains only the sigh
and whoever has not died
with his grey horse loses pieces
causes prophecies and fades away—down the hillside meanwhile
green tapes and miracles drag on). (27–31)

Elation is overpowered by destruction in "Carta de Bistriz" (*Pérdidas blancas*). Here, the poetic subject observes an apocalyptic scene tainted with sadomasochistic, homoerotic innuendos: a volcanic eruption, a hunt and the unheard crushing of bones through impalement by the "Terrible friend." Intertextually, the scene recalls Harker's betrayal of the count in *Dracula*: "A terrible desire came upon me to rid the world of such a monster. There was no lethal weapon at hand, but I seized a shovel which the workmen had been using to fill cases, and lifting it high I struck, with the edge downward, at the hateful face" (Stoker 54). Moreover, Haro Ibars's subject's emphasis on the abandonment and deception endured by the penetrated male dissolves any possibility of his appropriation of Harker's identity. In fact, rather than merely sympathizing with the plight of the vampire, the voice heard reveals itself to be none other than that of a male vampire himself. Claiming ownership of multiple burial coffins that metaphorically represent the forbidden body orifice, he takes on a collective identity that weeps in reaction to their implicit sexual penetration. Once again, a mockingly sacrilegious tone can be heard as holy lubricant enables the transgression of traditional corporeal boundaries:

> SE DESPLOMA UNA MONTAÑA—la cacería—nadie
> nadie escuchó el crujir de huesos cuando el Muchacho
> el Terrible amigo clavó su estaca Nadie
> escuchó el aúllar de mis cajas de tierra violadas por petróleo sanctus.
>
> (A MOUNTAIN COLLAPSES—the hunt—no one
> no one heard the crushing of bones when the Boy
> the Terrible friend drove his stake No one
> heard the howling of my earth boxes violated by holy oil). (1–4)

As the poem progresses, the male's appropriation of the vampire identity manifests itself through his personal aversion to the sun, and through his capacity to fly and transgress spatial boundaries in search of prey. Whereas anonymity masks his persona—he penetrates spaces as an unfamiliar face before the eyes of others—the poetic voice clearly identifies what paradoxically defines the ambiguity of his being. Suggestive of both the male sex and the intoxicating syringe, the *cuchillo*, is the constant focus of his gaze. The spilling of liquids and fusion of lead and blood further conflate the deviant acts associated with its penetrating presence:

> bueno es no ver más el sol es la vista y el olor
> de los humanos temblor de carnes
> ellos están reunidos en su bar
> andaré con pies de fieltro—siempre un cuchillo
> a lo lejos se desploma un vaso de leche no me conoce
> ....
> plomo de sangre descabellada la terrible
> bola de marfil.
>
> (Good it is not to see anymore the sun is the vision and the smell
> of humans trembling of fleshes
> they are gathered in their bar
> I will walk with felt feet—always a knife
> in the distance a glass of milk tumbles down it doesn't know me
> ....
> lead of mad blood the terrible
> ivory ball). (13–17, 20–1)

While the gay bar scene contemporizes this vampire tale, the dating of the "letter" itself—"Madrid, 1976"—directly grounds the reader back into the reality of *la movida madrileña*. In this manner, Haro Ibars explicitly identifies Madrid of the mid-1970s as analogous to Bistriz of the nineteenth century; consumptive, boundary-breaking, vampiric performances define the obscure hours of both spaces.

"Les belles heures de Vlad Dracul" (*En rojo*) immediately immerses the reader into the origins of Count Dracula, which many people consider the first vampire film to have been produced in France in 1897 (Murphy ix). The chaotic scene described within the opening verses destabilizes any sense of antiquity initially suggested by the title. Instead of recalling a past or even present monstrous experience, the poetic subject imagines a future, bestial existence within a noisy, congested, consumeristic urban society marked by broken storefront windows, groaning car motors, and impatience. The sense of individualism this initial imagery creates becomes more egocentrically nuanced when the male reveals himself to be the entity whose comportment determines the structure of the poem itself, and correlatively, the passage of time within the reality to come presented. This re-conceptualized future revolves around the poetic subject's sleeping and rising habits throughout a typical day. Thus, the significance of the title of the poem becomes clearer, despite the continued ambiguity as to whether or not the male has appropriated the voice of *the* Impaler himself:

> YA ESTARÁN ROTOS LOS ESCAPARATES
> y gemirán (pacientes) los motores
> y gruñirá con sorna la impaciencia
> cuando yo me levante a mediodía
> (la hora del mulé)
> Y escucharé a los perros de la muerte
> su aullido en los canales.
>
> (THE SHOP WINDOWS WILL ALREADY BE BROKEN
> and the [patient] motors will groan
> and impatience will growl with derision
> when I get up at noon
> [the hour of the mule vampires]
> And I will listen to the dogs of death
> their howling in the canals). (1–7)

While the male names a particular vampire breed—the *mulé*—in his elaboration of his daily routine, his own noon rising conversely relates to the nocturnal creatures' midday return to their deathbeds. As Miguel. G. Aracil notes in *Vampiros: mito y realidad de los no-muertos*, the *mulé* are "seres que durante el día suelen ser prácticamente inoperantes, pero al llegar la noche se incorporan de sus lechos hasta que suenan las doce campanadas del mediodía" (beings who during the day are usually practically inoperative, but when night comes they get up from their beds until the twelve midday chimes sound) (128). Other subtleties within the poem do lend support to the male subject's hybrid identity, one being his connection with the wild beasts of the night—the dogs of death. Furthermore, a strong parallel between the poetic subject's sexual desires and those of the *mulé* becomes apparent. A species of vampires evolving from the birth of a stillborn child or the violent death of an adult male, the *mulé* are characterized by an extensive sexual appetite more so than by a propensity for bloodsucking (Aracil 128). Rather than surfacing as a thirst-quenching substance, spilled blood in "Les belles heures de Vlad Dracul" marks hellish sexual penetration, a collective performance of spontaneous, sadistic fatal strategies. Nocturnal hours serve as the creatures' atemporal womb of blasphemous spectacle within which phallic beaks pierce forbidden corporeal orifices indistinguishable from black windows. The deviant blurring of bodies shifts back to the realm of the cinematographic with the light of day:

> Pavos sin rumbo pegarán sus picos
> a las ventanas negras Lunas/infierno
> habrá sangrado mucho en las aceras
> su maniquí de alta costura
> cuando en la noche/vientre me levante
>
> ....
>   cuando yo me despierte
> sin piernas entre piernas y sin ojos
> encima de mis ojos
> a la luz de nunca hora del té
> pues las colonias son ya de película.
>
> (Turkeys aimlessly will stick their beaks
> in the black windows Moons/hell
> will have bled a lot on the sidewalks
> its high-fashion mannequin
> when in the night/womb I get up
>
> ....
>   when I wake up
> without legs between legs and without eyes
> over my eyes
> in the light of never tea time
> for the colonies are already of film). (14–18, 23–7)

Besides utilizing allusions to Stoker's *Dracula*, Haro Ibars also borrows the titles of horror films to distinguish his monstrous poetic corpus, and consequently, to propel his male subject into the fantastical and equally intoxicating realm of hybrid being. It is in this sense in which the aforementioned works serve as a metaphorical big screen or still frame within which the Madrilean poet reconfigures masculine being. Overall, such intertextuality stresses the performability of identity and the power of personal agency:

the male subject abandons his role as spectator to enact his own rendition of his newly appropriated monstrous identity. *The Fearless Vampire Killers* (*Empalador*) serves as an example in which Haro Ibars appropriates the name of a 1967 Roman Polanski movie production, one of the most remembered vampire films for its portrayal of a gay vampire, the son of the count himself (Murphy 104). Campiness exudes from Polanski's scene of the grand ball in which identities blur and paradigms shift, vampire guests masquerading as humans, and humans being the minority in attendance (116-17). In Haro Ibars's poetic interpretation, rather than ballroom garb, decadent sweetness disturbingly masks the deviant collectivity, creating a pedophilically nuanced scenario. In accordance with camp aesthetics, the anomalous night wanderers' materialization as fleeting ice cream flavors and colors exaggeratedly connotes the vampires' seemingly innocent allure as "things-being-what-they-are-not" (Songtag 279), queerly alternating the poet's exploitation of fatalist strategies. Inevitably, the facade of childhood treats melts away to subversive performances of suicidal pleasures. A "sickly blue" suggestive of both male sexual arousal and a heroine trip gone astray metaphorically marks the pervasiveness of impending death, its inevitability concretized by the stench of past, destructive vampiric acts drifting from the men's bathroom. Furthermore, the paradoxical need to allow the dead "to rest" displaces those to whom the speaker refers to an ontological nonspace of unbeing:

> y aquella calle en sombras de otra hora hombre
> como de barquillo helados verdes al pistacho
> rosas a la fresa de ámbar a la vainilla
> o blancos blancos blancos de nata Satén en la ventana estremecida
> aroma a muerte en los urinarios y en la esquina de salitre
> le pregunta la hora un suicida a otro suicida
> pulsación de lo rápido en el terreno del más enfermo color
> el azul sin palabras para que puedan descansar los muertos.
>
> (And that street over there in shadows of another man-hour
> like of an ice cream cone ice creams green pistachio
> pink strawberry from amber to vanilla
> or white white white of cream Sateen in the shaken window
> scent of death in the urinals and in the corner of salty residue
> a suicide victim asks another suicide victim the time). (1-9)

Up to this point in the poem, the poetic subject's language locates him outside of the fantastical realm upon which he gazes. It remains unclear whether he is a vampire killer (in accordance with the title of the poem) or a vampire himself. As highlighted in the previously discussed poems, the male inevitably identifies with the anomalous clan, this time deeming himself ringleader of the blood-hungry prowlers. Evading the unremitting scrutiny of the public eye, he and his comrades conceal their forbidden homoerotic encounters and drug consumption within abject underground spaces, or the aforementioned tombs reminiscent of the clandestine spaces of the *movida madrileña*. Here, the collective boiling of their own bones in one cauldron elevates the monstrousness of their penetrating corporeal acts:

la calle está vigilada mis hombres deben pagar y pagan
una taza de té en el desierto una vena hinchada
ensalmos y cartones de lotería por casualidad
nos encontramos al salir del paso subterráneo por casualidad
hervimos juntos nuestros huesos en el caldero.

(The street is under surveillance my men must pay and they pay
a cup of tea in the desert a swollen vein
incantations and bingo cards by chance
we meet upon exiting from the underground pass by chance
we boil our bones together in the cauldron). (11-15)

"Epílogo (Le bal des vampires)" (*Empalador*) follows the intertextual lead of *The Fearless Vampire Killers*, in this case alluding to the original title of Polanski's 1967 parodic production.[6] Various parallels between Haro Ibars's poetic work and Polanski's work are evident. For example, the poetic subject's recollection of gluttonous celebration enjoyed by a collectivity of overlooked vampires mimics the film's climatic ballroom scene previously mentioned. Linguistically, his use of the diminutive underscores the ambiguity of the sexed bodies that populate the orgiastic scene and the artificiality of intelligible corporeality overall: *hombrecillos* (a naming suggestive of a lack of manhood) and *mujercillas* (a naming suggestive of physical grotesqueness) intermingle with the poetic subject. Sexual lust lures both the protagonist of the film and Haro's poetic subject into compromising situations. In the film, Professor Ambrosius's desire to rescue the beautiful Sarah leaves him in the grips of a vampire, Sarah herself. In Haro Ibars's work, the poetic subject, seduced by the feminine appearance of a fellow partygoer, inevitably participates in a homoerotic exchange. Hence, the poetic work of Haro Ibars proves itself to be more complex than the mere vampire/human charade. Within the subtext of vampirism, Haro Ibars manipulates gender signifiers, and in doing so, he underscores the artificiality of prescribed sexed identity overall. While the poetic subject maintains his partner's feminine identity through the use of the personal pronoun "she," her possession of a phallus—marked by the sperm that falls down the male speaker's back—suggests otherwise. The vampiric lover is an androgynous beast whose attractiveness, or seductive powers as an object of desire, becomes indistinguishable from penetrating sexual dominance. Intoxicating substances aid this reconceptualization of gendered identity:

En fiestas y cenas conocimos
hombrecillos achatados ellos eran sombreros
mujerzuelas coronadas de té muy ligero
ellas tienen los senos erizados de púas. El
....

---

[6] *The Fearless Vampire Killers* is the title that was chosen in the United States; the same film was originally released in the UK as *Dance of the Vampires*.

Ella se esconde entre la naftalina
se prueba ojeras en el armario más profundo
caravanas de esperma se despeñan por mi espalda.

(At parties and dinners we met
flattened little men they were hats
tarts crowned with very light tea
they have breasts covered with spikes. The
....
She hides among the naphthalene
she tries on rings under her eyes in the deepest closet
caravans of sperm fall over my back). (1-4, 7-9)

Conclusion

Speaking of a deceased gay friend in *De qué van las drogas*, Haro Ibars writes,

Vivía en un barrio obrero, en la periferia de Madrid, y su existencia no era ni mucho menos fácil; entre otras cosas, una homosexual mal asumida—no reprimida, sino convertido en espantajo de sí misma; los homosexuales de ciudad suelen aceptar la máscara grotesca que el sistema les impone.

(He lived in a working-class neighborhood, on the periphery of Madrid, and by no means was his existence easy; among other things, a wrongly assumed homosexual—not repressed, but rather turned into a scarecrow of himself; city homosexuals tend to accept the grotesque mask that the system imposes on them). (97)

Arguably, prescribed grotesqueness is what the Madrilean poet exploits throughout his monstrous poetic corpus. Penetrating the big screen, his male poetic subject becomes the imagined monster of conventional society, living the life of a queer vampire, hunting his corporeally liberating food of choice, and indulging in homoeroticism. Owing to his subversive behavior, life and death as conventionally perceived blur to the point of becoming indistinguishable. Continuous provocation of personal demise through corporeal wounding defines the poetic subject's celebratory attitude of "no regrets," or "living for the moment," a stance emblematic of the underground scene of Madrid during the late 1970s and early 1980s. The male vampire's mutilated corporeality as a penetrable, self-configured anomaly becomes his body politic in the most literal sense, visually recounting the chapters of his monstrous life choices. According to Paul Julian Smith, it is precisely these fatalist strategies that enable Haro Ibars to develop an alternative conceptualization of male being and to dismantle the gender dichotomy that alienates maleness from corporeality. The unveiling of and hunger for the male body has various consequences. Attributed a heightened consciousness of material presence, maleness incarnates a new form of sensuality. While the unyielding phallic presence is demythified through homoerotic wounding acts, the penetrability of the male body attains new significance as the desirable.

In *Our Vampires Ourselves*, Auerbach defines a social crisis as that which breeds vampires. Embodying societal fears and anxieties, the vampire figure is inherently political. With the death of Franco and the dismantling of his regime's ideological platform, Spain experiences a new sense of freedom, a fluid state conducive to the rebirth of the bloodsucking hybrid. The patriarch now absent, Spanish youths meander the underground scene of the capital, searching for a new understanding of selfhood. Becoming beasts of the night, Haro Ibars and his comrades sadistically transgress corporeal boundaries. In the epilogue of *Empalador*, Haro equates such violent and "unnatural" behavior to love itself: "Mi libro, [. . .] me parece muy bonito. Habla de vampirismo, de amor—que es lo mismo [. . .]. Adoro a los seres híbridos, a los humanimales que se evocan en la penumbra de los cuartos oscuros" (My book, [. . .] I think it is very nice. It is about vampirism, love—which is the same [. . .]. I love hybrid beings, humanimals that are evoked in the gloom of obscure rooms) (*Obra Poética* 138). Four years later in his regular column "Las tres viñetas" of the magazine *Combate liga comunista revolucionaria*, the Madrilean expounds upon his fascination with subversive creatures of the night:

> Bueno, el caso es que me gusta mucho el cine de terror; y que siento una pasión completamente literaria por los asesinatos sádicos, por quienes dedican su vida a la muerte, e incluso al genocidio. Ante el poder armado de los Monstruos en el Poder, Drácula me parece un ser enternecedor, una especia de cazador furtivo, condenado a chupar sangre en solitario, en su Castillo de los Cárpatos, porque no ha sabido ponerse al día y chupar los cauces establecidos.
>
> (Well, the thing is that I really like horror movies; and I feel a completely literary passion for sadistic murders, for those that dedicate their lies to death, and even to genocide. In the face of the armed power of the Monsters in Power, to me Dracula seems to be a tender being, a kind of poacher, condemned to suck blood on his own, in his Castle of the Carpathians, because he doesn't how to keep up to speed and suck the established channels). (12)

Whereas the reckless lifestyle of the *movida*'s vampires inevitably self-destructs, often in the most literal sense as evidenced by the AIDS epidemic and Haro Ibars's own premature death, the momentary pleasure of transcendental ecstasy in addition to the experience of rapture as concretized by the red still frame in *Arrebato* appear to have made the trip worthwhile:

> la catástrofe infinita de haber
> caído en la desgracia en el adiós sin pico ni plumas
> ni tampoco dientes ni desgarrar ni aullidos a media noche
> sin pecado ni médicos manchados ni puestecillos de periódicos
> ....

dulce la vida y la simiente la canción muerta el viaje
largo y suave por imágenes de heridas.

(The infinite catastrophe of having
fallen in the disgrace in the goodbye without beak or feathers
not even teeth neither shredding nor howling at midnight
without sin or stained doctors nor newspaper stands
....
sweet is life and the seed the dead song the trip
long and smooth through images of wounds).
("Laughing in my grave" [*Empalador*] 8–11, 27–8)

References

Aracil, Miguel G. *Vampiros: mito y realidad de los no-muertos*. EDAF, 2002.
Arrebato. Written and Directed by Iván Zulueta, Nicolás Astiarraga P.C., 1980.
Auerbach, Nina. *Our Vampires, Ourselves*. University of Chicago Press, 1995.
Case, Sue-Ellen. "Tracking the Vampire." *Writing on the Body*, edited by Katie Conboy, Nadia Medina, and Sarah Stanbury, Columbia University Press, 1997, pp. 380–400.
Cervera, Rafa. *Alaska y otras historias de la movida*. Plaza & Janés, 2002.
Haro Ibars, Eduardo. *De qué van las drogas*. La Piqueta, 1979.
Haro Ibars, Eduardo. *Empalador*. Banda de Moebius, 1980.
Haro Ibars, Eduardo. *En rojo*. Ediciones Libertarias, 1985.
Haro Ibars, Eduardo. "Las tres viñetas: El día de los monstruos (con desfile)." *Combate* liga comunista revolucionaria [Spain], Año 12, no. 347, May 31, 1984, p. 12.
Haro Ibars, Eduardo. *Obra poética*. Huerga y Fierro, 2001.
Haro Ibars, Eduardo. *Sex Fiction*. Hiperión, 1981.
Hoogland, Renée C. "Fashionably Queer: Lesbian and Gay Cultural Studies." *Lesbian and Gay Studies*, edited by Theo Sandfort, Judith Schuyf, Jan Willem Duyvendak, and Jeffrey Weeks, Sage, 2000, pp. 161–74.
Losilla, Carlos. *El cine de terror*. Paidós, 1993.
Mulvey, Laura. "Visual Pleasure and Narrative Cinema." *Film Theory and Criticism: Introductory Readings*, edited by Leo Braudy and Marshall Cohen, Oxford University Press, 1999, pp. 833–44.
Murphy, Michael J. *The Celluloid Vampires: A History and Filmography, 1897–1979*. Pierian Press, 1979.
Smith, Paul Julian. *Vision Machines*. Verso, 1996.
Sontag, Susan. *Against Interpretation*. Farrar, Straus & Giroux,1966.
Stoker, Bram. *Dracula*. Edited by Leonard Wolf. Annotated ed., C.N. Potter, 1975.
The Fearless Vampire Killers. Written and directed by Roman Polanski, Cadre Films, 1967.
Vilarós, Teresa M. *El mono del desencanto*. Siglo Veintiuno, 1998.

12

The Edges of the World in Classical Greece and Epic India

A Comparison of the Monstrous Races of Ctesias's *Indica* and the *Rākṣasas* of Vālmīki's *Rāmāyaṇa*

Albert Watanabe

While much has been written about the monstrous races at the edges of the Western world (often placed in India), one finds little on the theme from the Indic perspective. Sheldon Pollock's analysis of the *rākṣasa* (often translated as "demon") in Vālmīki's epic poem, the *Rāmāyaṇa*, presents a notable exception.[1] Drawing on J. Friedman's *The Monstrous Races in Medieval Art and Thought*, Pollock maintains that the *rākṣasas* function in a similar fashion to their Western counterparts. In this chapter, I wish to explore a more specific comparison between the monstrous races of the Greek writer Ctesias's *Indica* and the *rākṣasas* of Vālmīki's *Rāmāyaṇa*. I draw upon recent studies of Ctesias to compare with Pollock's analysis of the *rākṣasas*. While Pollock notes a few parallels of the Indic view of these *rākṣasas* with the monsters of the classical world, this chapter offers a detailed comparison of the monstrous races in Ctesias and the *rākṣasas* of the *Rāmāyaṇa*. Both Ctesias and Vālmīki place the monstrous in opposition to the norms of their respective societies, yet they also play with these oppositions, questioning these norms. The Indian epic takes us much further in this direction than Ctesias.

Ctesias (*c.* 441–394 BCE) was a Greek physician for the Persian king Artaxerxes II and the author of the *Persica* and *Indica*. These works have not survived and exist only as fragments.[2] Dominique Lenfant, in the introduction to her edition of Ctesias, dates the *Persica* to the 390s after Ctesias left the Persian court. It is unclear whether the *Indica* is earlier or later. For the *Indica*, Ctesias depends upon Greek and Persian sources. For Greek sources, the most significant is Scylax, who putatively was sent

---

[1] See Pollock (1987). A slightly revised version of this chapter appears in the introduction of Pollock (1991), pp. 68–84.
[2] I am referring to the fragments in Lenfant's edition from 2004. On Ctesias, see the introduction to Lenfant's edition, pp. vii–xxiv and Karttunen 80–5. On the *Indica*, see Lenfant (2004), pp. cxxxvii–clviii.

on an expedition down the Indus River by Darius I in the 520s BCE and who is the first to mention the monstrous races in India (Lenfant cxliii–iv; Karttunen 65–8). On the Persian side, Ctesias journeyed with the Persian king to the eastern parts of his kingdom and may have heard various information on India and may have seen the tribute sent to the Persian king from eastern vassal kingdoms.

It is also crucial to note here that for the Greeks and Persians of this time, India was the Indus River Valley bordered on the east by the Thar Desert (Lenfant cxxxviii–cxliii; Karttunen 157–60). Later we will discuss what connections can be made between these regions and the *Rāmāyaṇa* of north central India. Returning to Ctesias, the mention of these sources may give the impression that the *Indica* is a scientific ethnographical work, but I think that Lenfant is correct to point out that Ctesias's India is "une Inde fabuleuse" inhabited by monstrous races. For this reason, Ctesias could easily have drawn upon the Greek literary tradition on the wonders of the East.[3] He is our earliest major source for locating the monstrous races in India and giving us descriptions beyond just names (as Scylax did); these include the dogheads (*cynocephali* in F 45.40–3), pygmies (F 45.21–3), shade, or umbrella-footed people (*sciapods* in F 51a), *blemmyae* (those having no necks with their eyes in their shoulders in F 51a), *otoliknoi* or *panotii* (the big-eared people in F 51), the people who have no anus (F 45.44) and the Pandae, who bear children once in life and the children's hair turns from white to black as they age (F 52). These races then will pass through Megasthenes (*c.* 350–290 BCE) to Pliny (23–79 CE) and then into the Middle Ages.

Lenfant, in an article entitled "Monsters in Greek Ethnography and Society in the Fifth and Fourth Centuries BCE," characterized these races either as hybrids or as having an anatomical anomaly (i.e., often but not always having too many or too few body parts) (Lenfant 207).[4] Thus, in F 45.40–3, the *cynocephali* are part human but also have a dog's head, teeth, claws, and tail; they communicate by barking and have sex as dogs do. Pygmies are small, have long hair which functions as their clothes, and have penises which stretch down to their ankles (F 45 21). Thus, Greek ethnography, according to Lenfant, places these races at the edges of the world and changes individual anomalies into ethnic ones. However, the anomalies are not looked upon as disadvantages. For example, the *sciapods* use their feet to protect themselves from the sun. And the *cynocephali*, although they can only bark, still trade with other Indians understanding their languages and using gestures to communicate, receiving military weaponry from the Indian king in exchange. In spite of their height, the pygmies serve in the armies of kings because of their superior skill in archery. Ctesias uses these interactions with "real" Indians to give credence and a matter-of-fact quality to his accounts.[5]

---

[3] For a more comprehensive discussion of this point, see Romm, ch. 3; for Ctesias and this tradition, see pp. 87ff. Cf. also Wittkower.
[4] These two characteristics are also found in early portrayals of mythical monsters; on this point, see Clay (2003), p. 151.
[5] I am indebted to one of the anonymous referees of this chapter for this observation. Cf. Romm who notes "the matter-of-fact tone of the catalogue [of the marvel writers] helps balance the exoticism of

Furthermore, Lenfant contrasts Herodotus's attitude to these races with that of Ctesias (Lenfant 210–12). Whereas Herodotus either rejects or is skeptical of many of these races, Ctesias never questions their existence. While Herodotus links anatomical anomaly with moral degeneracy, Ctesias does not make this connection; in his estimation, both the pygmies and the *cynocephali* are most just. Thus, Lenfant argues that Herodotus adheres to the traditional model of the human as distinguished from the animal and the anomalous, while Ctesias questions these norms in raising paradoxes:

> The point here is to define the limits of the human and its attributes, but also to question certain moral norms (for instance, does the manner of copulating imply anything about the practice of justice?) or certain opinions (for instance, is it necessary to be beautiful to be just?). Ethnography, like myth, reflects the society that produced it and expresses a questioning of its norms. (Lenfant 212–13)

Before leaving the Greek world, it may be useful to say a little more specifically about where these races are located. Lenfant only says they are at the edges of the world. In Ctesias's India they inhabit the woodlands and mountains[6] along the river (e.g., the *cynocephali* live in inaccessible mountain regions, thus rendering them impossible to attack). In other words, these races do not live in the city-state, the polis, which defines the realm of the human and civilized. Friedman links Aristotle's well-known assertion of man as a political animal, a "city-state animal," with his notorious claim that some people are slavish by nature—these are the peoples who do not live in a city-state (Friedman 30). Friedman explains that the latter statement in the Middle Ages became a justification for the enslavement of those at the edges of the world. Nonetheless, this explanation may oversimplify the ancient Greek view. I think that Hayden White is correct in maintaining that the ancient Greeks also acknowledged that barbarians lived according to *some kind* of law and social order.[7] Hence, Ctesias,

---

the wonders themselves: The insistence on spare linguistic structures such as the simple assertion of existence, 'there is,' creates a veneer of clinical, dispassionate inquiry" (93).

[6] On mountains as habitations for these monstrous races, see Friedman who explains, "Generally speaking, monstrous men were placed on mountains because these features of the landscape, as Marjorie Hope Nicolson has well shown, were considered hostile and frightening. In Hayden White's words, 'desert, forest, jungle, and mountains' serve as 'the physical stages' on which the western European consciousness could act out fantasies of wildness and savagery. Thus, these places, and especially mountains, inspired great fear and distaste in medieval man" (148–9). Cf. Nicolson 39-9, White 6–7 and Hyde. This link between mountains and monstrous races seems valid for the medieval world, but evidence for this link in antiquity is rather sparse (most of the evidence points to the frightening aspect of mountains). The *cynocephali* may be the major example of this link in the classical world.

[7] As White asserts, "Most classical writers recognized that because barbarian tribes at least honored the institution of the family, they must live under *some kind* of law, and therefore were capable of *some kind* of order. This recognition is probably a way of signaling awareness of the uncomfortable fact that the barbarian tribes were able to organize themselves, at least temporarily, into groups large enough to constitute a threat to 'civilization' itself" (20).

in recording the customs and practices of the monstrous races, plays on and questions this opposition of polis and edges of the world.

Ctesias thus sets up various oppositions—polis versus forest or mountain, man versus animal, man versus the anatomically anomalous, and human morality versus the moral degeneracy of the monstrous. But instead of reinforcing the status quo, he raises questions about it by asserting the usefulness of the large foot of the *sciapods* or claiming that the *cynocephali* and pygmies are just. In this respect, Ctesias belongs to the Greek tradition of what James Romm refers to as "inverse or negative ethnocentrism," in which "foreigners [grow] not less but more virtuous in proportions to their distance from the Greek center."[8] This tradition is also closely related to that of paradoxographers. By having them perform banal actions, such as trading and serving in the army, Ctesias creates a matter-of-fact atmosphere in which to describe these monstrous races.

Let us now turn to Vālmīki's *Rāmāyaṇa*, which is one of the two major religious epics in Indian literature—the other being Vyasa's *Mahābhārata*. The *Rāmāyaṇa* relates the exploits of Rāma, an *avatāra* (an incarnation, literally, a descent) of Viṣṇu. Avatāras arise in the world, when there is some threat to destroy the world, specifically here the *rākṣasa* (demon) Rāvaṇa who has been granted protection from gods, animals, and other *rākṣasas*, but not man, because Rāvaṇa thought that they were too insignificant. The confrontation between Rāma and Rāvaṇa is brought about when Rāma is exiled to the forest and Rāvaṇa kidnaps Sītā, Rāma's wife, and takes her back to Laṅkā, his kingdom. Rāma then leads an army against Laṅkā, kills Rāvaṇa, and wins back Sītā.

Before turning to the *rākṣasas*, it may be useful to ask what was known to the Greeks about the literature of north central India. As mentioned earlier, for the Greeks, India was the Indus Valley. What information from north central India could pass through the Indus Valley to Ctesias and the West? The dating of literary works in India is notoriously difficult. The *Rāmāyaṇa* is dated from the sixth century BCE to the fourth century CE and the *Mahābhārata* from the fourth century BCE to the fourth century CE (Karttunen 147-50).[9] Both Lenfant and Karttunen are wary about distinguishing between earlier and later parts of the epic (Lenfant cl–clii; Karttunen 150). Nevertheless, it is rather intriguing to find "one-footed" (*ekapāda*) and "blanket-eared" (*karṇaprāvaraṇa*) races in both epics, which correspond to the *sciapods* and *otoliknoi* respectively in Ctesias.[10] Unfortunately, these races turn up in a list of names, and we learn nothing more about them. Outside of the epics, Indian sources

---

[8] See Romm 47. On the same page, he expands on this inverse ethnocentrism: "Whether these outermost tribes [. . .] were imagined in terms of 'soft' or 'hard' versions of primitive life, their extreme distance seemed to the Greeks to confer on them a unique ethical prerogative, licensing them to mock, preach to, or simply ignore the peoples of the interior. In their eyes 'normal' human values, as defined by those who imagine themselves at the privileged center, can appear arbitrary and even laughably absurd" (Romm 47). Romm also notes the closeness of this tradition to that of the paradoxographers (92).

[9] For the sixth century BCE date of the *Rāmāyaṇa*, see Goldman 14–23.

[10] For the *ekapāda*, see *Mahābhārata* 2, 28, 47 and *Rāmāyaṇa* 4, 39, 35; for the *karṇaprāvaraṇa*, see *Mahābhārata* 2, 28, 44 and *Rāmāyaṇa* 4, 39, 24.

also mention *śvamukha* (dogheads), which would correspond to *cynocephali*, but the earliest source is from the sixth century CE.[11] While these races should form the strict comparand with Ctesias's monstrous races, we have little more than names. Moreover, the dating of the Indian sources is also problematic. Overall, there seems to be little to compare between Ctesias and the *Rāmāyaṇa* in respect to the monstrous races. We are thus left with the *rākṣasas*.

It may be objected here that the *rākṣasas* are more mythological rather than ethnographic monsters. This distinction can be seen, for example, in Friedman's claim (pp. 24–5) that ethnographic monstrous races often have a basis in reality (e.g., the pygmies) or result from errors of perception (e.g., baboons as the basis for *cynocephali*) (Friedman 24–5).[12] Both Lenfant and Pollock place a greater emphasis on the imaginative than Friedman. I too agree with them in focusing on the imaginative in this chapter. On the Greek side, while Lenfant has been careful to distinguish between the ethnographic and mythological, she nevertheless observes in many places similarities between the two types.[13] On the Indian side, one may object that Pollock does not pay much attention to this distinction, but the *Rāmāyaṇa* and epic literature seem to blend ethnographic (in Friedman's sense) with the mythological.[14] We see this very clearly in the passage in which the *ekapāda* and the *karṇaprāvaraṇa* are mentioned. The context of the passage is the search for the abducted Sītā. Search parties are sent to each of the cardinal directions with a description of the peoples who will be encountered along the way. To the south are Rāvaṇa and the *rākṣasas* on Laṅkā. Thus, the *rākṣasas* are not distinguished from the *ekapāda* and the *karṇaprāvaraṇa* and form part of the peoples encountered at the edges of the geographical and moral world for India (Pollock, "*Rākṣasas* and Others" 270).[15] Let us now turn to these inhabitants at the edges of the Indic world.

---

[11] There are also Chinese accounts of dogheads. Karttunen suggests that "an actual people living in Northwest India" inspired these accounts (183–4). More specifically, David Gordon White assumes a central Asian source (Ephthalite Huns, Turko-Mongol, and Tibetan peoples), "who often identified themselves as the descendants of a primal union between a male-dog and a female human" (116).

[12] While acknowledging the role of "fantasy, escapism, delight in the exercise of the imagination," Friedman spends more time in supplying a historical basis of these races (24).

[13] Lenfant (1999) prioritizes the imaginary over the historical: "Even if ethnographers could have been inspired by actual monstrosities and were sometimes influenced by oriental iconography and legends, these were no more than a starting point for the construction of an imaginary world" (207). This imaginary world consists of the ethnographical "alchemy" of changing individual anomalies into an ethnic feature, but also showing that these anomalies are not disadvantages, as we have discussed above. On the similarity of ethnography and mythology, see pp. 197–8 and p. 213: "Ethnography, like myth, reflects the society that produced it and expresses a questioning of its norms" (Lenfant 213).

[14] Pollock (1987) acknowledges the predilection of scholars from the nineteenth and twentieth centuries to identify the *rākṣasas* with one or another of the indigenous Indian tribes, but wishes "to determine the signification of the *rākṣasas* in the imaginative world of the epic poem itself [...] the facts are in the first instance to be viewed as ideational ones. It is as generalized imaginative representations, large symbolic responses to important human problems, that the *rākṣasas* seem to be richest in signification, yet what are these but the responses and representations of a specific historical people—the traditional Indians" (266).

[15] As Pollock (1987) also explains, "[Laṅkā] is really to be looked for on no map; it is simply at the edge of the world, the moral no less than the geographical world, the Indian knew or could conceive of" (270).

In the *Rāmāyaṇa*, the *rākṣasas*, like their Greek counterparts, can also appear as hybrids or anatomically anomalous. Thus, Rāvaṇa has ten heads and Kabandha is a headless creature with one eye set in the middle of his stomach and with extra-long arms (3.65–9). The latter seems to be a combination of the *cyclops* and *blemmyae*. Whereas the Greek tradition has tended toward simpler hybrids (dog and human) and anatomical anomalies, the Indian tradition is much more complex. Furthermore, Kabandha is cursed to remain in this form until released by Rāma. Pollock thus compares Kabandha to the cursed races who are said to descend from Cain in the Middle Ages;[16] however, such a tradition is not found in the classical Greek world. Next, Pollock distinguishes these cursed forest *rākṣasas*, such as Kabandha, from "city" *rākṣasas*, such as Rāvaṇa, who live on Laṅkā. Pollock identifies the following characteristics of these "city" *rākṣasas*: (1) violence against the sacrifices of brahmans; (2) the ability to change into any form; (3) their aggressive sexuality (Pollock, "*Rākṣasas* and Others" 271ff; Pollock, *The Rāmāyaṇa of Vālmīki* 75ff).

First, let us examine the violence against the sacrifices of brahmans. When Rāma is a young man, the brahman Viśvāmitra asks Rāma's father to send Rāma to the forest to deal with the *rākṣasas* interfering with his sacrifices—sacrifices in the Indian world are regarded as maintaining the order in the universe. The *rākṣasas* living in the forest correspond to the Greek monstrous races outside the polis. But then the epic poet begins to blur this opposition between the forest and city. Pollock points out that Rāvaṇa and his subjects live in the city on Laṅkā, which Vālmīki describes with some of the same epithets used in describing Ayodhya, the home of Rāma. In fact, *rākṣasa* society has a similar organization to brahmanic society with "*brahma-rākṣasas*, who know the Vedas [. . .] and perform sacrifices" (5, 16, 2). One sees then that *rākṣasa* and brahmanic society are similar; according to Pollock, this similarity makes the *rākṣasas* scarier, because brahmanic society fears the lack of differentiation from the *rākṣasas* (Pollock, "*Rākṣasas* and Others" 271; Pollock, *The Rāmāyaṇa of Vālmīki* 75).[17] One further point: along with the *rākṣasas*, the ascetics live in the forest. The presence of the *rākṣasas* in the forest shows the breakdown of the order found in the city. Consequently, the ascetics withdraw from the worldly concerns of the city in search of spiritual transformation. Thus, in a certain sense, the *rākṣasas* offer a parallel to the ascetic, insofar as they both move away from the social order of the city.[18]

Having dealt with the first characteristic of the "city" *rākṣasas*, let us turn to the second and third characteristics—the ability to change form and unbridled sexuality. The scene of the abduction of Sītā illustrates these traits well. Śūrpaṇakhā, Rāvaṇa's sister, lusts after Rāma. Rather surprisingly, she does not transform herself into a beautiful woman, but remains in her repulsive form with beady eyes and hair

---

[16] See chapter five from Friedman.
[17] On this fear of a lack of differentiation, see Cohen 7ff.
[18] This movement is also reflected in the traditional stages of life in Hinduism: from the householder, one moves through a transitional stage, known as the *vānaprasthāśrama* (literally, the forest dweller stage) to the ascetic.

like copper in addition to her sinister voice (3, 16, 8–10). Throughout the passage, Vālmīki contrasts the *rākṣasī* with the handsome Rāma. Rāma jokingly fobs her off onto his brother, Lakṣmaṇa, and ultimately she is mutilated with her nose and ears cut off. Pollock points out that this is the punishment of fornicating/adulterous women (Pollock, "*Rākṣasas* and Others" 276, n30; Pollock, *The Rāmāyaṇa of Vālmīki* 79–80, n171).[19] Thus, again parallels are being drawn between the world of *rākṣasas* and humans; women violating the norms of sexual behavior are comparable to a *rākṣasī*.

Śūrpaṇakhā then tells Rāvaṇa of what happened to her, seeking revenge. She points out how attractive Sītā is as well. The lustful Rāvaṇa orders Mārīca to transform into a golden deer and lure Rāma and Lakshmaṇa away from Sītā. Rāvaṇa then appears as a wandering ascetic so as to be able to approach and abduct Sītā. In appearing in the form of an ascetic, Rāvaṇa undermines any sense of security for humans to be able to distinguish between ascetic and *rākṣasa*. In this passage, we also have an illustration of the standing epithet of *rākṣasas*, *kāmarūpin*, "able to take on any form at will" (Pollock, "*Rākṣasas* and Others" 272, 278; Pollock, *The Rāmāyaṇa of Vālmīki* 76, 82). But *rākṣasas* are not the only ones who undergo transformation; so do the gods, especially the *avatāra*, who manifests himself in whatever form is necessary to save the world. Viṣṇu has become Rāma to kill Rāvaṇa, who disdainfully refused to ask for protection against humans. There is a standard list of ten *avatāras*, which includes animal forms, a man-lion, a dwarf—thus, one sees that neither hybrids nor anomalous forms by themselves are a sign of the monstrous in India.[20] Furthermore, the serial transformations of the *rākṣasas* and the gods do not find a parallel in Ctesias or in Greek myth, where metamorphoses tend to have an anthropomorphic base.[21] Greek metamorphoses often tend to be a one-time thing: Daphne becomes the laurel and Lycaon the wolf. Perhaps the transformations of Zeus to seduce women (cf. n. 20) or of Proteus and Thetis, who use it as a means of protection, come closest to these changes in the Indic world. But, in general, the greater fluidity of the *rākṣasas* and the gods to transform themselves at will is not found in the Greek world.

One final note before concluding: Rāvaṇa is described as extraordinarily handsome. For Pollock, the *rākṣasas*' unbridled sexuality has the appeal of the forbidden to a society full of restrictions, especially for women:

> The *rākṣasa* is the essence of the Other. [...] His one reality is that of the fantasized alien, who at one and the same time is both feared and desired, who threatens mortal danger and yet is invested with an extraordinary, unsocializable sexuality.

---

[19] See also Erndl 69–72 and 81–4.
[20] And the gods do not always transform themselves for virtuous purposes; Indra appears to Ahalya in the form of her husband and seduces her (*Rāmāyaṇa* 1, 47, 15–31), reminiscent of Zeus and Alcmene. On this story, see chapter two from Doniger.
[21] As Buxton argues, "Insofar as Greek gods have a representational 'home base,' this must in most cases be taken as anthropomorphic" (189–90). In discussing the Indian gods, he writes: "Such beliefs are all of a piece with a holistic-integrative religious tradition in which 'there is no essential difference between human beings, animals and plants'" (Buxton 178–9).

It may be his very otherness that provides the source of both the fascination and the repulsion. (Pollock, "*Rākṣasas* and Others" 280-1)[22]

In conclusion, in the Greek world, certain oppositions are set up—polis versus forest or mountain, man versus animal, man versus the anatomically anomalous, and human morality versus the moral degeneracy of the monstrous. Ctesias somewhat undermines these oppositions, following the tradition of "inverse ethnography." He usually accomplishes this by the simple assertion of a positive trait, such as justice in the case of the pygmies and *cynocephali*, or the questioning of a certain characteristic, such as sexual position for the *cynocephali*. In the *Rāmāyaṇa*, Vālmīki posits similar oppositions: city versus forest, stable form versus the ability to transform, and purity versus uncontrollable sexuality. Yet, the constant undermining of them goes far beyond the paradoxes found in Ctesias in Greece. *Rākṣasas* live in cities and form a parallel society to that of brahmanical India; the gods as well as *rākṣasas* change shape and *rākṣasas* are as handsome as the heroes of the epic. It is especially this fluidity in changing at least their external appearance that makes it so difficult to distinguish gods, heroes, and *rākṣasas*. This ability to transform distinguishes the monstrous in the *Rāmāyaṇa* from Ctesias's perspective. For Ctesias, the monstrous is marked by hybridity and anatomical anomaly, whereas in the *Rāmāyaṇa* both gods and *rākṣasas* share these traits. Furthermore, the style of presentation of the two sources differs. Ctesias uses a matter-of-fact presentation which shows the monstrous races often in banal everyday situations such as conducting business and serving in the army, whereas the epic presents Rāma's heroic quest against the *rākṣasas* demonstrating how hard it is at times to recognize the Other. While the setting up of oppositions is common to both cultures, the constant undermining of them in the *Rāmāyaṇa* goes far beyond the paradoxes found in Ctesias.

References

Buxton, Richard. *Forms of Astonishment: Greek Myths of Metamorphosis*. Oxford University Press, 2009.
Clay, Jenny Strauss. *Hesiod's Cosmos*. Cambridge University Press, 2003.
Cohen, Jeffrey J. "Monster Culture (Seven Theses)." *Monster Theory*, edited by Jeffrey J. Cohen, University of Minnesota Press, 1996, pp. 3–25.
Doniger, Wendy. "Indra and Ahalya, Zeus and Alcmena." *Splitting the Difference: Gender and Myth in Ancient Greece and India*. University of Chicago Press, 1999, pp. 88–132.
Erndl, Kathleen M. "The Mutilation of Śūrpaṇakhā." *Many Rāmāyaṇas: The Diversity of a Narrative Tradition in South Asia*, edited by Paula Richman, University of California Press, 1991, pp. 67–88.

---

[22] On the attractiveness of the monstrous, see Cohen's sixth thesis "Fear of the monster is really a kind of desire" (16).

Friedman, John B. *The Monstrous Races in Medieval Art and Thought*. Harvard University Press, 1981.
Goldman, Robert. *The Rāmāyaṇa of Vālmīki, Vol. I: Bālakāṇḍa*. Princeton University Press, 1990.
Hyde, Walter W. "The Ancient Appreciation of Mountain Scenery." *Classical Journal*, vol. 11, 1915, pp. 70–85.
Karttunen, Klaus. *India in Early Greek Literature: Studia Orientalia*, vol. 65, Finnish Oriental Society, 1989.
Lenfant, Dominique. *Ctésias de Cnide. La Perse. L'Inde. Autres fragments*. Les Belles Lettres, 2004.
Lenfant, Dominique. "Monsters in Greek Ethnography and Society in the Fifth and Fourth Centuries BCE." *From Myth to Reason: Studies in the Development of Greek Thought*, edited by R. Buxton. Oxford University Press, 1999, pp. 197–214.
Nicolson, Marjorie H. *Mountain Gloom and Mountain Glory: The Development of the Aesthetics of the Infinite*. W.W. Norton and Co., 1959.
Pollock, Sheldon. "*Rākṣasas* and Others." *Indologica Taurinensia*, vol. 13, 1987, pp. 263–81.
Pollock, Sheldon. *The Rāmāyaṇa of Vālmīki, Vol. III: Araṇyakāṇḍa*. Princeton University Press, 1991.
Romm, James, *The Edges of the Earth in Ancient Thought: Geography, Exploration, and Fiction*. Princeton University Press, 1992.
White, David Gordon. *Myths of the Dog-Man*. University of Chicago Press, 1991.
White, Hayden. "The Forms of Wildness: Archaeology of an Idea." *The Wild Man Within*, edited by E. Dudley and M. Novak, University of Pittsburgh Press, 1972, pp. 3–38.
Wittkower, Rudolf. "Marvels of the East: A Study in the History of Monsters." *Journal of the Warburg and Courtauld Institutes*, vol. 5, 1942, pp. 159–97.

13

Satire and Monstrosity in African Diasporic Drama

Subbah Mir

Members of the African diaspora have produced a variety of dramas over time. Dramas of the African diaspora not only serve the purpose of entertainment and aesthetic pleasure but most of these plays also delve into serious geopolitical and social issues. The playwrights integrate African roots with modern issues in an effort to seek solutions to their sociopolitical problems. This chapter explores how and why the past is connected to the present in African diaspora drama in addition to probing what literary devices help in this aesthetic venture. I will establish that satire and irony, with their ability to both criticize and rectify the situation of African societies, are the backbone of African drama. Specifically, African writers deconstruct monstrosity via satire. The metaphor of monstrosity is the main literary device employed by many African playwrights for numerous reasons: first, it provides intellectual and aesthetic pleasure; second, it has the ability to "infect" and point toward "purgation" at the same time; and third, it is inextricably linked to human nature and (most importantly) to African roots in the form of the trickster god Esu. I conclude that African diasporic drama finds answers to sociopolitical problems by unearthing African roots. Moreover, it is through irony and satire that the reader is able to deconstruct various manifestations of monstrosity.

The primary plays I have chosen for this investigation are *The Tragedy of King Christophe* (1964) by Aimé Césaire, *The Eye of Gabriel* (1995) by Femi Euba (with a brief reference to his play *Dionysus of the Holocaust* [2002]), and *Joe Turner's Come and Gone* (2004) by August Wilson. Although Femi Euba is a Nigerian-born American scholar, many of his works are deeply rooted in African mythology. My theoretical framework includes Cleanth Brooks's "Irony as a Principle of Structure," Carl Jung's "Good and Evil in Analytical Psychology," Edward Said's ideas in the introduction to *Orientalism*, and the theories Euba presents in "Drama of Epidemic."

In his article "Irony as a Principle of Structure," Cleanth Brooks establishes irony as a ubiquitous device that serves the following powerful purpose in modern writing:

> There is the breakdown of a common symbolism; there is the general skepticism as to universals; not least important, there is the depletion and corruption of the very language itself, by advertising and by the mass-produced arts of radio, the

moving picture, and pulp fiction. The modern poet has the task of rehabilitating a tired and drained language so that it can convey meaning once more with force and with exactitude. (804–5)[1]

Thus, we can see the significance of irony in the present age in which symbolism is broken, the universal is criticized, and language has been "drained." Irony is born from "the acknowledgement of the pressures of context" (Brooks 804). Irony falls under the umbrella term of satire. Irony is one of the many devices that a satirist has at his or her disposal. As Jean Weisgerber explains, satire not only "require[s] a social background even when it exposes individual follies or vices, but its aim is to convince as many readers as possible that society, as matters stand, is inferior to what it should be" (160). By decrying the situation, the satirist is presenting a better standard, or is "purging through" (as Euba would say) imprecation. Weisgerber puts forth five main characteristics of satire: it is positive (in its venture for something better by bridging the gap between the real and ideal), indirect, theatrical, motivational in terms of intellectual effort, and it utilizes a whole range of rhetorical devices of which irony is one.

African diasporic drama makes use of all the five characteristics, which distinguishes it particularly as the theater of satire. Euba claims in his chapter "Drama of Epidemic" that "every black drama has a potential for satire, since satire is an inevitable and essential factor of survival, the concept nevertheless seeks to establish its satiric process as a theatrical device that significantly identifies the black dramatic expression" (121). Just as Brooks recognizes irony as a principle of structure, Euba similarly establishes satire as the driving force of black drama. According to Osagie, satire "strategically manages the rhetorical tools of irony, innuendoes, buffoonery, parody, paradox, allegory, wit, etc., to convey a socially transgressive message within temporal and spatial parameters established by society. Its ambiguous status as a verbal act that can be used to terrorize as well as to heal (cleanse) makes it both dangerous and a sanative element" (14).

The fact to be kept in mind is that satire cannot heal. It can be seen through investigation to lead toward purgation through the deconstruction of an apparent monstrous figure or happening. The reason satire is a backbone of black drama is because it fuses ritual, epidemic, artistic, and cathartic aspects to cure vices. The motives can be both stylistic, as initially outlined by Brooks, and political in nature as Euba underscores. In the satiric tradition in black drama, established through Yoruba ritual, Esu-Elegbara[2] is of prime significance. Esu is a sympathetic figure who employs his wit in order to lead people to a better situation. As an effective satirist, his focus is not on mischief, but rather on the rectification of social ills through scathing criticism

---

[1] This article was originally published in *Literary Opinion* in 1951. A revised form of the article appeared in the February 1962 issue of *College English*.

[2] The trickster god in Yoruba mythology who "as guardian of the crossroads, symbolizes chance, uncertainty, decision and fate" (Badejo 6).

applied with a blend of irony and wit (Sharrock 1965[3]). In essence, he castigates to "restore order." In epidemic drama, criticism fosters catharsis by aiming to expose vices through satire. In order to avoid conflating the Yoruba deity Esu with Satan, which is a common mistake, we need to understand the crucial differences between the Christian devil and Esu. This misperception also explains why black theater is epidemic drama.[4] Several historical practices depicted black slaves as devils by creating an invested knowledge of books and narratives such as *Heart of Darkness* and *Wide Sargasso Sea* in addition to many others in an effort to justify the acts of prejudice and cruelty perpetuated against them.

This phenomenon is connected to the long-standing "us versus them" debate that Edward Said explores when he posits that Orientalism "is not an airy European fantasy about the Orient, but a created body of theory and practice, in which, for many generations, there has been considerable material investment" (1802–3). This monstrous, invested knowledge spread like an epidemic through black drama. African and African American writers now have no choice but to purge this epidemic, either consciously or subconsciously, through satire. They have to *deconstruct* from within this hegemonic power structure. Satire in all of its divergent forms enables them to accomplish this goal. In this regard, Euba has explored black survival through satiric creations in four different genres: "The ritual, the historical, the political and the literary"[5] ("Drama of Epidemic" 126).

Euba in "Drama of Epidemic" first establishes black theater as epidemic drama before revealing satire as a way to deal with it. Satire represents a desire to cure the monstrosity in question by suggesting the destruction of a corrupt system epitomized by racism and mental slavery. This entire process is a satirical, aesthetic venture as well as a call for social reformation. It is not merely limited to what is satirized; rather, it is a procedure where the "satiric boomerang" can cause the satirist to be the satirized as well (Euba, "Drama of Epidemic" 123). Masks, the dramatic art of deception, two-pronged satire, and the so-called satiric boomerang form the basis of black theater. This is closely related to the concept of antiheroes in modern drama, which dramatizes braggarts, cowards, felons, liars, and other flawed individuals, because in reality human existence is full of imperfections and shortcomings. In this vein, Yoruba ritual mythology fills the gap between human flaws and struggles by providing the figure of a fate deity and master beguiler (i.e., Esu). Jung offers a psychological justification for such a deity that is both destructive and restorative like a military coup. In the aforementioned plays to be further analyzed, the satiric tradition firmly grounds the

---

[3] Roger Sharrock. "Modes of Satire." *Restoration Theatre*, edited by John Russell Brown and Bernard Harn, Capricorn Books, 1965, pp. 109–32.
[4] The term "epidemic drama" is borrowed from Euba's book chapter "Drama of Epidemic" and has been explained as something that is both good and evil, that infects and purges, like a vaccine, that infects to encourage immunity and purges you of the disease.
[5] It is hardly possible to separate one from the other in Black Drama. Nonetheless, as John Warton Lowe theorizes in the foreword to *African Modernity and the Philosophy of Culture in the Works of Femi Euba*, "Satire can be both dangerous and sanative, and that satire is myth, ritual, and history intertwined; none of these, however, are stable categories" (xiv).

supremacy of Esu in black drama as a combination of good and evil—someone who has the ability to both destruct and construct. Esu complements both tradition and modernity by serving as a bridge.

By taking satire back to its ritualistic roots in black drama, Euba presents Esu as a joining ritual symbolizing both destruction and purgation. He is the god of the crossroads. He is the one who is responsible for the blurring and merging of boundaries. It should be noted that Esu's malevolence is also suggestive of purgation just like black satire. By applying Carl Jung's philosophical framework for understanding good and evil, I see Esu as a representative of humanity with all of its existential weaknesses. According to Jung, good and evil are not distinctive, definite states of being; rather, they "are in themselves 'principles' and we must bear in mind that a principle exists long before us and extends far beyond us" (Jung 91). I will refer to Jung's explanation as the "Esu principle" in which one can discern the "relativity of values" (Jung 92) where "good and evil are only our judgement in a given situation" (Jung 98). It is the judgment of the onlooker that decides whether something is good or bad. From this vantage point, the concepts of good and evil are entirely dependent upon a given subject's perception. Relating the deconstruction of dichotomous morality based upon binary logic to the ritualistic figure of Esu, one can find his apparent harshness as suggestive of purgation, restoration, and catharsis linked to the completion of the epidemic circle.[6] As Euba hypothesizes in "Drama of Epidemic," "The drama of epidemic specifically acknowledges a black aesthetic which is based on the Yoruba concept of good and evil. As opposed to the biblical concept, both forces form complementary units embodied in Esu-Elegba, the trickster, god of fate, satire and satirist" (146). This non-dualistic vision of good and evil identifies Esu in everyone. Good and evil do not exist in neatly separated categories in distinct individuals as in fairy tales. Every human being exists in that gray area in which they are neither entirely good nor pure evil. Satire is an effective device for exploring this greyness, or rather human-ness, owing to its potential to reject, entertain, and facilitate a cure at the same time. Satire itself does not affect change directly, but rather it highlights and criticizes what is wrong in a given society. Nevertheless, satire does represent the possibility for meaningful change through dialogue. This is why satirical works are significant from a social and political standpoint:[7]

> In the plays based on or motivated by a historical idea, or plays that raise a political perspective, we move from the fictional individual in a ritual process to a fictionalized figure in history of factual life. The individual is indicted and satirized, through a historical process, by his fate more as a fact of history than as

---

[6] There are many concrete examples in Yoruba ritual plays like *The Story of Oxala* and *The Imprisonment of Obatala* in which Esu's words create tremendous hardships for the Yoruba gods. This device eventually serves the purpose of rectifying past actions and completing a circle.

[7] The reason why is their real-world relevance and desire to improve the situation. In the words of Nicholas Diehl, "Satires are works of fiction, but they are also veiled commentary on some aspects of the real world: satires satirize real-world targets" (Diehl 313).

a metaphysical entity. Furthermore, perhaps more realistically here than in ritual, the community or society is not only implicated but may also be affected by the satiric action. (Euba 131)

The Tragedy of King Christophe (1964) by Aimé Césaire, written in the context of the Haitian revolution, serves as a perfect example. Despite having a grandiloquent and megalomaniac personality,[8] King Christophe is a tragic hero stuck in his satiric fate. He attempts to form the recently liberated country of Haiti into a model of black rule but is disliked due to his extremist approach. He becomes paralyzed and shoots himself at the end of the play. His intentions are good, but his draconian methods are even harsher than slavery. In his analysis of the play, Hill explains, "Inheriting a country devastated by war, impoverished by colonization, with a vastly unlettered and un-skilled population bearing the psychological scars of slavery, Christophe is driven by the ambition to make free Haiti a showplace of black rule. In pursuit of his dreams he becomes an uncompromising tyrant who squeezes the last drop of energy from an already exhausted populace" (Hill, "The Revolutionary Tradition in Black Drama" 416). In this instance, Baron Saturday is the satirist that thwarts all of Christophe's planning. In order to render the satiric process effective, the playwright first establishes Christophe's commendable heroism in terms of his ideal vision, strong will, and fortitude.[9] The epidemic drama provides loopholes for his collapse through his flaws. The satiric ritual is then completed through his downfall. In this case, Hugonin's monstrosity, which manifests itself as "Baron Saturday" (Césaire, *The Tragedy of King Christophe*) by the end of the play, serves as a symbolic Esu. His songs are satirical barbs that mix sarcasm with opacity (e.g., "That's old Mister Whale / Under that white sail / Watch out Watch out for Mister Whale / He'll bite your head without fail" (Césaire, *The Tragedy of King Christophe* 16). His melodies are an ironic description of history and a satirical warning for the present. In fact, the play opens at a marketplace that is a sanctuary for Esu, because all roads cross and destinies interact in this space where the gains and losses of monstrosity are apparent.

Another way of looking at satire in the play is to take Christophe's god-like existence into consideration, which establishes him as a satirist in his own right. As the character himself declares, "My court is a theatre of shadows. But I read on the Blackboard everything that's written under their thick skulls" (Césaire, *The Tragedy of King Christophe* 51). Through his dialogues and actions, he is criticizing every malevolent being as a satirist. Although he is perceived as a monster, his desire is to form a great Haiti. Christophe acts much like Esu in an attempt to motivate the masses.

---

[8] From a linguistic angle, this phenomenon is also linked to coded and hermetic expressions describing Esu in Yoruban myth (e.g., Esu can throw a stone yesterday and / Kill a bird today" [Césaire, *A Tempest* 53]). This subject could be the focus of a separate linguistic analysis in the future.
[9] Euba in "Drama of Epidemic" mentions "Toussaint L'Ouverture, the hero of the slave insurrection for freedom in Haiti [as] the background inspiration in Aimé Césaire's *The Tragedy of King Christophe*" (155).

His actions and words are a concrete manifestation of satire.[10] From this perspective, the solution proposed for the incurable situation is that of "self-removal." In another sense, this "disappearing act" occurs when it is in the best interests of the country after the purgation of the epidemic of colonialism and slavery. Later in the text, however, Christophe loses his physical strength, becomes paralyzed, and eventually commits suicide. His paralysis before suicide reflects the genre of grotesque satire. In this regard, the following candid admission is especially relevant: "My knees are crushed. Envious fortune has struck me down"[11] (Césaire, *The Tragedy of King Christophe* 81). This is the aforementioned satirical boomerang when the satirist becomes the satirized in the final act of suicide. In this vein, Euba calls him "the worst satiric victim of his own vision as he falls" ("Drama of Epidemic" 133). In this manner, satire operates on multiple levels throughout the work.

Nonetheless, this same satirical process often fails to provide a sense of catharsis. The recurring question "Should Christophe have allowed the Haitian slaves to fail instead of making them work so hard?" haunts the reader-spectator. In certain scenes, "time" itself performs a satirical function in the sense that the quotidian existence of the satirized changes very little in Christophe's pre- and post-Haiti. Moreover, King Christophe is faced with the less than ideal choice of becoming either a despotic ruler or a failed leader. Here, satirical time offers "the choice between the two dehumanizing, satiric conditions of survival" (Euba, "Drama of Epidemic" 139). However, in a broader perspective, this theatrical technique is meant to arouse a desire for real freedom. As evidenced by Christophe's example, the satiric cycle may not always result in the desired outcome for the oppressed, but the playwright strives to purge the epidemic in a more general sense. The dramatist's apparent humanistic aspirations help to deconstruct Christophe's troubling monstrosity from an ethical angle. Satire may not be capable of bringing about an immediate change; however, the two-pronged grotesquery is suggestive of restoration.

According to Euba, "Through this grotesque expression, through this destructive aspect of satire or of epidemic process, comes the restorative—the hope for the future, the hope of eventual freedom" ("Drama of Epidemic" 136). Euba places this philosophy into dramatic form in his play *The Eye of Gabriel*. The play deals with a post-hurricane scenario on an island on the Gulf Coast of North America. Granma Congo represents African historical and ritual power as a follower of Esu—the god of crossroads. Tasha is an avid researcher from the north who is looking for answers to ease her troubled mind. Gran makes her see that she can eventually obtain these answers by following her African roots and religion. It is noteworthy how Euba attaches purgation to identity,

---

[10] He ironically calls Brelle a talker when he himself uses grandiose phrases. Christophe orders Brelle to be executed because "[Brelle] talks too much, Prezeau. He writes too much. But no blood, no blood! A peaceful death in his bed. [. . .] He's an old man. So gently [. . .] gently. [. . .] But quickly" (Césaire, *The Tragedy of King Christophe* 64). He also fires a sleeping, "poor tired peasant" because he was not contributing actively to the (re-)construction of Haiti (Césaire, *The Tragedy of King Christophe* 61).

[11] His permanent paralysis can be compared with the temporary paralysis of Herald Loomis discussed later.

and, consequently, to both history and religion. For example, Rebecca, another African American character, is lost due to her experimentation with a new religion that will forever remain foreign to her no matter how hard she tries to fit in.

The hurricane in *The Eye of Gabriel* is a tangible display of Rebecca's monstrous difference. Through her interactions with Gran Congo and subsequent empowerment by means of ritualistic enlightenment, Tasha is a source of future hope in addition to being a restorative force in the play. The entire episode of Granma Congo unfolds for the audience to see functions as a satirical form of turbulence that works toward psychological freedom and racial catharsis. As Osagie writes in the preface,

> Euba's use of satire is mostly deployed through what he calls an extended metaphor. Extended metaphors [. . .] do the job of not only identifying gaps in a relationship, a culture, an act, or an attitude, but also suggesting a possible resolution, a possible bridge in the seemingly impossible quagmire. [. . .] Esu, the Yoruba god of fate and the god of crossroads, becomes the ideal extended metaphor because he is an embodiment of the dialogism engendered in human relations. (xxiii)

The island on the Gulf Shores where the play takes place creates "crossroads" between the Caribbean, the United States, and Africa that highlight a kind of geographical, cultural, and psychological merging. Euba refers to it as "a play about generational passing of cultural power" (*The Eye of Gabriel* 2). Tasha (a Catholic), Rebecca (a Pentecostal), Matthew (a Baptist minister), and Hannah (an Esu follower) provide us with a microcosmic display of religious and traditional crossroad happenings. The apparent authority figure concretized in the image of Hannah's rocking chair evokes many different personal agendas.[12] However, satire brings forth Esu as the central figure and the real essence which the majority of them miss because the chair itself is laden with metaphorical connotations.

It is also ironic how Rebecca proselytizes for Christianity while simultaneously secretly believing that some miracle will happen to Hannah owing to her traditional "voodoo" power. Matthew and Rebecca advocate in favor of Christianity, but they are frightened by the power of traditional African religion as they never truly believe that Hannah has died. The alternating presence and absence of Granma Congo/Hannah on the rocking chair is an artistic device for "collapsing past and present time, thus creating a coalition between life and death, tradition and modernity, in ways that make the Yoruba metaphysical worldview digestible to an American audience" (Osagie 45). This theatrical tool creates a dramatic shape that allows for the deconstruction of various sorts of monstrosity. This device also places the dramatic action at the crossroads of many concepts such as life/death, tradition/modernity, African/American, experience/ naivety, past/present, and so on. As Osagie explains, Euba merges several different

---

[12] Some want it due to its religious significance, whereas others desire it as a cultural artifact. Some people believe in its miraculous essence, while others want to profit from it from a capitalistic perspective.

"Gabriels" at various times,[13] but the most important of these is Gabriel Prosser who incited a slave revolt. This slave rebellion is a satirical journey of restoration through monstrous massacre and destruction. By bringing the past into the present, Granma Congo establishes a particular point in time. Thus, this central African symbolic figure is "the eye of Gabriel" that drives the action and represents the meaning of the play.

Tasha, as a follower, is able to execute Hannah's mission only after she gets rid of her clouded and socially constructed sensibilities. The irony of Rebecca's mindset is that instead of grasping the essence of African history, tradition, and religion, she takes it too literally all along (e.g., sending the coffin to Africa or fighting to take Granma's chair) and is thus satirized when she renounces the multiplicity of the fate deity throughout the play. In this sense, "Her big error is that she discounts the metaphysical and therefore the metaphorical realm altogether. By interpreting Esu in only one way, a materialist reading, she misses the diacritic essence of god" (Osagie 51). Tasha is the one who finally realizes that it is not about personal resolution, but rather it is a question of black consciousness. She still has many battles to fight, but she at least is ready for the two-pronged satirical journey that is symbolized when Tasha "immediately hurries to put the object[14] in her bag" (Euba, *The Eye of Gabriel* 5). This object is the physical manifestation of Esu that concretizes the essence of black consciousness.

In contrast with Tasha, the Baptist church minister Matthew has satirically been defined as the "complex character capable of summoning up a mastery of various emotions, ranging from humble supplication through passionate denunciation to sadistic satisfaction" (Euba, *The Eye of Gabriel* 8). It is ironic how a church figure is a sadistic money monger. The monstrosity/epidemic in the play is evident from the depiction of the aftermath of the hurricane in addition to the conflicts between various people and Granma Congo. Even the very first interaction between Rebecca and Pastor is quite revealing:

> REBECCA (*Catching her breath*): Jehovah-jireh! . . . Stalking me, are you Pastor Matthew?
> PASTOR: My, my! Why should I be (*Quickly acknowledges TASHA*) God be with you, Sister. (Euba, *The Eye of Gabriel* 7)

The oozing wound of the epidemic is painfully transparent from the very start. It becomes hideous when the Pastor asks, "And how's the *new faith*, Sister Rebecca" (Euba, *The Eye of Gabriel* 8, my italics). Rebecca sometimes appears as a character who is a victim of self-parody. She seems to be the satirist and the satirized at the same time. As the narrator elucidates, "Rebecca halts and tightens up, clutching her Cross: her reaction is more to her prodded mind than to Hannah. Raises the Cross

---

[13] The angel Gabriel, Priest Gabriel, the brother Gabriel, Hurricane Gabriel, Hannah's great-grandfather Gabriel, and the historical Gabriel Prosser who all share the same name highlight the multiplicity of Esu. As the symbolic figure that Tasha places in her bag, Esu initiates a journey to rediscover black consciousness through ritual, tradition and satire.

[14] A miniature statue of Esu.

as if to hold an approaching demon in its tracks" (Euba, *The Eye of Gabriel* 10). She is essentially a victim of her own mind. However, there is a major difference between her agony and Tasha's. In Rebecca's religious worldview, there is a wide gulf between good and evil (i.e., God and the devil). Consequently, she is never able to find peace, a form of consolation, or a resolution to the conflict. Conversely, Tasha benefits from the two-pronged satire by going back to her roots. For Tasha, the hurricane is a deconstructed monster that symbolizes a new beginning similar to the act of breaking ground,[15] whereas it is a punishment culminating in death for Rebecca and the Pastor. The problem with Rebecca is that she is torn between her previous African religion and the new "White man's religion."[16] Pastor Matthew will be farther behind than Rebecca in terms of conflict resolution because he is the embodiment of hypocrisy and corruption. Above all, he is comfortable living in a constant state of hypocrisy. Euba offers no resolution or form of consciousness for the Pastor.

Gram Congo is the personification of a type of deconstructed monstrosity. Specifically, she is a symbolic Esu figure who wreaks havoc by refusing to enter the shelter because she is motivated by a larger purpose. When Tasha assumes that their conversation would continue after the hurricane, Gram Congo "smiles meaningfully" (Euba, *The Eye of Gabriel* 16). She realizes that she will only be present metaphorically, by means of a recorded voice, deconstructed monstrosity, manifestations of the Esu figure, the goals of Tasha's mission, and through the revival of black consciousness. How does deconstructed monstrosity work here? When Tasha asks, Gram Congo defines Esu as "E's de good and de bad, de right and left arm o'de law o' de universe, de powerful messenger o' de Almighty, guardian o' de gate, lord o' de crossroad, bringer o' change, and all de new beginnin's" (Euba, *The Eye of Gabriel* 37). When she asks for further clarification, "But what is he?," Hannah responds, "E's whatever you want 'im be. E's we all, ever'body" (Euba, *The Eye of Gabriel* 37). Hannah does everything in essentially the same manner as Esu. As opposed to being the embodiment of kindness who would give up her chair and land before death, she defends it tooth and nail just like Esu would do in the same situation. Hence, when Tasha calls him "LaBas the bad?," Hannah retorts, "Yeah, 'e do bad for good" (Euba, *The Eye of Gabriel* 32). Furthermore, Tasha complements Esu as "the good dissembler" (Euba, *The Eye of Gabriel* 32). Tasha agrees that "sometimes what we think is wrong is really some blessing in disguise. Sometimes our bitterest wrong is so logical and inevitable" (45). Hannah uses mockery and satire because she believes "we black people from Afric should know better, but we don't" (Euba, *The Eye of Gabriel* 36). That is why she does not want her chair to be in a museum: "And a don't wanna be in no museum, you hear me?" (Euba, *The*

---

[15] As Tasha asserts, "I met Gram Congo, and I knew immediately I just had to change the focus of my research" (Euba, *The Eye of Gabriel* 14–15).

[16] As the narrator underscores, "You can't handle it Becka, you jes' can't handle dis here r'ligion. A told you dat, way from de beginnin,', you can't handle whiteman r'ligion with de sp'rits of Afric—Is one or de oder, you can't do one and pretend to do de oder. See how you gone get yourself so confuse" (Euba, *The Eye of Gabriel* 42). Instead of going back to her roots, the irony is that she is trying to defeat "the enemies of blackness" (Euba, *The Eye of Gabriel* 44) as if she is completely pure in a realm in which evil exists outside of her.

Eye of Gabriel 50). She does not want papa LaBas to be merely another mundane antique. She wants it to have an eternal presence in black consciousness. This black consciousness is multilayered like Esu. As Susan-Lori Parks posits in "An Equation for Black People Onstage," "There is no one way to write or think or feel or dream or interpret or be interpreted. As African-Americans we should recognize this insidious existentialism for what it is: a fucked-up trap to reduce us to only one way of being. We should endeavor to show the world and ourselves our beautiful and powerfully infinite variety" (21–2). Euba explains this infinite beauty can only be accessed by being comfortable with one's roots. The deconstructed monstrosity paves a way for this process to occur. While having an argument with the curator Viney, Tasha reacts against this same limiting stance by exclaiming, "Oh yes, that's another bullshitting that you use to cloud your ignorance—anything that's not African is not considered authentic?" (Euba, *The Eye of Gabriel* 75). Authenticity lies in essence and conscience, not in materiality.

It is ironic how Rebecca and Matthew resist and negate Hannah, but they still believe in her powers. One of the many examples of this irony is when Tasha shouts, "Bullshit, Gabriel! You raped me!" (Euba, *The Eye of Gabriel* 66). Pastor Matthew interprets this deeply unsettling scene as the manifestation of the Archangel Gabriel. Another sort of irony is that they believe in these supernatural powers in a material way, not in the psychological and metaphorical sense in which they truly exist. This is why the satire moves away from Hannah (who is apparently dead due to her stubbornness when the curtain rises), to Rebecca and Matthew before the curtain closes (owing to psychological stubbornness of disbelief). Hannah's authenticity is established in her role as "the eye of [black] people" (Euba, *The Eye of Gabriel* 96)—the people who want to "see" and bring about a change through purgation of the epidemic.

This is the change that Amiri Baraka (LeRoi Jones)[17] wants black theater to bring about[18] and Euba links that "change" to a type of satire that this chapter has demonstrated is a reflection of deconstructed monstrosity. He theorizes that social transformation can be affected through "a call to the theatre for a satiric action that empowers and provokes through its satiric catharsis" (Euba, "Drama of Epidemic" 142). There is no promise of change, but instead a hope to defrost frozen thought. He associates African drama with a call to destruct supremacist and hegemonic cultural sensibilities. One example is Tasha in *The Eye of Gabriel* who is able to understand everything better after she can see the reality beyond the meta-narrative itself. Another intertextual parallel would be Walker Vessels who tries to eliminate slavery by cutting away his "White past" in *The Slave* by Amiri Baraka. As Euba contends, "For the revolutionary ideas are clearly bound up with the destructive and restorative processes of the epidemic concept, that is, the ritual destruction of white image and white values, and the cathartic satisfaction and 'sane' orientation of the black audience and the black race as a whole" ("Drama of Epidemic" 146). The direct or indirect presence of ritual

---

[17] It should be noted that Amiri Baraka was born Everett LeRoi Jones in 1934.
[18] As LeRoi Jones declares, "The Revolutionary Theatre should force change; it should be change" (Jones 210).

in black drama makes it clear that purgation is an impossibility without it—thereby making a respect for cultural values as the only available weapon. Consequently, this makes satire the ultimate backbone of black theater.

African diasporic drama has to face a double satirical challenge. In addition to problematizing the dominant meta-narrative, satire has to be comical yet meaningful. Through both "constructive deconstruction" and creative action, Euba's *Dionysus of the Holocaust* meets these criteria. It is an adaptation of Aristophanes's *The Frogs* that facilitates a cathartic eradication of a social disease through the fluidity of identity and memory of the past. The comic elements serve to lighten the satire of the prevailing epidemic in question. Whereas Aristophanes decries moral, social, and political corruption, Euba takes aim at racism. Owing to the polymorphous nature of both figures, Euba converts the Dionysian figure into the Yoruba god Esu[19]—which not only satirizes the rigidity of unidirectional stances but also brings the past into the present in order to force change. This "extended metaphor" "is an attempt to philosophize on the nature of art as already thinking, positioning, assessing, and evaluating (in other words, the performance of life, what it is and what it ought to be)" (Osagie 142). Dionysus takes on all the pain to purge the infection, to cure through imprecation. He tricks all humanity to "find themselves as humans regardless of race, culture, color or creed" (Euba, *Dionysus of the Holocaust* 11). In the play, the bag carried by Parakultus is satirically called a "load of culture" (Euba, *Dionysus of the Holocaust* 45). Until Dionysus performs a trick, it is always difficult for the servant to carry. As the narrator explains, it "will always be heavy for you to carry—until you've learnt the art of humanity and love" (Euba, *Dionysus of the Holocaust* 45). The play is full of satiric retorts between Afraks (the chorus of blacks) and Caucases (the chorus of whites), yet Euba still follows an inclusive approach and finishes the comedy with a compromise. However, a healthy compromise still involves following one's African roots.

A rediscovery of one's African roots does not mean migrating back to Africa; rather, it is about using the past to move forward in an effort to resuscitate this identity and rework on it. This process involves satiric intervention. August Wilsons's *Joe Turner's Come and Gone* has a strong satirical force in multiple realms,[20] for its ultimate call is the search for black identity represented through the symbolism of music. Loomis is searching for his lost wife from whom he became separated because of slavery. When he finds her, the wife is reunited with their daughter as Loomis claims to have found his "song." The lost wife symbolically satirizes the disenfranchisement of black people by trying to guide them toward a wholesome personal identity rooted in their pure African self. The realization of a personal identity is the end product of the arduous

---

[19] Euba establishes this metamorphosis between Esu and Dionysus from the very beginning when Dionysus dresses his servant Parakultus in multicolored robes, changes his name, and then changes position and dresses with him as part of a trick. Herakles describes him as "wearing a ridiculous youth-mask in name of deception" (9) to which Dionysus responds, "Well, am I not Dionysus, patron of the recreative process?" (9). He also creates a sharp contrast between a pure trickster (e.g., Hermelabas) and the one who deceives to reconstruct.

[20] It has already been established that the four genres (i.e., ritual, historic, political, and literary) cannot be neatly separated from each other in Black drama.

journey. For Loomis as well as for the entire black race, this involves both destruction and regeneration.[21] Evil is once again not something external that exists in opposition to good. Evil and good coexist through the conceptual force of Esu-Elegba.

Loomis, who comes "from all over. Whichever way the road take us that's the way we go"[22] (Wilson 10), is in essence an Esu follower, who apparently is looking for his wife but ends up resolving his conflict and finding his identity—like Tasha who is not deliberately searching for all of the answers that she finds to her questions. Loomis criticizes Christianity by questioning, "What's so holy about the Holy Ghost? You singing and singing. You thinking the Holy Ghost coming? [. . .] What he gonna do, huh?" (Wilson 32). Later, his grotesque self-paralysis contains a satiric streak. To be more precise, it is a depiction of a satiric form of monstrosity. It is undeniably destructive with his reminiscences about the slave trade, but it helps him embark on the journey of self-realization. As he cries out "My legs won't stand up!," he is ironically rising above the self toward a higher realization (Wilson 34). As a lost deacon who has suffered immensely, he is trying to come to terms with Christianity by challenging God. He eventually realizes, "You can't bind what don't cling" (Wilson 57). His identity is not given to him ready-made. He works hard to find "what does cling." His monstrous infection is cured through struggle and self-sacrifice:

> LOOMIS: I'm choking on my blood and all you got to give me is salvation?
> MARTHA: You got to be clean, Herald. You got to be washed with the blood of lamb.
> LOOMIS: Blood makes you clean? You clean with blood?
> MARTHA: Jesus bled for you. [. . .]
> LOOMIS: I don't need nobody to bleed for me! I can bleed for myself.
> MARTHA: You got to be something, Herald. You just can't be alive. Life don't mean nothing unless it got a meaning.
> LOOMIS: What kind of meaning you got? What kind of clean you got, woman? You want blood? Blood make you clean? You clean with blood? (*Loomis slashes himself across the chest. He rubs the blood over his face and comes to a realization.*) I'm standing! I'm standing. My legs stood up! I'm standing now! (*Having found his song, the song of self-sufficiency, fully resurrected, cleansed and given breath, free from encumbrance other than the workings of his own heart and the bonds of the flesh, having accepted the responsibility for his own presence in the world, he is free to soar above the environs that weighed and pushed his spirit into terrifying contractions*). (Wilson 580)

Herald Loomis discovers his identity through his satiric journey. Monstrosity initially makes him suffer before it eventually helps him to uncover his true self. After discovering his identity through the strange maneuvering of fate, he still needs to

---

[21] Ritual here is more psychic in nature than physical.
[22] The concept of roads and crossroads could be another intriguing future study in both the context of Esu and this play.

rework on it—not by going back, but by rising up and walking ahead.[23] What he does after the discovery could be the focus of another research study in the future. The evident goal of this current investigation is to highlight the significance of African diasporic drama in the context of deconstructions of monstrosity and calls for social transformation that attempt to create a better tomorrow.

As this exploration has demonstrated, African diasporic drama often assumes the shape of satire that operates according to the "Esu principle." It deconstructs representations of monstrosity by using a bi-pronged satire that paves the way for imprecation and catharsis. In all of the texts analyzed in this study, aesthetic pleasure is linked to the sociopolitical message of change. Historical memory, ritual, and the literary tradition are of prime significance in these plays because of the prevailing theme of social transformation. Real change is only possible through the destruction of the old system and the construction of a new one—that would make one take pride in their African heritage. By exploring the source of the infection, purgation is rendered possible through a strong bond with one's African roots. African playwrights have to criticize in order to purge. This is why satire, epitomized by Esu, is the prime force of African drama. I have deconstructed Esu's monstrosity by reflecting upon how good and evil coexist in addition to how negative events can ultimately lead to a positive resolution. The satirical journey of one individual, whether it be Loomis, Christophe, Tasha, or Afrak, can be read as a microcosmic representation of the entire black race, or of the human race for that matter. Although physical slavery is no longer prevalent, humanity still needs to find its song by ridding itself of the shackles of mental slavery in the form of cultural imperialism, racism, and xenophobia. Encouraging us to be comfortable in our own skin and cultural roots, African diasporic drama has the potential to forge a better path for all of humanity.

References

Badejo, Diedre L. "The Yoruba and Afro-American Trickster: A Contextual Comparison." *Présence Africaine*, vol. 147, no. 3, 1988, pp. 3–17.

Brooks, Cleanth. "Irony as a Principle of Structure." *The Critical Tradition: Classic Texts and Contemporary Trends*, edited by David H. Richter, St. Martin's Press, 2007, pp. 799–806.

Césaire, Aimé. *A Tempest*. Translated by Richard Miller, UBU Repertory Theatre Publications, 1986.

Césaire, Aimé. *The Tragedy of King Christophe*. Translated by Ralph Manheim, New York Grove Press, 1970.

---

[23] A similar idea is presented in another Caribbean play *Dream on Monkey Mountain* by Derek Walcott in which the protagonist Makak's intoxicated vision, which makes him see superiority in whiteness by abandoning blackness, is washed away at the end. In the final scenes, he reveals his intention to return to his roots: "Now this old hermit is going back home, back to the beginning, to the green beginning of this world" (Walcott 326).

Diehl, Nicholas. "Satire, Analogy and Moral Philosophy." *The Journal of Aesthetics and Art Criticism*, vol. 71, no. 4, Fall 2013, pp. 311–21.

Euba, Femi. *Archetypes, Imprecators, and Victims of Fate: Origins and Developments of Satire in Black Drama*. Greenwood Press, 1989.

Euba, Femi. *Dionysus of the Holocaust: Epic Satire on Race in Three Acts*. In *Black Drama*, Alexander Street Press, 2002. Electronic edition accessed on Oct. 19, 2017. https://search-alexanderstreetcom.libezp.lib.lsu.edu/view/work/bibliographic_entity%7Cvideo_work%7C3230186.

Euba, Femi. "Drama of Epidemic." *Archetypes, Imprecators, and Victims of Fate: Origin and Developments of Satire in Black Drama*. Greenwood Press, 1989, pp. 121–63.

Euba, Femi. *The Eye of Gabriel: A Play in Two Parts*. In *Black Drama*, Alexander Street Press, 2002. Electronic edition accessed on Oct. 19, 2017. https://search-alexanderstreet-com.libezp.lib.lsu.edu/view/work/bibliographic_entity%7Cbibliographic_details%7C3607602#page/1/mode/1/chapter/bibliographic_entity%7Cdocument%7C3877110.

Hill, Errol. "The Revolutionary Tradition in Black Drama." *Theatre Journal*, vol. 38, no. 4, 1986, pp. 408–26.

Jones, LeRoi. "The Revolutionary Theatre." *Home: Social Essays*, edited by Amiri Baraka, William Morrow & Co., 1966, pp. 210–15.

Jung, C. G. "Good and Evil in Analytical Psychology." *Journal of Analytical Psychology*. July 1, 1960. Electronic edition accessed through Louisiana State University's Digital Library on Nov. 15, 2017. https://edsaebscohostcom.libezp.lib.lsu.edu/eds/pdfviewer/pdfviewer?vid=0&sid=866171d6-bc19-47ac-83c6-25c2a25c1029%40sdc-v-sessmgr02.

Osagie, Iyunolu. *African Modernity and the Philosophy of Culture in the Works of Femi Euba*. Lexington Books, 2017.

Parks, Suzan-Lori. "An Equation for Black People Onstage." *The America Play and Other Works*, Theatre Communications Group, 1995, pp. 19–22.

Said, Edward. "Orientalism." *The Critical Tradition: Classic Texts and Contemporary Trends*, edited by David H. Richter, St. Martin's Press, 2007, pp. 1801–14.

Sharrock, Roger. "Modes of Satire." *Restoration Theatre*, edited by John Russell Brown and Bernard Harn, Capricorn Books, 1965, pp. 109–32.

Walcott, Derek. *Dream on Monkey Mountain and Other Plays*. Farrar, Straus and Giroux, 1970.

Weisgerber, Jean. "Satire and Irony as Means of Communication." *Comparative Literature Studies*, vol. 10, no. 2, 1973, pp. 157–72.

Wilson, August. *Joe Turner's Come and Gone*. Alexander Street Press, 2004.

14

How a Monster Became a Hero

An Understanding of Camusian Morality through the Absurdist Hero, Don Juan

Scott Truesdale

It was in 1616 that Tirso de Molina would write his most famous work, *El burlador de Sevilla* (*The Trickster of Seville and the Stone Guest*), a play which introduced the character of Don Juan to the world. This character would become one of the most iconic symbols of libertinism that remains to this day. De Molina's monstrous creation drew the attention of intellectuals from a range of fields, such as Michel Foucault who deemed Don Juan "the great violator of the rules of marriage" who was "driven, in spite of himself by the somber madness of sex" (qtd. in Stankeviciute 198). Echoing similar sentiments, the American sociologist David G. Winter maintains, "The theme of male power against female incorporation seems to run through both the early and the more recent versions of the Don Juan legend" (Stankeviciute 198). While Molina intended his work to be a religious condemnation of Don Juan's actions, treating the character as if he were a monster, French-Algerian absurdist Albert Camus observes Don Juan in a different light (The Trickster of Seville and the Stone Guest 2018). He brings him out of the shadows deeming him the archetype of absurdism who has accepted his place in the physical world without the illusions of a transcendent hope.

The immoral and at times violent character that De Molina intended Don Juan to be might seem a strange choice for Camus to idolize, as Camus was a man with strong moral beliefs who was far from being a nihilist. For instance, he speaks strongly against the act of suicide in *Le mythe de Sisyphe*. In *La peste*, he compares the horrendous actions of the Nazi regime to a plague that humanity is obligated to fight against. In *L'étranger*, it is evident that the absurdist Meursault must pay for his crime of slaying an Arab man. Hence, one can clearly see that Camus is by no means wishing to support a lawless world when he deems the libertine Don Juan an example for his readers to follow. Though an absurdist, Camus continuously fought for justice and equality in a universe in which he believed justice was nonexistent. While his absurdist worldview left him in a situation without predetermined meaning, Camus still contested the social injustice and the violence that permeated his era. This is especially apparent in his condemnation of the death penalty when he wrote in his famous essay "Reflections on the Guillotine," "None among us is authorized to despair of a single man, except after his death, which transforms his life into destiny and then permits a definitive judgment" (qtd. in Sheaffer-Jones 176). Even when his absurdist contemporary Jean-Paul Sartre was willing to at times accept violence as a means of achieving an admirable goal, as evidenced in his support of Stalin's Marxist regime, Camus was unwilling to forsake his conviction that justice should not be exempt from absurdist principles. Stepping outside the norm of many writers and philosophers of his time, Camus condemned political leaders such as Stalin who attempted to achieve utopic dreams by means of violence and moral injustice. As Ana Bazac reveals, "Camus a insisté seulement sur le fait que la théorie de Marx n'était pas scientifique mais un tas de prophéties, inévitablement contradictoires à la réalité" (Camus had insisted only on the fact that Marx's theory was not scientific but a pile of prophecies, inevitably contradictory to reality) (257).[1] This deeply implanted desire to instill a sense of justice in the world comes from Camus's conception of humanity. As Jill Capstick highlights, "The key term of Camusian ethics is the given value of human life" (453–4). This passionate desire to uphold the value of the human life might lead one to question how it is that Camus could admire a character such as Don Juan, whose own creator intended him to be a monster. In order to understand this conundrum, it is prudent to first comprehend the story of Don Juan according to Tirso de Molina and what good Camus saw in him that Molina did not.

Don Juan's story begins in Naples where he spent the night with the Duchess Isabela who believes that the man she is having intercourse with is her lover Duke Octavio. It is only at the first light of day that the duchess realizes the man is not Duke Octavio and screams for help. It just so happens that the one who comes to her rescue is Don Juan's uncle, Don Pedro. With the assistance of his uncle, Don Juan manages to flee while Pedro falsely convinces the king that it was not Don Juan but Duke Octavio who slept with Duchess Isabela. The king commands them to be placed in the dungeon until their wedding day.

Meanwhile in Tarragona, a young peasant girl named Tishbea happens to see a young man and his servant on the beach who appear to have survived a shipwreck. The man she rescues is none other than Don Juan. Tishbea restores him to health at her house where they make love. Don Juan and his servant flee Tishbea's home the following day. After catching up with them, Tishbea explains that she is angry about Don Juan's departure. Don Juan promises that he will one day marry her. Tishbea does not believe his lie and is so overcome with grief that she throws herself into the sea. This act leaves Don Juan to presume that she is dead. Consequently, the tragic loss of her life will now weigh heavily on his shoulders.

In this manner, Don Juan continues to interfere in the lives of others. Whether it be stealing a man's lover or his wife, Don Juan is constantly looking for sexual pleasure throughout his travels. His extreme passion for sexual intercourse goes so far that he

---

[1] All translations are my own unless otherwise indicated.

slays Don Gonzalo, an innocent father who caught Don Juan in the act of sleeping with his daughter. While Don Juan at first believes himself to have escaped the father's wrath, Don Gonzalo whispers with his dying breath that his spirit will haunt Don Juan until his death. This prophesy comes to fruition when Don Juan eats dinner in front of the tombstone and statue of Gonzalo. It is there that the ghost of Gonzalo comes to life and serves Don Juan a dinner of vipers and scorpions that he bravely consumes. It is after the dinner that the ghost touches Don Juan by the hand striking him dead instantly. The two then disappear completely to what most likely would be hell according to Tirso de Molina's version of the story.

Considering the story of Don Juan, one again might wonder how such a violent, self-centered, and libertine character could ever be considered a hero for Camus. However, by analyzing the absurdist worldview of Albert Camus, one finds that humanity is given only one life to live. Outside of our sensorial faculties, which are inextricably linked to the process of knowledge formation for Camus,[2] one cannot know if there is a transcendental world outside of the physical. Therefore, it is only logical that one experiences all there is to know of this fleeting life. Camus explains, "ce monde, je puis le toucher et je juge encore qu'il existe. Là s'arrête toute ma science, le reste est construction" (This world, I can touch it and I can judge that it exists. Here halts all my science, the rest is construction) (*Le mythe de Sisyphe* 36). Placing one's hope in metaphysical aspirations is foolishness for Camus because of our epistemological incapacity to understand the world outside of our sensorial capabilities. Therefore, Camus places value only on what is tangible, in what can be attained in this transient life. Consequently, Camus ponders in *Le mythe de Sisyphe*, "Pourquoi faudrait-il aimer rarement pour aimer beaucoup?" (Why would he [Don Juan] experience love a little when he could experience much love?) (99). The actions of Don Juan are sensible according to Camus since this is the only life of which he can be assured. Thus, it would be foolish for him not to experience the fleeting joy of every moment. Camus explains, "s'il quitte une femme, ce n'est pas absolument parce qu'il ne la désire plus. Une femme belle est toujours désirable. Mais c'est qu'il en désire une autre et, non, ce n'est pas la même chose" (If he leaves a woman, it is not absolutely because he desires her no more. A beautiful woman is always desirable. But it is that he desires another and no, this is not the same thing) (*Le mythe de Sisyphe* 101). In this passage, Camus is pushing humanity toward a hedonistic lifestyle in which the beauty and pleasure of every moment give meaning to our absurd existence.

It is the subjective projection of happiness into a world without metaphysical salvation. Camus knows that there is no way of escaping the human condition epitomized by birth, work, and death. Yet, he sees that beauty can be found within the present moment. Camus avoids Sartre's pessimistic notion that humanity is "condemned" to exist. He sees happiness where nihilists such as Samuel Beckett see

---

[2] In his essay "Rending Moments of Material Ecstasy in the Meditative Essays of Two Nobel Laureates: Le Clézio and Camus," Keith Moser explains that Camus is a sensualist philosopher par excellence.

life as actors without a script.[3] According to this morose vision of existence, we are all doomed to live in a senseless world with no hope or purpose where one must aimlessly wait for death. Camus attempts to confront "le néant" of existence with a hedonistic approach that searches for the artistic beauty of every moment. As the author avers in *Noces*, "Mais aujourd'hui l'imbécile est roi, et j'appelle imbécile celui qui a peur de jouir" (But today, the imbecile is king, and I call imbecile those who are afraid of joy) (18). Yet again, one might wonder if Camus's hedonistic approach to existence is supporting a lifestyle without morals, as Don Juan's character would seem to suggest.

In defense of his hedonistic ethos, Camus replies, "Mais l'erreur serait aussi grande d'en faire un immoraliste. Il est à cet égard 'comme tout le monde': il a la morale de sa sympathie ou de son antipathie" (But the error would be great to make [Don Juan] an immoralist. In this respect he is "like the rest of us": he has the morality of his sympathy and antipathy) (*Le mythe de Sisyphe* 102). It is clear from this passage that Camus is not calling for a lifestyle without morality. As previously stated, his works speak out against such a proposition. So, if he does not believe in the nihilistic approach that "if God does not exist then everything is permitted," then from where do justice and a sense of morality originate for Camus and his support of the monstrous Don Juan? It is clear that Camus found no moral comfort in the hope of religion or Christianity when he professes, "what I reproach Christianity with is being a doctrine of injustice" (qtd. in Sharpe 155). Camus came to accept that religion often established an "indifference to life" which led to metaphysical aspirations and a spiritual sense of salvation that left humanity in a state where injustice on earth was justified (Hoskins 146). A metaphysical realm of salvation, such as a biblical form of heaven, was bound to guide individuals toward a nihilistic point of view where the human in her or his present state has no worth.

Only after this present life did religion seem to offer hope or some form of justice, a flaw that Camus saw as unacceptable. Therefore, Camus found the Christian explanations of evil, free will, and the "fall" to be unsatisfactory. Gregory Hoskins underlines that whereas religion did not provide a concrete response for evil, Camus believed that "injustice, has its roots in the human condition" (148). Further developing this concept of injustice, Dilek Baskaya states, "Camus seems to argue that there are two sources of evil, which are, interrelated and inseparable: man and death" (33). Owing to his role in the French resistance during the Second World War, Camus witnessed the violence of which mankind was capable and the fact that this violence came uniquely from mankind, not from an omnipotent being. Given that he had witnessed the horrors of the Holocaust as well as the French-Algerian war, he knew the evil mankind could inflict upon others.

The second evil, death, is both inspiring and disheartening, as it steals from mankind the only thing that it possesses (i.e., life). Nonetheless, it also inspires us to live this one

---

[3] For a more comprehensive discussion of Beckett's profound nihilism, see John Valentine's essay entitled "Nihilism and the Eschaton in Samuel Beckett's *Waiting for Godot*."

life to the fullest. For this reason, Camus poses the question, "Avez-vous remarqué que la mort seule réveille nos sentiments" (Have you noticed that death alone awakens our feelings?) (*La Chute* 36). It is these two evils that left Camus with the conclusion that injustice comes from mankind. Moreover, the human condition provides no concrete epistemological answers to attain justice. This is where we find that Camus struggled his whole life to find a balance between his humanism and his desire for justice. Camus believed in humanity and its capacity to achieve great things. Even where his atheistic beliefs had overridden the ideologies of hope and an afterlife, Camus believed in the concrete element of humanism. As the Pied-Noir author explains in *La peste*, "l'homme n'est pas une idée" (Humanity is not an idea) (151). In comparison to many of his contemporaries who were searching for ideological utopias and salvation in religion, Camus believed in what he could see, feel, taste, and touch. These sensibilities led him to believe in humanity in its present state.

Even during the Second World War, Camus recognized the humanism of the Nazi soldiers and even criticized those who attempted to demonize them. In his *Lettres à un ami allemand*, Camus writes to those who served under the Nazi regime, "pour être fidèles à notre foi, nous sommes forcés de respecter en vous ce que vous ne respectez pas chez les autres. Nous voulons vous détruire dans votre puissance sans vous mutiler dans votre âme" (To be faithful to our faith, we are forced to respect in you what you do not respect in others. We want to destroy you in your power without mutilating your souls) (qtd. in Capstick 457). Throughout his years of writing, Camus strived to find the balance between the injustice created by humanity and the importance of the human life, the only force that presented any form of justice in the absurdist worldview. Being thrown into the chaos of existence without reason or purpose, Camus found that the one equality and form of justice humanity could embrace is that we are equally lost in the chaos of the human condition.

Each conscious, living person is forced to bear the load of existence on his or her shoulders. Consequently, we must choose to "revolt" against the reality of death which stands before us. This "égalité irréprochable de la mort" (irreproachable equality of death) led Camus to believe that death and the human condition were the two forces that provided humanity with a foundation for justice (*La peste* 214). Anyone who stepped outside of this foundation by taking the life of another was abolishing the only element that provided equality. It was this humanistic sameness that allowed Camus to see even the Nazi soldiers he revolted against as humans who deserved to be treated with justice when the war was over.

In transitioning from *Le mythe de Sisyphe*, one of Camus's earlier works, to Camus's book *La chute*, one finds that Camus seems to view Don Juan in a different light. While the character himself is never mentioned explicitly in the work, there are strong similarities between the lives of Clamence, Don Juan, and Albert Camus that are very much interlinked. Oliver Todd, writer of the biography *Albert Camus: A Life*, makes it clear that Clamence is very much a representation of Camus. In this regard, "When Olivier Todd once asked Jean-Paul Sartre, which of Camus' books he liked best he said: 'The Fall, because Camus has hidden himself in it'" ("Camus and His Women"). Todd's biography of Albert Camus reveals that Camus was in fact very much a womanizer, and he kept in touch with his lovers through letters and various visits that went as far as New York City. According to Oliver Todd,

> *The Fall* is the confession of a celebrated Parisian lawyer brought to crisis when he fails to come to the aid of a drowning woman. The "drowning woman" was Camus' second wife, Francine, who had a mental breakdown. As mother of his two children, Camus decided it would be more appropriate if her relationship with him was that of "a sister," allowing him erotic freedom.

For years, Francine appeared to go along with her role as one of Camus's mistresses, but eventually it became more than she could bear. As the unidentified author of the article from *The Guardian* entitled "Camus and His Women" reports, "Todd says that Francine said to her husband: 'You owed me that book,' and Camus had agreed." It is clear from this exchange between Camus and his wife that Camus is Clamence in *La chute*, who is desperately trying to find how to bear the guilt that arose from the strain he placed upon his wife.

In this same vein, Peter Roberts also notes that Camus "was suffering from writer's block. He was ill, with the effects of tiredness, depression and TB all taking their toll. He felt burnt-out and wondered what he had really accomplished in his life to date. His response was to begin writing some short stories, and this is how *The Fall* was born" (875). However, this side of Camus is in stark contrast to his earlier life. Camus's destructive actions in his marriage are hardly any different than the behavior of his idol Don Juan. In simple terms, Camus's romantic pursuits are no different from Don Juan's infidelity. However, another plausible interpretation is that Camus's reworking of the Don Juan myth has no direct correlation with *La chute*. In this sense, it is important to note that Tishbea in Tirso de Molina's *The Trickster of Seville and the Stone Guest* would most likely have been the inspiration for Camus's mysterious woman who tries to commit suicide by jumping into a river. The actions of Don Juan, which led to Tishbea's attempted suicide, and the woman who attempted suicide in *La chute* are both closely interlinked to Camus's own life concerning his affairs that led to the mental breakdown of his wife. As Camus comes to the realization of the price he and his wife paid for his actions, one must ask whether he still leaves his absurdist hero Don Juan on a pedestal for all to see, or whether his actions seem to change his perception of De Molina's monster.

In Camus's examination of justice and guilt in *La chute*, he highlights the fact that Clamence had lived a life similar to Don Juan's, outside the constraints of society. Clamence had never tried to bring harm to anyone, even if his actions did have negative consequences on others. His earlier life in fact was full of generous acts. As a self-proclaimed "judge-penitent," Clamence confesses that "je n'ai jamais fait payer les pauvres et ne l'ai jamais crié sur les toits" (I never made the poor pay and I never declared it on the rooftops) (Camus, *La chute* 24). Later, he adds, "j'adorais aider les aveugles à traverser les rues" (I loved helping the blind cross the street) (25). While the reader later discovers that Clamence performed all these good deeds in order to gain the attention of others, it is clear that Clamence's early life was not filled with great injustices. So, what moral law could he have broken that led to such severe self-condemnation? This question could possibly be answered given that there are only two options of living within the Camusian absurdist worldview, rebellion or suicide. As James Caraway posits, "The rebel, then, is the absurd man. The absurd man, the rebel, lives only on the basis of personal experience. He does not scorn reason; he uses reason but admits the irrational. [. . .] He sees that only this life has value" (129). Suicide, for Camus, can be one of two things, mental or physical. While the physical suicide is self-explanatory, the mental form is based on the desire to escape the physical world by vain means such as religious and transcendental explanations of existence that have no concrete basis. According to James Caraway, this conviction "reveals that life is the only value which the rebel realizes and that his actions will be for life" (129). As Caraway reiterates, "Thus, the only value which man knows is life. The rebel therefore rebels against death and for life. Whatever action is life-affirming will be that action which is ethical; that which is life-negating is not" (131). If this is the case and the only way for Camus or an absurdist to understand what is ethical is by interpreting if an action is life-giving or life-negating, then one must ask if the actions of Don Juan, Clamence, and consequently, Camus are life-negating. It is clear in *La chute*, in which Camus wrestles with his own conscious, that there must have been some essence of life-negation in his actions concerning the leaving of his wife.

The reason for this conviction lies in Gabriel Marcel's theory of being. According to Marcel, existence "c'est être en rapport avec le monde, du fait que notre corps y est situé. Exister est un attribut de l'être '"incarné'" (is being in relation with the world, the fact that our body is situated there. To exist is an attribute of an embodied being) (Feys 75). This theory coincides with Camus and his absurdist theory that we are all living beings who only possess one thing: life. As Sartre would also agree, the absurdist assumes that humanity has been thrown into the chaos of existence with no comprehension or means of understanding why she or he exists. Each person, according to Camus, is therefore left in a "situation" in which they do not have any objective reason for existence. Gabriel Marcel would agree with this viewpoint, but he would employ the word "incarnation" in place of situation. For Marcel, however, humanity lives in a broken world because of its incapacity to view conscious human beings as "others" and instead regarding them merely as machines. This idea of conscious, living beings wrongly transformed into machines leads to what Marcel terms objectification: "Le danger sera de considérer les êtres comme des objets posés devant le sujet, comme des choses qui lui sont étrangères, et inversement le sujet comme étranger à l'être. Fausse attitude que Marcel appelle 'l'objectivation,' le fait d'objectiver" (The danger will be to consider beings as objects put in front of the subject, as things which are foreign to him [her], and conversely the subject as a stranger to being. This distorted attitude is what Marcel calls "objectification," the fact of objectifying) (Feys 75).

Marcel theorizes that this loss of the human element leads to a world of machines in which any true connection with conscious others is completely lost. As the philosopher asserts, "Nous vivons dans un monde où le mot *avec* semble de plus en plus perdre son sens; on pourrait exprimer la même idée en disant que l'intimité semble y devenir de plus en plus irréalisable et qu'elle est d'ailleurs discréditée" (We live in a world where the word *with* seems to more and more lose its sense; we could explain this idea in saying that intimacy here becomes more and more unattainable and that it is discredited) (Marcel 36). In this planet of machines, the Other is completely lost in a world of mathematical equations where intimacy is nonexistent. The only way to escape this robotic relationship with others is to return to a viewpoint where she or he is no longer seen as a problem to resolve, but rather as a mystery to experience.

Marcel proposes that there are two ways of being in relation to others, viewing them as a *problème* or *mystère*. As Marcel outlines, "Un problème est quelque chose que je rencontre, que je trouve tout entier devant moi, mais que je puis par là-même cerner et réduire" (A problem is something that I encounter, that I find altogether in front of me, but I can discern and reduce it) (227). This theory of a problem is what Marcel calls primary reflection. It is when a subject encounters another conscious person but is unwilling to recognize their otherness. She or he deems the Other a mathematical equation that can be understood by a scientific formula. Marcel finds this to be a dangerous form of viewing the Other. A problem is something not to be known, but to be studied. It is an element that can be laid out before the observer and experimented. This form of relation with the Other, however, leaves no room for a true relation.

In a sense, it robs the Other of their consciousness, just as Descartes robbed animals of their own *Umwelt* when he deemed them "les bêtes machines."[4] In order to reestablish a relationship with the Other and restore their conscious identity, one must transcend the primary reflection that sees the Other as a problem and step into the realm of secondary reflection that views the Other as mystery. As Marcel hypothesizes, "Le mystère est quelque chose en quoi je suis moi-même engagé, et qui n'est par conséquent pensable que comme une sphère où la distinction de l'en moi et du devant moi perd sa signification et sa valeur initiale" (The mystery is something in which I am myself engaged, and which consequently is only thinkable like a sphere where the distinction of me and what is before me loses its signification and its value) (227). This secondary reflection redeems the Other's consciousness. It moves past the equations and objectification, thereby seeing the Other as one with which the subject is constantly engaged. Similar to how our consciousness is constantly developing, our engagement with the Other is in a state of continuous transition. It is through mystery that the Other is restored their sense of being and the subject is humbled. We realize that our perception of the Other is constantly in motion, thus it must be consistently reevaluated. Marcel proposes that objectification of the Other can only be avoided by transcending primary reflection, which sees the Other as a machine. By stepping into secondary reflection, we see the Other as mystery.

Considering Marcel's theories of being and objectification, it is possible that Camus feels the weight of guilt for his actions, because they have objectified the Other rather than viewed the Other as a true person. The women Don Juan, Clamence, and Albert Camus made love with were reduced to objects of pleasure, rather than persons who

---

[4] For a more in-depth explanation of the biosemiotic concept of an *umwelt* that transcends the pragmatic limitations of this current exploration, see Jesper Hoffmeyer's essay "Biosemiotics: Towards a New Synthesis in Biology."

are "beings." If this is the case, their actions would therefore be violating the absurdist's one rule of protecting life. While this would by no means be a physical taking of life, it would be a psychological act against another, as it negates regarding the Other as a conscious person. Clamence supports this theory in *La chute* when he declares, "I conceived at least one great love in my life, of which I was always the object. From that point of view, after the inevitable hardships of youth, I had settled down early on: sensuality alone dominated my love-life. I looked merely for objects of pleasure and conquest" (qtd. in Baskaya 38). This is evident in all Clamence's actions, as he continuously confesses his sins throughout the work. As the narrator (Clamence) confesses, "Quand je quittais un aveugle sur le trottoir où je l'avais aidé à atterrir, je le saluais. Ce coup de chapeau ne lui était évidemment pas destiné, il ne pouvait pas le voir. A qui donc s'adressait-il ? Au public" (When I left a blind person on the sidewalk after I had helped them across the street, I tipped my hat. This gesture of my hat was not evident to them, they could not see it. So, who was I addressing? The public) (*La chute* 52). Clamence's confession reveals that his previous righteous actions were only for his own benefit.

The people he used were merely tools for his own purposes. His actions objectified the Other, seeing him or her as merely an object that was calculable and without consciousness, an entity that could be exploited rather than known. This tension is created by Clamence's hedonistic passions, but also his desire to seek justice. It is an inner conflict that rages within Clamence all throughout the work, admiring the idea of justice yet longing for his hedonistic desires. As the narrator elucidates, "J'étais soutenu par deux sentiments sincères: la satisfaction de me trouver du bon côté de la barre et un mépris instinctif envers les juges en général" (I was supported by two sincere sentiments: the satisfaction of finding myself at the good side of the bar and an instinctive disdain toward judges in general) (Camus, *La chute* 22). As Camus struggles to understand his relationship with his wife, he finds his actions to be both right and wrong. He tries to find the balance between a hedonistic lifestyle, an existential remedy that led him to have multiple mistresses, and the injustice he practiced by objectifying his wife.

In his collection of essays *Noces*, Camus underscores the difficulty of practicing the duality of living a hedonistic life of "bonheur" and the justice that comes from respecting human life. As the writer-philosopher argues,

> "Notre tâche d'homme est de trouver les quelques formules qui apaiseront l'angoisse infinie des âmes libres. Nous avons à recoudre ce qui est déchiré, à rendre la justice imaginable dans un monde si évidemment injuste, le bonheur significatif pour des peuples empoisonnés par le malheur du siècle. Naturellement, c'est une tâche surhumaine. Mais on appelle surhumaines les tâches que les hommes mettent longtemps à accomplir, voilà tout" [Our task as humans is to find some of the formulas that will appease our infinite anguish in our free souls. We must stitch up what is torn, to render imaginable justice in a world so evidently unjust, the significant happiness for the people empoisoned by the misfortune of the century. Naturally, it's a superhuman task. But we call superhuman the tasks that men take a long time to accomplish, this is all] (Camus, *Noces* 112–13)

As Camus notes, the human task of finding happiness in this short-lived existence yet also achieving some sort of foundation for justice might be above the human capacity. In reference to Clamence, Peter Roberts asserts, "By his own admission and account of his actions he reveals himself to be a deceptive and manipulative man. He is egotistical, hypocritical, insincere, and selfish; and yet he is not without some redeeming features. He is as ruthless in deconstructing himself as he is in critiquing others" (878). Camus recognizes that while his hedonistic lifestyle was not as justifiable as he once pictured it, he could find equal fault in those around him.

Becoming a type of Don Juan and following his erotic passions also forced him to break with his own theory that "il peut y avoir de la honte à être heureux tout seul" (there could be shame for being happy alone) (Camus, *La peste* 190). As Clamence continues to confess his transgressions throughout the work, he obstinately admits that he does not want to give up practicing these faults. This situation is where Camus and all of humanity find itself. We wish to discover happiness within the absurdist world, yet we understand that possessing happiness alone only leads to shame and injustice (Davis 1018). Clamence's declaration "toujours est-il que le mot même de justice me jetait dans d'étranges fureurs" (It is always the word justice that throws me into strange tantrums) does not originate from a sense of hatred (Camus, *La chute* 97). Instead, he is struck by the overwhelming realization that he cannot achieve a life of total happiness without abstaining from justice, yet justice cannot be enforced without forsaking his happiness.

In conclusion, one might ask how Camus would have (re-)envisioned De Molina's monster after the aforementioned moral epiphanies that seem to have inspired the final pages of *La chute*. Tirso de Molina deemed his character as immoral and damned to hell, as is clearly noted in the denouement. Even if Camus's opinion of Don Juan evolved over time, his perception of the monster would still differ from De Molina's. Whereas De Molina saw a monster in Don Juan, Camus would see a man who was perfectly innocent, because there is no omnipotent judge to condemn his actions. Nevertheless, Camus would also see Don Juan as the most condemned of all monsters because he objectified the Other, stealing the only thing she or he possesses: life. In following the pursuit of pleasure, Don Juan knew that he would fail in his responsibility to the Other. Yet, if he would have remained responsible toward the Other, he would have been irresponsible to himself. For Camus, there is no escaping the innocence and the guilt that are found within every human being. Therefore, according to Albert Camus, Don Juan is "like the rest of us." We are all heroes. We are all monsters.

References

Başkaya, Dilek Başar. "From His Doctoral Thesis to the Fall: Evil through Albert Camus's Eyes." *Journal of Faculty of Letters / Edebiyat Fakultesi Dergisi*, vol. 33, no. 1, June 2016, pp. 29–41.

Bazac, Ana. "La révolte et la lutte: Albert Camus et Jean-Paul Sartre en dedans et en dehors de l'existentialisme." *Revue roumaine de philosophie*, vol. 54, no. 2, Oct. 2010, pp. 239–66.

Camus, Albert. *La chute*. Gallimard, 1989.
Camus, Albert. *La peste*. Gallimard, 1947.
Camus, Albert. *Le mythe de Sisyphe*. Gallimard, 1942.
Camus, Albert. *Noces suivi de l'été*. Gallmard, 1959.
"Camus and His Women." *The Guardian*, Guardian News and Media, Oct. 15, 1997, www.theguardian.com/books/1997/oct/15/biography.albertcamus.
Capstick, Jill. "Mastery or Slavery: The Ethics of Revolt in Camus's 'Les Muets.'" *Modern & Contemporary France*, vol. 11, no. 4, 2003, pp. 453–62.
Caraway, James E. "Albert Camus and the Ethics of Rebellion." *Mediterranean Studies*, vol. 3, 1992, pp. 125–36.
Davis, Olin. "Camus's *La Peste*: Sanitation, Rats, and Messy Ethics." *Modern Language Review*, vol. 102, no. 3, 2007, pp. 1008–20.
Feys, Robert. "Un Exposé De La Philosophie De Gabriel Marcel." *Revue Philosophique De Louvain*, vol. 53, no. 37, 1955, pp. 73–85.
Hoffmeyer, Jesper. "Biosemiotics: Towards a New Synthesis in Biology." *European Journal for Semiotic Studies*, vol. 9, no. 2, 1997, pp. 355–76.
Hoskins, Gregory. "Elements of a Post-metaphysical and Post-secular Ethics and Politics: Albert Camus on Human Nature and the Problem of Evil." *International Philosophical Quarterly*, vol. 47, no. 2, 2007, pp. 141–52.
Marcel, Gabriel. *Le mystère de l'être: réflexion et mystère*. Aubier, 1951.
Molina, Tirso de, and Gwynne Edwards. *The Trickster of Seville and the Stone Guest*. Aris & Phillips, 1986.
Moser, Keith. "Rending Moments of Material Ecstasy in the Meditative Essays of Two Nobel Laureates: Le Clézio and Camus." *Romance Notes*, vol. 49, no. 1, 2009, pp. 13–21.
Roberts Peter. "Bridging Literary and Philosophical Genres: Judgment, Reflection and Education in Camus' *The Fall*." *Educational Philosophy and Theory*, vol. 40, no. 7, 2008, pp. 873–87.
Sharpe, Matthew. "The Black Side of the Sun." *Political Theology*, vol. 15, no. 2, Mar. 2014, pp. 151–74.
Sheaffer-Jones, Caroline. "Effects of 'Phantasmatic Truth:' On the Reading of Albert Camus in Jacques Derrida's the *Death Penalty* Seminars." *Parrhesia: A Journal of Critical Philosophy*, vol. 26, 2016, pp. 176–93.
Stankeviciute, Kristina. "The Power Message of the Don Juan Figure." *Verbum*, vol. 1, no. 6, 2016, pp. 196–206.
"The Trickster of, and the Stone Guest." "The Trickster of Seville and the Stone Guest." *Gale Library of Daily Life: Slavery in America*, Encyclopedia.com, Sept. 3, 2018, www.encyclopedia.com/arts/culture-magazines/trickster-seville-and-stone-guest
Valentine, John. "Nihilism and the Eschaton in Samuel Beckett's *Waiting for Godot*." *Florida Philosophical Review*, vol. 9, no. 2, 2009, pp. 136–47.

Index

absurdity (Camus) 227–38
Alber, Catherine 100
androgynous monsters 50–9, 111–20, 126–7
Anthropocene epoch (the) 10, 60, 63, 74–5, 81, 105
anthropocentrism 4, 65–70, 75, 81, 87
Arens, William 41
authority (the essence of) 109–29, 153, 177, 219

Bantinaki, Katerina 102–3
Baraka, Amiri (LeRoi Jones) 222–5
Baudrillard, Jean 6–8, 24, 77
bestiaries 49–62, 116
biblical monsters 54, 57–8, 86, 90–6
biocentrism 4, 63, 71–84
Bloom, Harold 137–8
Boehrer, Bruce 87–8
Botting, Fred 130–1
Brayton, Dan 90–1
Brooks, Peter 131, 165, 179
Burley, Mikel 42–4

Camus, Albert 227–38
Canguilhem, Georges 132
cannibalism 4, 34–48
Carter, Angela 138
Céard, Jean 110
Césaire, Aimé 213, 217–18
Charlier, Philippe 132
Chodnovsky, Liza 133
Citton, Yves 25
Clasen, Mathias 29–30
Cohen, Jeffrey Jerome 1, 8, 69, 98–105, 132, 164–83, 209, 225
Colombo, Realdo 112
Corbett, Jim 105–6
corporality 5, 46, 64, 77, 109–30, 152, 155
Cox, Sandra 101–6

Crawford, Katherine 122
cross-species empathy 24, 68–72
Ctesias 204–12
Culler, Jonathan 158

Darwinism 3, 17–33
Dawkins, Richard 20, 31, 33
death (fear of) 44, 189, 219, 221, 228–33
De Beauvoir, Simone 179, 204
Derrida, Jacques 1–5, 11, 61, 63–84
Devun, Leah 111, 116, 119
diabolical monsters 39, 54–8, 86–96, 98, 125, 157, 215, 221
Diamond, Cora 42, 44
Diehl, Nicholas 120, 216
divine monsters 50–2, 55, 58–9, 96, 125
Don Juan (the myth of) 9–10, 227–38
Doucey, Bruno 74
dragons 50–2, 55, 58–9, 96, 125
DuBois, Page 139
Durbach, Nadja 64, 67
Duval, Jacques 109, 112

Egerer, Claudia 71
Empson, William 153–4
eroticism 22, 26, 38, 56–8, 187–203, 205, 209–11, 227–8, 232, 236
Esu (the deity) 213–26
Euba, Femi 213–24
evil (the notion of) 6–7, 39, 54–8, 86–96, 125, 148–61, 213–16, 221
evolution (theory of) 3, 17–33, 46, 60, 69

Fanchin, Gerard 76
Federmann, Reinhard 199
femininity (representations of) 6, 50–9, 117–19, 135–41, 147–62, 174–83, 210
Ffolliott, Sheila 122
Findlen, Paula 116

Foucault, Michel 3–5, 8–10, 38, 87, 109, 179, 227, 234
Frankenstein 6, 24, 28, 130–40, 147–62
freak show performers 5, 54, 63–70, 78–80

Gaita, Raimond 43
gender theory 109–30, 173–80, 188–210
Genette, Gérard 22, 33
ghouls 4, 34–48
Gilbert, Sandra M. 139, 141, 156–7
Gilman, Charlotte Perkins 165, 179–81
Goldhaber, Michael 25
Goldman, Robert 207
Goodwin, Paul 131
Gopnik, Adam 71
Goss, Theodora 78
Grant-Davie, Keith 167
Greek mythology 32, 50, 54–6, 204–12
Guerlac, Suzanne 65
Gurevich, David 133

Haro Ibars, Eduardo 187–203
hedonism 227–39
Herodotus 206
Hillenbrand, Laura 44
Hitchcock, Susan Tyler 130
Hoffman, Kurt Leroy 71
Hoffmeyer, Jesper 20, 234
horror films 29–32, 102–6, 189–203
Hull, David 21, 23
human-animal binary (the) 5–6, 58, 64–6, 69, 79–81
Hurst, Andrea 65
Hutcheon, Linda 139
hybridity 19–24, 36–9, 50–61, 87–91, 134, 138–40, 169–78, 182, 192–4, 198, 202, 205–11
hyperreality 6–9, 24, 77

Ibars, Eduardo Haro 187–204
Idelson-Shein, Iris 2, 5, 64, 78
immigration (monstrosity in) 8–11, 79, 101–5, 183–4
incel movement 147–62
irony (the device of) 102, 155, 213–24
Ishida, Sui 4, 34, 36

Johnson, Samuel 154
Jung, Carl 54, 213–16

Karttunen, Klaus 204–8
Katsman, Roman 133
Kellner, Douglas 7
Keret, Etgar 130–46
Kirkwood, Guy 78–9
Kleinhaus, Belinda 65
Kristeva, Julia 134, 142
Kubovy, Miri 137–8

Lamb, John B. 156
Lamming, George 86, 89
Landy, Joshua 22
Laqueur, Thomas 111
Lasch, Christopher 77, 80
Lawlor, Leonard 73
Le Clézio, J. M. G. 63–84
Leitao, David D. 134
Lenfant, Dominique 204–11
Lestel, Dominique 2–4, 17–33
Lévi-Strauss, Claude 49, 211
limitrophy (Derrida) 2–3
Litt, Toby 172–3
Long, Kathleen 109, 111
Loomba, Ania 86, 88
Losilla, Carlos 189
Louis-Combet, Claude 49, 58
Lumsden, Simon 66
Lupton, Thomas 93

Maffesoli, Michel 49, 61
Manokha, Ivan 9
Marcel, Gabriel 233–6
Marchesini, Roberto 132
Markale, Jean 49–50, 58–9
Márquez, Gabriel García 165–83
maternity (depictions of) 52, 130–46, 154–9, 179–80
Matsuda, Paul 173, 177
medicalization of the "monster" 93–6, 112
Melusine (the myth of) 49–62
Mendelson-Maoz, Adia 133, 137–8
Merrick, Joseph Carey 52–3
Midgley, Mary 43

Milburn, Colin   2, 4, 46
Milton, John   93–6, 132, 147–62
misogyny (manifestations of)   53–9, 93–6, 135–40, 147–62, 165–8, 174–83, 210
Moers, Ellen   131
Momaday, N Scott   165–70, 177
Monsaingeon, Baptiste   49, 60
monster (etymology)   49–54, 61–3, 67, 110
Montaigne   49–54, 61–3, 67, 110
Montuori, Alfonso   2
Morioka, Masahiro   38–40, 46
Moser, Keith   63–84, 104, 109, 229
Mulvey, Laura   131, 188
Murphy, Michael J.   158, 189, 197, 199

Namahira, Emiko   45
Nash, Richard   71–2
Neo-Darwinism   17–21
non-human personhood   9–10, 64–72
normality (history of)   40–7, 52–9, 64, 79, 110–19, 127, 138–40, 170, 179–80, 207

ogres   54–5
O'Keeffe, Timothy J.   154
Oliver, Kelly   65, 71
Olivier, Christiane   55
Osagie, Iyunolu   214, 219–20, 223

Pairet, Ana   58
Panopticism (Foucault)   9, 11
Paré, Ambroise   53, 110, 112
Parks, Suzan-Lori   222
Paster, Gail Kern   88
patriarchy   157–60, 175–6, 202
Paulson, William   7
Pennant, Thomas   94
Pentecostalism (representations of)   219–22
Plath, Sylvia   165, 176–83
Pollock, Sheldon   204, 208–12
Poovey, Mary   131
posthumanism   60, 86–9, 143
Preece, Rod   63

Quine, Willard Van Orman   43

racism   178, 215, 223–5
Richards, Evelleen   5, 64, 80
Ridon, Jean-Xavier   67
Rodger, Elliot   147–62
Romm, James   205, 207
Roussel-Gillet, Isabelle   66, 69
Ruskin, John   139
Ryan, Robert M.   156–7

Said, Edward   213, 215, 226
Salinger, J. D.   165, 179–84
Salles, Marina   66
satire (the device of)   213–26
scapegoating (the process of)   9, 56, 104–5, 181
Scobie, Alex   139
sea creatures   32, 50–9, 85–97
Seven Theses (Cohen)   98, 101–2, 165, 167, 170–1, 211
Sexton, Anne   165, 174–5, 179–80
Shakespeare   85–97
Shelley, Mary   6, 130–40, 147–62
Sherwin, Paul   131
Slater, Michelle   71–2
Smith, Norman R.   110
Smith, Zadie   182
Sontag, Susan   203
Spangler, May   58
Spiro, Mia   2, 64, 67
Spivak, Gayatri Chakravorty   131
Stibbe, Arran   2
Stoker, Bram   29, 188–203
subversion (monstrosity as)   40, 80, 168–70

Thibault, Bruno   74, 76
Thomas, Keith   87, 92
Topsell, Edward   86, 90, 93–6
Tournier, Michel   54–5
transgenderism   5–6

vampires   36–9, 98, 187–203
Vásquez, Mary S.   102–3
vegetarianism   34–48
voodoo   219–22

Wells, Herbert George 40-1, 46
Westerlund, Fredrik 76
White, Hayden 206, 212
Wilson, August 213, 223-6
Wilson, Edward O. 31
Wisnewski, Jeremy 42-3
witchcraft 57, 92-7, 174-5, 180
Wittkower, Rudolf 205

Wood, David 74
"Wounded Knee" (The battle of) 168

Yar, Majid 8
Yoruba mythology 214-25

Zapperi, Roberto 120-1
Zorach, Rebecca 116-17, 125

www.ingramcontent.com/pod-product-compliance
Lightning Source LLC
Chambersburg PA
CBHW072142290426
44111CB00012B/1954